EK
/IK

2v8/

Y0-BDK-038

H.D.Budden

BM/0vY4

(REPRINT
3×201)

THE
FAITH. OF A MORALIST

MACMILLAN AND CO., Limited
LONDON · BOMBAY · CALCUTTA · MADRAS
MELBOURNE

THE MACMILLAN COMPANY
NEW YORK · BOSTON · CHICAGO
DALLAS · ATLANTA · SAN FRANCISCO

THE MACMILLAN COMPANY
OF CANADA, LIMITED
TORONTO

THE
FAITH OF A MORALIST

GIFFORD LECTURES DELIVERED IN THE
UNIVERSITY OF ST. ANDREWS, 1926–1928

BY

A. E. TAYLOR

Verus philosophus est amator Dei.—*Augustine*

SERIES I
THE THEOLOGICAL IMPLICATIONS OF MORALITY

Considerate la vostra semenza.—*Dante*

MACMILLAN AND CO., LIMITED
ST. MARTIN'S STREET, LONDON
1931

PRINTED IN GREAT BRITAIN
BY R. & R. CLARK, LIMITED, EDINBURGH

PREFACE

THESE volumes contain the Gifford Lectures given in the University of St. Andrews in the sessions of 1926–27 and 1927–28 substantially as they were delivered, though I have restored a number of sentences and short passages which had, for the sake of brevity, to be omitted in the actual delivery, and have, in several cases, printed as a single whole what had, in delivery, to be subdivided into two lectures. The unstudied, even occasionally conversational, style naturally employed in addressing an audience of recent colleagues and personal friends I have thought proper for retention in the published volumes; the material could not have been systematically recast in a severer literary form without an expenditure of time impossible to one still fully engaged in actual teaching work.

I trust that the title I have, with some misgivings, adopted will mislead no one. It is meant to indicate two things—that the attitude assumed on the great ultimate problems discussed avowedly involves a "venture of faith", and that, as I think, the venture should be found natural by anyone who comes to these problems with the special presuppositions of a moralist. I shall not, I hope, be thought capable of the impertinence of asking my readers to be interested in an intimate personal

v

Confessio Fidei; even if I had that vanity, I should also, I trust, have the sense to understand that the terms of Lord Gifford's bequest preclude a Gifford lecturer from using his position as an opportunity for propaganda on behalf of his own *Privatmeinungen*.

But for an Appendix, a Supplementary Note to one chapter of the first volume, and a number of footnotes, the text stands as it was originally written. This will explain why no notice has been taken of Dr. Whitehead's *Process and Reality* and other valuable works published since the end of 1927. It should be mentioned that, for the same reason, the criticisms passed in several places on views of the late Dr. McTaggart were necessarily written before the publication of the second volume of *The Nature of Existence*, and that allowance must be made for the fact.

I have done my best to indicate the writers to whom I am conscious of serious obligations by the references appended in my footnotes. But I should like to make a further special acknowledgement of the great debt I owe to four writers in particular—Dr. Whitehead, the late Baron von Hügel, Dr. Edwyn Bevan, and Professor C. C. J. Webb. To Professor Webb's work I should have owed even more than I do if I had not deferred making acquaintance with the volume of *Studies in the Relations of God and Man* until my own manuscript was out of my hands.

I am specially under an obligation to my friend and colleague Mr. A. C. A. Rainer, Shaw Fellow in the University of Edinburgh, for valuable help in proof-reading and the preparation of an Index of Proper

Names for each volume. I trust the analytical synopses prefixed to the volumes have made the addition of an index of subjects superfluous.

I take the opportunity to explain that while references to Kant's works in general are to the volume and page of Hartenstein's second edition, the *Critique of Pure Reason* is cited by the pages of the original edition (first or second as the case may be). Two abbreviations have been occasionally used, *E.R.E.* for *Encyclopaedia of Religion and Ethics*, and *E.M.L.* for *English Men of Letters Series*.

A. E. T.

EDINBURGH, *May* 1930

I take the opportunity afforded by this reprint of correcting a number of small errors of the Press, due to my own defects as a proof-reader, with many thanks to the friends who have helped me to discover them. I would also here recant, or qualify, the remark made about the late F. W. H. Myers on page 255. On re-examination I find I have exaggerated the rarity of the references to God in *Human Personality*, and I have been assured by those who have the best right to speak that their comparative fewness and their vagueness do not represent the writer's deepest personal convictions. I hasten to accept the correction and to express my regret for any misconception. With respect to a similar qualification of certain references to Dr. Gore see the Prefatory Note to Series II.

A. E. T.

May 1931

CONTENTS

THE RELATIONS BETWEEN ETHICS AND DIVINITY

Illustration of this from the philosophy of Dr. McTaggart. The supposed absolute disjunction of fact and value a mistaken prejudice. It is true that very much which is actual is bad. This does not prove the hypothesis of the pessimist, but might suggest that the coincidence of fact and value is only accidental. Against such a view we may say (1) that it involves an unconscious false abstraction. What really has value is always the activity of a real individual. In a sense it is true that what we pronounce to have value is an universal, but it is an "embodied" universal, *in rebus*, not *post res*. And all judgements of value include a reference to *personal* activity. Illustrations from ethics and aesthetics. Discussion of the case of "truth-values". (2) The view that "ideals" have value but not existence is a consequence of an extreme logical "nominalism" which requires to be corrected by the Aristotelian doctrine of "analogous" predication. (3) In actual life, as it is lived by all of us, we find no separation between "facts" which are "given" and "valuations" which are "put on" the facts; the facts and their values are given together; both are found, neither invented. Or, rather, we have always "fact-in-valuation", never mere fact in isolation, nor mere valuation. Our "moral ideals" are not simply added by the mind to "the facts" *de suo*. We are no more justified in saying that our moral and religious life throws no light on the "actuality" than we should be in saying the same thing about the life-history of the species of organisms. It is more illuminating to know that the world is the *kind* of kinematical system in which the evolution of living species can take place than merely to know that it is a kinematical system. It may well be still more illuminating to know that the actual world is one in which artists, heroes, and saints have their place.

III. ETERNITY AND TEMPORALITY

The moral life a life of tension between the temporal and the eternal, only possible to a being which is neither abiding nor simply mutable, but both at once. What is characteristic of temporality is not the simple distinction of before and after, but the contrast of present with past and future. This contrast belongs not to merely physical nature but to the life of conscious conative creatures. The "dehumanised" mathematical time of classical kinematics is not *durée réelle*. Nature conceived as a mere kinematical system, has neither present, past, nor future. Hence Spinoza mistakenly calls the contemplation of such a system contemplation under the "form of eternity". It is really contemplation under a form of bare sequence. Temporality is the characteristic form of the study of that which has a history, *i.e.* of the object of the sciences of life and mind. An *organism* has a true history because it is a concrete individual using and feeding on an *environment*. Its responses to this environment depend on its "particular go", and its "particular go" is never independent of the route by which it has reached its present state. In conscious life the past is apparently never simply past and done with. On the other hand, past habit is never unmodifiable. Hence in man the possibility of the conquest of habit by intelligent foresight. In a rational life habit is present everywhere, but everywhere subordinated to foresight and plan. The plan, again, is not clear from the outset, but only discloses itself progressively to the agent himself. The past of *man* not a dead but a living past. To be aware of our life as temporal is already to begin to transcend the form of temporality. All human creation is an attempt to experience the fruition of good in a *now* where there is no consciousness of the no longer or not yet. Illustrations from intellectual and aesthetic enjoyment. Approximate conformity of these experiences to the classical definition of eternity by Boethius. They are only approximations because the good enjoyed in them is not the *bonum consummatum*. If the fruition of all secular good fails to attain this ideal we may reasonably infer that the ultimate good of man is non-secular and eternal, and that the *facts* of our moral being point to the Christian conception of the transformation and completion of nature by "grace". Now all secular good is defective, since it cannot be enjoyed as a whole simultaneously, and one part can only be enjoyed at the cost of surrendering others. But to acquiesce in this state of things and make it the rule to "live for to-day" would be both immoral and irrational. Even the man who lives for his "interest in this world" is morally far superior, as Butler rightly held, to the man who lives for the "passion" of the moment. Nor can it be an adequate account of the moral end to say that it is "betterment", "leaving things a little better than we found them". To say this would be to confess that good is incapable of attainment and morality a forlorn adventure. But in so far as a good beyond which there is no better is attained, life takes on the character of an eternity or abiding *now*. The strictly ethical life is neither merely successive nor wholly abiding. It is the life of advance from merely animal acquiescence in succession towards the whole and simultaneous fruition of a complete good. Ascent in the scale is attended by progressive "unification" of both good and virtue. Here morality makes contact with religion. Our own character answers to that of the good to which we aspire. The "soul" is one or many according as the good to which it aspires is one or many. The attainment of a fully unified personality depends on finding our principal good in God, the concrete unity of all good in its source. Impossibility of regarding the plurality of

goods as ultimate. The implication of morality is thus a double
one. It points to the existence of God as the absolute and final
plenitude of good, and to an eternal destiny for the moral
person whose aim is the fruition of the good. Importance of
"detachment" as an element in the moral life, equal importance of right use of "creaturely" good. Error of supposing that
complete attainment would mean the cessation of life itself long
ago exposed in principle by Aristotle.

The moral life, then, is one of endeavour towards an eternal
good. So far as the endeavour is successful, we achieve a communicated eternity. The goal lies beyond the bounds of the historical, but the advance to it is historical and implies the reality
of time, the characteristic form of the historical. Theories
which regard time as an illusion falsify our conception, and, if
acted on, spoil our practice, of morality. Time is the *stuff* out
of which a personal moral life has to be made, and made by
transcending time. The "natural" theology of a moralist is
thus incompatible with (1) secularism, the identification of
good with "worldly good", and with (2) all "theosophic" doctrines of the illusoriness of the moral struggle and the intrinsic
divinity of the human soul, since they rest on the denial of any
real difference of status between deity and humanity. In a
moral world moral progress must be real. A moral theology
must regard eternal life as something which has to be achieved
and may be lost by sloth. The moral life is a real adventure
which begins with "nature" and ends in "supernature". From
the ethical point of view this consideration is fatal to all types
of speculation about "reincarnation". Christianity strikes the
truly ethical note by its doctrine of *final* salvation and reprobation, rightly understood. Progress from and through nature
to supernature involves a right combination of "attachment"
and "detachment", and it is just this which makes the moral
life a difficult adventure. It is a hard task to cultivate the finite
good so long as it is the "best" for me and yet to let it go when
and because the better discloses itself. Illustration of this.
Hence the speculative puzzle of Green's *Prolegomena* that all
attempts to say what the moral ideal is appear to involve a
"circle". We have no "clear and distinct idea" of the good; it
discloses its character dimly and partially as we make advance
towards it. We cannot describe the goal of the moral pilgrimage because we have never reached it, yet the reality of the

pilgrimage involves the reality of the goal. The immediate and conscious aim of the good man may be for some definite and specific improvement in himself or his society, but the end really aimed at is a freedom from circumstance which involves the transcending of temporality. Again genuine moral effort is directed on the remaking not only of our "environment" but of ourselves as well, and of all the selves of our community. Unsatisfactoriness of Kant's formal doctrine on this point due to his forgetting that "practical reason" and moral personality are "in the making". My own "practical reason" therefore cannot be the ultimate source of the moral law. The moral law is discovered, not created, by *my* reason, and, for that reason, cannot be digested, in advance of experience, into a system of categorical formulae. Superiority of Aristotle's conception of "practical reason" to Kant's. The inevitable inference is that the reason which prescribes the moral law is one which is only gradually and partially communicated to us in proportion to our fidelity. Unless this were so, we could not feel unqualified "reverence" for it. Thus the ultimate moral legislator is the will of God. This means that we cannot distinguish in principle between the life of discharge of duty and the life of "faith". In all genuine moral life we "walk by faith".

Inadequacy of the treatment of evil in most works on ethics. (Plato and Kant are exceptions to the rule.) Moral badness is neither mere "atavistic" reversion to type nor mere disregard for reasonable rule. Our experience of personal guilt is *sui generis* and distinctively human. (1) It involves dissatisfaction with our self and self-condemnation, and differs in kind from any discontent with our surroundings. (2) It has a peculiar indelibility; guilt cannot be "worked off and paid for" by subsequent "making good" or by the infliction of a penalty, and this sense of the indelibility of guilt cannot be explained away as "morbid" or as the effect of non-ethical "theological" superstition. (3) The sense of guilt regularly accompanied by a demand for our own "punishment". Retribution essential to a genuinely ethical theory of punishment. Recognition of this in the Christian doctrine of "forgiveness of sins". The distinction between forgiveness and mere "condonation". (4) Significance of the universal association of guilt with "pollution". This is no mere accidental association. As civilisation advances particular acts may be removed from the category of the morally "dirty", but the sense of sin as polluting is intensified and becomes more inward. We come to demand the cleansing of the "thoughts of the heart", *i.e.* the remaking of the natural self from its centre. This is inconsistent with any ethics which reduces morality to beneficent social activity. Fallaciousness of the criticism which deprecates "purity" as a "negative" virtue. Any morality has its negative side. Unsatisfactoriness of an ethic of mere "efficiency". (5) What we feel to be out- raged by sin or dishonour is not an impersonal law. The out- rage is felt as personal treason against a person, yet not against our own personality as it actually is, but against a real per- sonal embodiment of our ideal of good, treason against a "living God". Impossibility of accounting for this by regarding God as an "imaginative personification" of the impersonal, like, e.g., Britannia or "Humanity".

Moralists in general concern themselves almost wholly with the analysis of the "good for man" and leave on one side the problem of providing an adequate motive for the devoted pur- suit of it, though the great practical need of life is just such a motive. This is justifiable as a rule of method, but it makes it impossible to regard such moral philosophies as entitled to the position of directors of human action. We have to face the question whether such adequate motivation can be found apart from actual contact with a superhuman reality. Kant tells us that early education is to train us to substitute rever- ence for duty for "inclination", but he never explains how, on his theory of human nature, the lesson is to "get home". Spinoza's attempt to explain how the transition from "bond- age" to "freedom" is begun involves a formal self-contradic- tion. And the course he actually recommends would be more likely to lead to *acedia* than to "intellectual love of God". What we really need is an ideal which is an efficient as well as a final cause, and such an ideal is impossible if value and exist- ence are really ultimately disjoined. Actual advance in good must be a response to a movement initiated and sustained by the eternal and divine. Morality itself then leads us up directly to the "theological" problems of grace and nature, faith and works. These problems are, in fact, simply one special form of the more general problem of divine "transcendence". We have to note that no pure "immanence" philosophy can take morality with sufficient seriousness. Denial of divine "tran- scendence" leads to Pelagianism in theory and self-righteous- ness in practice, denial of divine "immanence" to antinomian- ism. In moral practice you cannot rise above your present level by "lifting yourself by your own hair", nor by the strength of an ideal which is only "your own ideal". The initiative in remaking of personality cannot come simply from within the personality which is to be remade. In this sense all genuine morality presupposes the supernatural as its environment and nutriment. This does not mean that person- ality can be remade without genuine personal effort and hard work. But the hour of "vision" in which the inspiration for the work comes is one of a vision in which we look outward, away from ourselves. We do not find our route for the future from contemplation of the route of the past; the complete "ideal" is itself apprehended, however indistinctly. A natural theology which takes the moral life seriously should present three characteristics. It must regard God (1) not merely as Creator but as Redeemer and Sanctifier and (2) as the lover of men. This may be anthropomorphism, but it is unavoidable anthro- pomorphism. (3) It must regard the life of God as essentially an activity of self-communication, as is done in the orthodox doctrine of the Trinity. This makes it impossible to set "natural" and "historical" or "revealed" theology in sharp opposition, or to deny the reality of "revelation" on *a priori* philosophical grounds.

The problem of the destiny of the individual man is second- ary and dependent; God, not immortality, is the primary interest of an ethical religion and theology. From this point of view, metaphysical arguments for the "natural immortality" of the human mind are of little value, besides being incon- clusive. This is equally true of the alleged experimental proofs furnished by "spiritualism". Examination of McTaggart's objection to "moral" arguments for immortality. It can only be sustained if we accept the ultimate separation of value and fact, as McTaggart does, in principle, by excluding God from his metaphysics. Our problem is whether the moral nature of man indicates his destination for a future beyond the grave, and, if so, what light it throws on the quality of this future. In any case, we must not expect the light to be other than very dim. We may consider first (1) the argument from the *con- sensus* of mankind, (2) the appeal to the widespread *wish* for continuance. As to (1), the *consensus* seems in fact to be much more general than is often asserted, and thus to be at least a suggestive fact of human nature. As to (2), it may be urged that the existence of a wish is no proof that it will be gratified, and even that this particular wish is only a masked form of the instinct of self-preservation. But there are very grave difficul- ties in accepting this second statement; it seems insufficient to account for the *specific* beliefs of humanity about the "unseen world". The future, as contemplated by mankind in general, is not the kind of future we can suppose to be keenly desired. It may be said that we are dealing with a primitive impulse more deep-seated than conscious wish, but can we really think of "unconscious impulse" as capable of the effects the theory ascribes to it? The more old-fashioned "naturalistic" explanation of the facts by appeal to dream-experiences involves a similar difficulty. However such beliefs in the mere continuance of life beyond death originate, they are non-ethical. A genuine moral argument for immortality must be one to the effect that the destruction of human personalities would make the moral end unattainable. If *this* can be proved, the proof will be sufficient for those who believe in the absolute objectivity of moral obligation, though for no others. This is, in substance, the position of Kant.

We may fairly argue from the reality of a function to the reality of an environment in which it finds its use. The question at stake is whether the moral life presents us with functions which demand the "other world" as an environment, *i.e.* whether the "good" is such that it *cannot* be obtained "in this life". Is this world a home or a place of pilgrimage? This is not a merely speculative problem, since our rule of conduct is necessarily and profoundly affected by our answer. In the last resort the question is whether it is ever morally justifiable to sacrifice known "worldly good", except in the prospect of winning more good of the same kind. Mill, for example, regards such sacrifice as an unfortunate accident due to bad social conditions and never justified except by the prospect of creating a greater amount of "happiness". It is demanded as absolutely necessary in any moral scheme which aims at the "remaking" of personality, and no compensation "in the same kind" is contemplated. Is devotion to the temporal improvement of human society a sufficient justification of the moral imperatives? If not, the moralist, who is committed to holding that they are justifiable, must look to the "beyond" for the justification. Professor Laird's argument in favour of the "secularist" position summarised. Its vulnerable point is that it is only valid against one who says "Let us eat and drink for to-morrow we die", not against one who says "To-morrow will see the end of us all, therefore eating and not-eating are alike futile". Professor Laird himself holds that *all* "imperatives" are moral, that no imperative commands the impossible, and that the supreme imperative is to "make the best of yourself". He is bound to consider whether, without the "beyond", *this* imperative does not command the impossible. If it does not, the moral good must involve full mastery not only of our circumstances but of our "moods and passions", the completion of the making of our personality, and this involves transcendence of temporality and all finite loyalties. So the "well-being" we really desire for our successors is a better *personality*. The "paradox of humanitarianism" to which this leads. We cannot overvalue the temporal "good" of mankind, provided that there is something we value still more, the "remaking" of mankind. And that requires the surrender of every temporal good "when the time comes". Yet, unless the moral imperative is self-stultifying, complete surrender must achieve the "saving" of the moral self. This means that the moral good is a personal life not expressible in terms of duration, and yet intensely real, and not affected by death. Such a life involves at once enrichment and "purgation", and there is no good reason to think of the purgation as ended at death. Moral superiority of the Christian conception of the "last things" over oriental theories of "reincarnation". No reason to think that spiritual "adventure" could be absent from the "life to come". Bearing of this on the difficulties suggested in *Appearance and Reality*. The *possibility* of a "final reprobation" cannot be excluded from an ethical theory of the life to come.

If the moral life is marked by the tension between the temporal and the eternal, there must be an element of "other-worldliness" in practical moral living, and we have to ask what kind of other-worldliness is morally legitimate. The same problem recurs in aesthetics. Here, too, by universal consent, "earthiness" or "worldliness" is incompatible with the highest achievement. The good man and the good artist must both be "men of this world" and yet "unworldly". Illustration of the combination from the work of Shakespeare (*Macbeth, The Tempest, Antony and Cleopatra*). Life is equally spoiled by concentration on a merely manageable "success" and by forgetting the duty of the moment in concentration on what lies beyond all moments. The right rule is to make the very using of temporal good itself an act of devotion to more abiding good. The "flesh" is not simply to be suppressed in the interests of the "spirit", but converted into its minister. The only way to succeed in being a "good man" is to aim at being something more. Not to do so leads to the degradation of morality into a mere respectability, which is not likely to remain even respectable. It is fatal in principle to sever the life of the "divine something in man" from the "work of *man*". Other-worldliness is either the death of all morality or the vital breath of moral life, according as it is of the wrong or the right kind. Ambiguity of the statement that all duties are "social". The great "social" virtues themselves seem only to flourish best when human society is not made the *supreme* object of loyalty. Humanity is best served by those who do not make it their "god". "Religious" and "secular" duties may be the same duties, but it makes all the difference whether they are discharged in a "religious" or in a "secular" spirit. It is generally

true that the duties arising from an embodied loyalty will only
be discharged to the height when they are "consecrated" by a
supreme "unembodied" loyalty. The "other" world is to "this"
world as "form" to "matter". "It is the death of idealism to
transfer its ideals to the future" (Bosanquet). If this means
that time and imperfection are illusions, it is merely false. A
practical ideal *necessarily* involves reference to the future. But
a sound ideal is a pattern which can persist with growing enrichment into a new and unfamiliar future. "The other world
is only this world rightly understood". The truth or falsehood
of the saying depends on what we mean by "understood". The
process of acquiring moral personality, like that of learning
to appreciate art, is one in which what begins by being the
"other" and unfamiliar becomes increasingly dominant in the
pattern of the "world" of our habitual interests, and what was
at first familiar becomes strange, intrusive, and "other". The
"real" world is hierarchised; the pattern of the whole is repro-
duced in the parts with varying degrees of distinctness. A subordinate pattern is not understood until it is discerned to be
subordinate. Error of Professor Alexander on this point. Thus
it is not true that the other world is this world understood, if
you mean to imply that this world can be understood by taking
as its dominant pattern one which can be detected by abstractive consideration of a restricted selection of characters, as
is done, *e.g.*, when the saying is used as a sufficient disproof of
the reality of miracles, grace, revelation, a future life. Practical
bearing of this on the conduct of life. We only come to a right
understanding of "this" world by incorporation of patterns
originally felt to belong to the "other" and "unfamiliar".
Understanding is not the same as the elimination of complexity. Every partial pattern has an "other" beyond it. Hence we
only come near to grasping the pattern of the whole by looking
for it in the rich concrete reality of spiritual life. This is the
final justification of our refusal to accept an ultimate dualism
of fact and value. Values are the dominant features of the
pattern of the whole, and therefore must permeate and shape
the course of actuality. Fragmentariness, dependence, and contingency are more characteristic of the "created" than error or
sin. The moral growth of the individual as an example of the
integration of partial patterns.

IX. The Goal of the Moral Life   .   .   .   386

The allegation that the moral life is, from its very nature,
one of aiming at the unattained and that with attainment
morality itself would simply disappear. The "antinomy" of the
moral life as stated, *e.g.*, by Bradley. "Morality is fighting
against evil, but if evil were destroyed there would be nothing

left to fight; hence morality is trying to annihilate itself." We cannot meet this allegation by saying that the moral life is a fighting not for victory but for the sake of the fight. Good is not made good by the fact that some men prefer evil. Men will not fight hard unless you convince them that they are contending for something worth fighting for. It is thus of the first importance to consider whether, after all, the fundamental aspiration of morality is self-destructive. This might be true if we could accept such an account of morality as H. Spencer's (as Bradley does not). Spencer's theory, in fact, contradicts itself, and is also based on a grave misreading of the facts of life. The sense of moral obligation does not in fact grow weaker as social life "evolves". It would be truer to say that the standard becomes more exacting and is more closely lived up to. Spencer's error seems to be due to the assumption that morality is simply putting right what is amiss and that there is only a limited amount of wrong social relation to be put right. Arbitrariness of these assumptions. It would be as reasonable to say that science is simply the correction of errors and that, since the number of errors to be corrected is finite, science will vanish from a "fully evolved" human life. (Cf. the thesis of Avenarius.) Spencer also confounds obligation itself with the awareness of it, and this with consciousness of disagreeable effort. Now morality is no more the mere righting of wrongs than science the mere correction of errors. Even in a society where there are no "abuses" there would remain the work of embodying the love of each for all in the detail of daily life. Bradley may, however, intend the criticism to be directed more specially against Kant, who makes the same sort of initial assumption as Spencer in a subtler form, by holding that it is of the essence of morality to be a struggle against "inclinations". If this is a sound position, a moral "rational theology" would have to reject the conception of a final "beatitude". Kant has forgotten that the final elimination of "inclination" would not really amount to the confusion of man with God. Fruition and aspiration may be blended, and such a life would be definitely man's and not God's. Green's view on this sounder than Kant's. There might well be progress in fruition in a life where there was no longer progress towards fruition. Life "in Heaven" would be life by "vision", but the vision might be capable of ever-growing enrichment. And those who see most might well have the "social service" of helping others to see. This would also leave room for endless spiritual adventure. To identify morality simply with the struggle against evil is like identifying art with the acquisition of technique. The main business of the social life is not simply to learn how to love rightly, but to love, and this may well persist in a state where we have no longer to unlearn unloving or foolishly loving ways. Bosanquet's depreciation of morality as the sphere of "claims and counter-claims" a mere caricature, resting on the notion that finite individualities are necessarily repellent of one another. This is really true of the shallow, not the rich, personalities. In a heaven of beatitude, the moral life would be transfigured but not transformed into something non-moral. We need to employ the Aristotelian distinction between a "process" and an "activity". If we do so we shall see that there is nothing irrational in anticipating a state in which the process of forming character is over, while the activity issuing from character remains. Such a view, no doubt, implies that progress *in* good, though not progress towards good, persists "in Heaven" and affords justification for the conception of our present state as one of "probation". It also implies the presence of an irreducible element of succession and temporality in the life of all "creatures", an element which may "decrease indefinitely" as we ascend higher in the scale of being. Hence a knowledge which leaves no place for surprise seems possible only to the Creator. Hence there would be room for "practice" as well as "contemplation" even in Heaven.

I

INTRODUCTORY

O Wisdom, coming out of the mouth of the Highest, reaching from the beginning even unto the end, graciously and mightily ordering all things, come to us and teach us the way of understanding.—Antiphon of December 16th.

THOSE of us who are from time to time honoured by the invitation to lecture on Lord Gifford's foundation are placed under a definite restraint in the choice of our subject-matter by the fact that each of us is acting as temporary substitute for a permanent Professor of Natural Theology. We are instructed to deal, as such a Professor would be bound by ordinance to deal, exclusively with "natural" theology, and natural theology is a name with a well-known history and an established significance. The phrase was introduced into the vocabulary of educated men by Cicero's contemporary, the famous *littérateur* and antiquarian M. Terentius Varro,[1] for the express purpose of discriminating an account of God and divine things which makes the claim to be strictly true from two other accounts of the same matters which advance no such pretensions, the *mythical* and the *civil* theologies. Mythical theology meant acquaintance with the tales of gods and their doings told in, or implied by, current imaginative literature. Since the Periclean age, the current opinion in "enlightened" circles had been that these stories are the mere inventions of poets,[2] whose only aim is to entertain

---

[1] Augustine, *De civitat. Dei*, vi. 5.

[2] Cf. Euripides, *Heracles* 1346 ἀοιδῶν οἴδε δύστηνοι λόγοι, Isocrates, xi. 38 ἀλλὰ γὰρ οὐδέν σοι τῆς ἀληθείας ἐμέλησεν, ἀλλὰ ταῖς τῶν ποιητῶν βλασφημίαις ἐπ-

and amuse. Civil theology is knowledge of the various feasts and fasts of the State Calendar and the ritual appropriate to them, such as is imparted, for six months of the year, by Ovid's *Fasti*. The whole of this cultus, it was held, is the manufacture of legislators aiming at social utility and convenience. But *philosophic*, or *natural*, theology is a different thing. It is the doctrine of God and the divine seriously taught by scientific philosophers as an integral part of a reasoned theory of φύσις, *natura*, the reality of things. It thus makes a definite claim, well founded or not, to be genuine ἐπιστήμη, to give us truth, in the same sense in which geometry or arithmetic does so. The ground to be covered by such a doctrine of God had already been marked out with some precision by Plato in the tenth book of the *Laws*; it is the same ground to which, in the main, natural theology has confined itself ever since Plato's first erection of it into a scientific discipline.

It was Plato's conviction that there are three fundamental truths about God which cannot be denied, or even called in question, without poisoning moral life, personal and corporate, at its sources. They are these: (1) God, a perfectly good and wise supreme mind, exists and is the author of all "becoming", of all *we* call "nature"; (2) God controls all the events which make up nature for ends worthy of His perfect wisdom and goodness; (3) God exercises a moral government of mankind in accord with a law of sovereign and inflexible justice which ensures that each shall receive his deserts—a thesis from which the immortality of the human self follows as a corollary. From Plato's time to our own, the natural, rational, or philosophical, theologian has remained in principle true to this programme:

ηκολούθησας, οἱ δεινότερα μὲν πεποιηκότας καὶ πεπονθότας ἀποφαίνουσι τοὺς ἐκ τῶν ἀθανάτων γεγονότας ἢ τοὺς ἐκ τῶν ἀνθρώπων τῶν ἀνοσιωτάτων κτλ.

God, Providence, Judgement to come have been and are his special themes; his confession of belief might be said to be, *credo in unum Deum, vivum et remuneratorem*.[1] Thus, to take one or two typical examples, we may consider first the general scheme of the great classic work of the golden age of Scholasticism on our subject, the *Summa contra Gentiles* of St. Thomas.[2] We are told there (*S.C.G.* i. 9) that the knowledge of God accessible to the human mind independently of specific revelation may be brought under three heads. We may consider (1) what may be asserted of God in Himself, *quae Deo secundum seipsum conveniunt*; (2) what may be asserted about the procession of the creatures from God, *processus creaturarum ab ipso*; (3) and about the ordination of the creatures towards God as their end, *ordo creaturarum in ipsum sicut in finem*. The starting-point of the whole inquiry will therefore be the demonstration of the *existence* of God, *consideratio qua demonstratur Deum esse*. In accord with this scheme, the first book of the work is given to the consideration of the existence and attributes of God, the second to God's relation to the historical world of finite "creatures" as its creator, the third to His fuller relation to the creatures as their "good", His providential government, His eternal moral law, and His action as judge and as bestower of grace. Only the last book falls outside this scheme,

---

[1] See the continuous exposition of this elementary theology in *Laws* x. 893 B 1-907 D 1, and compare the brief statement, which we may fairly call Plato's personal "confession of faith", *Ep.* vii. 335 A 2 πείθεσθαι δὲ ὄντως ἀεὶ χρὴ τοῖς παλαιοῖς τε καὶ ἱεροῖς λόγοις, οἳ δὴ μηνύουσιν ἡμῖν ἀθάνατον ψυχὴν εἶναι δικαστάς τε ἴσχειν καὶ τίνειν τὰς μεγίστας τιμωρίας, ὅταν τις ἀπαλλαχθῇ τοῦ σώματος· διὸ καὶ τὰ μεγάλα ἁμαρτήματα καὶ ἀδικήματα σμικρότερον εἶναι χρὴ νομίζειν κακὸν πάσχειν ἢ δρᾶσαι.

[2] Thomas gives his reason for confining the argument to "natural" divinity at *S.C.G.* i. 2. A Christian cannot appeal, in controversy with Mohammedans or "Pagans", to the authority of a "scripture" acknowledged by both parties: unde necesse est ad naturalem rationem recurrere, cui omnes assentire coguntur; quae tamen in rebus divinis deficiens est.

since it is concerned with the "revealed" doctrines of the Trinity, the Incarnation of the Word, the Sacraments, and the final state of the penitent and impenitent —all matters in relation to which the function of human reason is no longer positive demonstration, but the mere dialectical dissolution of objections raised by "infidels" against the authoritative teaching of the Church.[1]

In the same way, the first half of Butler's *Analogy*, which bears the sub-title *Natural Religion*, takes as its topics in order, *The Future Life, The Government of God by Rewards and Punishments*, the moral character of this government, the conception of our present state as one of probation, the moral freedom of man (ch. 6, *On the Opinion of Necessity*); the *existence* of God being treated as outside the argument on the ground that it is not disputed by the Deists, against whom the whole treatise is directed. So the famous *Boyle Lectures* of Samuel Clarke[2] deal in order with the existence of God, the attributes of God as Creator and Moral Governor of the world, the certainty of a "state of rewards and punishments", as truths assumed to be capable of formal demonstration, and then proceed to argue "dialectically" for the necessity of a specific divine revelation and to dismiss the objections urged against the claims of Christianity in particular to be this revelation.

Kant's conception is, to all intents and purposes, the same (*KdrV*[2] 659 ff.). With his usual quaintly pedantic

---

[1] *S.C.G.* iv., *Proemium*, Restat autem sermo habendus de his quae nobis revelata sunt divinitus ut credenda, excedentia intellectum humanum. . . . Probanda enim sunt huiusmodi auctoritate sacrae Scripturae, non autem ratione naturali; sed tamen ostendendum est quod rationi naturali non sunt opposita, ut ab impugnatione infidelium defendantur.

[2] The full title is "A Discourse concerning the *Being and Attributes of God*, the *Obligations of Natural Religion* and the TRUTH AND CERTAINTY of the *Christian Revelation*. In Answer to Mr. *Hobbs, Spinoza*, the *Author of the Oracles of Reason*, and other Deniers of Natural and Revealed Religion. Being sixteen Sermons Preached in the Cathedral-Church of St. *Paul*, in the years 1704, and 1705, at the Lecture founded by the Honourable *ROBERT BOYLE*, Esq.".

fondness for exhaustive formal classification, he begins his criticism of speculative theology with the time-honoured distinction between a purely rational and a revealed knowledge of God. Rational theology is then subdivided into two types, the *transcendental*, that of the strict Deist, who admits only the existence of a *first*, or *supreme*, or *necessary* being with a character wholly unknown and unknowable, and the *natural*, that of the Theist, who holds that some light on the character of the Supreme Being can be derived by analogical reasoning from the known character of the human mind. (Hume, we observe, would thus rank in Kant's classification as a Theist, since he admits at least a "remote" analogy between the Supreme Being and the human mind.) Strictly speaking, Kant goes on to say, such a natural theology may take either of two very different forms. "Natural theology concludes to the attributes and existence of an author of the world from the structure, order and unity, found in this world, a world in which we have to assume two kinds of causality with their rules, Nature and Freedom. Hence natural theology ascends from this world to the supreme intelligence as the principle either of all natural or of all moral order and perfection; we call it in the first case physico-theology, in the second, *moral* theology. "But, he adds, since we understand by the word *God* not an "eternal blindly-working nature," but a supreme being "who is to be thought of as the originator of things through his intelligence and freedom", in rigid accuracy we ought to deny that the mere Deist has any real belief in God, though courtesy leads us to express ourselves more gently by saying that the Deist believes only in a God, the Theist in a *living* God. At bottom, then, natural theology means for Kant the doctrine of God as free intelligent creator and moral ruler of the Universe, and we may note that on *his* classification the doctrine of Spinoza is a "true atheism".

It is, of course, no more true of ancient than of modern philosophers that they have spoken on these themes with a single voice. Of old, as to-day, the pure sceptic concluded that knowledge in such high matters is impossible to man; the Epicurean vigorously asseverated[1] that we can be sure of the existence of the gods, but still more vigorously that we can be sure that there is neither providence, moral government of mankind, nor life to come. But properly speaking an atheistic theology, or a theology of simple nescience, is still a theology, though it may be a poor one. Even to say that mankind is temporarily incompetent to decide the issues Plato had raised is to admit at least the competence of human intelligence to take cognisance of them. The court may find itself unable to reach a decision, but the questions have at least not been raised before the wrong tribunal. To get clean rid of theology we should need to maintain that its problems are not merely unanswerable by human intelligence, but are not even questions with an intelligible meaning, that they are mere strings of insignificant vocables with none of the characters of a genuine question beyond the rising pitch of the final syllable or the printed mark of interrogation after the concluding word.

It is, no doubt, conceivable that a man might take up this position; there seem even to be philosophers[2]

---

[1] Epicurus, *Ep.* iii. (Usener, *Epicurea,* § 123) θεοὶ μὲν γὰρ εἰσίν· ἐναργὴς γὰρ αὐτῶν ἐστιν ἡ γνῶσις; Κύριαι Δόξαι 1-2, τὸ μακάριον καὶ ἄφθαρτον οὔτε αὐτὸ πράγματα ἔχει οὔτε ἄλλῳ παρέχει, ὥστε οὔτε ὀργαῖς οὔτε χάρισι συνέχεται· ἐν ἀσθενεῖ γὰρ πᾶν τὸ τοιοῦτον. ὁ θάνατος οὐδὲν πρὸς ἡμᾶς· τὸ γὰρ διαλυθὲν ἀναισθητεῖ. τὸ δ' ἀναισθητοῦν οὐδὲν πρὸς ἡμᾶς.

[2] The sceptics, whose views are represented for us by Sextus Empiricus, may serve as an example. Hobbes, again, seems to hold that "natural reason" requires us to make no theological assertion beyond that of the existence of an unknowable cause of the world.

who must be presumed to have adopted it if they are
to be supposed alive to all the consequences of their
principles, though such philosophers seem to be a small
minority.   If I held the view myself, I should not, of
course, be attempting the delivery of a series of Gifford
Lectures, since it is the only theological position which
seems to be ruled out by the terms of Lord Gifford's
bequest.   So long as the questions which give rise to
theologies are allowed to be genuine questions with an
intelligible sense, it is open to a lecturer on the foundation to treat them with complete freedom, provided only
the freedom is combined, as it always should be, with
sincerity, candour, and courtesy. He may contend that
human intelligence is debarred by its own inherent limitations from finding any answers to its own questions,
or again that in the present state of our information any
answer would be premature. Or he may find solutions
of some or all of the problems in an actual existing
theology or philosophy, or in a new philosophy or
theology of his own. He would be within his rights if
he saw fit to argue that the true answers to the questions
have been already given in the Catechism of Trent, the
Thirty-nine Articles, or the Westminister Confession,
that they are contained in the Christian, Jewish, or other
Scriptures, the Hermetic writings, the works of Mrs.
Mary Baker Eddy, or the *Philosophie positive* of Comte.
The only restriction on his freedom is the highly proper
one that when he finds the solution to a problem in the
dogmas of an existing theology or philosophy, he must
offer *reasons* for holding that the dogma in question
is true; he must not stifle examination of its truth by a
mere appeal to extra-rational authority.   He may be
as orthodox, by any given standard of orthodoxy, as
he pleases; only he must not allege the orthodoxy of
his convictions as sufficient proof of their truth.   He

may be as "unconventional" as he chooses, but he must have something better to urge on behalf of his unconventional positions than the bare fact that they are "heresies".

If the subject-matter of a course of Gifford Lectures is thus limited by certain justifiable restrictions, none, fortunately, are laid upon what it is the fashion to call, by a metaphor from the national game of Scotland, the speaker's "approach" to his subject. He may, if he is a professional philosopher, directly attack the metaphysical problem of the nature of "ultimate reality," or the "epistemological" problem of the characteristics of genuine knowledge and the conditions of its possibility. If his interests lie in either the exact or the descriptive sciences, he may choose to discuss the initial postulates, the special methods, and the present achievements of his own study, and the worth of the contribution it can make to a fully integrated and co-ordinated reaction of the human person against the total environment in which human life has to be lived. If his concern has been more with the study of man than with inanimate or infra-human nature, he may speak to us, out of the fullness of his knowledge, and beyond it, of our human past. He may seek, I know not with what success, to throw light on the truth and worth of religious convictions and practices by considering them in their first beginnings, as part of the still crude and inarticulate response of the nascent human intelligence to its bewildering surroundings, and discussing their social value as creating, supporting, or transforming the corporate life of the family, the clan, the horde. Or he may survey the customs and beliefs of men at a higher stage of development; he may attempt to reconstruct the thought of Israelites or Babylonians, Egyptians or Iranians, Greeks or Romans, about man's unseen lords and his dimly surmised destiny, may exhibit its significance for the culture of these peoples, and invite us to consider what legacy from these old religions might yet profitably be carried over into our own vision of the world, and what we shall do well to reject as a *damnosa haereditas* of error and folly. We might, again, be addressed by a poet, or other artist, anxious to discuss the question what witness, if any, his own art bears to the reality of the unseen things. The Gifford foundation has already been fruitful in our Scottish Universities, and not least in St. Andrews, in work by men of acknowledged eminence along most of the lines of which I have spoken, and we must hope that it will continue to bear like fruit in the future.

It is hardly necessary to state, before an audience in the University where I so long and so recently had the honour and happiness to teach, that I cannot undertake work of the kind I have been describing; you will all know that I possess none of the qualifications. I must not attempt even to attack the fundamental issues of metaphysics and epistemology, and to offer you anything in the way of a novel conception of the nature of reality or of knowledge. I am only too conscious that any positions I have so far been able to reach by inquiry in these remote and difficult regions are provisional and tentative, and, I suspect, may not be too self-consistent. I can well believe that others are more fortunate, but, for my own part, the more I reflect on the deliverances of philosophers with a system, even those for whom I feel the highest reverence, the more readily do the words rise to my lips, *mirabilis facta est scientia tua ex me; confortata est, et non potero ad eam.*[1] I cannot promise anyone who may care to attend these lectures any new and startling information, or any

---

[1] Ps. cxxxviii. (Vulg.) 6.

particularly original fresh "orientation" in thought. What I propose to attempt is something less ambitious, though perhaps not without its use.

Since it has been my business in life for many years, and will remain so until my days for business are over, to introduce young people to the study of moral philosophy, it is most fitting that I should approach the questions which a Gifford lecturer is expected to consider from the side of ethics. There, if anywhere, I ought to be least out of my depth, or perhaps it would be more modest to say, sticking most strictly to my last. Such a treatment may be further recommended by a rather different consideration. No living theology has ever arisen from mere intellectual curiosity. The serious theologies have always come into being as the fruit of reflection upon lived and practised religions; hence the truth we all recognise in the saying that *pectus facit theologum*. And though a richly living religion is always something much more than a rule of conduct, it is never, for those whose religion it is, less than this. A religion we can accept means, among other things, a guide by the light of which we can face all the tragedy and all the comedy of life joyously and undismayed, without frivolity as without misgivings. The march of events in our own country and our own life-time has been sufficient to prove that the old combats which used to be waged between the professors and the assailants of our own religion, the Christian, over such problems as the discrepancies between Scripture and geology or astronomy, the date and authorship of the Pentateuch, the books of the prophets, or the Pastoral Epistles, were mere insignificant engagements between outposts. The infinitely serious issue for the whole future of European civilisation is that of the soundness of the Christian ideal of human character and the Christian rule of life.

If we can still maintain that in that rule and ideal we have something absolute and permanent, authoritative for Europeans of our own age no less than for Jewish and Hellenistic communities of the first century, or for our own ancestors of the thirteenth or seventeenth, it is certain that the Christian religion will survive uninjured any criticism it may yet have to encounter from biologists or anthropologists. If the finality of the Christian ideal of personal character and the Christian rule of conduct cannot be maintained, no temporary success of the apologist in rebutting this or that ill-considered "scientific" or "historical" criticism can alter the fact that the Christian faith, as a religion, is under sentence of death. And it is a chief symptom of the mental condition of our age that this precise issue is being pressed upon us with a wholesomely relentless insistence. As recently as the years of my own boyhood, the most prominent of the unfavourable critics of Christianity in our own country were usually the most anxious to declare that their quarrel was with bad science and false history, not with a bad ideal of life or a false rule of conduct. At the present moment the sons and daughters of the men of my own generation are expressly urged, by persons whose intelligence and conscientiousness are undisputed, to break with the whole moral tradition of Christianity, precisely on the ground of its inadequacy to furnish a rule of life for a society which, so it is assumed, has outgrown its past. The spirit of man, we are told on all sides, has "found new paths," and we must walk in them.

Indeed something more is at stake than the fate of a particular historical faith, however dear or august. Not Christianity only, but religion itself, is on its trial. It may quite well be that the future philosophical student of history will yet find the most significant and disquieting of all the social changes of the "Victorian age" to be the combination of universal state-enforced primary education with the transference of the work of the teacher to the hands of laymen under no effective ecclesiastical or theological control. The effect of this successful laicisation of education has inevitably been to raise the immediate practical question whether moral conduct, the direction of life, does not form a self-contained domain, and ethics a wholly autonomous science, neither requiring support or completion from religion, nor affording rational ground for religious convictions of any kind. The gravity of this practical issue can hardly be exaggerated. Something more momentous than even our national existence is at stake; the question is that of an ideal of life for the whole of future humanity. It is idle to hope, as some of our contemporaries perhaps are hoping, that the secularisation of education may at least leave religion in being as a graceful and desirable embellishment of life for the exceptionally sensitive and imaginative souls. It is of the very nature of a living religion to claim the supreme direction of effort and action. If the claim is disallowed, religion itself ceases to be real; if it is allowed, it is idle to dispute the right of religion to be made the foundation of education. A wrong answer to the question about the relations of morality and religion, once generally accepted, is certain, sooner or later, to be made the foundation of an educational policy, and adoption of a radically vicious educational policy means shipwreck for the spiritual future of mankind.

I propose, then, to discuss this question of the relations between morality and religion. I do not, of course, mean the subordinate historical question of the ways in which the actual ideal of character cherished, or the actual level of practice attained, by a given community

at a given date has been affected for good or bad by the
religious usages, traditions, and convictions of the community. Even had I the inclination to conduct an inquiry of the kind pursued in the mid-nineteenth century
in well-known works by such writers as Buckle and
Lecky, I have not the necessary minute erudition. The
question I would seek to answer, if I can, is definitely
not historical, but critical and philosophical. It is, in
fact, that which is raised, though inadequately, in
Kant's second *Critique*, and more simply presented by
Plato in the *Philebus*. What is the true character of
the "good for man"? Would successful prosecution of
all the varied activities possible to man, simply as one
temporal and mutable being among others, suffice to
constitute the "condition" which, in Plato's words,[1]
"will make any man's life happy"? Or have we to confess that, at the heart of all our moral effort, there is
always the aspiration towards a good which is strictly
speaking "eternal", outside the temporal order and incommensurable with anything falling within that order?
Is the world where we play a part for our three-score
years and ten what Wordsworth called it, to Shelley's
disgust, "the home of all of us," where we must "find
our happiness, or not at all," or is it, as others have
told us, a far country from which we have to make a
tedious pilgrimage to our genuine *patria*? In language
more fashionable to-day, have we as moral beings only
one "environment," a temporal, or two, a temporal and
an eternal? If the eternal exists, what light is thrown
on its character by our experience of the struggle to
attain to it? What kind of thing must it be, if it is
indeed the goal of all our human aspiration? As a
second question, if our true good is a "thing infinite

---

[1] *Philebus* 11 D 4 ὡς νῦν ἡμῶν ἑκάτερος ἕξιν ψυχῆς καὶ διάθεσιν ἀποφαίνειν τινὰ
ἐπιχειρήσει τὴν δυναμένην ἀνθρώποις πᾶσι τὸν βίον εὐδαίμονα παρέχειν.

and eternal," is it conceivable that it can be attained by a one-sided movement of endeavour on our part, or must we think of our own moral effort as a movement of response, elicited and sustained throughout by an antecedent outgoing movement from the side of the eternal? Is the reality of what Christian theologians call the grace of God a presupposition of the moral life itself? These are the questions to which we have in the first place to find an answer, when we undertake to discuss the relations between morality and religion and the bearing of specifically moral experiences on the issues of natural theology.

The attempt to answer these questions will naturally lead on to a further third question, that of the degree in which "autonomy" can rightly be ascribed to moral science in particular, or to science in general. If we should find that the basis of a sound rule of conduct and a true ideal of character have themselves to be sought in the eternal realities which religions claim to disclose, we shall be driven to reconsider the well-known grounds on which Kant proclaimed the "primacy of the practical reason", and to ask whether they do not prove something Kant would not have been willing to grant, the "primacy" not of ethics, but of divinity. We shall be face to face again with the claim made in the famous metaphor of St. Peter Damiani [1] that theology, the knowledge of God, is the rightful mistress; "philosophy" and "science", the whole body of our systematised knowledge of the creatures, only the handmaid. Manifestly, such a claim should neither be admitted nor rejected without careful scrutiny. Religion is, to put it bluntly, by no means an accommodating neigh-

---

[1] *De divina omnipotentia*, v. (Migne, *Patrolog. Lat.* cxlv. 603) "quae tamen artis humanae peritia, si quando tractandis sacris eloquiis adhibetur, non debet ius magisterii sibimet arroganter arripere, sed velut ancilla dominae quodam famulatus obsequio subservire."

bour: grant her a single inch, and she will promptly demand an ell, or rather, not an ell, but the whole compass of sea and land. She will have nothing at all, or else the supreme direction of all the activities of life. And we cannot well allow that claim without conceding a corresponding claim to primacy for theology, the organised body of our religious *knowledge*. To admit religion into life but exclude theology from science, fashionable as the compromise has been in recent times, would be like conceding the importance of the physician as a practical director, but dismissing physiologist and pathologist as impostors. Yet on the other side, theology is clearly not entitled to dictate to the student of morals, or of anything else, either his point of departure or his point of arrival in his investigation of the facts of life. Unless the investigation has been genuinely free from such interference, the witness of ethics, or any other study, to theology becomes worthless in the degree in which the evidence has undergone preliminary manipulation. We are thus compelled to deal in the last place with the double question: (*a*) What is the kind and degree of autonomy which may reasonably be claimed for any science? (*b*) under what limitations is it possible to claim some kind of primacy for theology?

.The discussion of these questions ought not to demand any very minute or profound acquaintance with the technicalities of professional philosophy, or the special systems of individual philosophical thinkers. The issues to be faced are the same which confront any man who has become conscious of the duty of playing a man's part in the business of active living and the necessity, if he is to live in a way worthy of a man, of playing that part consistently and on intelligible principle. None but those who are content to drift through existence without any attempt to understand it can

ignore them or be indifferent to them. What they most
demand for their profitable discussion is not so much
information, or erudition, or even dialectical ingenuity,
as openness to the whole wide range of suggestion with
which all our active experiences are pregnant, combined
with the sound and balanced judgement we popularly
call common sense—the *esprit juste*, to speak with
Pascal, rather than the *esprit de finesse*.

In actual life these qualifications do not seem to
be more liberally distributed among metaphysicians,
psychologists, or constructors of theoretical systems of
ethics than among their neighbours. Hence, for our purpose the thought of great makers of literature who have
been also great readers of the human heart may be
much more important than the speculations of the professed metaphysician or psychologist. In particular, I
venture, at my own peril, to think that the popular
estimate of the authority attaching to the deliverances
of the psychologist by profession in matters of morals
and religion is grossly exaggerated, probably in consequence of an elementary fallacy of confusion. The
psychologist manufacturing, on the basis of his laboratory experiments, an artificial *schema* of the human
mind is too often confused with a very different person,
the reader of individual human character. Yet all of us
probably know able psychologists whose verdicts on
character or interpretations of motive we should never
dream of trusting in an affair of any practical moment,
and must certainly know many a man whose judgements of his fellows and insight into the possibilities of
life we should accept as highly authoritative, though we
are well aware that he knows nothing of the highly
abstract science of psychology, and would very possibly
be merely puzzled if he tried to study it. When we wish
to confirm or correct our reading of human life, it may

safely be said, we do not commonly think of turning in the first instance to the works of the metaphysician or psychologist, or, if we do, the metaphysician or psychologist whose view of life we trust is trusted because he is something more than a specialist in metaphysics or psychology. We all attach great weight to Shakespeare's interpretation of human life, or Dante's, or Pascal's, or Wordsworth's; even when we reject their testimony, we at least do not reject it lightly. I believe it would be safe to say that Plato is the only metaphysician to whose verdicts on things human we ascribe anything like this significance, and the reason is manifest. It is that Plato was so much more than the author of a philosophical theory; he was one of the world's supreme dramatists, with the great dramatist's insight into a vast range of human character and experience, an insight only possible to a nature itself quickly and richly responsive to a world of suggestion which narrower natures of the specialist type miss. If I am found in the sequel appealing to the testimony of "moralists", I trust it will be understood that by moralists I do not mean primarily men who have devoted themselves to the elaboration of ethical systems, the Aristotles, or even the Kants, but men who have lived richly and deeply and thought as well as lived, the Platos, Augustines, Dostoievskys, and their fellows.

Similarly the psychologist who can teach us anything of the realities of the moral or religious life is not the Professor who satisfies a mere intellectual curiosity by laboratory experiments, or the circulation of *questionnaires* about the dates and circumstances of other men's "conversions", or "mystical experiences". A man might spend a long life at that business without making himself or his readers a whit the wiser. So long as he looks on at the type of experience he is investigating simply from the outside, he can hope to contribute nothing to its interpretation. He is in the position of a congenitally blind or deaf man attempting to construct a theory of beauty, in nature or art, by "circularising" his seeing and hearing friends with questions about their favourite colour-schemes or combinations of tones. The psychological records really relevant for our purpose are first and foremost those of the men who have actually combined the experience of the saint, or the aspirant after sanctity, with the psychologist's gift of analysis, the Augustines and Pascals, and next those of the men who have had the experiences, even when they have been unable to analyse and criticise them, the Susos and the Bunyans. Mere analytical and critical acumen without a relevant experience behind it should count for nothing, since in this, as in all matters which have to do with the interpretation of personal life, we can only read the soul of another by the light of that which we know "at first hand" within ourselves. To put the point in a paradoxical way, when we try to interpret the life of another, we are in much the situation we should occupy if we had to light a candle to see the sun, and if the apparent luminosity of the seen sun were directly proportional to the brightness of our candle. *Wär' nicht das Auge sonnenhaft, Wie könnte es das Licht erblicken?* may perhaps—I am not confident on the point—be meaningless in the physical world, but is strictly true in the moral.

One final observation before I attack my problem directly. We are to be concerned in our discussion with "natural" theology, and the very name suggests to us, as it did not to its inventor,[1] a contrast with "revealed" religion and theologies claiming to be based on "revelation". For the purpose of exhibiting the point of the

---

[1] Cf. C. C. J. Webb, *Studies in the History of Natural Theology*, pp. 10 ff.

contrast, we may be provisionally content to understand by a "revelation" any kind of spontaneous self-disclosure of a divine reality, as distinct from an attainment of knowledge about divine things reached purely by effort from our own human side. It is manifestly possible to hold more than one view of the relation of natural theology, as we have defined the phrase, in accordance with the precedent set by Varro, to a theology founded on revelation. One formally possible view, indeed, we may exclude at once, the view that a genuine natural theology and an equally genuine revelational theology might be in real contradiction. Such a contradiction would prove that either the natural theology had not been reached by the right use of human intelligence, and so was not "natural" in the sense in which we are using that word, or the revelation on which the revealed theology was based no genuine self-disclosure on the part of the divine, and therefore no true revelation. But two possibilities still remain. We might conceive that a revelation, if there is such a thing, would leave the results won by the aid of "natural human reason" standing without modification, merely supplementing them by further knowledge not attainable by unassisted human effort; again, we might conceive that the effect of revelation would be not merely to supplement "natural" knowledge, but to transform it in such a way that all the truths of natural theology would acquire richer and deeper meaning when seen in the light of a true revelation.

Whether there is any subtle disloyalty to reason involved in such conceptions of the supplementation, or enrichment, of natural theology by revelation, and if there is not, in which of these alternative ways we ought to conceive the relation of the two theologies, will be topics for future consideration. At the outset I am concerned only to mention the simple fact that, as matter of history, natural theology has never been found an entirely adequate expression of the attitude of devout souls to their world. It may fairly be doubted whether any man has been able to live and die nobly solely in the strength furnished by a "natural" religion or theology. Even if we consider the cases of intensely religiously-minded philosophers who have been markedly out of sympathy with the institutional cults and traditions of their community—a Plato, for example, or a Spinoza—it is not difficult to see that the practical faith with which they have confronted the issues of life and death has regularly gone far beyond the limits of legitimate deduction from the professed principles of their philosophy. And in Christian societies natural theology has only been pursued with steady devotion by men who, in point of fact, were earnest believers in an historical self-disclosure of the divine, and active adherents of a positive institutional religion. It has been a factor in the great institutional and traditional religions of the world, not a rival to them. The attempt of the Deists of the eighteenth century to erect what they called the "religion of nature" into a rival of historical and institutional Christianity was, as we all know, a short-lived failure. Partly, the champions of the "religion of nature" were insincere; their alleged devotion to "natural" religion was often no more than an excuse for practical irreligion and worldly living. Partly the being proposed for worship in the "religion of nature" was found too thin and insubstantial an abstraction to evoke genuine adoration in a rational creature. Even when the "religion of nature" did not begin in irreligion, it speedily lapsed into it. To-day, I take it, few of us would quarrel with the title of one of Blake's *brochures*, *There is No Natural Religion*. Men who feel the need of religion

as a guide, but cannot reconcile their intellectual convictions with unqualified acceptance of any of the institutional religions around them, fall back on some kind
of tentative personal faith which has its roots in one of
the great historical religions; from this they take what
they can and leave the rest. Men who in the eighteenth
century would have been among the more devotionally-
minded Deists enroll themselves now as the advanced
"Modernists" of Christianity or Judaism. They thus
bear impressive witness to the truth that worship, like
all the specifically human activities, morality, art, the
pursuit of knowledge, and the rest, is a supra-individual
activity, needing for its maintenance at a level of steady
and vigorous efficiency all the support afforded by
organised fellowship, definite institutions, and a great
historical tradition.

It is a curious paradox, when one comes to reflect,
that an age as alive as our own to the necessity for association, common interests, shared work, in the prosecution of science, and the value of a great inheritance
of tradition for the production of living art, should
tend to be suspiciously resentful of the suggestion that
the same conscious fellowship in a great community of
the living and the dead is equally important for the
soul's religious life. We readily admit that the discovery
of a great truth or the creation of a great poem, picture,
or symphony, by a solitary, alone in a society which
cares nothing for science or art and has no inheritance
of tradition in either, would be something like a moral
portent. Yet it is not uncommon to find estimable
writers expressing themselves, with a touch of contempt and a curious disregard of the historical facts,
as if there must be an actual opposition in principle
between a living personal faith and an institutional
religion, or as if the men of supreme insight and genius

in religion were so many flowers blossoming alone in a desert, owing nothing to the educative influence of association for a common purpose with the like-minded among the living, and less than nothing, if that were possible, to the traditions which bind a living generation to the like-minded among the dead.

In sober fact things are not thus. Religion, like science, requires a communal background. What Royal Societies are to the one, Churches are to the other. Organised and accumulated tradition plays the same part in both as the conservator of sanity and protectress against the tragedy of merely futile effort. No one can deny that institutions, traditions, conventions, have their very real dangers in all departments of life, but in all they are indispensable. They are edged tools, if you like, but necessary tools. You cannot, to be sure, conserve sanity in thought, art, or living, without some risk of occasional cramping of genius. But without some organised protection of sanity the world would be filled not with men of genius, but with "cranks", faddists, and lunatics. The real enemies of spiritual life in all its manifestations are not conventions and traditions, but conventionalism and traditionalism, outward respect for the letter of traditions, or the form of institutions, which are no longer alive. This must be my excuse, if excuse is needed, for frankly approaching the study of the moral and religious life in no spirit of affected neutrality and aloofness, but from the point of view of one moulded by education in a definite moral and religious tradition, and actively partaking in the common worship of a definite historical community. There is no reason why such historical loyalties need make clear-sighted critical study impossible. If the difficulty were insurmountable, the effects would be felt far beyond the bounds of a study of religion. It should be possible, and there is abundant evidence that it is possible, for an intelligent man to be a loyal and whole-hearted Scot, Englishman, or Frenchman without being blinded to the defects of the national character or institutions. Where will is morally upright and intelligence alert, the loyal citizen, indeed, is more likely to hit the mark with a criticism from within than the benevolent and intelligent foreigner, who must, to the end, remain an "outsider" to so much. And it is even so with the organised life of religious communities. You must be an *insider* if you are to have full comprehension of their real weaknesses as well as of their strength. In a world where the best of us carry about so much of the *fomes peccati*, men are naturally not prone to carry on the work of quiet criticism from within in public; they prefer to descant on the mote in a brother's eye, and to keep a decent silence about their troubles with the beam in their own. Such merely polemical criticism is seldom of much benefit to a man who honestly wants to understand. What the faults of the Christian Church are is probably better known to its devoted workers than to the smart non-Christian journalist, and though I have often listened, I trust in a spirit of willingness to learn, to trenchant "exposures" of the errors and sins of my own branch of that Church from representatives of other branches, I confess I have found the quiet comments of loyal supporters from within more enlightening. A "philosophy of religion", to be of any value, must not come from the detached theorist "holding no form of creed, but contemplating all"; it must be the fruit of patient and candid self-criticism on the part of men living the life they contemplate, each in his own way, but each ready to learn, alike from the others and from the outsider.

II

ACTUALITY AND VALUE

Io ti farò veder ogni valore.—DANTE.

ὡς ἀληθῶς τὸ ἀγαθὸν καὶ δέον συνδεῖν καὶ συνέχειν οὐδὲν οἴονται.—PLATO.

WE are now to attack the first of the questions we have proposed for examination. Does morality, if its claims are to be justified to the critical intelligence, involve any presuppositions which point beyond itself? Does it supply its own *raison d'être*? If not, does it receive its missing completion in the activities, however we define them, which are commonly called religious? To ask the question is to make the assumption that we are starting on our inquiry with some provisional definition, or at least description, both of morality and of religion. Such an initial statement may be highly tentative, as all "definitions in use" are bound to be. It will certainly need illumination, and probably need correction, as our discussion proceeds, since the distinctive characters of the merely ethical and the specifically religious attitudes towards life can only emerge gradually in the course of the argument. Thus any formula from which we may start must appear, in the first instance, more or less arbitrary; its true significance and its justification, like that of "real" definitions in general, can only be discovered from the use to which it is put. No harm will be done if we consciously follow the practice, so often adopted by Aristotle, of beginning with a current definition which needs immediate correction, if only it leads us directly to the raising of a problem relevant to our purpose. Accordingly, I propose to make such a start on the present occasion from a brief and trenchant saying of the late Professor Bosanquet which has the double merit of setting the contrast between mere morals and religion in high relief and of leading straight up to what is, in principle, the most formidable issue we shall be called on to encounter.

"In morality", says Bosanquet, "we know that the good purpose is real, in religion we believe that nothing else is real." [1] On the face of it, the sentence calls for a certain amount of interpretation. There is, for instance, apparently an intentional contrast, of which the precise character is left unexplained, between the "knowledge" said to be characteristic of morality and the "faith" distinctive of religion. On this we need not dwell, since we find on consulting the context of the sentence that morality also is held by the writer to depend on a kind of faith. It is plain, again, that neither "knowledge" nor "faith", as the words are being employed by Bosanquet, means *mere* intellectual assent to a proposition as true. No one would call a man virtuous on the strength of his mere speculative assent to the statements that lewdness and cruelty are bad, generosity to a successful rival, and fairness to a formidable antagonist good. Nor should we think a man religious simply because he believed it to be true that God exists and that God's kingdom will some day come, in the same way in which he believes that there is a President of the Argentine Republic, or that cancer will some day be suppressed by medical science. The knowledge and the belief spoken of must both be taken to mean a *scientia* or a *fides sapida*, a knowledge and a belief which affirm themselves in prac-

---

[1] "The Kingdom of God on Earth" (*Science and Philosophy*, p. 346).

tice by dominating and regulating the whole lives of those who are in earnest with them, a knowledge and a belief operative to "good works".

Once more, the second half of the statement might be criticised on grounds which appeal with special force to many of those whom we all recognise as most sincerely religious. To say that *nothing* but the "good purpose" is real at least *seems* inconsistent with any vivid sense of the tremendous actuality and vitality of sin, as well as of fruitless physical and moral pain, and it might be urged that the influence of the various religions on life and character has been, and is, purifying and elevating precisely in proportion to their insistence on the reality of these antagonists of the "good purpose" and the duty of consecrating life to a "holy war" against them. And manifestly a "holy war" is something very different from a sham fight. If there is "really" no enemy to be overcome, the injunction to put on the "whole armour of righteousness" must appear no more than a dull and impious jest. It would seem that any religion which affirms the *exclusive* reality of the "good purpose" must lead to some indifferentist or antinomian apotheosis of "things as they are". Such a religion, as we see in the cases of the merely lewd or cruel nature-worships of the ancient and modern East, may be potent for deadly moral and spiritual mischief; at its most harmless, as I think we see from the working of what is quaintly miscalled "Christian Science", it is powerless as an inspiration to active moral good. In short, we might be asked whether, on the proposed definition, we should not have to give the name religion to the unethical eroticism of a Persian Sufi and refuse it to the faith of a Paul or an Augustine.

This is a difficulty felt keenly by others than the merely unspeculative. It lies at the root of the lifelong

polemic of my honoured and lamented friend Dr. Rash-
dall against the traditional conception of divine in-
finitude, and largely explains the violent revolt of so
acute a thinker as Antonio Aliotta against Theism
itself.[1] To admit the existence of God, according to the
brilliant Italian philosopher, is equivalent to converting
the "good fight" into a mere parade manœuvre, since if
God is, the issue of the combat is already decided, and
hence history becomes a mere pageant. Thus Aliotta's
reason for renouncing the Theism with which he began
his career is precisely that Theism implies the very conviction with which Bosanquet at least *seems* to identify
religion. It is true, to be sure, that Bosanquet's real
meaning was probably not quite what some of his
critics have taken it to be. Whatever may be the case
with some of the recent Italian Absolutists, Bosanquet
cannot be supposed by those who knew him to have
intended to deny the actuality of evil, or to belittle the
significance of those experiences of struggle and conflict
which have led moralists and saints to speak so constantly in metaphors borrowed from the battlefield.[2]
Whether, in the end, his statement may be not so understood as to be true we may have to consider later on. At
present I am concerned only to maintain that, like the
saying of Parmenides about the impossibility of thinking
of "what is not", it is a dark and a hard saying, not to
be taken at its "face-value". If there is a sense in which
whatever falls outside the "good purpose" can be said
to be unreal, it must also be true that "what is unreal
is in a sense real", as Plato[3] maintained that, with all
respect for Parmenides, "what is not in some sense
also is".

---

[1] See Aliotta, *La guerra eterna* (ed. 1), pp. 156 ff.
[2] Though I think it true that, judged from a Christian standpoint, his "sense
of sin" is *inadequate*.
[3] *Sophistes*, 258 D 5 ff.

The value of Bosanquet's antithesis for my own purpose is independent of these obvious strictures. I quote it because it leads directly to a criticism which goes much deeper. By the use of the word *real* it raises the whole familiar problem of the relation between fact and value. Religion, it might be said, at any rate so far answers to the proposed definition that it certainly rests on the conviction that something is absolutely real, or, in plainer language, is "bed-rock *fact*". It may be hard to say just what that something is, but it is clear that *some* existential proposition or propositions must be at the foundation of every religious faith. Every such faith is a faith *in* someone or something, and so presupposes at least certain conviction that this someone or something *is*, and is a very active reality. And this is where a religion differs from a morality.[1] Morality, we are often told, has to do exclusively with values or ideals and is unconcerned with fact or reality. It deals entirely with what "ought to be" to the complete exclusion of what is. A moral conviction is a belief not in the actuality or reality of anything, but a belief in the *goodness* of certain things, or, if you prefer the alternative form of statement, in the *rightness* of certain kinds of conduct. What the moral conviction affirms is not a *Sein* but a *So-sein*, or perhaps we should even say, a *So-sein-sollen*. Hence it is never allowable to reason from the admitted goodness or rightness, the moral value, of any state of things, to its actuality, nor from its admitted badness to its unreality, any more than we may reason from "this is the only right thing to do" to "this is always done", or from "this is abominably wrong" to "this is never done". In a word, no ethical proposition is ever existential and no

---

[1] As Baron von Hügel was fond of observing, morality deals with an "Ought", religion with an "Is", and no amount of "Ought-ness" will make "Is-ness".

existential proposition ever ethical, and the one serious fault of Bosanquet's antithesis is its identification of morality with a knowledge of an existential proposition, "the good purpose is real". It may quite well be the case that whatever is is very bad indeed. Mephistopheles may be right in asserting that

alles was entsteht,
Ist werth—dass es zu Grunde geht,

and Kant may even have been justified in his uneasy suspicion that the history of the world has never recorded the performance of a single act of genuine moral value.

If this absolute and rigid divorce between fact and value can be maintained, it must follow at once that there can be no religious, and *a fortiori* no theological, implications of morality. It might still be the case that some or all of the propositions asserted by natural theologians are true and capable of being proved, or at least rendered probable, but knowledge of the moral nature of man will yield no grounds for believing in any of them, nor will any of them assert anything about the unseen which has significance for the personal moral and spiritual life of man. Natural theology, at best, will give us indications only of an "architect of the universe", not of a just judge of men, still less of an unseen friend and father. For, on the hypothesis, premisses drawn from ethics, being wholly non-existential, can never yield an existential conclusion, nor premisses drawn from the natural sciences, since none of them are assertions of value, any conclusion which asserts goodness or value. Hence, even if the philosopher finds himself able to assert any convictions about the being of God or the destiny of man, these convictions cannot be expected to dignify life by opening new vistas of spiritual values to be achieved. His natural theology will be at most Deism, in Kant's sense of the word, not Theism.

An illustration may be taken from the philosophy of the late Dr. McTaggart.[1] McTaggart was notoriously attached to one of the great traditional doctrines of Platonic natural theology, the dogma of the native immortality of the human soul, and much of his work is devoted to a gallant attempt to establish its truth. But he accepted, at the same time, the other, very un-Platonic, dogma of the irreducible antithesis between fact and value. Hence he contended that all "moral" arguments for man's immortality—all, that is, which are based on analysis of the "good for man" and the conditions of its attainability—are merely irrelevant. His own highly ingenious arguments are drawn entirely from metaphysics, metaphysics being considered simply as a body of true assertions of matter of fact about the structure of the existent. The practical consequences of this attitude are curious and instructive. The immortality which McTaggart's reasoning establishes, if we accept that reasoning as valid, and as the only valid ground for any conclusion on the matter, is virtually equivalent to a mere unending survival of numerically identical human persons, and the prospect opened up to us by the demonstration seems not to be of a kind likely to make any difference for the better in the quality of our interior life.[2]

Eternal life, conceived in the Christian sense, as a life in which human personality is transformed as it

---

[1] The remarks which follow were written long before the appearance of *The Nature of Existence*, vol. ii., and are necessarily based on two earlier books, *Studies in Hegelian Cosmology* and *Some Dogmas of Religion*. I do not see that the case is substantially altered by the publication of the posthumous second volume of *The Nature of Existence*.

[2] *Some Dogmas of Religion*, pp. 16 ff. I do not think the truth of the criticism affected by the fuller exposition of McTaggart's theory in *The Nature of Existence*, vol. ii.

gazes on the living and perfect good, into the likeness of that which it beholds, immortality, conceived after the fashion of Plato, as a life in which we are united by a complete interpenetration of mind by mind, with the best of our fellows, these are visions of a life which is not merely "future", or "endless", but of ever ascending *quality*, a "new" or "changed" life; it is to such transfigured life, not to an indefinite more and more of an existence which men of high purpose have already weighed in the balance and found wanting, that the "divine something" in man has always aspired. McTaggart's purely non-ethical arguments, even if we accept them as demonstrative, really hold out no hope that *this* aspiration can ever be realised. Deathlessness *might* be no more than a condemnation to the weary burden of mutability and temporality without even the hope of release, to say nothing of escape into worthier life. In his earlier work the one *definite* promise McTaggart holds out to us is no more than the prospect of an infinite sum of pleasures, a prospect which to many of us suggests boredom rather than felicity, and if it is true, as is urged in his later writings, that "nothing is too bad to exist", it would seem that, after all, pure metaphysics cannot guarantee even the Hedonist's sorry substitute for human good.

If there is none but an accidental conjunction between reality and value, the Is and the Ought, any conceivable theology must share this fate, since every theology will be a *mere* statement of fact, a theology for the irreligious. Where there is nothing to adore, there is no religion, and no man can adore a bald fact as such, irrespective of its quality, any more than he can really adore an ideal admitted to be a mere figment of his own imagination. The possibility of genuine worship and religion is absolutely bound up with a final coincidence of existence and value in an object which is at once the most *real* of beings and the good "so good that none better can be conceived", at once the Alpha, the primary and absolute source of being, and the Omega, the ultimate goal of desire and endeavour. Only such an object can be adequate to the worship of a rational creature, for no other can rightly make the demand for the last and utter surrender which is worship in the spirit. Qualify the reality of the worshipper's *numen*, and his self-surrender becomes properly and necessarily hedged about by reservations and conditions; worship degenerates into an unhealthy admiration for the work of his own hands or his own brains. Take away the value, or set limits to it, and worse happens. We can at least admire or respect a mere ideal which we know to be our own creation, or at least we can admire or respect the exalted mood in which we created it, by contrast with the more common-place moods of every day. But in mere fact as fact what is there to respect? Mr. Russell, to be sure, once wrote a too-much-belauded essay on the *Worship of a Free Man* whose freedom is based on emancipation from the belief in any intrinsic connection between worth and fact. But I suspect that the title of the essay was only one of Mr. Russell's little ironies. In truth, his "free man" *worships* nothing, or, if anything, himself. He *despises* fact for its brutal stupidity and revenges himself on it by becoming the Narcissus of his own dreams.[1] The masters of the interior life would have told the writer that the one way to find yourself, no less than to find God, is to look *away* from yourself, and that "disdain" is a poison, not a food for the "free" soul.

Our very first step in our discussion, then, must be to show, if we can, that the supposed rigid disjunction

[1] Cf. B. Russell, *Philosophical Essays*, 66, 70.

of fact from value is, after all, a mere prejudice, too hastily conceived by philosophers who neglect the true business of "dialectic", repeated and thorough criticism of their own assumptions. It is worth while to remind ourselves how very modern this dogma is. We may trace it back, in the first instance, historically, to Kant's first *Critique*, where the purpose of the smashing assault on speculative theology, and, indeed, of the whole *Dialectic of Pure Reason*, is to divorce value completely from fact by denying that the "ideals" of speculative reason have any contact whatever with genuine knowledge.[1] Of course, in making this denial Kant is consciously rejecting the convictions which had been at the heart of the two great traditions which had dominated earlier philosophical thought, the Socratic doctrine that the ἀγαθὸν καὶ δέον, "the good and the ought", the supreme principle of valuation, is also the cement, so to say, by which the structure of the existent is held together, and the Christian doctrine that God, the source from which all creatures proceed, is also the good to which all aspire and in which all find their justification. We all remember Kant's own dismay at the apparent success of his undertaking, and his strenuous efforts, after putting asunder what "God and nature" had joined, to bring the disconsolate halves together again by invoking reason "as practical" to undo the work of reason "as speculative". Perhaps some of us, however, are not careful enough to observe that this reconstruction of a broken bridge is no "second thought", but is carefully prepared in the *KdrV*. itself; the *whole*

---

[1] I think we may take it as a result finally established by the work of Adickes and other scholars on the structure of the *KdrV*. that the *Dialectic*, as a whole, is the earliest and crudest section of the whole book. For the really fruitful ideas of the critical philosophy we must go elsewhere, to the ripest paragraphs of the *Analytic*. See the results of investigation as summed up in the *Commentary* of my colleague, Prof. N. Kemp Smith. The *Dialectic* is, in fact, vitiated throughout by the persistence of the Cartesian devotion to "clear and distinct ideas".

critical philosophy was never intended to be learned from the "transcendental Dialectic" alone and the interpretations of Kant based primarily on the *Dialectic* are all misinterpretations. If we are in error in denying the severance of fact and value, then we are, at least, erring in very good company and may take heart from the reflection.

Now what is the substance of the case we have to meet, when the problem is reduced to its simplest terms, and freed from all false dialectical subtleties? I will try to state it in my own words, but as fairly and forcibly as I can. It amounts, so far as I can see, to this. Plainly (*a*) we cannot argue straight away from the actuality of the actual to its goodness. The world is full of bad conduct, bad science, bad art. It is arguable—though I do not know how proof or disproof could be reached —that bad men and bad deeds are more common than good, and it is, at least, certain that very good deeds and very good men are both rare. We all understand how Mr. Pecksniff's mind worked when, as his biographer tells us, he said of anything very bad that it was "very natural". At any period we like to consider, there has been more bad art of every kind than good, more loose reasoning than accurate; great moral, scientific, artistic achievement is not common. If we consider the *cursus ordinarius* of nature, when all allowance has been made for sentimental exaggeration, it is undeniable that it is attended by a great deal of suffering and wretchedness, and much of this, we must agree, is decidedly very bad. The bad obviously is an actual feature in the products both of nature and of human art, no less than the good. Nor can we assume, with the lighthearted optimism of some of the eminent "Victorians", that the bad is regularly instrumental to a greater good, or that the normal trend or bias of nature and of human society is towards the steady minimising of the bad, possibly to its elimination. (We do not, indeed, see enough of the actual to be able to deny this as a possibility, but we see too much to be able to affirm it as a probability.) At most the advance of "evolutionary" science *may* perhaps have shown that it is probable that, in the region of the actual directly accessible to our own observation, there has been "progress" in the neutral sense of fairly steady development along continuous lines, but we cannot assume that the same thing has been true in regions of unexplored space and unrecorded past time inaccessible to our investigation, nor that the proposition will hold good of the unknown future. It might further be urged that much of the progress we can detect is only progress in this neutral sense of accelerated movement in the same direction. It has not been proved, and there is much to make us doubt, that it has equally been progress in the sense of advance towards the *better*. Our own experience of the life of Europe since the opening of the present century might, indeed, suggest an uneasy doubt whether the "advance of civilisation" may not have been progressive only in the sense in which a physician speaks of a patient's progress towards dissolution or a moralist of the "rake's" progress in debauchery.

Our verdicts, indeed, are inevitably passed on short views, whereas to pronounce on such a question with confidence, we should need to take the long view of spectators to whom the whole recorded history of man, or even the whole definitely ascertained physical history of our solar system, would be as yesterday by comparison with the vast immensity of pre-history. This is true; but we know enough to forbid any hasty inference from the actuality of a feature of the existent to its goodness. And it may be added that we are no less debarred from arguing in the reverse way that what is not actual and never will be actual cannot be good, and better than anything which is, or will be, actual. The best in what is actual has its recognisable defects; were there no other, its very impermanency would be a defect. Even when good only passes away to give place to better, we must always think how much better still it would have been if we could have had both goods—*e.g.*, the ardour of youth and the wisdom of age—at once. The flower may fall only to give place to the fruit, and we may perhaps confess that, since we cannot have both, it is better to have the fruit without the flower than the flower without the fruit. Yet when autumn comes, we miss the flower. The Callipolis of Socrates' dream never existed in history, and there is no ground to suppose that it ever will, but a man would have to be an extreme *Realpolitiker* if he took this as *proof* that its institutions and life are inferior to those of London, Paris, Berlin, or Chicago. We should understand, if we did not accept, the view that all our "ideals" are no more than dreams, if it were added that the dream is often nobler than waking life, where it is too frequently the ugly or sordid dreams that "come true".

This, so far as I can see, is really the whole of the case in support of the alleged rigid separation of fact from value. It should, of course, be noted that the most such arguments allow us to assert is that the conjunction of fact with value is "accidental", that there is no inherent reason why what is actual should also be good, or what is good also actual. Nothing in what has been said compels us to go to the further length of pessimism, to hold that the good, from its very nature, must be unreal, and the actual by an intrinsic necessity, evil or imperfect. As I have said, I regard it as the most important problem in the whole range of philosophy to examine this alleged want of connection between reality, actuality, existence, or being, and goodness or value in a spirit of thorough criticism. I can do no more here than offer very imperfect and tentative hints towards such a truly critical examination, but I dare not do less. I cannot reconcile myself to the view that philosophy is a simple pastime for the curious, with the same attractiveness, and the same remoteness from all the vital interests of humanity, as the solution of a highly ingenious chess problem. If philosophy were really that and no more, I confess I should have small heart for the devotion of life to such "fooling". I am content, with Plato and Kant, to be so much of a "common fellow" as to feel that the serious questions for each of us are "What ought I to do?", "What may I hope for?", and that it is the duty of philosophy to find answers to them, if she can. If none can be found, so much the worse for philosophy, but her incompetence is not to be assumed lightly. I proceed, then, to offer some considerations which may fairly suggest that the connection between existence (or actuality) and value is not accidental (or extrinsic). Even if these considerations fall short of demonstration they may still have a real work as tentative "aggressions", and indicate the lines along which abler thinkers than myself may yet be able to reach a true solution of the problem.

(i.) It seems clear, to begin with, that most of the writers who insist on the radical separation of value from actuality are victims of an insidious fallacy of diction, a false abstraction due to convenient but ambiguous habits of speech. This particular point has been argued with admirable fullness and lucidity by Professor Sorley in his work *Moral Values and the Idea of God*,[1] but I may be allowed, in view of its

[1] *Op. cit.* pp. 139 ff.

importance, to dwell on it again. When we speak of virtue, art, science, health, as having *value*, it is never virtue, art, science, health, "in the abstract" to which we mean to refer, but always the actual virtuous conduct, artistic production, true thinking, healthy bodily functioning of persons conceived as existent, either in fact or *ex hypothesi*. The candid utterances, generous acts and impulses, the creation or appreciation of beauty, the comprehension of truth, the vigorous performance of the physical functions of life by existents—in fact by persons—are the real objects to which we are ascribing the possession of value; we are not predicating value of the logical "concepts", virtue, beauty, knowledge, or health. These, as the logician studies them, have been mentally isolated from all relation to the concrete individual existents in whose lives they appear, but it should be evident that in this process of abstraction they have been deprived of their specific value by being, legitimately enough for the logician's special purpose, cut loose from "existence". (In fact, the *concept* virtue, for example, has *no* specific ethical value; the value it has is merely that of being a "clear and distinct idea", and this value for classificatory purposes is common to it with the *concept* vice. So the health which has a value not shared by disease is not the "concept" health, but health exhibited in the functioning of existent organisms.)

No one could seriously maintain that there would be intelligible meaning in the statement that health has a value not shared by disease, if there were no actual living organisms. It is only a system which contains living organisms of which we can say that it is "better" if these are healthy and enjoy the exercise of their organic functions than if they are diseased and only perform the vital functions with pain. *Health is good* is only an abbreviated way of saying that it is good that *organisms* should live in a state of health, bad that they should live in a state of disease. *Pleasure is good* means nothing, or means that pleasure enjoyed by existents who can feel is good. So the knowledge we pronounce good means the active discovery and contemplation of truth by intelligent minds. And if it is suggested that not only knowledge but *truth* is good, I would reply thus. On the supposition that it is logically possible that there might have been a purely physical universe, containing no minds as constituents and contemplated *ab extra* by no transcendent mind from without, it would still be the case that some relations and interactions subsist between the constituents of such a universe and some do not, and if, as the common materialist holds, there was once a time in the past of the actual world when there were no minds, still there were certain events, and no others, which were then happening, and the common materialist believes it possible, in a general way, to say what those events were, *e.g.* to reconstruct in outline the story of the formation of our solar system. In a sense, then, if there could be, or ever has been, a world without minds or persons, there is a truth about that world. But this is not the "truth" of which we can intelligibly say that it has value.

What is really meant when truth is called a value is that *knowledge* of the true is good, the lack of that knowledge bad, the false conceit of it, acceptance of the false as true, worst of all. And by calling knowledge good, we do not mean that a particular pattern of black marks on a white surface, or a particular sequence of articulate noises, as such, is good. There would be no reason to ascribe any special value to a printed copy of Newton's *Principia* surviving in a world where there were not, and never would be, any minds to apprehend the meaning of the printed marks, or to the noises made by a gramophone repeating the propositions of the *Principia* on a mindless planet. If we could suppose the gramophone to be started on its work and all existent minds then to be annihilated, we should, I take it, not judge that it made any difference to the goodness or badness of such a state of things whether the event which annihilated the minds also affected the working of the gramophone or not. It would be as reasonable to ascribe "economic value" to a mass of precious metal supposed to be located somewhere on an uninhabited and wholly inaccessible planet.

We can, indeed, call one hypothetically assumed system in which mind is not actually present better than another, but I feel sure that when we speak in this way it is always with reference to the *future* of the two imagined systems. We judge that in which feeling and thought are expected to "emerge" and to get fair play better than that which either leaves no room for their appearance, or provides no chance of their adequate development. In a word—to condense my point into a formula—the knowledge we value as good is primarily always "knowledge in act", the life of an existent individual intelligence discovering or contemplating truth. It is only in a secondary sense that we go on to ascribe value also to knowledge in proximate or remote "potency to act", as when we speak of value in connection with knowledge a man has acquired but is not actually using, or even in connection with the contents of a library not actually accessible to the student. We say it is good that the library should still exist, because we trust that its stores will yet be utilised by someone, and will incite to fresh actual pursuit and enjoyment of knowledge. Hence the notoriously low value we set even on knowledge actually before the mind, when it is mere "erudition" which does not stimulate to further intellectual activity. To quote some pertinent words of Professor Eddington, "if we consider a world entirely devoid of consciousness . . . there is, so far as we know, no meaning whatever in discriminating between the worlds A and B. The mind is the referee who decides in favour of A against B. The actuality of the world is a spiritual value. The physical world at some point (or indeed throughout) impinges on the spiritual and derives its actuality solely from this contact."[1]

Now what is true in this case is equally true in the less obvious cases of the values we ascribe to great art and good moral practice. What we commend is not courage or temperance "in the abstract", an "universal" concept, but the characteristic life of a courageous or temperate man. What we condemn is not cruelty or adultery "in the abstract", but the characteristic acts and desires of cruel or adulterous men. Adultery "in the abstract" is *good* with the only goodness an "abstraction" can have; it is an admirable example of a "clear and distinct idea", and that is all there is to be said about it.

We may, indeed, say in a sense which is both true and important that in our moral judgements we are ascribing values to universals, and that the judgements would not be genuinely ethical unless this were so. But if the statement is not to prove a source of danger-ous error, we must at once add that the "universal"

[1] A. S. Eddington in *Science, Religion and Reality*, p. 211. It may seem, at first, as though we have been confusing two theses: (*a*) value belongs only to the individual and existent; (*b*) value always involves reference to mind. The sentences quoted from Dr. Eddington indicate the intimate connection between the two apparently distinct theses. It is precisely because the two "physical worlds" A, B, of which the writer speaks, are purely constructions of the physicist and there-fore consist of de-individualised "concepts" that existence and value are both meaningless when predicated of them. We shall have much more to say on this point in the sequel.

which has value—other than the merely logical value of a "clear and distinct idea"—is always the universal embodied *in rebus*, not the universal *post res* of the nominalist logicians. "Mercy is good" does indeed mean more than "this, that, and the other merciful acts are good"; it means that these acts are good not incidentally, because, for example, they happen to have been also pleasant or profitable, but because they are *merciful*, and for no other reason. But the statement does not mean that mercy is good, apart from its exercise in act. What is good is, in Aristotelian language, the universal mercy as constituting the "form" of the merciful man's acts, not as detached, for the purpose of the logician, from its function as the form of those acts, and "informing" the *intellectus possibilis* in the logician. As the great schoolmen of the thirteenth century were rightly careful not to make nonsense of the doctrine of perception by confusing the "form of lapideity" as it exists in the stone I see or touch with the "form of lapideity" as it exists in the eye which sees the stone, or the intellect which has "collected" the concept of a stone from sense-experiences, so we need, no less imperatively, to distinguish between the mode of being of moral "universals" as they are the "forms" of virtuous acts and their mode of being *per abstractionem* in the thought of the student of ethics contemplating the virtuous conduct of another party. It is as "forms" of the good acts of virtuous agents, and only as such, that they can be said to have specific moral value, and as such forms they are not "abstracted" from their setting of concrete individuality. The abstracting is done by the contemplating intellect and affects only the universal *post rem*. (In short, the primary meaning of *mercy is good* is that the mercy shown by the merciful man is good, not that mercy as contemplated by the "disinterested spectator" is good. If the act of contemplating and approving mercifulness, performed by such a spectator, who is not himself at the time engaged in the exercise of mercy, is good, as it is, it is only good *because* showing mercy is good. The "disinterested spectator" *recognises* the already existing goodness of the act he rightly approves, he does not *bestow* the value on the act by his approving contemplation.)

The same thing appears to me no less true of all the values of art. What we really regard as so very good is beauty as constituting the characteristic form of the beautiful thing, beauty as *existing* in the poem, or symphony, or portrait, not beauty as a "concept", detached from the individual things of beauty in which it is embodied. Here, once more, those of our contemporaries who are insistent in denying that "universals" exist, while they are equally sure that "value" belongs to the non-existent universal, seem to me mere victims of a vicious logical nominalism. A character in one of Mr. Lowes Dickinson's books suggests that it would make no difference to the *value* of a great picture if it were painted by an artist in a state of complete unconsciousness, and sunk, as soon as it had been painted, to the bottom of the sea.[1] It would be hard to find a better example of the double view that the universal, and only the universal, has value, but that it also has no actuality. And yet it is noticeable that the example does not succeed in that *complete* separation of value from actuality at which the speaker is manifestly aiming. What is spoken of here as beautiful is after all not "beauty in the abstract", but beauty as "informing" a particular picture. And we note too, that though the speaker is careful to exclude any reference to the

---

[1] G. Lowes Dickinson, *The Meaning of Good*, p. 110.

enjoyment of a possible *spectator* of the picture, he has
not eliminated all reference to individual persons and
their activities, as he should have done; he has kept
the artist and his activity, though he reduces this to the
minimum by imagining the activity to be unconscious.

Now why, we may ask, should the artist be brought
into the illustration at all? For the purpose of the
argument would not an arrangement of colours, or of
light and shade, effected by unguided natural processes,
have served as well, or better? Why, then, is a painter
to be brought into the hypothesis, though an unconscious one, unless the writer secretly feels that the
beauty we value as *good* must be the characteristic
"form" of a personal activity, even though the activity
is, inconsistently, imagined to be entirely "unconscious"? I seem to detect here an involuntary confession
that the good beautiful thing must be a thing *made*
by someone, a concession which might lead to some
far-reaching consequences, if we went on to bring it into
connection with the undeniable fact that a situation
not brought about by any known human, or even
animal activity, such as a sunset or a thunderstorm,
may be exceedingly beautiful. I trust I shall not be
misunderstood here. I am not for a moment defending
what I regard as the wholly untenable view that truth,
or beauty, or moral goodness is "subjective", in the
sense that we can make propositions true, things beautiful, acts right, by thinking them so. I am not denying
that there are truths which no man knows, truths which,
it may be, no man ever will know, beauties which have
no human spectator, heroisms and delicacies which
no man's actual conduct has exhibited. I should be the
first to admit that truth, beauty, goodness are not
created but discovered by their spectators. My point
is a different one and has a double edge. It is (1) that

the truth, beauty, goodness to which we ascribe worth are in all cases "concreted", embodied in individuals of which they are the constitutive forms, and that our ascription of worth is only significant in view of this embodiment of the "universal" in the individual; (2) that in all such judgements of value the reference to *personal* activities is always more or less explicitly present.

This is clearest in the case of judgements about moral worth, where it is always explicit personal activity that is pronounced good or bad. Even Mr. Lowes Dickinson's Dennis has not suggested that the character or conduct of a man going through the business of life and performing "good works" in a state of complete somnambulism could intelligibly be said to have moral worth. He apparently allows that the somnambulist would have neither virtues nor vices, though he conceives that he might paint a beautiful picture, forgetting perhaps that it seems to be of the essence of all art to be *mimetic*, or representative of something. As for aesthetic values themselves, as I said, the introduction of the "unconscious" artist *seems* to imply that the same consideration holds good, though not so obviously. For it seems to be implied that we cannot properly call "natural objects" beautiful unless we think of them also as the works of a divine artist, or at least allow ourselves to imagine "nature" as an artist, though an "unconscious" one. In the case of truth, which is commonly classed along with beauty and moral goodness as a "value", reference to personal activity might seem to be absent, but this absence is only apparent. For (1), as I have said, what we really mean by calling truth a value is that the *knowledge* of truth is good, ignorance or error bad. If we are to speak of truth at all in a mindless universe, manifestly we cannot mean truth in what Aristotle calls the primary sense of the word, the sense in which we call *judgements* true. We must mean truth in that very vague sense in which the mediaeval logicians reckon truth, along with unity and goodness as one of the "transcendentals", when they lay it down that *quodlibet ens est unum, verum, bonum*. Even so, we have not really got away from the reference to mind, since, as St. Thomas explains[1] what is expressed in the statement that any *ens* is *verum* is *convenientia entis ad intellectum*, the intrinsic *knowability* of being. This is actually pre-supposed by the formula itself, when it treats *verum* as a predicate of *ens*. The formula, in fact, asserts just what the philosophers who detach value from existence are anxious to deny. "Values" not concreted in actuality would not be *entia*, and therefore, according to the Thomistic doctrine, would be entitled neither to be called *vera* nor to be called *bona*.

Also (2) it would be a paradox to say that all truths, because equally true, are equally valuable. By this I do not mean merely that a proposition may be true and yet be unimportant from its want of relevance to the special interests of a particular person. (Thus, for example, the statement of Mr. F.'s aunt in *Little Dorrit*, "there's milestones on the Dover road", was irrelevant to the immediate concerns of the hearers, though it might have been important enough to any one on the Dover road with a day's walk before him, who had to decide where he would break it for a meal.) Quite apart from this difference in accidental importance for particular individuals, there is an intrinsic difference between pro-positions, all equally true, in respect of their purely

---

[1] *De Veritate*, q. I, art. I, resp. "Convenientiam vero entis ad intellectum ex-primit hoc nomen *verum*. Omnis autem cognitio perficitur per assimilationem cog-noscentis ad rem cognitam. . . . Prima ergo comparatio entis ad intellectum est ut ens intellectui correspondeat: quae quidem correspondentia adaequatio rei et intellectus dicitur, et in hoc formaliter ratio veri perficitur."

theoretical significance. Some of them throw a flood of light on a wide range of the knowable, others do not. Every branch of knowledge has its illuminating truths and its merely curious truths; the value of the two is widely different, though they stand on the same footing in respect of being true. Reference to the highly personal activity of understanding is implicit in this inevitable distinction between knowledge which, apart from its so-called "practical" consequences, is valuable as highly illuminating and knowledge which has not this value. But if value always involves some kind of reference to the activities of persons, it cannot be true that value and existence (or actuality) are only accidentally conjoined. Indeed, it should be a truism to say that *ex vi termini* a value must be a good, and that, again *ex vi termini*, a good must be something that can be possessed and enjoyed by someone or something. In this respect it is with all values as with those of the economist; an article cannot intelligibly be said to be "worth" so much if there is no one *to* whom it is worth that price. Ice, for example, is valueless in the solitudes of Antarctica. St. Thomas (*loc. cit.*) may again be allowed to illustrate the point for us. He explains that *quodlibet ens est bonum* is meant to express the appropriateness of *entia* to appetition, as *quodlibet ens est verum* expresses their appropriateness to intellection. Hence both dicta convey a reference to mind, which unites in itself the *vis cognitiva* and the *vis appetitiva*. If there were no intelligence, nothing could have "truth-value", if there were no appetition, nothing could have value at all.[1]

[1] *Loc. cit.* "alio modo secundum convenientiam unius entis ad aliquid; et hoc quidem non potest esse nisi accipiatur aliquid quod *natum sit convenire cum omni ente*. Hoc autem est anima quae quodammodo est omnia, sicut dicitur in iii. *De anima*. In anima autem est vis cognitiva et appetitiva. Convenientiam ergo entis ad appetitum exprimit hoc nomen *bonum*."

(ii.) Again, consider some of the consequences which seem to follow immediately from the admission of either truths or the knowledge of them into the list of values. A truth, even a truth as yet undiscovered, is a proposition,[1] and it should have been quite evident, ever since Plato wrote the *Sophistes*, that to be significant at all, and therefore to be a proposition, an utterance must always be, directly or indirectly, an assertion about τὸ ὄν, what *is*. Everyone can see that this is so with singular propositions, and with "particular" propositions, which are equivalent to groups of singular propositions whose subjects are as yet unspecified. That "some men are mathematicians" is only significant because the statements that "*this* man (say Legendre) is a mathematician" and that "*that* man (say Gauss) is a mathematician" are also significant. And the subject of a singular proposition, being a "this", can never be simply non-existent; "this *nothing*" would be an unmeaning noise. (Hence the universal recognition that singular and particular propositions have always "existential import", with its necessary corollary that in strict logic a "subalternate" proposition can never be inferred simply from its *subalternans*.)

It is true that everyone who tries to treat logic seriously finds himself driven to deny that the universal proposition has direct existential import. But the consequence is that, if we consider closely, the "universal" reduces to something less than an actual proposition. It becomes what Russell and Whitehead call a "formal implication" not between propositions but between "propositional functions". That is, the true meaning of the statement "all men are mortal" can only be given

---

[1] At least this is the case with the truths contemplated by the philosophers who have most to say of truth as a "value". On the possibility of non-propositional truth and knowledge there will be some remarks to be made in our final lecture.

without excess or defect in the form "that x is a man implies that x is mortal". This again means, to state it more precisely, that "is mortal" is true of *any* subject of which "is a man" is true. To make a genuine proposition out of this blank form it is necessary that we should replace the symbol x, on both its appearances, by one and the same name or denoting phrase, indicating one individual *this*. Only when we have done so have we passed from asserting a relation between mere "propositional functions" to asserting a relation between *propositions*. And when we take this step, the propositions which figure in the (now "material") implication are seen at once to have existential import.

Thus, though we often utter the words that man is mortal, we never really mean no more nor less than we say. As Russell has remarked, we should not expect to find the decease of Man recorded in the *Deaths* columns of the *Times* or the *Morning Post*. On the other hand, we mean more than was supposed by Mill when he took the statement to be no more than the assertion of "is mortal" about each and every individual man who has actually lived in the past, is living now, or will live hereafter.[1] When I say that all men are mortal, I may not know that Botticelli is the name of a man and a Florentine; like the young gentlemen in *Punch*, I may believe that Botticelli is the name of a wine or a cheese. Yet I mean my assertion to cover the statement that *if* Botticelli is a man—which I hold not to be the case—Botticelli is also mortal. The subject of which something is asserted in the universal proposition is thus neither a definite collection of determined indi-

---

[1] *Logic*, bk. i. c. v. § 2: "When we say, all men are mortal, the meaning of the proposition is, that all beings which possess the one set of attributes possess also the other". Cf. bk. ii. c. iv. § 3: "A general truth is but an aggregate of particular truths; a comprehensive expression, by which an indefinite number of individual facts are affirmed or denied at once".

viduals, nor yet the "universal" or "concept" of which such individuals are "instances". It is *any* individual, known or unknown, of whom a certain statement is true, and what I assert is that a second statement also will be true of such an individual. If there should be *no* such individual, if, for example, there never should be any actual man, the statement (in this case, that all men are mortal) seems to me to lose its claim to be regarded as true. I see no way of successfully disputing the old dictum *nullius sunt nullae proprietates*.

The statement, often made by formal logicians, that *all* assertions are equally true of the "null-class" seems to me only a disguised way of making this admission. If you can assert a pair of contraries of the same subject, the distinction between truth and falsity loses its meaning so far as that subject is concerned; truth and falsehood cease to be *opposed* values, and so cease to be values at all. A genuine assertion with a *meaning* always makes a "claim", well-founded or not, to be true and not to be false. For that reason, I should say, it is impossible to make a genuine assertion about the merely non-existent. If that is not "the expense of spirit in a waste of shame", what is? I confess I cannot enter into the state of mind of those agreeable and entertaining persons who suppose themselves to be recapturing the spirit of Plato's philosophy when they discuss propositions about the "round square" and other such impossible "objectives". My own conviction is that Plato would have dismissed the topic with the single remark that, since there are no round squares, nothing can be significantly said about the "round square", and that human life is too short to be further curtailed by an expenditure of breath with no meaning behind it. Even the statement that there are no round squares is not, properly speaking, a statement *about* round squares, but rather a confession that we have tried hard to make such a statement and found it impossible. We can make no statement which proves on analysis to be, in the terminology of Frege, all "function" without any "argument". Here again scholasticism puts the point excellently: "Being is in a certain way affirmed about not-being, in so far as not-being is apprehended by the intellect. Hence the Philosopher says in the *Fourth* of the *Metaphysics* that the negation or privation of being is in one sense called being; hence also Avicenna says, at the beginning of his *Metaphysics*, that no enunciation can be made except about what is. For that about which the proposition is made must have been apprehended in the intellect."[1]

At the cost of a seeming digression I should like here to explain what I take to be the source of confusion in the minds of those who think that the merely non-existent can be the subject of a significant judgement of value. It is the old and deadly error of supposing that a word must be either simply *univocal* or merely *equivocal*, the same fatal error which Spinoza commits when he assumes that either will and understanding, when they are ascribed to God, mean precisely the same thing as will and understanding in ourselves, or the double employment of the same words is as purely accidental as the double use of the vocable *dog* for the friend of man who guards our houses and a group of stars in the nightly sky.[2] In exactly the same way, it is often assumed that "existence" or "actuality" must either mean exactly what it does when we discuss the question whether the sea-serpent exists, or whether Prester John actually existed, that is, occupation of a definite region in the historical series of spatio-temporal events,

---

[1] St. Thomas, *De Veritat.* q. 1, art. 1, ad sept.
[2] *Ethica* i. 17 *Scholium.*

or mean nothing at all. Then, since "ideals" clearly must not be said to exist in *this* sense, it is asserted that "ideals" or "values" simply do not exist at all. Under the baneful influences of an evil nominalistic tradition, inherited from the senility of a scholasticism which had lost its vigour, the great Aristotelian conception of the "analogous" use of predicates has been allowed to fall out of our modern thought, with disastrous consequences. It is simply not true that the alternatives, univocal predication—equivocal predication, form a complete disjunction. This is plain from the elementary examples produced by Aristotle himself, when he wants to illustrate the meaning of analogy. When I say that a wise adviser and director is a physician of the soul, I am manifestly not predicating "physician" of such a man in the same sense in which I say of Mr. Jones, or Mr. Smith, Fellows of the Royal College of Surgeons, that they are able and experienced physicians. But it is equally plain that the use of the word "physician" here is no mere historical accident of language, as it is a mere historical accident that I call a certain group of stars "the Dog", rather than "the Cat" or "the Dodo". My soul is, indeed, not a body, and it is not dieted with albuminoids or carbohydrates, nor dosed with tonics or aperients. But there is a real appositeness in the metaphor I use. But for an historical accident I might call the group of stars a cat, a dodo, a hyena, or anything you please, as appropriately as I call them a dog; all that matters is that, whatever word I use, it should be understood which group I have in mind. But it is a *happy* and well-chosen metaphor I am using when I speak of a physician of souls, or call the wise statesman who brings his country safely through perils and disorders the "pilot who weathers the storm". The one is not κυρίως, in the strict sense, a medical man, nor the other a seaman, but it is true that the one stands to his "penitent" as the physician to his patient, the other to the nation as the pilot to the vessel and its company. Analogy in the strict sense, "analogy of proportionality", is a genuine feature in the structure of things. So again is analogy in the looser sense. As Aristotle observes, a surgical implement is not surgical in the precise sense in which an eminent operator is surgical, but again, it is no accident of language that we use the same epithet in both cases.

To take a less trivial illustration, the very word *life* itself, or, as Aristotle says in this connection, "existence", is not strictly univocal. When we say that what the best type of friend desires is neither entertainment nor advantage to be derived from his friend, but that friend's *existence*, that he prizes that friend's existence, even if he is henceforth to exist in conditions which preclude all possibility of further intercourse, what we mean, as Aristotle says, is that the good man finds a high intrinsic value in his friend's thinking and perceiving. Even the "Waring" whom we expect never to see again has not vanished, the world has not lost the value it gets for us from his presence in it as an alert and benign intelligence: "In Vishnu-land what avatar?" It would be another matter if our friend's mental activities of all kinds were irreparably annihilated. In a sense he might still be, but not in the sense in which our affections find their satisfaction in his being. Such being as he might still retain if he only continued to breathe, to be nourished and the like, in a state of complete "paralysis of the higher centres", would not be what we mean by the life of a *man*. In the case of a man, to be means to be alive, and to be alive in the special way in which "human beings"—the very phrase bears witness to the soundness of Aristotle's contention—are said to be alive. The hopelessly demented or paralysed are not what we mean by the very expressive slang phrase "live men". The man who only *is* in the sense in which a log or a stone is, if there is such a man, may fairly be said to "be no longer".[1]

If the existence, then, which we ascribe to the individual as a *proprium* is not an univocal word, is it merely a word which has an accidental plurality of unconnected senses, like *box*, or *dog*? Clearly it is something more than this. We can say of whatever is an individual and of nothing else, that it is actual, exists, or has existence, as the logicians recognise when they assert that the universal proposition differs from the singular or particular in not having "existential import". And if we ask what we mean by individual here, I can find no answer but that implied in the Aristotelian account of "primary substance", that the individual is that which can figure in propositions as subject, but never as predicate, or, to use Frege's terminology, that which is an argument of functions, but never itself a function of any argument. Clearly we have no right to assume without examination that only what we commonly call "fact", that which can be located and dated by reference to an interval in the spatio-temporal series, is thus individual. If we meditate the reasons which have led Professor Whitehead to make a sharp distinction between *events* and *objects* and to insist that location and date belong properly to events, to objects only secondarily, in virtue of their "ingredience" into events,[2] we might even be led to the very different view that *individuality* is precisely the feature in things which resists our attempts to locate and date it. It is at

[1] Cf. Aristot. *E.N.* 1170 a 32, τὸ δ ὅτι αἰσθανόμεθα ἢ νοοῦμεν, ὅτι ἐσμέν (τὸ γὰρ εἶναι ἦν αἰσθάνεσθαι ἢ νοεῖν).

[2] See *Concept of Nature*, c. vii. pp. 143 ff.

least clear that the assumption that the individual must always mean that which occupies a definite, *i.e.* a de-limited, spatial and temporal interval has no real claim to be admitted as true without careful and searching criticism. It is conceivable that individuals may be of many types and that "existence", as asserted of them, may have as many shades of meaning as there are types of individual. This possibility forbids us to assume that the existent is simply that which can be located and dated, and consequently forbids us also to assert that "values" and "ideals", since they have admittedly no date or location, must merely be non-existent, not-actual, "what is not".

(iii.) These considerations, however, are only pre-liminary to the point on which I would rest the main weight of the case for refusing to admit the ultimate severance of value from existence. The point on which I would lay the chief stress is that any such severance falsifies the facts of real life, where existence and value appear always as distinguishable, but always as con-joined. The moral life is inevitably misconceived and its suggestions misread, if we start by thinking of the attitude of the man who is ordering his life as *Mensch mit Menschen* on the analogy of the attitude of a super-physicist or super-chemist to a laboratory problem. If we make this mistake of confusing the man who is seeking a rule of life to live by with that of a theorist speculating about the activities of the good life as lived by someone else, it is not unnatural to imagine such a theorist as first having the facts of life given, "thrown on the screen", "presented for his observation", and then bringing to them a scheme of valuation freely im-posed by himself from the outside. Thus we come to think of the facts, or realities, as one thing, the valua-tion put on the facts by the "observer" as another independent thing, and so the question arises whether the valuation is not wholly personal to the observer, and so arbitrary, and devoid of all foundation in the facts, as we call them. But when we are addressing ourselves to the primary moral problem of living, facts and valuations do not present themselves in this neat antithetical fashion, as the given on one side, and the interpretation subjectively put on that given on the other. In life as we all, including the laboratory worker himself, live it, *all* is given, facts and valuations together, in an undivided whole. We find ourselves not passive spectators of a scene presented to our contemplation, but actors in the drama, taking our part in response to the suggestions of our environment, which is at least human, moral and social, as well as biological and physical. The living moral tradition of our community, the equally living tradition of the scientific, artistic, or religious group into which we have been initiated, are embodied schemes of valuation, but they are also as much facts and part of the given to which we have to make our response as the pressure of the atmosphere, or the gravitational "pull" of the earth. Our respect for our parents, our love for our friends, our loyalty to our country, our adoration of the divine, all are specific responses to specific features in an actual whole which is, in the first instance, given and not made. We are from the first creatures with a moral as well as a physical "environment", and the values of the moral life are themselves the constituents of the environment, not afterthoughts, or "psychic additions", of our own personal creation.

I may perhaps illustrate my meaning by a reference to the similar status of the so-called "secondary" qualities of sensible things, and again to what Professor Alexander and his admirers call "tertiary" characters. In

spite of the utterances of a whole series of eminent philosophers, from Galileo and Descartes down to our own
age, it ought to be patent that, whatever the ontological
status of the greenness of the leaf and the redness of the
rose-petals, they are no "psychic addition" made by the
percipient subject to a given consisting simply of so-
called primary qualities. The green colour of the grass,
the crimson of the rose, are there in the world as it is
given to us through the eye, no less than the shape of
the blade or the petal. It is not my mind which, in knowing the grass or the rose, puts into it a green or a red
which was not there; on the contrary, it is from an indefinitely rich and complex given that I come to single
out these particular elements for separate contemplation. In this matter, once more, the greatest scholastics,
I think, showed themselves better analysts of the facts
than their successors of the more modern world. St.
Thomas, for example, if I understand him rightly, as
very possibly I do not, teaches a doctrine of perception
which a thoroughgoing realist might accuse of containing the germ of the later heresy of representative perception. He holds to the Aristotelian formula that when
I see, for example, a rose there is an actual presence of
the "form" of the rose in my own sensibility, the *species
sensibilis*. But he is very careful to avoid the mistake
of supposing that the rose I see is the same thing as this
"sensible species". The "species" plays a necessary part
in the work of perception, but it is the *instrument* by
which seeing is effected (the quo *videtur*), not the *object*
seen (the quod *videtur*). What I see is the "form of the
rose" embodied in the actual rose, not the "form of the
rose" as present in my eye or my mind. This "form" *is*
present there, or there would be no vision, but of the
"form" as present in me I have no perception at all; I
perceive, *through its instrumentality*, the corresponding

"form" as existing in the rose. The sensible species is thus, in the *causal* order, a mediating link between me and the rose; in *the order of perception and knowledge* I apprehend the rose itself without awareness of any intervening *tertium quid* whatever.[1] Now this may not be a wholly satisfactory analysis. I own I am tempted to say, with what a Thomist would probably regard as a leaning to an *outré* realism, that there is really no evidence that anything *psychical* intervenes in the causal order between the physiological processes in retina, optic nerve, and cerebral centres, and the perception of the rose. But at any rate the recognition that the "sensible species", if it is a psychical reality, is not itself apprehended by sense, would have been enough to keep the theory of knowledge off the false track on which it has been sent for so many generations by the unhappy influences of Descartes and Locke. We may at least say that a sound theory must retain as a minimum of realism the Thomist distinction between the *quod* and the *quo* of perception.

The mistake of thinking otherwise would hardly have been made if philosophers and men of science had always drawn the important distinction, on which John Grote used rightly to insist,[2] between the philosopher's attitude to *his* given and that of the positive sciences to theirs. The philosopher interested in analysing knowledge as a whole must inevitably take as his ultimate antithesis that between the knower-agent, on the one side, and the whole, as yet undifferentiated, continuum of the known-and-interacted with, on the other. And there can be no doubt on which side of the antithesis the colour of the grass or the rose falls. It is not a knowing,

[1] Cf. *De Veritat.* q. 10, art. 8, ad sec. "in visione corporali aliquis intuetur corpus, non ita quod inspiciat aliquam corporis similitudinem, quamvis per aliquam corporis similitudinem inspiciat."

[2] *Exploratio Philosophica*, pt. i. c. i.

or an acting, but a fact known and reacted to, a feature
in the continuum; not a response, but a percept which
may provoke responses of different kinds, according as
the percipient finds the colour pleasing or unpleasing,
stimulating or depressing. It can only be mistaken for
something else when we have first committed the
blunder of confusing this most elementary antithesis of
knower and known with the entirely different antithesis
between the constituent of the known which I gradually
learn to recognise as my own body and those constituents which I call foreign bodies. Then it becomes possible to argue, plausibly but fallaciously, that since the
mechanical interactions between bodies can be understood without taking their differences in colour into
account, and since, in the interests of exact science, we
should like, if we can, to reduce all interactions between
bodies, even in the case where one of them at least is
alive and sentient, to the mechanical type, the colour
which can be disregarded by "rational mechanics" is
not really there, and must therefore be an "addition"
made by the mind to the given. Or it is argued by philosophers of a different school, with equal disregard of
concrete realities, that since we can, for various special
purposes, break up the given into small fragments of
simple and homogeneous quality, it was given in that
form, and we get the really monstrous doctrine that the
real or given consists primarily of detached *sensa* which
knowledge somehow pieces together; the awkward
problem then arises, with what justification the piecing
together is done. If we would only look at the facts of
life without this artificial distortion of perspective, we
might see at once that what is given is neither a configuration devoid of sensible quality, nor a number of
qualitatively definite disconnected *sensa*, but a single
most imperfectly discriminated whole, in which shape,

colour, size, odour, sound, are all present from the outset, and that progress in knowledge means, not making
unauthorised additions to this whole, but becoming increasingly sensitive to distinctions within it.

In the same way the "presentation-continuum" itself
is not the whole of what, in the first instance, is given.
It is given itself as one with its setting, all of a piece
with elements which will be afterwards detached for
separate consideration as making up our specifically
human and social *milieu*. The mother's protecting care
is given in infancy along with and in the same sense as
the mother's features, or the bloom on her cheeks. And
to myself it seems clear, again, that the beauty of the
rose is no more read into, or added to, the fact of the
rose than its colour. Both are, in the first instance, *found*,
not brought, though, as the colour seems not to be found
except by creatures with eyes, so the beauty, too, is not
found by the man who has not the "inner eye" by which
beauty is discerned. At least the artists of the world
have commonly spoken and borne themselves as if it
would be the death of artistic endeavour to discover that
their work has been a process of inventing and not one
of finding.

Now all this seems to be no less true of our moral
"ideals". As I do not add either the tints or the beauty
of the rose or the sunset *de meo* to a rose or a sunset
"given" without beauty, or even without colour, but
find the colour or the beauty *in* the given, so I do not,
by an "act of valuation", make Jonathan's affection for
David or the self-devotion of Marcus Curtius, the humility of St. Francis, or the patient labour of Darwin
good; I find the goodness there in them. Presumably,
I should have had no moral "ideals" at all if I had not
begun in childhood by accepting "as a little child" the
moral tradition of my community with its witness to the

fact that qualities like these are "objectively" good, exactly as iron is hard and lead soft. And any tradition of living would soon cease to be a living tradition if men could be persuaded that it consists of "valuations" manufactured by themselves and imposed on the "real facts" of life from outside. A tradition thus degraded would lose all its power of inspiring to fresh endeavour and better action. The ideals of good which in actual history move men to great efforts only move so powerfully because they are *not* taken to be an addition imposed on the facts of life, but to be the very bones and marrow of life itself. Behind every living morality there is always the conviction that the foundation of its valuations is nothing less than the "rock of ages", the very bed-rock out of which the whole fabric of things is hewn. The mere suspicion, phrase it as we will, that "divinity gives itself no concern about men's matters", that "the universe is sublimely indifferent to our human distinctions of right and wrong", that "facts are thoroughly non-moral", when it comes to be entertained seriously, regularly issues in a lowering of the general standard of human seriousness about life. Serious living is no more compatible with the belief that the universe is indifferent to morality than serious and arduous pursuit of truth with the belief that truth is a human convention or superstition. In short, if one is thoroughly in earnest with the attempt to separate the given, the fact, from the superadded value, one will discover, on the one hand, that what one has left on one's hands as the bald fact has ceased to be fact at all by the transference of every item of definite content to the account of the added, and, on the other, that the "value" has lost all its value by its rigorous exclusion from the given. What confronts us in actual life is neither facts without value nor values attached to no facts, but fact revealing value, and dependent, for the wealth of its content, on its character as thus revelatory, and values which are realities and not arbitrary fancies, precisely because they are embedded in fact and give it its meaning. To divorce the two would be like trying to separate the sounds of a great symphony from its musical quality.

The point I am anxious to make, then, is one which would be generally admitted, so far as the mere epistemological problem is concerned. I do not believe that anyone who has seriously faced that problem will be disposed to deny that in our knowledge of the actual world it is quite impossible to make a hard-and-fast distinction between a kernel of reality or fact which is given as such once for all, and an interpretation, more or less doubtful, superadded by the apprehending mind. There is no specific datum of sense which can be isolated in this fashion, any more than it is possible, in the study of biological development, to mark off a primitive datum, as the given and original endowment of the organism, from the effects of interaction between this datum and its environment. Whatever we assign, in some specific investigation, to the organism as originally there, antecedently to a particular process of development through interaction, itself, on further examination, turns out to presuppose earlier processes of development by which it has come to be what it is. Everywhere in our biological science we are confronted by the distinction between developing organism and conditioning environment; but I suppose it is never possible, on either side, to accept any feature of a situation as simply given material for development, with no history of internal development of its own. So in the genetic study of the growth of our knowledge of the corporeal world around us. However far back you trace a man's cognitive relation to this world, you find in it the two relatively opposed factors of passive reception of given data and active interpretation of the data, but their apparent independency is only apparent. We never reach any actual stage in the mental growth of the individual man or the society so primitive that we could say of it, "here all is passive reception of a given with no element of disturbing interpretation", any more than we can expect, at the other end of the process, ever to achieve a "scientific understanding of nature" in which everything should be interpretation, and nothing uninterpreted given fact. There is no reason to believe that even the simplest beginnings of anything we could recognise as human cognition present us with purely passive reception of the merely given. Recognition, comparison, discrimination, whereever they show themselves, are already incipient interpretation, and even the crudest human apprehension of the bodily world involves them all. We may fairly doubt whether some such processes are not characteristic of the perception of the lowest organisms to which we can attribute any perceptiveness. If they are not, then we have, at least, to say that so-called "perception", in creatures to whom it is a purely passive receptivity, must be so radically different from the perception of man that the development of such organisms belongs, like the formation of the earth's crust, to the prehistory, not to the history, of intelligence, and that with the first dawn of human perception we have a real discontinuity on the psychical side, a genuine emergence of something wholly novel, which is only very superficially masked by the mere temporal continuity of the sequence of physical and biological events.

What is thus generally allowed to be true of cognition is, I would contend, equally true of all the reactions of man against the wider world in which he

finds himself placed. Our moral "ideals" are not something added by the mind *de suo* to "facts" or "things-as-
they-are". As all human perception is already intellectual interpretation, so all human practice is already
reaction guided by the light of a tradition, however
rudimentary, of the good, and all human art production inspired by recognition of beauty as a character
of things. The conception of our ideals of good as simply
derived from an earlier life of merely blind appetition,
so that primarily "good" means only "what a man
happens to be lusting after", is thoroughly unhistorical.
So far as our personal memories carry us back in the
reconstruction of individual experience, or our historical
researches in the reconstruction of human experience
at large, we never reach a stage at which appetition is
more than *relatively* "blind", *i.e.* uncontrolled by a
tradition of the good which presupposes intelligence.
If we *could* get real evidence that in fact there was a
time in the life of the individual or the community
when the blindness was absolute, once more we should
have to regard this time as belonging to individual
or communal prehistory, and to recognise that there
has been, with the dawn of *guided* appetition, in each
of ourselves, or in humanity at large, a real, though
masked, discontinuity. Purely blind appetition, if it
exists at all, is qualitatively infra-human. The history
of humanity, as T. H. Green rightly insisted, is a history of developing intelligence, not of the production
of intelligence out of something else. The really given
is a whole situation which includes ourselves, with our
definite endowment of more or less coherent schemes
of value, our hopes and fears, our choices and avoid-
ances. The history of man is no tale of the superim-
position of an edifice of "mental construction" on a
basis of *mere* givenness; it is the story of the gradual

clarification and progressive definition of apprehensions, contacts with the "given", cognitive and practical alike, which have been there all along in vague and implicit form, in any life we can recognise as being qualitatively of a piece with our own.

If this is so, it is merely arbitrary to assume that while our physical structure and its history throw real light on the general character of the system of realities which includes human organisms among its constituents, our moral, aesthetic, religious being throws no light whatever on the nature of this reality. We have every right to hold that, however we conceive of the real, we must not think of it in terms which could make the actuality of this richly diversified life a mere unintelligible mystery. There must be at least as much to learn about the inmost character of the real from the fact that our actual spiritual life is controlled by such-and-such definite conceptions of good and right, such-and-such hopes and fears, as there is to learn from the fact that the laws of motion are what they are, or that the course of biological development on our planet has followed the lines it has followed. It may be that this is a grave understatement. Without prejudice to the issues which are still ground of dispute between the mechanist and the vitalist, we may, I take it, fairly say that there is no likelihood that science will ever return to the point of view of the best seventeenth-century thinking, the point of view from which the one and only thing of first-rate importance to be said about the real is that it is a geometrical system. The development of evolutionary biology has at least had the result that we now recognise that it is more illuminative to know that the real exhibits itself as a realm where there is room for life and sentience than to know that it forms a kinematical system. It is such a system, but the important thing is that it is the *kind* of kinematical system in which living organisms can find a home. May it not well be even more important to know that it is a system in which moral, artistic, and religious aspiration can flourish and find adequate scope? On any theory the real must always remain very mysterious to our apprehension, but it *may* be that we come nearer to understanding its character when we know that it is the environment of organic life than when we merely know—if we do know it—that it is a closed energetic system, and nearest of all when we know that it is at once the stage and inspiration of the artist, the hero, and the saint. Our geometrical knowledge may be very much clearer and more articulate than our knowledge of life and sentience, and this again much clearer and better articulated than our knowledge of our own moral being, which is, as Shelley said, a "mystery, even to ourselves"; the knowledge we can have of God may be still more unclear and inarticulate. And yet it may well be that, for all its dimness, it is just this knowledge which brings us most directly into contact with the very heart of reality. Spinoza's ideal of a "theology" demonstrated, after the fashion of Euclid, as a consequence of self-evident premises may be the supreme vanity of vanities, and yet it may still be true that *perfecta scientia Deum scire*, that the knowledge of God is the most real knowledge we have.

III

ETERNITY AND TEMPORALITY

Τὸ μὲν γὰρ δὴ παράδειγμα πάντα αἰῶνά ἐστιν ὄν, ὁ δ' αὖ διὰ τέλους τὸν ἅπαντα χρόνον γεγονώς τε καὶ ὢν καὶ ἐσόμενος.—PLATO.

Heav'n
Is a plain watch, and without figures winds
All ages up.   VAUGHAN.

WE have decided, for reasons stated in our last lecture, that it is permissible to look to our personal experience of the life of aspiration after the good for indications of the true character of the actual. What is actual, we hold, must at least have such a character, the *So-sein* of the *Seiendes* must be such, that I can say, *What I ought to be, that I can be*. This, as we see at once, is what Kant meant by his famous saying that *I ought* implies *I can*. But Kant's formula is in one way defective. He is thinking, as he too often is throughout his ethical writings, rather of the single performance than of the *So-sein* which reveals itself in the performance. He means primarily What I ought, at this juncture, to *do*, that I can *do*, if I choose. Hence it is on *my own* nature as a morally responsible being that the principle, as Kant conceives it, throws a direct light; any consequences it may have for the understanding of the realm of the real as a whole are only reached, in the second *Critique*, "with windlasses and with assays of bias". But when we remember that on Kant's own theory, no less than in actual fact, deeds are only prized as having intrinsic and absolute worth so far as they can be taken

67

to be effects revelatory of a character or quality of the doer who is their "free cause", we see that the ultimate moral imperative is not "do this", but rather, "be this"; the tree must first be a good tree, if it is to bring forth genuinely good fruit. Hence the second of the supreme human problems is misstated in Kant's well-known enumeration of them;[1] its true form is not, What acts ought I to do, but What manner of man ought I to be? Indeed, we might fairly say that Nietzsche has given the perfect expression for the supreme "categorical imperative" in his injunction *Werde der du bist*, if only we are careful to remember from the first that I do not, at the outset, know *wer* or *was ich bin*; I am a riddle to myself, and it is only through the process of the *Werden* that I, slowly and painfully, gain some insight into my *Sein*. Even in the artificially isolated "physical realm" of natural science, what we study is never a *mere Werden*, a mere succession of barely particular events which just "happen"; we are dealing everywhere with successions which exhibit pervasive "universal" characters, or patterns, events in which, in the terminology of Whitehead[2], *objects*, that is "universals *in re*", are situated, "becomings" which, in the significant language of Plato,[3] are γενέσεις εἰς οὐσίαν. Still less is any morally significant act a mere event which happens. The piquancy of the disparaging epigram that human life is "one damned thing after another" is wholly due to its glaring falsity as a description of any life but one which would be morally worthless.

There is a famous passage in Plato's *Timaeus* in which this point is made very strikingly. The Pythagorean Timaeus is there giving a pictorial account

---

[1] *KdrV.*[1] 805 (= *KdrV.*[2] 833).
[2] *Principles of Natural Knowledge*, pp. 82 ff.
[3] *Philebus*, 26 D 8.

of the "soul" which, as he teaches, animates the whole physical universe. God, he says, made it by mixing certain ingredients, as the master of a feast mingles the wine and the water for his guests, in the great mixing-bowl. The ultimate ingredients of the mixture are two, the *same*, "the being which is undivided and always self-same", and *the other*, "the being which becomes and is divisible in bodies" (*Tim.* 35 A 2). They are, in fact, just object and event, the eternal and the temporal. In the great world-soul, according to Timaeus, these ingredients are wrought into a perfectly stable compound. *Our* souls contain the same elements, but the brew is not of the same quality; we are made of the "seconds" and "thirds" (*ib.* 41 D). We may certainly take the meaning to be that in our case the resulting compound is always more or less unstable. In the world-soul, he means to say, eternity and temporality are together, in permanent interpenetration and equilibrium; in our human spiritual life there is a tension between them, more or less acute according to the quality of the individual life.

These remarks of Timaeus, divested of their trappings of imagery, may furnish a suitable text for some reflections on what, as I take it, is the most patent and universal characteristic of explicitly moral life wherever it is found. As morality becomes conscious of itself, it is discovered to be always a life of tension between the temporal and the eternal, only possible to a being who is neither simply eternal and abiding, nor simply mutable and temporal, but both at once. The task of living rightly and worthily is just the task of the progressive transmutation of a self which is at first all but wholly mutable, at the mercy of all the gusts of circumstance and impulse, into one which is relatively lifted above change and mutability. Or, we might say, as an

alternative formula, it is the task of the thorough transfiguration of our *interests*, the shifting of interest from
temporal to non-temporal good. It is this which gives
the moral life its characteristic colouring as one of
struggle and conflict never finally overcome. When the
conflict has not yet begun, or at any rate has not become
conscious struggle, there is as yet only the pre-moral,
or incipiently and unconscious moral, life of the natural
or animal man; if it finds completion in the entire transformation of the self and its interests from temporality
into the supra-temporal, the strictly ethical level of life
has been passed, and with it the *merely* human level.
Es strebt der Mensch, so lang er lebt, and we may add
that, *so lang er lebt*, man is always striving towards
something which he not merely has not reached, but of
which he only knows in the dimmest and vaguest way
what it is. The "Form of Good" may be "the master-
light of all our seeing", but if we are asked *what* it is,
though the better men we are, the less hopelessly vague
our answer may be expected to be, the best of us has
nothing like a "clear and distinct idea" of what he would
be at. Really to say what "the good" is, we should need
to be in fruition of it, and if we had the fruition, our life
would have become, in Aristotle's language,[1] no longer
that of man, but that of the "divine something" in man.
Or to speak more Christianly, to know what "glory"
is, we should need to be ourselves already "in glory".

"Now", says an apostolic writer, "we are sons of
God, and we know not what we shall be." The thought
finds an unexpected echo when our great master of
human experience, without any trace of theological
prepossession, wants to bring home to us the mingled
pathos and comedy of a distracted mind. "They say
the owl was a baker's daughter. Lord, we know what

[1] *N.E.* 1177 b, 27-28.

we are, but know not what we may be!" Its philosophical form is the thesis on which T. H. Green has so much
to say in the *Prolegomena to Ethics*,[1] that in all moral
progress to a better, the driving force is aspiration
after a best of which we can say little more, at any stage
of the process, than that it lies ahead of us on the same
line of advance along which the already achieved progress from the less to the more good has been made.
As usual, when we are trying not to rubricate knowledge already won, but to anticipate, poetry has here
the advantage over technical philosophy as a medium
of expression, for the reason that poetry can convey so
perfectly the sense of the tentativeness with which we
have to grope our way in the half-light which is, after
all, our "master-light".

> Shape nothing, lips; be lovely-dumb;
> It is the shut, the curfew sent
> From there where all surrenders come
> Which only makes you eloquent.

Or again:

> I know not what my secret is;
> I know but it is mine:
> I know to live for it were bliss,
> To die for it divine.

Yet the not uncommon experience is misread when,
as seems to be the case in Professor's Alexander's surro-
gate for theology,[2] it is interpreted simply as evidence
that the life of the mind is a stage on the way to the
evolution of something of which we can say nothing
whatever, except that it is, and must always remain,
the blankly inconceivable. The point of the experience
is precisely that though we could never say articulately
what the goal of the journey is without having reached
it, yet at every fresh step we are finding ourselves in a

[1] Green, *Prolegomena*, pp. 178 ff.
[2] Alexander, *Space, Time and Deity*, bk. iv. *passim*.

land which is no mere "strange country"; as the familiar hymn puts it, we are getting "a day's march nearer *home*", losing ourselves, quite literally, to find *ourselves*. It is not altogether true that manhood is *etwas das überwunden werden muss*; it is rather true that it is something which has to be *won*. So at least the moralist who really believes in morality must hold; if science or metaphysics profess to prove anything else, *he* can only retort, "so much the worse for them". That is the moralist's special way of becoming "a fool for Christ's sake".

Let me devote the rest of this lecture to an attempt to make my meaning clearer. And, first of all, let me offer some remarks—at a later stage we may find it necessary to return upon them—on the most tormenting of philosophical questions, the meaning of the notions of time and eternity. I begin, as "better known to ourselves", with Time, or, as I would rather say in this connection, Temporality.

Temporality.—We must begin by an attempt to get our minds clear on some important distinctions. Nothing I have to say at this stage has any bearing on the puzzles which may be raised about methods of *measuring* intervals of duration, or *locating* events temporally. It is with duration and succession as features of human moral life, not with the question of their measures or magnitude, that I am now concerned. Again, what we have to consider is not the mere fact of *successiveness*, the relation of "earlier" and its converse "later", as we find them in the course of physical events, but something very different, the distinction between *past, present*, and *future*. If we confine our attention to the events of the physical order taken, by an artificial and legitimate abstraction, apart from all reference to the way in which they affect the emotional and conative life of individual experients, we may fairly say that

though there are in "nature", as thus conceived, everywhere relations of before and after, there is neither
past, present, nor future. To introduce *these* distinctions
is to make explicit or concealed reference to the individual experient and his interior life of action and purpose, exactly as the same reference is introduced whenever we speak of "right" and "left", "before" and
"behind", "above" and "below". In a purely physical
world where there were no experients, there might be
earlier and later events, but no event would ever be
present, past, or future. Again, within the experience
of an individual experient, there may be a before
which is not properly to be called a past, and an
after which cannot rightly be called a future. I
must at least register my own conviction that the
purely "instantaneous" present, the "knife-edge", as
it has been called, is a product of theory, not an experienced actuality. The briefest and most simple and
uniform experiences we have "last", even if they only
last for a fraction of a second, and they are never merely
"static"; there is transition, and thus the before and
after, within them. For example, whenever we listen
to music, there is a before and after relating any two
immediately successive notes;[1] if there were not, or
if the relation were not actually constitutive of the
experience but merely "inferred" somehow "on the
basis of" the experience, we should have no apprehension of melody. But, equally certainly, we should
have no apprehension of it if we could not apprehend
the two notes and their successiveness, with its "sense"
as an ascending or descending interval, in a single
pulse of present experience. And I should say that

---

[1] And, for the matter of that, the individual single note, as heard, has always
its characteristic "protensity", as it has been called. We no more hear instantaneous sound than we see "mathematical points".

when we are listening to music in the proper mood, and with the right kind of appreciation, we appear to take in a considerable stretch of the successive as all alike there in one apprehended present, in spite of our definite awareness of elaborate relations of before and after between its constituents. If it were not so, I do not see how we could ever have come by awareness of a musical phrase—for example, any characteristic theme or *motiv* of Beethoven or Wagner—as a whole and a unit.[1] And more generally, though I cannot argue the point here, I should assert the *change* is actually "sensed", not, as some suppose, merely "inferred" from a succession of experiences all internally "static". It is, then, with the distinction of past from future and both from present, not with that of before from after, that we are now concerned. The point for us is not merely that events can be contrasted as earlier and later, but that they can be contrasted as "no longer" and "not yet".

Now *this* distinction is manifestly based directly on our own experience of ourselves as striving and active beings. The "future", the "not yet", is the direction taken by a conation in working itself out towards satisfaction (or towards being dropped, because it is persistently thwarted). The "not yet" is that towards which *I* am endeavouring, or reaching out. Its opposite, the "no longer", is that from which *I* am turning away. You might, indeed, conceivably try to get rid of the reference to action by distinguishing the two directions as those of anticipation and memory, prospect and retrospect respectively, if it were not that the very use of the familiar words *pro*spect, *retro*spect, brings back again the very reference on which I am dwelling. Strictly speaking, this antithesis only gets its full mean-

---

[1] The apprehension of a spoken syllable will, of course, illustrate the point equally well.

ing within the sphere of effort which is, at least, incipiently moral. In physical nature, as conceived by the "classical" kinematics of the nineteenth century, there is really neither past, present, nor future, no emergence of the *not yet* into the *now*, nor fading of the *now* into the *no-longer*. In dehumanising our experience to the "limit of opakeness", as we have to do if we mean to think in terms of the classical kinematics, we try to think away *these* distinctions and to retain only a bare sequence of later or earlier, which is neither *within* the present, nor yet *from* the past, *through* the present, *to* the future. Bare sequence of this kind is not succession as we actually apprehend it in the concrete case, where the "passage of nature" regularly comes to us as one factor in a striving and forward-reaching personal life. Just because such sequence as a science of kinematics can contemplate is bare sequence, thus artificially detached from its setting, it is never even real sequence, and kinematics is a science of abstract possibilities, not of actualities. The "flow of time" contemplated in classical mechanics is not "real" time, and its intervals are no *durée réelle*. In trying to conceive a world where simple successiveness is everything, we are inevitably driven to imagine a succession which is not real succession and a temporality which is not real time. We talk, indeed, of the "everlasting hills", and of the "most ancient stars", but only by an anthropomorphism which a strictly mechanical science is bound to reject. What has no present, and therefore also neither past nor future, cannot properly be said to "last" either a short time or a long time, to be recent or ancient. In a world where there was nothing but movement, or nothing but "matter" and movement, duration would have lost its meaning.

It is with the appearance of something which we can

call, by more than a "legal fiction", effort and purpose that the distinction between past, the direction of that from which effort is moving away, and future, the direction of that to which effort is tending, first becomes really significant, and, in becoming so, gives significance to the motion of the present, the "moment" which is not only "*a* now" but *now*. Time, we may say, as it actually is, is the characteristic form of the conative, forward-reaching life. So much, at least, we must all have learned from M. Bergson. This will enable us to understand why, though Spinoza, whose ideal for the sciences of the living organism and the living spirit was that they should all be reduced to the study of complicated kinematical configurations, could insist that it is vital to true thinking to contemplate its object "under a certain form of eternity", the tendency of an age which, like our own, has derived its ideal of science largely from the modern development of evolutionary biology, is rather to think it obvious that the "essence of true thinking" is to contemplate its object under a form of *time*, to write the object's life-history—exactly what Dr. Whitehead is trying to do by introducing the conception of "organism" into physics itself. Spinoza's thought is that so long as the durational form still affects our results, our thinking is missing its mark. Thinking which was thorough, through and through what thinking professes to be, would see the *facies totius universi* as something which has no history. The thought more familiar to our contemporaries is that really adequate knowledge, knowledge which is through and through all that knowledge ought to be, would see everything as something that *is having* a history, and a history which is never complete. We shall have to return to the point in the penultimate lecture of our course, and may then find that both conceptions sin by that commonest of all intellectual errors in philosophy, over-simplification. But for the present the point I want to make is simply this. What Spinoza calls "eternity" is precisely what might more truly be called the bare form of mere sequence, the contemplation of one kinematical pattern or another as the kaleidoscope of the universe turns in a "mathematical time" where there is neither present, past, nor future. He thinks he has eternalised a life-history by merely making it unhistorical. He reduces real action to a string of "configurations", and a mere configuration has no history, except by a misleading metaphor.

When we come to deal with the sciences of life and mind—I mean these sciences themselves, not the hypothetical kinematics into which they are sometimes sublimated by a crude metaphysics—we are dealing with processes which have a genuine form of temporality just because they disclose the activities of historical individuals, beings whose life is a *streben*, a reaching out from a past to a future. The route by which a mere configuration of points or of mass-particles has reached a given shape may be immaterial to the further succession of its shapes, the route by which an organism or a personality has become what it is is all-important, for the organism or person is charged with all its past and pregnant with all its future. Of it we may truthfully say, inverting a well-known line of Tennyson, that all it has seen is a part of it. This is why the organism, and still more the person, has a history in a sense in which a mere configuration has none. It may be, of course, and we shall yet have more to say on the point, that there is no actual reality which is a mere configuration of the kind contemplated in text-books of kinematics or dynamics. In that case we should have to say, and we should have the support of eminent living physicists in saying it, that Spinoza's ideal of knowledge is in principle unattainable, even in the sciences of the "inorganic"; physics and chemistry would be no less irreducible to complicated applications of rational mechanics than physiology and psychology. This is, in fact, precisely what Dr. Whitehead, for one, is saying very eloquently at the present moment. But *if* actual physical processes really are nothing more than changes of configuration in kinematical systems, or transactions between *kinetic* systems, then we should have to say that, in principle, when you know what the configuration, or the system of mass-particles, is "at any instant t_o", you know all that it has in itself to become; or, rather, the very motion of "becoming" is too deeply infected with historicity to be applicable to such a pattern. If it seems to us to "change", that is only because we have mistakenly treated it as having some unity and individuality of its own, whereas it is, in truth, only an arbitrarily selected piece of an indefinitely larger pattern. The more we widen our consideration to take in more of the pattern, the more does the appearance that it exhibits any change or development vanish.

The case is altered the moment we come to deal with the lowliest thing which displays a concrete individuality of its own. The simplest organism, recognisable as such, for example, differs from a mere configuration or a mere kinetic system by the fact that it has an *environment*, specifically distinguished from and opposed to itself, and lives upon this environment by "assimilating" material drawn from it, whereas the mere configuration or kinetic system has merely "surroundings", but no true "environment".[1] This duality

---

[1] And consequently Goethe's well-known thesis that "Natur hat weder Kern noch Schale" is *not* true of "organic nature".

in unity of organism and environment is fundamental for the understanding of transactions between them. A mere configuration, or a mere assemblage of mass-particles, as I say, has no "environment"; it is always itself a constituent part of a wider configuration or system, singled out for consideration in virtue of some "subjective" interest of our own, theoretical or practical. An organism is not, in like manner, a subjectively selected and artificially isolated constituent of its own environment. The antithesis between the two is significant for the organism itself, as well as for the student of it. A true organism, we might say, is always *Athanasius contra mundum*. It, as much as the student of it, has its "world" and stands over against that world, not, perhaps, necessarily in the cognitive opposition of knower to known, but at least in the practical opposition of user to used, feeder to thing fed on.[1]

Without this opposition, significant, as we are saying, in the highest degree for the organism itself, the organism would not have the sort of specific individuality it actually has; to use the terminology of a recent eminent occupant of this platform,[2] it would not be the special sort of "substantial unity" of its environment which, in fact, it is. Being the sort of "substantial unity of the environment" which it is, however completely its life may seem to be made up of responses to solicitations directly supplied by the environment, the responses are never completely determined by characters in the environment alone. How the creature will react to these solicitations depends also on the

---

[1] And, be it noted, the relation of organism to environment is not, like that of one kinematical system to another with which it interacts, a one-level relation; the transaction is not a mere "exchange". The organism "assimilates" what it receives from the environment; the environment receives excreta from the organism, but does not "assimilate"them.

[2] Dr. C. Lloyd Morgan. The reference here is to language used in Dr. Morgan's spoken Gifford Lectures. For the thought see *Life, Mind and Spirit*, lecture iii.

sort of creature *it* is, on *its* "particular go", and its "particular go" never seems to be quite independent of the route by which it has reached its present state, as that of a mere "energetic system" is held to be independent of the route by which it has come to its present condition. Certainly, the higher the creature ranks in the scale of evolutionary development, the more hopeless would it be to attempt to say how it will respond to the situation, on the strength of mere knowledge of its present condition. As we ascend in the scale, what the creature will do now is found to depend increasingly, in more ways than one, on what it may have done before. All that men of science have to teach us about the importance for a creature's life-history of the formation of routes of special permeability for the transmission of influence from the environment, or for initiated responses to such influence, or, at higher levels, about the importance of the formation of physiological routine and psychological habit, serves to illustrate the point. But it is also illustrated by the apparently antithetic facts which indicate that established routine and habit never become absolutely rigid. We observe apparently casual and unaccountable deviations from the most fixed established routine and habit in the lives of all lower organisms which we can subject to individual examination, as well as in our own, though in their case the interpretation of these deviations is necessarily tentative and ambiguous. (Indeed, I should be curious to know from competent observers whether even the "decapitated" frog of the laboratory is really quite as much of a piece of clockwork in its behaviour as it is made, for a legitimate purpose, to appear in the text-books which condense the results of countless individual observations into a summary formula. Are we not dealing, even here, with something like a "journalistic" exaggeration?) In our own case we can often see what the interpretation is.

We are not absolutely under the sway of the most thoroughly organised habit or the most constant of associations. At the lowest level of what we recognise as distinctively human conduct, the line of response which has not been usually followed in the past, the train of associations which has not been common, may sporadically reaffirm itself, as, to take a trivial example from my own experience, I occasionally find myself, for no discoverable reason, heading a letter with an address at which I have not resided for a quarter of a century. It does seem to be a fact of conscious human life, that, thanks to the pervasive omnipresence of memory, the past is real in our human "world" as it is not at lower levels. As F. H. Bradley says somewhere in one of his numerous scattered essays, the mere fact that a conscious response *has* once been made at some time seems of itself to be a possible cause of repetition. So much seems to be true not only of ourselves but of, at any rate, those higher animals who are at the nearest remove from us. With them, as with us, it is a misleading metaphor to compare the establishment of habitual responses to the demands of the environment with the process by which the river digs out its own bed. Thus, to appeal to the example I have just given, I may perhaps make the mistake of dating a letter from the long-abandoned address twice at an interval of several years. During the interval I had perhaps never once made this mistake, though I had written and dated hundreds, or even thousands, of notes and letters. If the production of a habit, physical and mental, were really on all-fours with the formation of a river-bed, such complete disuse of the old reaction and repeated discharge of the new ought to have made the mistake impossible. The stream may depart from its formed channel because there is a present obstacle which blocks it; it will not diverge merely because there was once in the past a now long-removed obstacle at this particular place. With me, the mere fact that I used, twenty or twenty-five years ago, to date my letters from a particular address seems to be of itself a possible sufficient basis for doing the same thing now, unreasonably and in the teeth of a habit developed by the regular practice of years.

Further, as we all know, it is just this possibility which makes the conquest and control of habit by intelligent purpose and precept also possible. In the life of a reasonable man we find neither random spontaneity nor servitude to habit dominant. What we do find is a combination of habit and spontaneity, and a combination with a definite character. (Though we must not call this character a "law", if we mean by law anything for which we could supply a general "blank" formula.) We find habit everywhere, but habit subservient to foresight. What a man does at this present juncture, if and so far as he is a reasonable man, is primarily designed to meet the individual demand of this individual situation, and the demand of the situation must be taken to mean the call made on the agent in this situation by a coherent plan of purposive living. (Thus the "demand of the situation" will be different for different agents.) The character of the plan itself, as I have tried to indicate, is not known, even to the agent, fully and definitely from the outset; it reveals itself progressively as he meets and faces successive situations. An upright man has a certain "ideal" before him. His purpose is, in all situations—what they will be is largely unknown to him—to conform himself to the "holy" will of God, to promote the true good of his social group, to "keep his honour untarnished", or something of that kind. In spite of all that Kant has said about the clear and infallible guidance afforded by the categorical imperative of duty, no man knows in advance what particular line of conduct will, in some unrehearsed contingency, most surely conform to God's will or keep a man's honour bright. That is precisely what you can only discover, with any approach to certainty, when the contingency is upon you. Hence it is that, even of those with whom we are most intimate, we so often can say no more, if we are asked how we suppose they will act in some difficult position, than that we do not know what they will do, but are sure that their act, whatever it is, will be the act befitting a true Christian, or a high-minded man. We are sure that they will do nothing common, or mean, or unbefitting, and we are sure of no more. And when we say this, we do not mean to be uttering a triviality, or giving expression to the non-moral partiality which is ready to approve anything done by a friend because it is done by him. We mean that when the act in question has been done (and it may prove to be a complete surprise to us) we shall be able to see that it was the right and reasonable thing to do. Our judgement of approval is genuinely ethical and genuinely "synthetic".[1]

There is thus perpetual novelty, adjustment to the requirements of the moral ideal in a changing and unforeseeable environment, in all typically moral action, and, as I have said, even the precise character of the ideal itself only becomes partially and gradually clear

[1] Of course I am not denying the obvious fact that the lessons of the past all through play a part of fundamental importance in directing intelligence to the response demanded by the new situation. If the situation presented no recognisable analogy with anything in the agent's past history, intelligence would presumably be helpless to cope with it. But the lesson of the past is not one which can be got "by rote".

to us in the very act of meeting the demands it makes upon us. What demands it would make in a totally unfamiliar situation—as, for example, if I, with my special past history, should suddenly be called upon to exercise judicial functions on my own sole responsibility for some social group, I cannot even guess. But the point is that all that is ever handed over to the control of mere habit is the execution of the details of my act; the combination of the details, which is the important thing, is exactly what is always more or less novel and unique. If, for example, I have to write a letter of instructions to a subordinate about the way in which some practical task is to be executed, the mere formation of the marks on the paper is matter of habit, and the more completely so the better. The less I need give my attention to the spelling of the different words, or the grammar of the different sentences, the more fully can I concentrate my mind on the main problem of making my instructions reasonable and indicating them promptly, unambiguously, courteously and in the way likely to obtain hearty and willing co-operation from this particular subordinate. But the command over spelling and grammar which makes this concentration of attention on the main problem possible is itself dependent on memory, and so only itself possible in virtue of the fact that, in conscious human life, we are not at the mercy of mere "customary association", that standing source of irrelevancy. Everything depends on the principle that what has once been present may be present again, or perhaps it would be more exact to say, that what has once been operative may be operative again, apparently for no reason beyond the fact that it has once been operative and that it is relevant that it should be operative once more; recollection is not a mere function either of the recovery or of the frequency of experienced conjunction. To put the matter in a sentence, a human past may sometimes be a "dead" past; it is never safe to say of it, as we can perhaps say of the past of the lower animals, that it is dead and buried. This consideration has its important bearing on the quality of our moral life. Whether we like it or not, there are no more characteristic or common features of our human moral life than remorse and repentance. It may reasonably be doubted whether an "animal" is capable of either.

One might, indeed, possibly suggest that a well-behaved dog does exhibit something which looks like remorse, when it commits a fault for which it has usually been punished in the past. It is uneasy and shows its uneasiness; apparently, too, it has some kind of expectation of punishment. But I would take the opportunity to utter a humble protest against the over-hasty making of inferences about the mental life of animals in general from the behaviour of the few which we have not merely domesticated, but admitted to special intimacy with ourselves. It seems to me quite possible that the association of the house-dog, for example, with man may go a long way to humanise and moralise the dog and may make it something more than "only a dog". Before trusting confidently to conclusions about the capacities of animals based on the behaviour of our domestic friend I should like to be satisfied that the same behaviour is found, in some degree, in the dog in a state of nature, or the dog who has only associated with men markedly less moralised than ourselves. And even our most highly humanised dogs seem, at any rate, incapable of rising above the level of a rather crude remorse to anything like what we call, in the language of morality and religion, genuine repentance. Contrition —the first step to a true repentance—seems hardly to enter into their lives.[1] They may feel very uneasy until they have first been punished for an offence and then treated once more with the old friendliness. But when the offence has been "paid for", no dog seems to trouble himself about it. The mere fact of having offended does not seem to be felt as a man feels a past misdeed, a past stain on his honour, and often, ridiculously enough, a mere past piece of social *gaucherie*, as something which remains, after all "payment", a living and uneffaceable reality. "What I did is worked out and paid for" is a phrase we think characteristic of the attitude of the habitual criminal to his crimes; *pereunt et imputantur* is the language of morality; "my misdeeds prevail against me" is the cry of spiritual religion.

I might go on to illustrate my point further by dwelling on the way in which, in virtue of our possession of social tradition and history, the course of life of any one of us may be determined by a past which is neither, strictly speaking, his own, nor that of his own ancestors. Here we have a real difference between human and animal life, which remains real even if we take the most generous and least critical view of the facts which are sometimes alleged to prove the efficacy of so-called "racial memories" in the life of the animal. Our possession of recorded tradition, in the widest sense of that phrase,

---

[1] It is important not to confuse *contrition*, as Mill seems to do in his language about the "internal sanction" of morality, with regret or remorse. Regret may be felt for mere unfortunate circumstances. I may, for example, regret that I am not well enough off to do someone a social service which I should like to render, or that I have not the social influence which would procure him some advantage. It, to use Butler's distinction, concerns our "condition" rather than our conduct. Remorse, in our language, seems to mean exclusively dissatisfaction with one's own conduct, but it is a dissatisfaction which need have nothing to do with the moral quality of the conduct. Genuine contrition involves absolute and unqualified self-condemnation of one's conduct, and of one's personality, so far as expressed in that conduct, as *evil* or *sinful*. Hence its connection with the second stage of repentance—confession. The essence of confession is that it is recognition that an act which is absolutely to be condemned is my personal responsible act, and that, in condemning the act, I am condemning myself, so far as the act expressed myself, as guilty and evil without excuse.

makes it possible for us, as it is for none of the lower
animals, to be guided in the shaping of our own present
and future by almost any record from the past, even
from a past that goes back into "geological time". It
might be rash to say of any event known to have
occurred in the earth's past that it is really over and
done with, that it will never again be relevant to the
shaping of the future. In the merely inanimate world,
according at least to the conceptions of "orthodox"
mechanics, the past seems to shape the future only in
so far as it has not passed, but has persisted during the
interval. In the merely animate world, the past which
shapes a future seems to do so by the persistence of its
contribution in the way of a series of effects through an
interval. In the world of intelligent human action, the
remembered past seems to be able to mould the future
directly and immediately, striking, so to say, out of its
own remote pastness, even though there has been no
continuous persistence of itself or its effects through
the interval. When remembered, it *lives* again in "ideal
revival" in a more real sense than the makers of the old
psychological terminology ever intended. In a purely
physical world there would be no past, because there
would be no present; in a world of mere perceptions,
impulses, and instincts there would be only a dead past
holding the present in the mortmain of habit; in the
life of men, as intelligent and moral persons, and not at
any lower level, we have a living past. The outward and
visible sign of this is that man, at his lowest, has *traditions* where the animals seem to have only *instincts*.

I fear I have dwelt only too long on what must seem
painfully obvious and familiar. But I have done so for
a purpose. I would make it the more fully clear what
is implied by saying that *time* is the characteristic form
of the life of moral endeavour. It is plain, I hold, that

apart from our personal experiences of endeavour and its gradual satisfaction, we should know nothing of past and future, though we might still be able to distinguish before and after. The past, let me say it once more, means that from which *we* are turning away, the future that to which *we* are turning. And I think, though to say this is to anticipate a little, if we were asked what a present, or "now", is, as it is actually lived and experienced, we should not be far wrong in saying that whatever we experience as *one* satisfaction of endeavour is experienced by us as *one* "now", as a present in which the before has not sunk into the past, and the after is not waiting beyond the threshold of the future.

But if the temporal is strictly and properly the form of the life of conscious appetition, it should follow that in being so much as aware of our life as temporal at all, we are already beginning to transcend the form of temporality. For what is it we are endeavouring to do in even the humblest and most rudimentary striving after a positive end? As the psychologist says, we are endeavouring to keep before consciousness, and, if we can, to intensify, an experience we find agreeable to ourselves. If there really is a still lower level of conation where the endeavour is only to banish from consciousness an experience found disagreeable,[1] we may, at least, fairly say that this level is passed by the human baby at a very early stage in its career, and does not concern us as students of morals. Now to endeavour even to keep an agreeable condition of bodily wellbeing, like that of the cat before the fire, steadily in consciousness, is already to be trying to transcend the merely temporal form of the experience. We want to

---

[1] But the truth rather seems to be, as is stated in Stout's *Manual of Psychology*[4], p. 113, that "appetition is primary and aversion derivative"; aversion arises "with regard to any situation incompatible with the desired end".

have the pleasant sense of warmth, to have it thoroughly, and to have it in a "now" where there may be a before and an after, but where we are not conscious of a no longer or a not yet. If we are aware of the not yet, that means that the thorough satisfaction of our endeavour has not been reached; if we are aware of a no longer, satisfaction is palling or fading. When satisfaction is at its height and fills our being, the sense of past and future is lost in a rapture which is all present, so long as it lasts.

At a higher level than that of mere animal enjoyment, such as we may get from basking before a good fire, or giving ourselves up to the delight of a hot bath, we know how curiously the consciousness of past and future falls away, when we are, for example, spending an evening of prolonged enjoyment in the company of wholly congenial friends. The past may be represented for us, if we stay to think of it at all, by whatever happened before the party began, the future—but when we are truly enjoying ourselves we do not anticipate it—by what will happen when the gathering is over. The enjoyment of the social evening has, of course, before and after within itself; the party may last two or three hours. But while it lasts and while our enjoyment of it is steady and at the full, the first half-hour is not envisaged as past, nor the third as future, while the second is going on. It is from timepieces, or from the information of others, who were not entering into our enjoyment, that we discover that this single "sensible present" had duration as well as order. If we were truly enjoying ourselves, the time passed, as we say, "like anything". I have heard that the late R. L. Nettleship was in the habit of dwelling on this familiar expression as indicating the real meaning of "eternity". The same thing appears to be true of the "aesthetic pleasures", and of the enjoyment of unimpeded intellectual activity. When our thought is moving readily and successfully, without being brought to a halt by any baffling obstacles, towards the solution of a problem which interests us and to which we are equal, the experience of advance from the statement of the problem to its solution is, of course, an experience of before and after, or it could not be a conscious advance, but it is a movement within a conscious present, from a before which has not faded into the past, to an after which is not felt as belonging to the future.

So again, if I may trust my own experience, which is not that of a *connoisseur* with any very special aptitude, but is, perhaps, all the more significant for our present purpose on that account, when our consciousness is really *filled*, as it can be, with the movement of a piece of music, so that the music is, for the time, our "universe". The "movement" is movement, and we apprehend it as such, but within limits which presumably vary with personal responsivity to the special "appeal" of music, the apprehension of a musical unit is sensibly simultaneous. It is not an attending first to one note or chord, then to the next, but an attentive awareness of the *form* of a whole phrase which is taken in as a whole, and felt as all *now* here. Everyone, I take it, apprehends a short and striking phrase of two or three notes or chords in this way, as a unit; most men can apprehend a larger phrase with a really marked form of its own, a "theme" from one of Beethoven's symphonies, for example, in the same way; a real musician, I suppose, would have the same apprehension of a whole "movement" as all present at once as a characteristic of his normal experience. It is, I imagine, experiences of this kind which Nietzsche had in mind when he said that *alle Lust will Ewigkeit*, and whatever the meaning of that verse may have been, it has always seemed to me

that experiences of this kind—they are most common,
I believe, in an intense form, when one is listening to
music which really masters one, but they are found also
in the enjoyment of drama and other forms of art [1]—it
has always seemed to me that they give us the key to
the famous and classic definition of eternity by Boethius,
that it is *interminabilis vitae tota simul et perfecta
possessio*, "whole, simultaneous, and complete fruition
of a life without bounds".[2] What the definition excludes, as being proper to temporality, we note, is not
the before and after, but the not yet and no longer
which would mark an experience as *not* the "whole
and complete" satisfaction of endeavour.

We all know the sort of criticism which has been
directed against this language by Hobbes, and by
numberless smaller men than Hobbes, the objection
that the *"nunc stans* of the schoolmen"—Boethius
uses no such words—is an unmeaning phrase. I should
reply that the sort of experiences of which we have
been speaking, *while they last*, conform exactly to the
definition. When, for example, we are enjoying the
music with heart and soul, in the first place we are
engrossed by it; it is the *total* field of awareness, or,
at least, of full awareness;[3] next we have a satisfaction
of endeavour which not only fills the whole soul, but
is also at once (*simul*) and complete (*perfecta*). And
there is a further feature of the experience which
corresponds to the clause *interminabilis vitae*. While

---

[1] Notably when we are following the movement of a powerfully wrought scene
in a drama as actual spectators in the theatre.

[2] *De Consolatione Philosophiae*, v., pros. 6. Cf.

> " Then long Eternity shall greet our bliss
> With an *individual* kiss;
> And Joy shall *overtake us as a flood*."

[3] "I have no life, Constantia, now but thee,
> Whilst, like the world-surrounding air, thy song
> Flows on, and fills all things with melody."

the experience lasts, one really does seem to have been "translated" into a world of beautiful sound which is "without bounds"; one has a sense that one always has been, and always will be, floating on the tide of harmony. (I trust my language will not sound affected; it is the best I can find to render a not unfamiliar experience faithfully.) There is, to be sure, illusion here, because, in the first place, we all have other interests than those which are satisfied by listening to music, so that we cannot get a *perfecta vitae possessio* in that way, and, in the next place, we are embodied intelligences, with nervous systems subject to fatigue and exhaustion; the flesh proves itself weak, even when the spirit continues ardently willing. But we can at least imagine the removal of these limitations. We can imagine a kind of life in which all our various aims and interests should be so completely unified by reference to a supreme and all-embracing good that all action had the same character of completeness which is imperfectly illustrated by our enjoyment of a musical pattern; we can also imagine that nervous fatigue and its consequence, the necessity for the alternation between attention and remission of attention, were abolished. And in both cases, the method by which we succeed in imagining such a state of things is the legitimate, and often indispensable, one of "passing to the limit" of a series of which the law of formation is familiar and the initial terms known. If the limit were reached, experience as a whole would be a single enjoyment, at once completely centralised and steadily advancing; would it not thus have lost the elements of the no longer and the not yet? Would not "whole and complete life", really analogous to a "movement" in some great symphony, be the entrance into "the joy of the Lord", the real achievement of that complete and *simultaneous* fruition of a life without bounds of which Boethius spoke?[1] I think it would, and the further point I would make is that in the specific experience of the moral life we already have to do with endeavour which, from first to last, is directed upon the attainment of such a form of fruition, and yet, while it retains its specific character, can never finally reach its goal. If we are justified in treating our own existence and peculiar *So-sein* as moral beings as capable of throwing any light whatever on the character of the actual and real as a whole, we might then reasonably infer that we may argue, here as elsewhere, from the existence of a function to the reality of an environment in which the function can find adequate exercise. If the pursuit of temporal and secular good must inevitably fail to satisfy moral aspiration itself, we may fairly infer that there *is* a non-secular good to which moral endeavour is a growing response. In so far as such a good can be apprehended and enjoyed at all, temporality, with its antithesis of not yet and no longer, is itself progressively relegated to a secondary place in the life of enjoyment, time is actually swallowed up in eternity, the natural life in one which is, in the strict and proper sense of the word, supernatural, morality in religion. The conception of a realm of "grace" as transforming and completing the realm of "nature", so characteristic of Christianity, will then appear as suggested, and indeed necessitated, by the known facts of our moral being themselves.

Now, is secular good, obtainable under strictly temporal conditions, an object really adequate to

---

[1] I may be allowed to remind the reader of the great classic exposition of the thought in St. Augustine (*Confessions*, ix., x. 23-26, the scene at the window in Ostia).

evoke and to sustain this aspiration which gives the moral life its specific character as moral? In plain words, can a satisfactory morality be anything but what is sometimes called by way of disparagement an *other-worldly* morality? And if not, how precisely ought we to conceive the relation of the this-worldly to the other-worldly? In principle, I believe, the greatest moralists have always answered the first of these questions in one way. If there could be such a thing as a life of purely secular or temporal enjoyment, its special and characteristic feature as temporal would be precisely that its various goods or objects of aspiration *cannot* be had all together by anyone. They must be had one after another, on the condition that some are always not yet, and others no longer. This is the point of the familiar epigram already mentioned which describes a strictly worldly life as "one damned thing after another". (For reasons which will appear immediately, I make no apology for the vulgar, but really relevant epithet.) The delights of childhood, of youth, of mature manhood, of an honoured old age, are all good. Some of each class are among the best goods we know, but some must always be forfeited that others may be gained.

> All things are taken from us, and become
> Portions and parcels of the dreadful past;
>
> There's something comes to us in life,
> But more is taken quite away,

and utterances like these may not be the whole of the truth, but there is only too much bitter truth in them. We cannot have the ripe wisdom, assured judgement, and reflective serenity of maturity at its best without leaving behind the ardours and impetuosities and adventures of act which belong to youth, and these, again, you cannot have without losing much of the *naïf* wonder, the readiness to be delighted by little things, the divine thoughtlessness of childhood. All are good, yet none can be enjoyed except in the season of life appropriate to each, and the enjoyment is always tinged at once by regret for what has had to be given up and unsatisfied aspiration after what cannot yet be. One could not be happy, as the fable of Tithonus was devised to teach, in an immortality of elderliness, but one would be no less unsatisfied with an immortality of childhood, or youth, or mid-manhood. It would be as bad to be Peter Pan as it would be to be Tithonus, and even an unending prime would hardly be more desirable. To a deathless Olympian the sage might reasonably give the counsel of our own poet—

> The best is yet to be :
> Grow old along with me,

and, from the nature of the case, the counsel would be impossible to adopt.

We may say the same thing of the common, or social, good. In our generation it should be superfluous to insist that men as groups, or even humanity as a whole, always have to pay the price of temporal good won by the loss of temporal good. However much we gain in the way of good by what we call advance in civilisation, something which is also good has to be surrendered. Life is made more secure, but, in the course of becoming more secure, it loses its quality of adventure, and becomes tame and commonplace. Order is won, but at the cost of some real loss of individuality and initiative. International understanding and good feeling are promoted, but the "good European" has lost the passionate devotion to the *patria* which could inspire an

Athenian of the age of Pericles, or a Florentine of the age of Dante. Even those of us who, like myself, are keenly alive to the necessity and the duty of being "good Europeans" can hardly feel that the thought of Europe makes us, as the thought of England made Words-worth's ideal warrior, "happy as a lover". Science "grows from more to more", and at each stage in the growth it becomes increasingly harder for the man who gives himself to the scientific life to be more than a specialist with a range of vision as lamentably contracted as the field of a powerful microscope. And so it is everywhere.

> We say that repose has fled
> For ever the course of the river of time,
> That cities will crowd to its edge
> In a blacker incessanter line,
> That the din will be more on its banks,
> Denser the trade on its stream,
> Flatter the plain where it flows,
> Fiercer the sun overhead.
> That never will those on its breast
> See an ennobling sight,
> Drink of the feeling of quiet again.

It is simply not the case that

> The old order changeth, giving place to new,
> And God fulfils Himself in many ways,

in the sense in which the words seem to have been understood when they were uttered. The new order does *not* simply take up into itself all that was good in the old and enrich it with further good, merely letting the bad slip away; it is won by the definite surrender of positive good, not by the mere elimination of defects, and the surrendered good is not reconquered. No doubt the vulgar epithet in the saying about life I have twice quoted is prompted by the sense that there is always this element of surrender clinging to every stage of

what we call progress. A more sentimental temperament reacts to the same situation by the development
of the *décadent* pessimism which tries to find the secret
of the goodness of the mutable in its very mutability—

> the very reason why
> I clasp them is because they die !

The logic here is, however, manifestly at fault. If the
summer's rose withers, so does the "stinking weed";
the worth of the perfume cannot really lie in that which
is common to it with the stench.

It might, of course, be said, that since all temporal
good is thus only "for a time", and it is not evident that
there is any good but that which is temporal, the reasonable attitude to life is that of the Epicurean; we should
live in the moment while it lasts, giving ourselves no
concern with what is beyond our immediate reach:
carpe diem, quam minimum credula postero. "Let us
enjoy the good things that are present, and let us
speedily use the creatures, like as in youth. Let us fill
ourselves with costly wines and ointments, and let no
flower of the spring pass us by." "Remove sorrow from
thy heart and put away evil from thy flesh, *for* childhood and youth are vanity."

> ὁ δαίμων, ὁ Διὸς παῖς . . .
> μισεῖ δ' ᾧ μὴ ταῦτα μέλει,
> κατὰ φάος νύκτας τε φίλας
> εὐαίωνα διαζῆν.[1]

But we only adopt such an attitude at the cost of a
breach with both morality and rationality, and since
men are, after all, moral and reasonable beings at heart,
"looking before and after", it is not surprising that the
Epicurean never is consistent. Lucretius may assert
in round words that, because we are merely ephemeral

---

[1] Euripides, *Bacchae*, 416 ff.

creatures, our concern is only with the moment, but he finds it necessary to preach on the text *nil igitur ad nos mors est* with a vehemence and at a length which shows that the sermon is delivered to himself as much as to Memmius. Horace never succeeds in disguising the fact that Lalage and the cask of Massic are the merest vain devices for concealing a "skeleton in the cupboard". A man, being a man, *must* "look before and after"; he cannot be really indifferent to the claims of the good that has to be left behind, or the lack of the good which is not yet to be had. Just in so far as he takes life seriously, his whole aim is to find and enjoy a good which is never left behind and never to be superseded. What his heart is set on is actually that simultaneous and complete fruition of a life without bounds of which Boethius speaks. As he grows more and more intelligent and moralises his life more and more completely, the nature of this underlying ethical purpose becomes increasingly apparent. As compared with the man who has no definite aim beyond getting the satisfaction of the moment, the man who has concern for what Butler calls his "interest in this world", even if that interest is taken to be limited to the securing of long life, health and comfort, has gone some way in the direction of overcoming the mere successiveness and temporality of incipient experience; the man who has learned to care for the well-being of a family or a house, still more the man who cares for the good of a wider, richer and more permanent community, or the man who cares first and foremost for the great so-called "impersonal" goods, art, science, morality, which can survive the extinction of a nation, an empire, a race, has proceeded further along the same road.

Yet it should be plain that even the last-named never really reaches the end of the road, if all he really achieves can be adequately described in terms of mere successiveness and temporality. So long as there is wrong to be put right, error and ugliness to be banished from life, the individual or the community is still only on the way to the possession of the heart's desire, and has not yet entered on the enjoyment of the inheritance. The best men often contrive to reconcile themselves to the prospect of spending their life in the arduous effort to make the pursuit of the unattained good a little less difficult for their successors. It is enough for us, they say, if those who are to come after us start on the pursuit at a point not quite so remote from the goal as that where our own efforts began. But to make this acquiescence seriously possible, it seems necessary to forget that, in a human history dominated by the form of successiveness, the result is still to leave every succeeding generation infinitely far from attainment.

The best type of Utilitarian, who makes his good in practice of the removal of abuses, is a fine type of man, but it is hard to think that human history as a whole could have much value, or a human life much interest, if nothing is ever achieved beyond the removal of abuses. If our moral achievement always ends only in the attainment of the slightly better, that of itself is proof that we never attain the good. A good which is to give life all its value cannot simply be a goal which lies ahead of us at every step of our path and, in fact, recedes indefinitely as we approach it. It must be something which is actually being had in fruition through a present which does not become past. And just in proportion as such abiding fruition of good is a feature in our actual experience, that experience is taking on a form which transcends the moral, if by the moral we mean, as Kant, for example, did, the sphere where endeavour is always towards the simply future and unrealised, and the dominant attitude is that of struggle. If human life, under the most favourable of circumstances, were a mere succession of increments of "betterment", it would be, in principle, a failure to achieve good; "meliorism" is only a foolish *alias* for pessimism.[1] If life is not a failure, then it cannot be an adequate account of the moral life to say that it is one of advance towards a future fruition which never becomes present. There must be another side to the facts. "A man's reach must exceed his grasp." Our experience must be something more than a progress in which the best we can say of every stage is only "not yet good, but rather better". There must be a sense in which we can be really in fruition, permanently established in a good beyond which there is no better. In the measure in which this can be truly said of any life, we may also say of that life that it is already shot through with the distinctive character of eternity and is an abiding *now*.

The distinctively ethical life, then, falls somewhere between these limits. It is not merely successive; if it were it would not even be a life of serious endeavour towards good. It is not simply a life of present and eternal fruition, from which succession and conflict have fallen away, for then it would be something more than ethical. In proportion to its moral worth, it is a life which is undergoing a steady elevation and transmutation from the mere successiveness of a simply animal existence to the whole and simultaneous fruition of all good which would be the eternity of the divine. As we rise in the moral scale, under the drawing of conceptions of good more and more adequate to sustain intelligent aspiration, living itself steadily takes on more and more a "form of eternity". For, in proportion to the level we have attained, each of our achieve-

[1] *Le meilleur est l'ennemi du bien.*

ments becomes more and more the reaction of a personality at once richer and more unified to the solicitation of a good, itself presented as richer and more thoroughly unified. As we rise in the moral scale, we more and more cease to have many goods with rival claims upon us, and come nearer to having one ever-present good, just as—we have learned it long ago from Socrates and Plato—we cease to exhibit a plurality of virtues, or excellences, relatively independent of one another, and come to display the "unity of virtue" in every single act. He that is joined to the Lord is *one* spirit.

Here we make a contact with the sphere of religion. There is the closest correspondence between our character and the quality of the good to which we respond in action. So long as we are moved to respond only to goods which must be had one after another, our character itself must show a corresponding want of unity; it must fall apart into phases and moods with no profound underlying unity. To the old Platonic question whether the soul is one or many we can only reply, as in effect Plato does, that it is as its desired good is. If it has many goods, it is itself many, its personality is loose-knit and incipient. It will only have a real, and not a merely ideal, inner unity of personality when its good is one and all-embracing, a real and living single good which is the source of all goodness and leaves nothing of the good outside itself. That is to say, unity of personality and interest will only be attained, if at all, by a soul which has come to find its principal good in God. If God, the concrete unity of all good in its one source, is not real, the complete unification of personality in ourselves, the very goal of all education of character and all moral effort, cannot be real either, and the supreme purpose of the moral life will be a self-baffling purpose. That "intrinsic goods", as they have been called, are an ultimate and irreducible plurality is just now something of a popular thesis with moralists, and there is great excuse for it as a salutary reaction against the view that all good is of some one kind.[1] But if the plurality is really ultimate, it should be an inevitable corollary that genuine moral personality is unattainable. Our growth, as we enrich our lives with more and more that is good, should be in the direction of multiplication and dissociation of the self. Such a view seems flatly at variance with the known facts of the moral life which fully bear out the familiar Socratic-Platonic contention that it is *bad* for character to exhibit the dexterity of the "quick-change *artiste*". It is only under the influence of the "pathetic fallacy" that we allow ourselves to think of the world as a stage "where every man must play a part"; to treat it as a stage where the best man is the man who has the widest repertory of different parts would be to invite practical shipwreck. In the world of life, to be "everything by turns and nothing long" is to be at the bottom, not at the top, of the ladder.

I conceive, in fact, that this doctrine of an ultimate irreducible plurality of goods would never have been maintained but for the prevalence of the logical error we have already had occasion to mention, the error of ignoring the reality of "analogical unity". Since it is clear that we can say of such very different things as bodily health, mental distinctions, self-forgetful virtue, that they are all good, it has been inferred, on one side, that the goodness we ascribe to them must be some one identical common quality, present alike in all of them, though in different degrees of "intensity", or with

---

[1] I am thinking, it will be seen, largely of the type of doctrine made popular by Prof. G. E. Moore's *Principia Ethica*.

some further specific *differentia* in each case, so that the various goods form a plurality of irreducible, and perhaps co-ordinate, species of a genus *good*. This assumption is easily shattered by criticism, and the critic is thus prone to suppose that he has shown that *good* has no unity *at all*, and must be a merely equivocal term. Both positions rest on the uncriticised assumption that predication must either be universal, as when I call both rodents and ruminants mammals, or merely equivocal, as when I call the domestic animal and the constellation both by the name "dog". In the first case, the rodents and the ruminants have in common not only a name, but a group of characters which the name indicates. Both are, for example, vertebrates, red-blooded, four-limbed. In the second, the household animal and the constellation have nothing in common but the name, and that they have even this in common is due to a mere historical accident. Now, these alternatives are not exhaustive, as we might all have learned from Aristotle, if we had not been blinded by bad nominalistic traditions to the force of his doctrine of analogical predication. Virtue and health are both called good, not because they have a core of identical "common characters", further specially determined in each case, but because virtue is *related* to one term x_1 in the same way as health to a different term x_2. Virtue is the efficient living of the social and intelligent life, just as health is the efficient discharge of physiological function. There need be no further correspondence in character between social function and physiological function to make the ascription of goodness in both cases highly significant. In fact we see that the very qualities which justify us in calling one thing good may equally provide the justification for calling a second bad, and, again, may be wholly irrelevant to the goodness or badness of a third. A good knife must be sharp, but a good poker blunt, a good mattress must be hard, a good pillow soft.

And yet the various goods of life are not simply a collection or aggregate; they form a hierarchy. What at one stage of mental and moral development seems complete satisfaction[1] of aspiration sinks, for the man who is living at a higher level, to the position of a mere pre-condition of getting satisfaction it cannot itself provide, or may become indifferent, or even a positive hindrance. At the highest attainable levels of human personal activity what we find in the moral heroes of our race is not diffusion of attention and endeavour over a vast multiplicity of radically incongruous objects of aspiration, but an intensely unified and concentrated endeavour towards a unified good. Ends not capable of finding their place in this unity have sunk to the level of mere pre-conditions, or of things which may, or perhaps must, be dispensed with, though at a lower and less human level any one of them may have been, in its time, a temporary substitute for the actual *summum bonum*. Mere dispersion is the characteristic moral condition of the amateur in living, as mere concentration on the partial is that of the fanatic. This is why I cannot but feel that, when all is said,

[1] May I take the opportunity of explaining that by using the notion of "satisfaction" I do not mean to suggest that everything which is actually desired by anyone is good, and good *because* he desires it. I know only too well that most of our desires are *vain* desires, desires for that which will *not* satisfy. When I speak of the good as the "satisfactory", I mean that it is that which contents men who are what they *ought* to be, and will content me when I am what I ought to be. (This is my reply to the old criticism of Professor G. E. Moore, who accused me (*Principia Ethica*, p. 160) of the "vulgar mistake" which he has taught us to call the "naturalistic fallacy". Unless Prof. Moore would regard it as "fallacy" to deny the unsupported allegation that there is no connection between "existence" and "value", I think I may confidently plead not guilty to the accusation, though I own I should have expressed myself more carefully if I had anticipated the misinterpretation. I am not anxious to defend a passage written thirty years ago, but the whole purpose of the argument of which Prof. Moore quotes a part was to *deny* that to enjoy and to approve are the same thing.)

the life of a man like Goethe, with its manifold but imperfectly co-ordinated and hierarchised responses to so many of the aspects of the total human environment, must be pronounced second-rate by comparison with the life of a man like Socrates. It is not only the specifically saintly man who can truly say of himself *"One* thing have I desired of the Lord".

It is clear that the implications of this tendency to unity and concentration of aim are double, according as we fix our attention on the character of the good aspired to, or on the aspiration itself. On the one hand, full achievement of the aspiration which lies behind all moral advance is only possible if there really is a good by the quest and attainment of which human endeavour will be finally unified and made single of aim. The moral quest will be self-defeating unless there is an object to sustain it which embodies in itself good complete and whole, so that in having it we are possessing that which absolutely satisfies the heart's desire and can never be taken from us. The possession must be possession of a "thing infinite and eternal", and this points to the actuality of God, the absolute and final good, as indispensably necessary if the whole moral effort of mankind is not to be doomed *ab initio* to frustration. On the other hand, if the effort is to reach its goal, the *possession* of the supreme good on our part must also be itself final; we must be able to look forward to having the infinite good, and to having it in perpetuity. But in such a fruition our own being would have been lifted above the level of successiveness; we should ourselves have passed from temporality to eternity, and the life we know as characteristic of morality, the life of effort, struggle, defeat and renewed endeavour, would have been transfigured into one of rest and enjoyment.

Thus morality itself seems to imply, as a condition of being something more than a mere crying for the moon, an eternal destiny for the human person, and so far as life becomes an endeavour to adjust the self to such a destiny, it would be ceasing to be merely ethical and taking on a specifically religious character. It would become our moral duty, and our highest moral duty, to aim at being something more than merely good neighbours and loyal citizens of the State.

This statement must, of course, not be misinterpreted. To say that a life which aims at nothing *more* than being a good moral life is itself morally defective is not to say that we can be content with less than this. I suppose there is no moralist of the first order who has not preached the supreme duty of cultivating a right detachment from the best and dearest of temporal goods. Even family affections, the "dear love of comrades", or selfless devotion to the cause of our class or our country, become snares, if we elevate family, friends, class, or country into goods to which all and every consideration must be sacrificed. From the point of view of religion this is to make them into "idols"; from the most strictly ethical point of view there are always things we must not do, even for the sake of wife and son, friend or country. I may lay down my life for my friend or my country; I shall not, if I am a truly virtuous man, think myself free to serve my friend by a perjury, or my country by an assassination. The mere admission that there are such limits to all temporal loyalties is a confession that no object of such loyalties is the supreme and final good. But this is not to say that these loyalties are not, in their place, imperative. There is no moral right to set a limit to loyalty to good, except on the ground

that the limit is demanded by loyalty to better good.
And thus the true detachment is not cultivated by
simply turning our backs on secular good and temporal
duties, but by service and fulfilment, always with the
condition that we make the discharge of the duty
and the enjoyment of the good instrumental to the
attainment of the non-temporal highest good of all,
that we serve and enjoy temporal good without losing
our hearts to it. Half this lesson is well and wisely
preached by T. H. Green, when he ends his *Introduction to Hume* [1] with the warning not to despise
Hume's doctrine because of the secular character
of the morality recommended by that philosopher,
since "there is no other genuine enthusiasm of humanity" than one which has travelled the common highway of reason—the life of the good citizen and honest
neighbour—and can never forget that it is still only
"a further stage of the same journey". The other and
equally indispensable side of the same truth is that the
moral aim of humanity always is to be something more
than a mere good citizen and honest neighbour, and
that the man who has seen no glimpses of the way
beyond is not likely even to get as far on the way as
thorough good citizenship and honest neighbourliness.
Indeed, the metaphor of the journey, as Green uses it,
is not quite adequate, for the true business of man is
not to pursue the temporal good first and the non-
temporal afterwards, but, as Green would, no doubt,
have agreed, to pursue both at once and all through
his life, to be something more than citizen and neighbour in the act of being both, and to be both all the
more efficiently that he is all the time aiming at the
something more. It is just this impossibility of really
making the right service of temporal good and the

[1] T. H. Green, *Works*, i. 371.

right detachment from it fall apart into two successive stages of a journey which, more than anything else, makes worthy moral living the hard thing it is, and, by making it hard, saves it from degenerating into a mere routine and gives it something of the character of perennial adventure.[1]

A few final words on a difficulty of fundamental principle. It may be said that life itself can only be thought of as a process of *never* completed "adjustment of organism to environment". If the adjustment were ever complete and no new readjustment ever demanded by variation of the environment, would not life cease automatically? Without the impulsion supplied by the pain or discomfort due to disturbance of adjustment, and the support of the effort towards better adjustment by attendant pleasure, what would there be to keep life, or at any rate conscious life, going? The thought is one which has been often expressed, but never better than by Hobbes in the

---

[1] I do not deny that there may be, for some persons, a vocation and a duty to renounce temporal good which it may equally be a duty for others to use. I am not denying, for example, that it may be right for some persons to give themselves to lifelong celibacy and poverty, though I am sure that such persons are a minority. What I do mean can be illustrated by a simple example. Suppose a man feels in early life a strong attraction to the life of a religious order, I should say that the attraction, however strong it is, is not of itself sufficient proof of "vocation". Before a man decides that it is his duty to follow it, he ought most earnestly to consider whether his action may not be a disguised shirking of moral obligations which no one is at liberty to disregard. If he has parents who are likely in their old age to need support and tendance which there is no one but himself to supply, he cannot ask himself too seriously whether *for him* the adoption of the so-called "religious life" may not be no more than the making void of the commandment to honour father and mother. This need not be so, of course; but there is always the danger of self-deception on the point. It is true that Christ calls on men "to leave father and mother", if need be, for His sake. But one needs to be quite clear that, in one's own case, the act really is done *for His sake*, not as a yielding to the tendency to do what demands the minimum of effort. The "conventual life", I should say, is all the more likely to be a man's real vocation if he does not find the prospect of it too attractive to "flesh and blood". Cf. the sober judgement of St. Thomas (*S.T.* ii.ᵃ ii.ᵃᵉ q. 101, art. 4 ad 4ᵗᵘᵐ) that—contrary to the opinion of certain persons—to enter a monastery, leaving one's parents without proper support, is to "tempt God", *cum habens ex humano consilio quid ageret, periculo parentes exponeret sub spe divini auxilii*).

famous words in which he denies the very possibility
of a *summum bonum*. "Nor can a man any more live,
whose Desires are at an end, than he whose Senses
and Imagination are at a stand".[1] The obvious inference would be that the "eternity" of which we have
spoken is only another name for nothing. Everything
is "becoming"; nothing is "being"; things are always
in the making, nothing is ever finally made. What have
we to say to this highly popular way of thinking?

All I need say at the present point is that the reasoning rests on a grave *petitio principii* long ago exposed by
Aristotle in the *Nicomachean Ethics*.[2] Aristotle, it may
be remembered, has there to consider the bearing of a
similar theory on the question of the worth of pleasure. It was an argument of the anti-Hedonists in the
Platonic Academy that pleasure cannot be "the good",
because pleasures arise always and only in connection
with γενέσεις, processes of *transition*. We feel pleasure,
it was said, whenever the organism is in process of recovery from a preceding disturbance of its normal vital
equilibrium; when the equilibrium has been re-estab-
lished, the pleasure drops. We feel it, then, not when we
are, physically, "at our best", but only while we are
getting back towards our "best" from a condition in
which we are "not ourselves". This thesis was then
generalised into the statement that what we enjoy is
never *fruition*, but always *movement* towards a still
unreached fruition. When good is actually attained, full
enjoyment ceases. Though the argument was originally
meant only to prove that feelings of pleasure are not
"the good", it can obviously be used equally to support
the view that *life* itself, in any sense of the word in
which life has value and interest for us, is incompatible with full fruition, "man never is, but always to be,

[1] *Leviathan*, c. 11.   [2] *E.N.* 1158 a, 7 ff.

blest". Aristotle counters the argument, as you may recollect, by insisting on the radical difference between "becoming" (γένεσις), the process by which "adjustment to environment" is effected, and "activity" (ἐνέργεια), the exercise of a fully formed function, and actually maintains that, even in such cases as the enjoyment of appeasing felt hunger—the very cases which might seem to give the strongest support to the theory he is rejecting—the facts have been misread. Even in these cases, he urges, what directly occasions pleasure and is enjoyed is not the "recovery" from disturbance of the organic equilibrium, but the underlying discharge of function, which has not been inhibited or disturbed. He means that, for example, the "gusto" with which the hungry man relishes his meal is only indirectly dependent on previous "depletion". It is, strictly and directly, simply enjoyment of the normal vital functioning, which has persisted unimpaired all through, though masked by the superimposed special local inhibition of hunger.[1] Hence, on Aristotle's own theory, the connection between enjoyment and processes of transition to more satisfactory "adjustment" is incidental and indirect; such transitions are only attended by enjoyment because they involve the gradual removal of an inhibition. An activity, a vigorously discharged functioning, with no inhibition to be overcome, would be much more enjoyed. This is why Aristotle speaks of the life of God, a life liable to no inhibitions of function and never involving improved "adjustments", and thus including no experience of "transition", as the supreme example of enjoyment absolute and unbroken (χαίρει ἀεὶ μίαν καὶ ἁπλῆν ἡδονήν, he says, whereas our human pleasures are never pleasures unmixed[2]). As psychologists know, there is no theory of the conditions of pleasure-pain

[1] *E.N.* 1157 b, 35.   [2] *Ib.* 1154 b, 26.

which does not encounter grave difficulties,[1] but the Aristotelian type of theory, which connects pleasure, and enjoyment generally, with unimpeded functioning, or activity ($\dot{\epsilon}\nu\dot{\epsilon}\rho\gamma\epsilon\iota\alpha$ $\dot{\alpha}\nu\epsilon\mu\pi\dot{o}\delta\iota\sigma\tau o\varsigma$), seems, at any rate, to be attended with fewer difficulties than any other, and may prove to be absolutely right. (The only serious difficulty I feel about it myself is that it is hard to say what "unimpeded activity" we can suppose to account for the intense enjoyment of "sweets" which seems to be generally characteristic of palates not artificially schooled. And, for anything I, who am a layman in such matters, know, the *physiologists* may have discovered, or may yet discover, a complete answer to the question.) If the Aristotelian theory of enjoyment should be the true one, it would follow that enjoyment is not bound up with "becoming";[2] Spinoza's assertion—wholly inconsistent, by the way, with his own famous doctrine of the intellectual love wherewith God loves Himself—that we can enjoy nothing but becoming, "*transition* to greater activity", will become simply false.[3] The transcendence of the form of successiveness involved in fruition of the good simple and eternal will be also entrance upon the one experience which would be, through and through, "pure delight". "They do rest from their *labours* and their *works* follow them" will be neither more nor less than the literal truth.

---

[1] See the discussion in Stout, *Analytic Psychology*, ii. pp. 268 ff.

[2] Cf. Stout, *Manual of Psychology*[4], p. 118.

[3] *Ethica*, iii. *ad fin.* Affectuum definitiones, 3. Si enim homo cum perfectione ad quam transit nasceretur, eiusdem absque laetitiae affectu compos esset. (Cf. iii. 11 *schol.* per laetitiam . . . intelligam passionem qua mens ad maiorem perfectionem transit.) It might be urged that the definition is expressly given as that of *laetitia* as a *passio*, and should not therefore be extended to cover the "active" *laetitia* of iii. 58 and later propositions. But it should be observed that in iii. 58 itself the *existence* of this "active" *laetitia* is inferred from iii. 53, and that the proof of iii. 53 depends immediately on the definition in question.

SUPPLEMENTARY NOTE TO III

DR. McTAGGART'S DOCTRINE OF TIME

As has been already explained the references in the preceding pages to McTaggart's views were written before the publication of the posthumous part ii. of *The Nature of Existence*; (the essay of 1908, referred to in that volume (p. 23, n. 1) as expounding McTaggart's doctrine, much in its final stage, I had no doubt read at the time of its appearance, but not subsequently). It is therefore necessary to consider how far the comments of the text are affected by the full publication of McTaggart's view.

I admit at once that the position adopted throughout the post-humous volume is more in accord with what seem to me to be the implications of a sound religion and morality than that commonly favoured by idealists who pronounce time "unreal". For McTaggart holds strongly that, though time is itself "unreal", it is not a *mere* illusion. There is a real ordered series (the *C-series* as McTaggart calls it) of which the temporal order is a "mis-perception"; evil also is a reality. And McTaggart believes himself able to show further that the "*C*-series" has a sense corresponding to the temporal direction from past to future, and a "last term". This last term is a state of personal existence from which all evil, except the "sympathetic pain" arising from awareness of the evil which has preceded in "pre-final stages", has disappeared. (*Op. cit.* c. 65, p. 431.) Moreover, though this "final stage", when attained, is experienced as non-temporal, it inevitably appears from outside itself as something yet to be attained in the future, and as duration which has a beginning, but not an end. Hence, as against the usual versions of Spinozist and Hegelian doctrine, the Christian conceptions of the blessed hereafter are the truer; the Christian conception of Heaven is as nearly true as it is possible for any conception of the "final stage" on the part of persons who are not enjoying it to be, whereas the rival view—that the universe, in its "pre-final stages", is, and can be seen to be, perfectly good—is false, and makes ethics unmeaning. Christians, in fact, have been right all along, only that they are bad metaphysicians, and therefore cannot see why they are right. (*Op. cit.* c. 61, pp. 367-371.)

It will be seen that McTaggart thus concedes a great deal of what is contended for in the present volume. But there are important reserves which indicate that his position is by no means so "Christian" as he supposed it to be. Thus (*op. cit.* p. 432) we find the love of God specified, by the side of the pleasure of swimming, as a good which may exist in any of the "pre-final stages", but must disappear in the final; God can be loved everywhere *except* "in Heaven". (This is because, according to McTaggart, belief in the existence of God is an error, just as belief in the existence of water is an error. In the "final stage" there are no errors left. Consequently, in that stage, no one believes in the existence either of God or of water, and therefore no one can enjoy either swimming or loving God.) Since Christianity is not the only considerable religion which makes the *essentia* of the joy of Heaven to consist in the vision and love of God, McTaggart clearly overrates the support religion can give to his conceptions.

Now I think it not difficult to see that the divergence between McTaggart's anticipations for mankind and those of the greater ethical religions is determined in advance by his general attitude towards Time. On McTaggart's view, successiveness is itself an illusion, though an inevitable one. The illusion arises from "misperceiving" as successiveness what is really a logical relation of inclusion between the consequent terms of the "*C*-series" and their antecedents. (See *op. cit.* c. 60.) It follows that each of us is really an "eternal" being, in his own right, though it is only in the "final stage" that he becomes fully aware of his own eternity. There is no difference in reality, in this respect, between any one person and any other, and therefore, in McTaggart's scheme, there can be no God, no one who is *the* "eternal" being "who only has immortality". In the great ethical religions, on the other hand, the distinction between *the* one strictly eternal being and all others is fundamental, however we express it, and consequently it is fundamental that "passage" should be a real characteristic of the "creature". Successiveness, therefore, cannot be a mere "misperception" of a logical relation; it must be something inherently real in the constitution of the "creature", like "unactualised potentiality" in the philosophy of St. Thomas. This makes it desirable to re-examine McTaggart's final statement of his reasons for pronouncing Time "unreal". We need to do this carefully, all the more because McTaggart holds (p. 4) that whereas the positive results of the volume are only highly probable, the negative conclusions are demonstrated.[1]

---

[1] I think myself that this is an exaggerated confidence. Negative conclusions based on the incompatibility of a proposition with the principle of "Determining Correspondence" explained in vol. i. do not appear to me demonstrated, since—though I cannot argue the point here—I believe it can be shown that there can be no such relation as that described by McTaggart. The reasons alleged for regarding Time as "unreal" (*op. cit.* c. 33), however, are entirely independent of the theory of "Determining Correspondence", and thus might be demonstrative, even if that theory prove false or insignificant. Proof that there is no such relation would thus be fatal to McTaggart's reasons for holding that whatever is real is a self, or a part of a self, but would not affect his proofs that there is really no time.

McTaggart begins by distinguishing carefully between the distinctions *earlier-later* and *past-present-future*. A set of terms related only as earlier-later forms what he calls a *B*-series; terms related as *past-present-future* form an *A-series*. Time, if there is Time, requires the reality of both *A*- and *B*-series, and of the two the *A*-series (past, present, future) is the more important. On these points, as will have been seen, I am in full agreement with him. From these premises McTaggart develops a *reductio ad impossibile*. If there really is a temporal series, its generating relation cannot be simply *before-after*; it must be an *A*-series. An *A*-series is inherently self-contradictory and so impossible. The proof of the minor is sought in the ancient ἀπορίαι connected with the notion of *change*. This is the general character of the argument; we must now examine it rather more in detail.

As its author presents it, the argument consists of two stages: (1) There cannot be time without an *A*-series; a *B*-series by itself would not be sufficient to constitute Time. (2) And there cannot be an *A*-series. *Ergo.*

(1) is proved as follows. There could be no Time if nothing changed.[1] But if there is no past, present or future, nothing changes. The "earlier" and "later" events of a *B*-series always have been, are, and always will be, in precisely the same unchanging relations of priority and posteriority to one another. Each term in the series "from the dawn of time", as we say, to its close (if it has a close), occupies just one and the same position in the series. Change can mean only one thing, that a certain term in the *B*-series is differently determined by the terms of the *A*-series. *E.g.* the death of Queen Anne was once in the remote future, then in the near future, then in the present, then in the near past, and it is still becoming more and more remotely past. We conclude, then, that the *B*-series alone, if it exists, must be temporal, since its generating relation, before-after, is temporal, but it is not enough to constitute time, since it does not contain the sufficient conditions of change, which are to be found in the *A*-series.[2] This establishes our first proposition.[3]

(2) The second is established by considering what the generating relation of an *A*-series would have to be. In the first place, it must be a relation to some term which itself is not a member of the series, since, "the relations of the *A*-series (past, present, future) are

---

[1] McTaggart adds that, if anything changes, everything else changes with it, since the relations of every other thing to the changing thing are in some way modified by the change. But this further contention is irrelevant to the immediate argument.

[2] *Op. cit.* p. 13.

[3] In order to state the argument succinctly, I pass over here some five pages of polemic, directed merely against Mr. Russell.

changing relations", but the relation of a term of the series itself to other terms of it is unchanging. The A-series would thus be defined by the fact that each of its terms has, to an X which is not a term of the series, one, and only one, of the three relations of being past, being present, being future. All the terms of the A-series which have to X the relation of being present fall between all those which have to X the relation of being past, and all those which have to X the relation of being future. And it seems not easy to identify any term which fulfils the conditions thus required of X. But the still more fatal difficulty, the difficulty which forbids us to assume that there may be an X with which we are unacquainted, and which plays the required part, is that the characteristics of being past, being present, being future, are incompatible, and that *every* term of an A-series would have to possess them all. All of them are successively in the future, in the present, in the past. The only exceptions would be for the first and last terms of the series, if it is held that it has such terms. And even they would need to have at once two incompatible determinations. If there ever was a first event, or first moment of time, it was once present, and is past; if there can be a last, it is future, and will some day be present. To put it crudely, the present event is distinguished from past and future events by being at the present moment, but presentness is a characteristic of *every* moment. To try to distinguish *this* moment from any other by saying that it is the *present* "present moment" lands us at once in a "vicious infinite regress". An A-series is thus intrinsically impossible, and therefore temporality is an illusion.[1]

Now with some part of this criticism, as I have said, I should myself agree. I agree with McTaggart that Time cannot be reduced to a mere relation of before and after, the mere ghost of time. If our experience could be reduced to a "knife-edge", from which the relation *before-after* were merely absent, I agree that the very word "time" would be meaningless, because we should have no acquaintance with succession, and also, I should add, an experience of before and after in which the before did not fade into the past, nor the after "emerge" into presentness, would not be what we mean by "experienced" or "lived" time. There would indeed be successiveness within the content experienced, but not within the experiencer. We should be looking on at something we could call the "history" of the world around us, but *we* should have no history of our own. And I think I should further agree that McTaggart is right in saying that the determination of the terms of his A-series can only be effected by relation to an X which is not itself a member of the series. But with this my agreement ceases.

[1] *Op. cit.* pp. 19-22.

I think it possible to say what this all-important X is; it is the living, percipient, finite subject of experience. The *now* present, or "present" present, is whatever enters as a constituent into *my* act. I do not pronounce it actual because it is determined as present, but present because it is actual. It is the distinction between "act" and "potentiality" which must be taken as fundamental, and as the source of the temporality of our human experience.

What is more, if I were all "act", without any unrealised potentiality, I might observe a succession in things around me, but the succession would fall entirely within a "present". I could then say of myself, "Before Abraham was, I am". The secret of the puzzle which McTaggart goes on to develop is precisely that I do not merely *observe* the successiveness of events; my own being is immersed in successiveness. I am a γιγνόμενον, but a γιγνόμενον conscious that the end to which I aspire is γίγνεσθαι εἰς οὐσίαν. This, as I see the matter, is just the fundamental "surd" or "irrationality" involved in the existence of beings with a real history. That it cannot be "rationalised" away, that is, cannot be analysed into a complex of "clear and distinct ideas", is not, as McTaggart seems to suppose, a proof that successiveness is an illusion. On the contrary, it is *the* proof that the historical world of individuals is not a methodical fiction but a genuine fact. The contradiction McTaggart finds in the fact that what *was* present becomes past, and what *was* future present, would exist if the X by relation to which these distinctions are made were itself something all "act", without any "potentiality", but the X is myself, and I am not *actus purus*. All that McTaggart really proves is that if I were the suprahistorical God, there would be no past or future for me, because there would be none in me.

I conceive that it may be objected that the distinction between potentiality and act cannot be the foundation of the threefold distinction, past, present, future. It might serve to distinguish present from not-present, but how is it to distinguish past from future within the not-present, since the actual becomes potential, no less than the potential actual? May we not reply that this is never a complete account of the matter? The actual which is reduced to potentiality is not reduced to the same potentiality which was there before the actuality. We say that a very old man has fallen back into a "second childhood", but the "second" childhood is not an identical recurrence of the former. It is a "potentiality" with a difference. And the growing domination of physics by the "principle of Carnot" seems to show that, on a closer view, nothing in the history of the universe ever repeats itself identically. At most there are partial imperfect repetitions which may be treated as identical recurrences, relatively to some particular human purpose.

The traces of the past are really ineffaceable, and it is fully compatible with such indeterminacy as is requisite for morality that they should be so. Saul's past neither constrains him to disobey the heavenly vision, nor forces him to obey it. But whether he disobeys or obeys, in neither case will he be the same character he would have been if he had not been a party to the death of Stephen. The act may "make him a worse man", or a better; what in any case is false, is that "it will make no difference".

I should take objection to the whole conception of Time as we are familiar with it in our experience as being an "*A*-series" of momentary events which are successively present, as I should to the conception of change as some kind of "relation" between an event M and another event N, upon which McTaggart's whole chapter is founded. Change, I should say, is not a relation between one experienced event and another; the change *is* the event, and I hold that we have a direct and "irrationalisable" experience of change itself. We do not "experience M", then "experience N", and infer that there has been a change; "M changing into N" is a formula which is the first attempt at rationalising a refractory experience which is *sui generis*. (M persisting as M is itself one form of this experience.) "Becoming" is falsified by the attempt to rationalise it into a string of tiny atoms of "being"; it is *not* "being misperceived", and therefore the attempt to find the reality of it in a purely logical relation, made by McTaggart, is wrong in principle. That becoming is not being, and yet is not an illusion, any more than being is, is, in fact, the consideration which seems to me fatal to every form of "panlogism" in philosophy, and if the rejection of panlogism is what is meant by "irrationalism", I suppose I must be content to accept the name of irrationalist.

It may be said that, by this account, it follows that each of us has his own individual "personal" Time. I should admit this, and frankly concede that a "universal" Time is an impossibility, and a "common Time" a makeshift, devised for specific necessary purposes, like a common creed, or a common party programme. The "lived" Time of each of us is a "perspective" peculiar to himself; but the point I want to insist on here is that it is a perspective of a becoming, not of a stable being. That is to say, with Whitehead, and against McTaggart, I want to make a real distinction between the super-individual fact, "passage", or "becoming", and its "measure". McTaggart's arguments are formally directed to disproving the existence of the measure; what he really needs to do, if Time is to be made a "misperception" of a series generated by a purely logical relation, is to disprove the reality of "passage" itself. And that "passage" is real each of us is a living proof to himself, since he also "passes".

IV

FURTHER SPECIFICATION OF THE GOOD
NATURE AND SUPERNATURE

More! More! is the cry of a mistaken soul; less than all cannot satisfy Man.
BLAKE.

WE have so far tried to find the inmost meaning of the
moral life of man by regarding it as an endeavour towards an eternal good made by a creature who, in so
far as he achieves the end of his endeavour, achieves
also a derivative, or communicated, eternity. The point
on which I propose now to lay stress is precisely the
communicated or derived character of the eternity thus
attainable by man. As I read the story of the "ascent"
of humanity, it is throughout a tale of the ways by
which a creature who, being a creature, starts at a level
of mere secularity or successiveness, advances towards
an "eternal state", in proportion to, and in consequence
of, the eternity of the contemplated good which all
along inspires all specifically human endeavour. In
other words, though the goal of human aspirations
would lie beyond the bounds of the historical, the advance to it is strictly *historical*, and the reality of the
advance implies the reality of *time*, the formal character
of the historical. Any metaphysical theory or theological speculation which reduces time, in the end, to
the status of an illusion must falsify our whole conception of the moral life, and, if seriously acted on, taint
our moral practice itself with insincerity and superfici-

ality. Any metaphysic and any religion for which the moral life provides inspiration must hold fast to two positions which it is difficult, but absolutely vital, to keep together in one "synoptic" view: (1) that time as we know it in our personal life—not the ghost of it we retain in our kinematics—is truly real, is, in fact, we might say, the very stuff *out of* which our life has to be made, though only the *stuff*; (2) that we only make a genuine human life out of this stuff in proportion as we transcend it, as a "more eminent" form is superinduced upon it. Temporality is there just to be overstepped.

> Man hath all that Nature hath, but *more*,
> And in that more lie all his hopes of good.

It will be seen, then, that on such a view there will be two antithetical false conceptions against both of which the natural religion and theology of a moralist will have to be in perpetual protest. One of these views is that which we may follow general usage in calling "naturalism", or "secularism", the theory which treats the form of temporality not merely as real, but as so deeply ingrained in all our experience that it is hopeless to dream of getting beyond it. From this point of view our whole conception of the moral life of man as a re-generation and re-making of the self in the likeness of a contemplated eternal good would have no meaning whatever. The only good for man would be a purely "creaturely", or temporal, or this-world good; what in his more exalted moments he takes to be his pilgrim-age to a land of promise would be only a roaming in a wilderness where he is destined to lay his bones. The generation of Israelites who fell in the desert would be the type of all the generations of men, with this difference, that there would be no Joshua nor Caleb in the host of adventurers who have gone out of the spiritual Egypt.

Of this type of view I have already said all that it seems in principle needful to say. I would only add now that its most plausible defenders seem usually to evade the surely imperative task of showing how it can be made to agree with the notorious facts of human moral inspiration. A recent eminent precursor of my own in the tenure of this lecture told us repeatedly that his own position was naturalistic "enthusiastically" and "to the core". But I observed that in the published volumes dedicated to the exposition of the position, though there was much patient and valuable discussion of the satisfactoriness of the scheme in biology and comparative psychology, the confrontation of it with the recorded moral and spiritual *history* of man was, to say nothing worse of it, perfunctory. And I note that, in the very last paragraphs of that work, the mere "ephemerality" of humanity is set over against the abidingness of God, apparently in fixed and final antithesis. "In our passing life we touch the fringe of immortality, when we acknowledge God as ultimate substance."[1] No doubt; but the question is whether nothing is permitted to me but a touching of the fringe. Can Moses not "enter into the cloud" and remain there? Is the promise *Io ti farò veder ogni valore*[2] kept to the ear and broken to the hope? Do we only touch the hem of the garment in our most favoured moments, or can we be grafted into the wine-stock and live with the life of the vine of eternity? *Sentimus experimurque nos aeternos esse*, "we perceive and know of a truth that *we* are eternal".[3] The words are those of Dr. Lloyd Morgan's favourite philosopher; are they only words with no substance? We may fairly expect the preachers

---

[1] C. Lloyd Morgan, *Life, Mind and Spirit*, p. 313.
[2] Dante, *Paradiso*, xxvi. 42.
[3] Spinoza, *Ethica*, v. 23, Scholicum.

of naturalism to know and speak their minds on the issue.

The other type of view against which the serious moralist is, as it seems to me, equally bound to register his protest, needs more special consideration, because of the attraction it has always had for just those thinkers who have been most alive to the eternity of the good to which man aspires. It is the view which, in one way or another, contrives to reduce the temporal in the moral life to the position of an illusion by treating eternity as a character which inheres in man from the first, so to say, in his own right, not derivatively. This is the conception which appears in all those philosophies and religions which treat the human soul as a "fallen" divinity whose task is to recover its original place among the rest of the "gods". We find the religious expression of it, for example, in the well-known verses inscribed on tablets discovered in the graves of Orphic sectaries in Italy and Crete, where the soul of the deceased recites its celestial pedigree and claims, as of right, to take its place in the heavenly home to which it has found its way back,[1] and, again, in many of the gorgeous fragments of Pindar in which the same theme is elaborated. The appeal of the Pythagorean preaching of "transmigration"—in itself a mere naturalistic speculation about the kinship of man with lower animals—to souls really touched to fine moral issues, has also always been based on a further conflation of this inherently non-ethical belief with the Orphic conception of the fallen god who makes his way back to his first estate by slowly ascending the stages of the hierarchy of lives, from mollusc to man, and from humanity back again to divinity. In our own days we meet the same

---

[1] See the texts as given by O. Kern, *Orphicorum Fragmenta*, as fr. 32 (pp. 104-109).

idea among all the confusions and incoherencies of what calls itself theosophy, and, in more reasoned form, in the various metaphysical systems of those thinkers who, like Dr. McTaggart, resolve the universe into a vast collection of persons, all equally "unoriginate" and equally endowed with native eternity. Not all these various forms of belief openly and avowedly treat time as a mere illusion. But all, I venture to say, make an assumption which should lead in consistency to that position. They all abolish any real distinction of status between divinity and humanity. According to all of them, we, who suppose ourselves to be men, are really all along gods. There is no question of our becoming something which we are not "by nature"; our whole history is only the story of our coming back to a status which we had in the beginning, or even of the discovery that we have, and have always had, the status. Thus there is no real progress in the spiritual life of man; it is a mere climbing back up a ladder from the top of which we have fallen, or, perhaps, a waking from a mere dream of having fallen.[1]

One would be loth to speak hardly of any creed which has had at least the merit of fixing men's minds on the mark of a very high calling; yet I think it must be clear that all views of this kind, by making advance, at bottom, an illusion, must, if one is in earnest

---

[1] In the philosophical literature of the world this type of view finds its most perfect expression in the neo-Platonic version of the fall and descent of the soul as set forth by Plotinus. According to him, as his latest editor puts it (Plotinus, *Enneads*, iv. ed. Bréhier, p. 215), "our salvation is not to be achieved, it has been eternally achieved, since it is part of the order of things. Passion, suffering, sin, have never touched more than the lower part of the soul". Christianity, too, as traditionally presented, has its doctrine of the "fall". But then the "fall" is a *real* one which affects the soul to its centre and needs to be repaired by a *real* "work of grace". It is no service to the understanding either of Christianity or of Plotinus to obscure the point that neither sin nor grace, as conceived by Christians, has any place in a consistent neo-Platonism. In Plato himself there is no obscuring of the distinction between humanity and deity, and, perhaps for that reason, he contemplates a possibility of real "damnation" for the "wholly incurable".

with them, gravely impair the seriousness of our moral striving. The very reason why endeavour is so serious is that it is endeavour to become what we have *never* been, to rise above and out of our very selves. If we are really ourselves divine, and have been so from the first, it seems fairly obvious that we need not take the moral struggle so tremendously in earnest; we may surely trust nature to reassert herself in the long run, *expellas furca, tamen usque recurret*. Whether we run in the race with our might, like men contending for masteries, or saunter along the track, we may fairly count on reaching the goal sooner or later. At most all we can effect by taking life so hard is to get a little sooner where all of us are bound to get in the end, and it might be argued that since we are sure of reaching our destination, there is no need for hurry; we can all well afford to loiter, as we are all prone to do, among the flowery meadows on the way. Thus the doctrine of the native and original divinity of the soul, though it begins by an apparent complete break with naturalism, seems, when duly thought out, to lead to a naturalistic morality. It is perhaps significant that "theosophists" are notoriously hostile to the missionary effort to substitute practice of the Christian rule of life for rules based on puerile or lewd nature-worships, and, again, that Dr. McTaggart should once have come perilously near the suggestion that since we are all bound to reach "perfection" in the end, no matter what way we take through life, we may as well, in practice, take as our moral "criterion" pleasure, a thing we *can* miss.[1] This is as though one should say "all roads through the wilderness of the world end in the Celestial City. But the traveller is pressingly recommended to take the route by

---

[1] McTaggart, *Studies in Hegelian Cosmology*, p. 127.

rail[1] which leads through the populous and fascinating city of Vanity, and by no means to omit a long stay in its attractive neighbourhood."

If we are to be genuinely in earnest with a high ethical rule of living, it would seem to be indispensable that we should be convinced that there is something really at stake in moral effort, and that the something which may be won or lost is no less than the supreme good which makes life worth living. What we endanger by sloth must be something more than a quantity of interesting and agreeable incident; it must be the life of the soul itself. Eternal life itself must be something which conceivably may be missed, and, for that reason, the eternity to be achieved by right living must be something not inherent in humanity from the start, but something to be *won*, and therefore something communicated and derivative. Hence humanity and divinity cannot simply be equated by a theology which is to be true to the demands of ethics. The divinity accessible to man must be not *deity*, but *deiformity*, transfiguration into a character which is not ours by right of birth, but is won by an effort, and won as something communicated from another source, where it is truly underived and original. In plain language, we break with the presuppositions of the moral life equally whether we eliminate the natural or the supernatural from our conception of things. To think of the moral life adequately, we must think of it as an adventure which begins at one end with nature, and ends at the other with *supernature*. Whether, before it can reach this end, it must not itself be transformed into something which is more than mere morality, is an issue we shall have to face later on. For the present, I aim

---

[1] Cf. Hawthorne's story of the *Celestial Railroad*.

simply at making it a little clearer what I mean by the transition from nature to supernature, and removing some objections which may possibly be entertained to the very conception of a "supernatural".

I would first, however, interpose two remarks intended to call attention to the point that the objection I have taken to the types of theory I have classed together, as obliterating the distinction between divinity and humanity, is not captious or frivolous, but obvious and serious.

(1) Theories of this type seem to lead inevitably to the doctrine of successive reincarnations, in one of its numerous forms, since they are manifestly inconsistent with full acceptance of the apparent facts about the humble beginnings of our own personal existence in conception, birth and babyhood. So we find that not only the unphilosophical, but the metaphysicians themselves, when they commit themselves to a theory of this kind, regularly treat reincarnation either as an integral part of their doctrine, or as an almost certain inference from it. They constantly convert language like that of Wordsworth's great *Ode*, where our birth is called a "sleep and a forgetting"—language which the poet himself was careful to explain as imaginative symbolism [1]—into a record of supposed actual fact. That the facts are not actual cannot, we must admit, be demonstrated, but it is at least obvious that such a reading of the observed facts about growth and development, in the individual or the group, involves a reversal of what *looks* like the natural interpretation. What we seem to see, as we watch the growth of a child's mind and character, is a process in which an

---

[1] "I think it right", he says, "to protest against a conclusion, which has given pain to some good and pious persons, that I meant to inculcate such a belief. It is far too shadowy a notion to be recommended to faith, as more than an element in our instincts of immortality."

originally almost indefinitely plastic "raw material" of tendencies, dispositions, aptitudes, receives steady determination into personality and character with definite structure. We *seem*, at least, to be watching the actual making of a personality. And, again, there are only too many cases in which life seems to take a wrong turning. In this we *seem* to be watching the dissolution and degradation of a promising moral personality into the merely non-moral, under the influence of passion or sloth. The moral of *Richard Feverel*, "he will never be the man he might have been", does seem to be the moral of not a few actual lives. Indeed, which of us can be sure that it may not be the moral of his own?

On any type of pre-existence theory, this impression must be wholly mistaken. There is no authentic process of growing *into* personality, since what we have mistaken for the plastic material of a personality has, in fact, been itself already fully shaped by the supposed past.[1] And the same thing will be true of the history of human social groups. Society will not really be, as it appears to be, something which has grown up, by stages still in the main traceable, from indeterminate beginnings. Behind every such apparent beginning there will lie concealed the formative work of a presumably endless past; thus everything which could be called, in the now fashionable phrase, "emergent evolution" must be a pure illusion, from the point of view of what I might name the "Orphic" theory of personality. The indifference to history often shown by philosophers who favour metaphysical speculations of this type will be the natural consequence of their conviction

---

[1] It is not without significance that Dr. McTaggart, the author of the subtlest and most sustained argument for this type of theory in our own literature, was also an adherent of through-going "determinism". See *Some Dogmas of Religion*, c. 5.

of the complete unimportance of everything temporal.[1]
But this indifference to the historical leads at once to a
breach with the attitude of practical morality. It takes
the tragic note wholly out of life.

It has often been objected to theories of pre-existence
that they outrage our natural feelings by their implication that the *innocence* which is the great charm of infancy is a mere illusion. The "innocent" infant, we are
asked to believe, has often really behind it, stamped on
its soul, though in "invisible ink", the past of a rake,
a harlot, a swindler, a murderer. Such a thought, it has
been said, is an outrage on "a mother's feelings". This
appeal to maternal feeling—I do not know why a *father's*
feelings are usually left out of the count—may look like
a piece of mere sentimentalism which should have no
weight with the serious philosopher. But it is, perhaps,
worth while to consider whether the argument may not
be a popular and rhetorical way of making a real point.
To me it seems that this is the case, and that the moralist has, at least, as vital an interest as the evolutionary biologist and the genetic psychologist in insisting
on the reality of time, development and the historical
"emergence" of the new from the old, the richer in
content from the poorer, the definitely organised from
the plastic.

---

[1] It must not be forgotten that I do not pretend that it is demonstrated by this
reasoning that time and "emergence" are not illusions. I am only urging that the
antecedent probability is very much against a theory which requires us to treat
characters apparently so universal and significant as illusory. It is reasonable only
to accept a metaphysic of this kind if we find ourselves driven to it by the most
cogent logical necessity, and this, I venture to think, is not the case. I would add
that strict logic appears to require that, with the abandonment of the admission
of actual "indeterminateness" into the structure of the historical should be
coupled the denial that there was ever a "first moment"; time must be a series in
which there is no first term. It does not seem to me clear that an actual "infinity
a parte ante" in which every stage is thus perfectly determinate is even conceivable, and on that ground I should regard the view that time is a series with a
first term as, at least, the *opinio potior*. But I cannot argue the case here. (I may,
perhaps, refer to Dr. C. D. Broad's article "Time" in *Encyclopaedia of Religion
and Ethics*.)

As I have suggested in a note to the last paragraph, if we look at the arguments for pre-existence seriously we ought to see that they are all also arguments for a series of past existences which has *no* first member. If any human personality ever begins with a genuine infancy, there is no antecedent reason why what I suppose to have been the beginning of my own history as a person, some fifty odd years ago, should not have been what it seems to have been, a genuine first beginning. If it is impossible that I should have begun then, the same impossibility must attach to any earlier first beginning, however far back you locate it in an unrecorded past. We must assume, therefore, an ultimate plurality of persons who are one and all metaphysical "absolutes" and have never really grown to be anything at all. Dante's lovely description of the new-made soul, as it comes from the hands of the Creator,

> l' anima semplicetta che sa nulla,
> salvo che, mosa da lieto fattore,
> volentier torna a ciò che la trastulla,[1]

will describe nothing, for no soul has ever been an *anima semplicetta*; personality and character have had no real growth. And similarly the point will be taken out of Blake's reflection that "every harlot was a virgin once", since there will be just the same ground for adding that the virgin was also a harlot once. Now this means that we commit ourselves once for all to the fatalistic doctrine of the eternally fixed and unalterable "metaphysical" character, the doctrine of all others most fatal to genuine moral seriousness. There will be no such thing as real moral advance in goodness to be achieved or real moral degradation to be dreaded, since, on the theory, in whatever I do I am only show-

---

[1] *Purgatorio*, xvi. 88-91.

ing myself what I always have been and always must be. Our life will be not merely a stage-play, but a puppet-show. The prayer *cor mundum crea in me, Deus*, will be senseless, and in its place we shall have nothing better than the dreary confession—

> For a new soul let who so please pray;
> We are what life made us, and shall be;
> For you the jungle, and me the sea-spray,
> And south for you, and north for me.

It is a well-known doctrine of the great schoolmen that one of the inherent limitations of divine omnipotence is that "God cannot will that God should cease to be God", just because of God's intrinsic and underived eternity. But on the "Orphic" theory we may say much the same of every one of ourselves; Judas cannot will to cease to be Judas the traitor, nor Caiaphas to become anything but Caiaphas the hypocrite. Yet, unless Judas can will to become loyal or Caiaphas to become sincere, neither is truly a *moral* person, any more than either could be a moral person if he were fettered by an astrological horoscope to his "star". No one has employed the imaginative mythology of reincarnation with more splendid effect than Plato, but we have to observe that his moral earnestness forces him to break with the central thought of Orphicism just when he appears to be asserting its positions most unreservedly. The text on which the great myth of Er the Pamphylian, at the end of the *Republic*, is based is the saying[1] that "it is a momentous issue, far greater than men think it (μέγας ὁ ἀγών, οὐχ ὅσος δοκεῖ), whether we are to become good or bad", and the momentousness of the issue is expressed in the myth itself, when its main point is made to be that the "luck" (δαίμων) of our next life is one which we shall *choose*

[1] *Republic*, 608 B.

for ourselves, the wisdom of the choice, with the consequent felicity or misery of the life, depending on the degree of singleness of mind with which we now pursue wisdom and virtue.[1] Still more completely does the moral break the bounds of the imaginative story when the aged Plato, in the *Laws*, has to vindicate the reality of the moral order against the belief in indifferent gods who leave men's conduct unregulated. We are then told simply that the "kingdom of nature" and the "kingdom of ends" are unified by the establishment throughout the universe of a single law of what we might call spiritual gravitation. Souls, like liquids, "find their level", though, unlike liquids, they find it by rising as well as by sinking. A man tends to "gravitate" to the company of his spiritual "likes". And this, of itself, ensures that, through all conceivable successions of lives and deaths each of us will always be in a "social environment" of the like-minded, and so "will do and have done to him what it is meet that such a one should do or endure".[2] The genuine reality of moral ascent and moral decline, which the pre-existence doctrine taken seriously must tend to deny, could hardly be asserted more impressively.

One might even add, if a momentary digression may be pardoned, that traditional Christianity shows its

---

[1] *Ib.* 617 E οὐχ ὑμᾶς δαίμων λήξεται, ἀλλὰ ὑμεῖς δαίμονα αἱρήσεσθε.

[2] *Laws*, 904 C: "For as each of us desires and as he is in his soul, so and such, to speak generally, he is coming to be. Thus all things that have a share in soul change, and the source of the change they have in themselves, and as they change, they are transported, in accord with the ordering and law of destiny. . . . 'This is the doom of the gods in heaven', O boy, or lad, who deemest thyself overlooked by gods, that as a man becomes worse he makes his way to the company of worse souls, as he becomes better to the better, and thus, through life and all deaths, suffers and does that which it is meet that the like-minded should suffer from their likes and do to them. . . . In this judgement thou shalt never be passed over, though thou be ever so small, and hide in the depths of earth, or exalt thyself and soar to the sky: the penalty that is due thou must pay, while thou art still here among us, or, after thy passage hence, in the house of Hades, or, it may be, by removal to some region more desolate still."

moral superiority to theosophies of the Orphic type by
precisely the very doctrine which is often made matter
of reproach against it, its teaching on Heaven and Hell.
Since these theosophies repose in the end on an unethical metaphysics, it is not surprising that they hold
out the prospect of an unending alternation of temporary "heavens" with temporary "hells"; they all envisage
the possibility that the Christ of this incarnation may
be the Caiaphas of the next, and the Caiaphas of to-day
the Christ of to-morrow. And why should this not be
so,[1] if nothing is definitively won by moral victory or
irretrievably lost by moral defeat? It seems to me that,
in its substance—I say nothing now of disfiguring accidental accretions—the Christian doctrine of a *final*
salvation and reprobation springs less from theological hardness of heart than from seriousness of moral
conviction. It is the supreme assertion of the conviction that choice is real and that everything is staked
on the quality of our choice. If happiness depends on
character and character is genuinely made by our
choices, we cannot refuse to contemplate the possibility that character, and with it happiness, may be
lost beyond the power of recovery by sufficient persistence in choosing evil or sufficient indolence in choosing
good. If we choose the worse long enough, or even
neglect to practise choice of the good, we may conceivably end by making ourselves incapable of effective
choice of the better, just as surely as by choosing good
with sufficient persistence we may come to be incapable
of choosing its contrary. One may legitimately *hope*
that, by the mercy of God, no man will ever throw him-

---

[1] It may very well be so, even on Dr. McTaggart's version of the theory. For
though he holds that we are all predestined to an ultimate Heaven of goodness
and happiness, he also holds that, in the enormously long series of lives which
precede this "ultimate stage", there may be any degree whatever of fluctuation
both in happiness and in virtue (*Nature of Existence*, ii. pp. 473-7).

self away beyond all possibility of recovery. But only
the morally indifferent would lightly deny that the thing
may be done, and that I myself, if I am careless enough,
may be the man to do it. Indeed, the more I allow
myself to imagine that personality is something made
once and for all, the more likely I shall be to draw
the inference that I am, and must be, what "life" has
made me, and so to desist from any real effort to become better than I now am.

Even if it were true that this cessation from effort
does not mean, as in the moral life it does, that one does
not remain long even at one's present level, the prospect of "staying where one is" would, I take it, be a
fairly formidable "hell" to a thinking man fully alive to
his actual moral and spiritual lack of order and comeli-
ness. It may be an element in God's blessedness that
He cannot so much as wish to be other than He is; our
worth as persons, and consequently our happiness, is
bound up with the aspiration to become what we actually are not, to be "divorced from the poor shallow thing
which now" we are. We have to put on divinity, and
the putting on is a process in which temporality, though
increasingly subordinated, is never finally left behind.
Our task as moral beings is to lead a "dying life"; to
rest on our oars would mean a "living death", a very
different thing.

(2) My second observation arises out of the first.
Just because, in the moral life, conscious pursuit of a
good definitely envisaged as supra-temporal grows out
of, or emerges from, pursuit of a good which presents
itself to the aspirant, in reflection on his aspirations,
as temporal, progress in the moral life itself depends
throughout, as has already been said, on a right combination of attachment with detachment. It is this
which, more than anything else, makes a life of real

moral success exceedingly difficult. It is not difficult
to become wholly absorbed in the pursuit of some end
definitely limited and circumscribed by temporal and
secular conditions, and thus making a clear and definite appeal to imagination; to become, for example,
simply engrossed in the work of one's profession, in
cultivating the social graces, amenities, and affections
within the limit of one's family circle, or group of
friends, or in pursuing one's chosen "hobby". It is
a comparatively easy thing to map out a definite plan
of action and to say, "My aspirations shall be carefully
restrained within these limits and directed on what
is clearly capable of being compassed by reasonable
effort, within a reasonable time and with ordinary good
fortune. I will not run the risk of frustrating modest
and rational anticipations by indulging indefinite
desires and unclear aspirations after an infinite which
remains always in the clouds. My rule shall be carefully
to measure my coat according to my cloth, to demand
of life and of myself no more than they can be reasonably expected to accomplish, to know what I am equal
to, and to seek nothing beyond it." This is, in principle,
the counsel of Epicurus, and if "safety first" were
really a practicable rule of moral living, it would be the
right counsel. It means definite self-chosen attachment
to the known, familiar and finite; such detachment as
the Epicurean rule advises, or permits, is no more than
a "counsel of prudence". An Epicurean will try to be
cool in all his attachments, because reflection on human
experience has taught him that unforseeable adverse
fortune may at any moment deprive him of all he
cares most about, and time, in the end, must take all
things away. But his rule has no place for the spirit
of adventure which freely hazards the certain for the
always uncertain hope of a better to come. It is no part

of his wisdom of life to turn his back on the "unit", which may be had for the taking, for the chance of the "million" which it is always very doubtful whether he will win or miss. The call of the desert is inaudible to him, or if, by any chance, he ever catches it, his philosophy prompts the response, *quittez les longs espoirs et les vaines pensées*. Hence the secret fascination of the Epicurean creed and its preachers in literature, Horace and the rest of them, for all of us in our too frequent unworthier moods. Its appeal to the maxims of "safety first" and the "bird in the hand" comes home to us precisely *because* it is a proposal to make the great refusal *per viltà*, and there is so much *viltà* in all of us. We are uncomfortable in the presence of a Pascal, who insists on reminding us that *il faut parier*, and that the stake we must hazard in the game of life is ourselves. But a morality of unconditional obligation—and no other morality deserves the name—depends on frank recognition of the fact that its way of life cannot be anything but a "wager", with myself for the stake, in a game where I cannot see the cards before they are played.

There is, again, a kind of detachment which I conceive it is not unduly hard to practise, when the first plunge has been taken, the detachment which leads a man out into the Thebaid. Since none of the more palpable objects to which men attach themselves, family, wealth, power, knowledge, is an absolute and all-satisfying good, it is, at least, a simple and intelligible rule that one will turn one's back on them all, and treat what is, at most, second-best as though it were not good at all. It may, indeed, require iron resolution to lead the life of a Brand, but, at any rate, the man who braces himself to such a life has gained something very real by his simplification of the practical problem.

He escapes the most agonising difficulties of all, those which come of genuine perplexity. His rule, if only he can live up to it—and habituation can do much to remove the obstacles—is simple and unambiguous. The trouble is that the moral life itself is not a simple matter, and that over-simplification, whatever form it takes, leads to failure. The supremely hard task is that of bringing the "right measure" into life, effecting just the right adjustment of attachment with detachment. It is eminently hard to cultivate the particular and finite good heartily, because it is good and so long as it is the best for me, and yet to be able to let it go, in spite of its fully appreciated goodness, neither sullenly nor recklessly, but freely and gladly, when the better has disclosed itself and its call is imperative. No simple rule can be given for this,[1] and yet it is the secret of all high moral attainment.

Let me take a simple concrete example, to illustrate my meaning from a problem which most of us have to face in everyday living. Think of some of the things which are implied in the right ordering of what we call "romantic" sexual love. The problem is not at bottom, as it is sometimes made to appear in superficial works on ethics, no more than that of keeping an elementary physical appetite within safe and decent bounds. If it were only that, it would be without its most formidable moral difficulties. When, in the dawn of adolescence, the "young man's fancy lightly turns to thoughts of love", he must be a very poor kind of young man if, from the very first, the promptings of mere animal "passion" are not so overlaid with characteristically human affection and imagination that they are, for the most part, only in the background of consciousness.

[1] "Ah, what a dusty answer gets the soul,
When hot for certainties in this our life."

Most of us, I suspect, are barely aware of them during the romance we call "love" and courtship; it is later on that we become fully awake to them. Still, of course, they are there, if only as undertones, and I should go further and say frankly that they ought to be there. The ends which they serve in any distinctively human life, even a prosaic and unimaginative one, are clearly *moral* ends, and include, at the least, the life of mutual trust and companionship in the joys and sorrows of earthly existence, the *consortium totius vitae*, and the bringing up of a new generation to be decent and useful members of the great fellowship of the living and the dead. These ends are not likely to be effectively attained where the primitive *physical* drawing of youth to maid, and maid to youth, is not adequately strong and real. That is not likely to be a wholly sound family life which has not begun with "passion", and though "passion" itself, felt for a *person*, is already physical desire in process of sublimation and translation into the super-physical, it demands the physical basis. When there is no call of the body to the body, there is no sufficient foundation for "true love". Now, the wrong, or at least inferior, kind of detachment is prompted by recognition of these facts and by the true reflection that the facts presuppose a physical condition and mental mood which, in the nature of things, cannot last. Physical charm and the ardours of physical desire belong to joyous youth and lusty prime; to any man the time must come, sooner or later, in the order of nature, when the grace and charm which stirred him have taken their place with the *neiges d'antan*, or when, even if they were less evanescent than they are, advancing years would compel him to confess of himself, "I take no pleasure in them". It is true and certain enough that

> beauty cannot keep her lustrous eyes,
> Nor young love pine at them beyond to-morrow.

Romantic passion may be the delight of a season; it cannot be of itself the business of a life. So it is easy to say, "Because this cannot satisfy beyond its season, it is clearly not the one abiding good, and a good which is not abiding is what I will have none of". But we can all see readily that the man who simply cuts romance and passion out of his life—except when he does so in strict duty at the summons of an imperative greater good, and even then he is paying a very real price for the greater good—is maiming his whole moral being. He is cutting himself loose from the whole circle of the experiences which do most to moralise the great majority of human beings, declining a high spiritual adventure. But a man may also maim his life by undue attachment. If no one will ever get all the moral wealth that may be got out of the life of family ties and responsibilities, unless he begins with the ardour and passion of the lover, it is true that no one will make the best, or anything like the best, of such a life who simply remains the youthful ardent lover all his life long. He will end by wearying himself and the object of his ardours; indeed, these ardours only minister to his moral being so long as they are spontaneous and unprompted. When the relation needs to be maintained by conscious effort, as it some day must be, if it is to last through the physical and mental changes of a lifetime, it may become a clog, instead of a support to the soul. "Some love too little, some too long."

Thus the problem life sets us is that of a steady progress in the conversion of passion ennobled by affection into affection intensified by its connection with passion, but the element of passion steadily tends to recede into the background of a mellow and golden past. It is good, in season, to have been the romantic lover, but it is only permanently good on condition that one reaches out to what is beyond, that the actual experience of ardent youth is made a stage on the way to the different experiences of a perfect middle age and later life. And the task of so living in the present while it lasts that one is helped, not hindered, in the advance to the future is so easily spoiled by the natural human reluctance to meet the new and untried that it demands unremitting vigilance and unrelaxing effort to escape the danger of moral sloth.

This is but one example of the problem which is raised by all the relations and situations of the personal moral life. To evade any of them is detrimental; to rest in any of them as final equally spoils them. All have to be used, as good in their measure, and all have to be transformed. It is because, with advancing years, we all tend to grow weary of the progressive transformation, and try to put off our harness, that middle age is attended, for all of us, with grave danger of moral stagnation. We all want to say to ourselves, "I have now come to the point when I may stand still; I want to be no better, no wiser, no more responsive to the call of moral adventure, than I am now. Henceforth let my life be a placid backwater." But to yield to the suggestion is moral death. Here is the special witness of the moral life to man's position in the universe as a creature whose being is rooted at once in time and in eternity.

This difficulty in finding the right adjustment of attachment to detachment is, of course, primarily a practical one. But, like most serious practical difficulties, it has a theoretical problem behind it. The theoretical difficulty has found clear expression in the sections of the *Prolegomena to Ethics*, in which T. H. Green dwells on the apparent "vicious circle" involved in every attempt to make definite and articulate statements about the character of the good for man, or moral ideal. The same point is illustrated equally by another great work on ethics of the same date and proceeding from the same group of thinkers, F. H. Bradley's *Ethical Studies*, where we find the relatively simple ideal of faithful discharge of the "duties of our station", on which we could fall back with confidence so long as we were concerned merely with the refutation of the deliberate pleasure-seeker, or of the fanatic for a formulated code of "categorical maxims", proving itself inadequate under more searching criticism. Green's way of stating the difficulty has, for my present purpose, the advantage of being the boldest, and so making the point hardest to overlook. All the moral progress of individual man, or of societies, has found its inspiration in a "divine discontent", a sense of a best which is beyond all the good that has so far been achieved. It is the men who will be content with nothing but the best whom we have to thank for every serious advance which man and society have actually made towards even a moderately "better". If the merely "relatively better" were enough to content us, it would not be apparent why we should take even the first steps beyond the measure of good already attained, for this is itself already a "better" by comparison with something we have left behind us. The moralist who is in earnest with life is, necessarily and on principle, an *intransigeant*; he means to aim not at the rather better, but at the absolute best. And it is the tragedy of the moral life that not only is the best never actually achieved at a

specific date and place, but that you cannot as much
as make it really clear to yourself with any detail what
the best is; you do not possess a "clear and distinct
idea" of what you would be at.

From the point of view of the devotee of the "geometrical method", the life of unremitting moral
endeavour, which we at least confess with shame we
ought to be leading, however lamentably we fall short
in our practice, is an unending aspiration after a
je ne sais quoi, just as the life of the profound thinker
or the great artist seems often, even to himself, to be
one perpetual attempt to express the ineffable, or
convey the incommunicable.[1] To the question, "But
what is it all about, and just what is it you would have?"
neither moralist artist, nor metaphysician has any
definite answer to give. In the case of the moralist,
in particular, any attempt to say precisely what it is
he wants to do, or wants his society to be, leads
straight either to the idle amusement of constructing
a "New Jerusalem", or to the serious mischief of trying
to force the "New Jerusalem" of one man's dream on
the multitude who are quite unfit to inherit it. And
we all know from experience that these Utopias of the
doctrinaires, even at their best, have the fatal defect
that the one thing they cannot guarantee is the one
thing which matters; you may describe the walls of
the city down to the smallest of the gems which glitter
in them, or its police arrangements down to the size
and material of the most insignificant button on the
coat of the humblest official, but you cannot ensure
that the inhabitants shall be "true Israelites" in whom
there is no guile. Your Eden may be cunningly and

---

[1] Plato, *Ep.* vii. 341 C ῥητὸν γὰρ οὐδαμῶς ἐστιν ὡς ἄλλα μαθήματα, ἀλλ' ἐκ
πολλῆς συνουσίας γιγνομένης περὶ τὸ πρᾶγμα αὐτὸ καὶ τοῦ συζῆν ἐξαίφνης, οἷον ἀπὸ
πυρὸς πηδήσαντος ἐξαφθὲν φῶς, ἐν τῇ ψυχῇ γενόμενον αὐτὸ ἑαυτὸ ἤδη τρέφει κτλ.

strongly fenced, but no fence will keep out the old serpent. And yet, without the inspiration of the vision, you are certain to leave the old Babylon pretty much as you found it. There is no moral institution of all we inherit of which we can honestly say that, as we know it, it is worthy to be eternised because it gives us the best. However much we may appreciate its "spirit", the spirit comes to us always encumbered with a "letter" which it has not wholly informed, and we are incapable of saying in advance how this letter is to be permanently kept from becoming a *dead* letter. Moral traditions and institutions are always in process of transformation while they are alive, *because* they are alive; the attempt to provide them with an eternalised expression beyond which imagination is forbidden to travel would be, in principle, to kill them.

This is equally true of all attempts to imagine what attained perfection, or felicity, completed humanity, would be in an individual personality, as we may learn from consideration of the different pictures of the life of Heaven on which men have tried to feed their souls. I am not referring merely to the infinite dreariness and moral emptiness of the common "spiritist" revelations of our future, with the dreadful prospect they disclose of an eternity of aimless gossip and twaddle. In this kind the best, no less than the worst, are but shadows. Must we not, if we are quite candid, say even of Dante's Paradise, that though, for a moment while we are under the immediate spell of the poetry, it may seem to leave nothing to be desired, yet, when we reflect, if we take the imagery as more than symbolic of things the poet himself cannot really envisage, the spell is broken? We are in a world where the inhabitants seem to have nothing in particular to do, and where we feel that the intrusion

of the visitor from earth must have provided the beatified spirits with a welcome relief from monotony. It
is not surprising that Green should decide that there
is no way out of his "circle". What the best, which has
all along been the inspiration of moral effort, may be,
we commonly say, at any time, most inadequately
by pointing to the little better which has so far been
attained and saying that the best is that which has
inspired the achievement, and that advance to a better
state still means progress along the same road. What
the windings and turnings of the road may be, and
what new prospects each of these may disclose, we do
not know. We can only say that no advance will be
made by simply retracing our steps.[1]

Now, one sees at once what the mere "reformer",
with his insistence on immediate and visible practical
"results", is likely to say to such a declaration. His
objection, in fact, might be fairly summarised by the
mere grumble, "Toryism", in spite of the fact that
in practice Green was a zealous late nineteenth-century
Radical. If the critic designed to be more explanatory,
he would clearly have something not wholly unplaus-
ible to say for himself. What he might say, with fair
plausibility would, I conceive, be much this: "I fully
accept your statement that moral progress is not to be
made, in my personal life or in that of society, by
simply turning one's back on the route by which the
slow but real progress of the past has been achieved.
I agree with you that the spirit of all that is good in
existing practice and actual institutions ought to be
conserved. But the problem which confronts me is to
know how much, in our inheritance, is 'spirit' and how
much is 'letter'. Is a proposed modification of my personal rule of conduct, or of the social rule of the com-

---

[1] Cf. *Prolegomena to Ethics*, pp. 183-4, 351, 404.

munity, which involves a marked and visible departure from established convention, really a surrender of the spirit of morality, or only revision of a letter which has become obsolete? To adopt your own metaphor of the journey, is one always really going back on one's track whenever one seems to be doubling? The road itself, you know, may wind, in spite of Bunyan's denial; or, again, the traveller may have missed the obscure right path some way back, and his one reasonable course now may be to make for the road again across difficult open country. Whether this is his case or not could only be certainly discovered from careful study of a good road-map, and, by your own confession, even if Bunyan possessed such a map, you do not. This being so, can you complain that your directions seem to me a little like the bad and unsafe rule of always following 'one's own nose'?" This, as I take it, is the substance of Professor Hobhouse's grievance against the whole social theory of Green's distinguished continuator, Bosanquet, and there is an apparent good sense about the complaint which finds an echo in the hearts of many of us.[1]

Yet it is no less apparent that the "ordnance survey map" of the road which mankind, or each of us, has to take through human life is certainly not to be had. It is not merely that the detailed Utopias which have been imagined by one enthusiast after another are all unsatisfactory, though I confess I have never examined one of them which did not seem at least as likely to prove a "hell on earth" as a "heaven below". The root of the difficulty lies deeper. It is vain to set yourself to picture a temporal "heaven on earth", because earth is temporal and heaven is eternal. Since the future is hidden from us, you can

---

[1] L. T. Hobhouse, *Philosophical Theory of the State*, pp. 80 ff.

never know that if you succeeded in setting up your
Utopia you might not find that you had surrendered
better for worse; you do not know the price which might
have to be paid for it. And, again, you do know at
least one thing about a temporal Utopia, that because
it is temporal, it could only be reached to be deserted
again. Once set up, it would cease to be a "better"
ahead. The attempt to depict an actual eternal felicity
is more hopeless still, because to know what it is one
would already have had to put off temporality and put
on eternity in one's self, and none of us has ever done
this. We cannot describe the goal of our pilgrimage
because we have never reached it. And yet we cannot
say, with Bunyan's Atheist, "there is no such place
on the map", and abandon the journey, because to do
so would be to cease to be serious with life, and that
we dare not do, so long as we remain moral. It is
moral aspiration which has humanised the human
animal, and we dare not believe that the humanisation
of man is an illusion, or a bad joke. The goal may be
out of sight, but a goal there must be, or

> There's nothing serious in mortality;
> All is but toys.

Green's problem of the apparent moral "circle", then,
seems to show us morality transcending itself and
passing into religion and worship in several ways,
some of which I will try to indicate briefly.

(1) As Green himself reminds us, the immediate
conscious demand of the man who is bent on bettering
himself, or his society, may be, for something quite
inconsiderable, the correction of a particular tendency
or habit in himself which prevents him from being in
some particular what he approves of being, the removal
of some little impediment to the successful prosecution

of a communal aim.[1] At our own level of moralisation,
for example, the man who takes in hand to reform his
life may be already conscious of nothing more than
that it would be better for him to get up an hour
earlier in the morning, to smoke one cigar a day less,
or to pay his small bills a little more promptly as they
come in; the man who wants to leave society "rather
better than he found it", may start with nothing more
"transcendental" than the desire to check some small
waste in the spending of the local rates, to make some
particular legal procedure a little less dilatory and
expensive, or to secure for the community some hours
more of sunlight in the year by the introduction of
"summer time". But if you are in earnest with the
spirit of "reform", though you may begin with the
conscious intention of some one such definite minor
correction, you do not stop there. The putting right
of this or that defect does not prove to be a panacea
for our human failure to make the best of life. The more
you have succeeded in setting right, the more you
find calling out for further treatment. Any earnest
sense of the necessity for putting anything to rights
can lead you, if you are logical and resist sloth, to the
remaking of life as a whole. With each limitation surmounted, you become conscious of further limitations,
still to be surmounted, of which you had never dreamed.
Thus it is those who have made most, not those who
have made least, progress in the moral conquest of
themselves and their surroundings who are most
keenly alive to human imperfection and finitude.
The slave who, with some effort, has broken one link
of his fetters is more gallingly aware of the chain that
still binds him than the slave who has never dreamed
that he may be free. Behind the whole process, and

[1] Cf. *Prolegomena to Ethics*, pp. 250-5, 265, 325-7.

giving it all its value, there is what an American might
call the "urge", towards complete emancipation, but
it is only as we steadily loosen one shackle after
another that we discover that nothing less than complete freedom would satisfy the impulse which led us
to break the first link. To become increasingly conscious of ourselves as finite and fettered is only the
other side of becoming conscious of ourselves as made
for, and destined to, freedom and self-mastery. But
complete freedom and self-mastery lie beyond the
horizon of temporality. So we end by making the
discovery that what we began by mistaking for a mere
attempt to adjust ourselves a little better to supposedly
hard-and-fast conditions of our temporal environment
is really the effort to transcend time and mortality
altogether. The *larva* might fancy that its business
on the leaf is merely to become a bigger and fatter
larva; its true aim in feeding on the leaf, if it only knew
it, is to turn into the *angelica farfalla*. You must become something more than "mere man", on pain of
otherwise becoming something less.

(2) Next—and this is a point on which it is all-
important to lay full stress—genuinely moral effort
after a "better" is always double-edged. If the effort
has "moral" quality, what moves us is never simply
dissatisfaction with our *environment*, or, in Butler's
phrase, our "condition"; there is always also dissatisfaction with *ourselves*, or, as Butler puts it, "our conduct", and the character of which that conduct is the
expression. We will not merely that the course of things
shall be different, but that we ourselves will be different.
There is nothing "divine" about a discontent which
is not also dissatisfaction with ourselves, in fact, self-
condemnation. The eastern rhymester's longing to
shatter the "frame of things" and make it anew, "nearer

to the heart's desire", has no moral quality, so long as
it does not put the heart itself at the very head of
the list of things to be shattered and remade. The making of a personality, like that of an omelette, requires
the breaking of eggs, and the first egg to be broken
is a man's own heart. Hence the superficiality of all
attempts to identify true moral progress with any mere
scheme of "social amelioration", or the moral ideal
with a well-constructed "social system". The builders
of the vulgar Utopias are all concerned only with
providing for the "heart's desire" of very imperfectly
moralised beings, the securing of felicity for men who
remain unenlightened and "unregenerate". The trouble
is that so long as one remains still the "natural man",
desiring as good only that which is good in part and
for a season, no satisfaction of such desires will yield
felicity. The merely "natural" man has only the choice,
at best, between satiety and disappointment. To
achieve felicity, one must first learn to set one's heart
on a good which can neither cloy nor be taken from
one, and no such good is discovered or desired without
a real travail of the soul. There is no genuine regeneration of society but one which is based throughout on
this transformation of personal aim and character.
Happiness, as Kant truly says,[1] would mean for each
of us that the course of the world should conform
completely to his "will and wish", but the conformity
is impossible so long as our "wills and wishes" remain
what they are, in many respects, even in the best of us,
sensual, foolish, peevish. We have to learn to care intensely for so much that, at first, had no attraction for
us, and to cease to care greatly about so much we all
begin by prizing highly.

Yet it is equally true that the activity from which

[1] *KdprV.* I. Th. ii. B. ii. *Hptstck.* (*Werke*, Hartenstein[2], V. p. 130).

all moral advance springs is directed outwards as well as inwards. The progressive transformation by which mankind are humanised and moralised is not only a transformation of the self. The Stoic who limits himself to the endeavour to "make a right use of his presentations" (ὀρθῶς χρῆσθαι ταῖς φαντασίαις), misses the mark by one-sidedness as much as the mere "social reformer" who dreams of regenerating the world without first being regenerated himself. It is not only that the outward march of events has to be subdued to human purposes by an increasing control of "nature" built on patient study of "nature's" ways, and, again, that there must be steady correction of hampering social habits and conventions, if the "course of events" is to be shaped into conformity with a sane human will. This is true enough, but it is only half the truth. The other half is that the genuinely moralised spirit is itself a *missionary* spirit. What the good man wants to have of the world, he equally wants his neighbour to have, but, beyond this, what he wants to be, he wants his neighbour to be also, and his neighbour's name is Everyman. The moral aim is not merely that society shall be rightly ordered in external matters and my own will intelligent and virtuous, but that all men's wills shall be as my own in these respects. The good man could not find the best on which his heart is set in a world where men's dealings with one another were outwardly conformable to a right rule, and his own, but his own only, further inspired by a genuine devotion to the rule for its own sake. If the best is really to be achieved, we need to add that it must be in a world where *all* men, not only "one strong man in a blatant land", in Kant's formula, reverence duty in their hearts as well as conform to it in their outward acts. It is not enough that I should myself "reverence the moral law";

if the world is to be what it must be before the good
man can pronounce it what he would have it, *all* men
must bow in a common reverence. So it becomes no less
a part of the life "from duty" to set other men forward
on the way of desiring the truly supreme good than
it is to desire it myself with all my heart. It is quite
impossible to rest in the curious Kantian compromise
which tells me to promote in myself the spirit of reverence for duty, but to be content with assisting to promote my fellow-man's "happiness". Indeed, the compromise is incompatible with Kant's own final word
on "happiness", that happiness means a state in which
the rational will is actually realised in the course of
events.[1] So long as any man's will falls short of being wholly reasonable and humanised, the course of
events which realises the rational, *i.e.* good, will cannot
realise that man's will, so that I *cannot* propose to make
another "happy" without winning his will for goodness
and rationality. Kant might have learned something
on this matter from the saying of Epicurus, "If you
would make Pythocles happy, seek not to add to his
possessions, but to moderate his desires".[2] It is a badly
maimed account of the truly good will to say only, as
Kant sometimes does, that its object is that every man
should be made happy to the degree in which he is
deserving of happiness, and as a consequence of his deserving. So much might be secured in a world where
no man had any virtue and no man was happy, or even
in one where all men were very vicious and consequently very miserable. It is secured in Dante's horrible
picture of a Hell where the torments are ingeniously
graded according to the ill-deserts of the inhabitants.
But it would surely be a very doubtful morality which
could find a universe consisting of one vast Dantesque

---

[1] *Kdpr V. loc. cit.*   [2] Epic., Fr., 135 (Usener).

Hell "very good". (In fact, if a universe so constituted could be very good, one might say, in Dante's own words, *uopo non fosse partorir Maria*.) If Kant's formula were really the last word of morality, there seems to be no reason why a final shutting up of all creatures in condemnation, because all have been dis- obedient, should not be a perfectly satisfactory con- clusion to history. It cannot be the supreme object of the good will that all of us should be "as happy as we deserve": it would be, at any rate, a less patently faulty formula to say that the good will wills that we should be made deserving of happiness and should attain the happiness we have been enabled to "merit". (I do not say that this statement is beyond criticism, but it is at least better than Kant's own.)

Even Kant's own statement seems to require that we should transcend the limitations of Kant's presenta- tion of morality. Kant himself allows that a will which could effect the subordination of the whole course of history to a moral demand that the happiness of individuals shall be a consequence of their moral worth, and proportionate to that worth, cannot be the will of any finite creature. It must be a will backed by omnipotence, or, at least, a will which is supreme over the whole temporal order and wields every part as a wholly plastic instrument for a moral end. Thus it must be a living supreme divine will into conformity with which our own wills grow in proportion as we become what we ought to be.[1] And this consideration seems to lead us at once to grave dissatisfaction with Kant's own fundamental moral principle of *Autonomy* of the Will, as he himself states it. According to his own account, the reason why it is only reasonable and proper to pay unconditional reverence to the com-

[1] *KdprV.* I. Th. ii. B. ii. *Hptstck.* (*Werke*, Hartenstein[1], V. 131).

mands of the moral will is, in the last resort, that the moral will is *my own* will, "as rational", so that in obeying it I am obeying a law which I impose on myself. I am to be wholly submissive because in submitting I become my own master. It is true that Kant guards himself, as I think some of his critics, Neo-Thomist and otherwise, sometimes forget, by an important *distinctio*. My will, according to him, is *legislative* in the moral world, but it is not *sovereign*, for the very reason that it is bound by its own commands.[1] The moral world of persons is a constitutional realm with a Parliament, and it may be—it was Kant's opinion that it not only may be, but is—a monarchy in which God is the constitutional monarch. (In any case, Kant is clear on the point that *I* am not monarch.) But this *distinctio* does not wholly remove the difficulty it is intended to meet. What the difficulty is we may see from consideration of another Kantian thesis. When Kant is anxious to establish the point that a morally good will cannot derive its goodness from the character of the *results* it produces, he rightly urges against all forms of utilitarianism, that the good man's attitude in the presence of the known moral law is one of unqualified reverence, and that such reverence cannot be felt for any *product* of our own action. We cannot, in fact, unless we are idolaters, worship our own handiwork.

This should have prompted the further question whether, without falling into the priggishness which is a peculiarly detestable kind of idolatry, anyone can worship *himself*. Now, if the good will is no more than *my* will, or, to put it more precisely in the way in which Kant puts it, if there is no more profound and ultimate reason for my reverence for it than that it is

---

[1] *Grundlegung zur Metaphysik der Sitten*, ii. (*Werke*, iv. 282).

my own will, does not absolute reverence for the good will and its law of duty degenerate into self-worship? Are we not at least on the brink here of a paradox which is inevitable in any living morality, however simple? If the commands of the good will were *merely* the commands of some external power foreign to myself, if my own will did not "go along" with them, in obeying, I should be no more than a slave. I might think obedience prudent, or expedient, but I could not obey with the joyous self-surrender of adoration. But, again, if these commands were only the commands of *my* will why should I reverence and adore? The power which sanctioned the command might surely at any time dispense with its own injunctions, on the principle *sit pro ratione voluntas*. The peculiar moral attitude seems only fully intelligible if we agree with Kant that the commands of morality are absolutely reasonable, but part company with him by immediately adding, as something more than an "open possibility", that they do not originate in a reason which is "my" nature, that they come from a supreme and absolute reason into likeness with which I have to grow, but which remains always beyond me. What "my" reason does, and does always only imperfectly, is to *recognise*, not to *create*, the obligations it is my duty to fulfil. It is just because the reason which is the source of the moral law is not originally mine, nor that of any man or all men, that I can reverence it without reservations.

This is only another way of saying what Kant, and other "rationalist" philosophers too often forget, that man himself and man's reason are always things "in the making", never things finally made and once for all there. We do not come into the world rational; we have to achieve our rationality slowly and partially, with labour and difficulty. The moral law by which our conduct is to be judged is not, from our birth, written in indelible characters on the tables of the heart. It is gradually disclosed, as we gradually grow into humanity. Its primal seat, then, cannot be in a reason which is already ours by possession, but must be in that "reason" into conformity with which we are slowly growing. Only by some such conception do we escape the intolerable dualism of Kant's account of man's nature as compounded of a rationality which is already full-grown and perfect, and an animality which never grows into anything better at all. And only so do we find a place in our schemes of morality for some of the qualities which, when we are not under the domination of preconceived theory, we all recognise as the ripest fruits of spiritual growth.

(3) A moralist may be permitted to feel a special interest in this last-mentioned point and to leave it to the metaphysician to deal more fully with the formal difficulties inherent in an exaggerated dualism of "reason" and "inclination". What, we may ask, is the right moral attitude to the old problem of Job, the problem of the apparently wanton and pointless suffering and disaster life so often brings with it? It does not require very profound moral insight to understand that the practically sane attitude is neither that of stupefaction and moral paralysis, nor that of embittered "revolt". The spectacle of an eminent novelist shaking his fist at the "president of the immortals" because his heroine has come to the gallows is not morally edifying, and is, moreover, a little comical to anyone who remembers that, after all, it is not God, but the novelist himself, who "creates" the heroine and deliberately contrives her hanging. There is more to be said for the Stoic "resignation", which

takes refuge in a grim refusal to lower one's head under the "bludgeonings of chance", when the attitude is genuine, and not—as I suspect is more often the case—mere self-conscious theatrical "pose". But I think we all know of a better way, which is followed in practice by thousands of humble souls under burdens more grievous than those which send the sentimentalists of literature to whining or cursing, according to temperament, and the literary Stoics to admiration of their own fortitude. It is possible to do better than to abstain from complaints or to cultivate pride; it is possible, and we all know of cases in which it is finely done, to make acceptance of the worst fortune has to bestow a means to the development of a sweetness, patience, and serene joyousness which are to be learned nowhere but in the school of sharp suffering.

> Count each affliction, whether light or grave,
> God's messenger sent down to thee; do thou
> With courtesy receive him; rise and bow;
> And, ere his shadow cross thy threshold, crave
> Permission first his heavenly feet to lave;
> Then lay before him all thou hast . . .
>   . . . Grief should be
> Like joy, majestic, equable, sedate;
> Confirming, cleansing, raising, making free;
> Strong to consume small troubles; to commend
> Great thoughts, grave thoughts, thoughts lasting to the end.[1]

There is the nobly ethical attitude to affliction, which does not merely safeguard moral good already won against degradation, as the Stoic resignation may do, but makes trouble itself the direct means to further enrichment. But this attitude is possible only on one condition: the affliction must be regarded as "God's messenger". One must really believe that "whom the

---

[1] Aubrey de Vere.

Lord loveth, He chasteneth". Is such an attitude possible in a life directed by the Kantian maxims? To my
own thinking it is not. The point of the situation is that
it is precisely the heavy afflictions which can be converted into the means to the greatest moral enrichment.
And the sting of these afflictions lies just in their apparent wantonness, their seeming utter unreasonableness.
If we come, in this life, to see any reasonableness in
them, we do so only because they have already borne
the fruit they can bear only on condition that they are
first gladly accepted in all their apparent unreasonableness. Unless I mean by the "reason" I worship with
unqualified reverence something more than the "reason
I have now in possession", I own I do not see that we
could admit this morally most fruitful attitude towards
afflictions into a scheme of morality which is, *ex hypothesi*, to be a life "by the sole dictate of reason", and
I note that I have found nothing in Kant's writings of
any period to suggest that he himself dreamed of any
attitude towards such visitations which goes beyond
the "Stoic" retreat of the tortoise into its shell. Yet,
if he did not, he was blind to the highest.

I should infer that here we have a concrete illustration of the way in which the moral life itself, at its best,
points to something which, because it transcends the
separation of "ought" from "is", must be called definitely religion and not morality, as the source and
inspiration of what is best in morality itself, and that
the connection between practical good living and belief
in God is much more direct and vital than Kant was
willing to allow. I cannot doubt that morality may
exist without religion. An atheist who has been taught
not to steal or lie or fornicate or the like is, probably, no
more nor less likely, in average situations, to earn his
living honestly, to speak the truth, and to live cleanly,

than a believer in God. But if the atheist is logical and
in earnest with his professed view of the world, and the
believer equally so with his, I think I know which of
the two is the more likely to make irreparable and
"unmerited" grievous calamity a means to the purification and enrichment of personality.

(4) Again, we can see that the assumed identity
between the right and the rational does not permit, as
it should if the legislative moral reason were my own,
in the sense of being an endowment which I have,
and eternally have, in possession, of an inference which
is absolutely vital to Kant's theory of the "categorical
imperative" as a sufficient moral *criterion*. The injunctions of the good will, to which we must at all costs
be loyal, cannot be digested, in advance of experience, into an articulated code of precepts sufficient to
guide the upright man's steps, no matter how slippery
the places where they have to be set. We are familiar
enough in daily life with the truth that when we try to
decide in theory what would be the dutiful course of
action in a situation which has never confronted us in
our practice, we most commonly find ourselves beset
with considerations for and against every proposed
course, considerations which we may balance endlessly
against one another without coming to a conclusion.
And yet we know that if we live in the dutiful spirit,
when the responsibility of deciding rightly is thrown
upon us, we can trust that it will bring with it the light
necessary for the decision. The voice of enlightened
conscience does not make itself audible until the duty
of deciding is laid upon us. There could probably be
no worse preparation for right action than careful an-
ticipatory study of systems of casuistry; to know with a
justified confidence that you can trust your "conscience"
does not mean that you know in advance what the de-

liverances of "conscience" will be.[1] Similarly, I should say, I may and do often feel a justified confidence that my friend will acquit himself as a man should in some situation of great "difficulty" and grave responsibility. But this need not mean, what only the muddle-headed "determinist" takes it to mean, that I know what my friend's decision will be before it has been made. In many cases, especially when my friend is a man of riper experience and higher moral wisdom than myself, his decision may take me by complete surprise.[2] He may do what I expected he would refuse to do, or may take a line different from any of those which presented themselves to me in anticipation. My confidence is not that I know what he will do, but that I know that whatever he does will be seen, *after* it has been done, by myself or by others of more penetration, to be the act of an upright and honourable man. (Just so my confidence in a man's skill in chess, or his humour in repartee, does not mean that I know by what move he will counter his opponent, before the move is made, or what he will say in reply to a challenge before he has opened his mouth.)

There is nothing new in the particular point which I am here urging. On the contrary, Kant's reliance on the "imperative" as a *criterion* has always been felt to be the very weakest point in his ethical doctrine. I should actually be inclined to say that many of his critics have fallen into the mistake of supposing that a successful attack on the value of the "imperative" as a

---

[1] Mark Rutherford, *Clara Hopgood*, c. 5: "You are asking for a decision when all the materials to make up a decision are not present. It is wrong to question ourselves in cold blood as to what we should do in a great strait; for the emergency brings the insight and the power necessary to deal with it. I often fear lest, if such-and-such a trial were to befall me, I should miserably fail. So I should, furnished as I now am, but not as I should be under stress of the trial." Yet this position clearly needs some qualification, unless we are prepared to deny that *counsel* is ever of practical use in a moral difficulty.

[2] On this point compare the moral of Browning's *Iv̀an Iv̀anovitch*.

criterion of itself disproves its very different claim to be an adequate formulation of the supreme *principle* of right action, and that much of their criticism simply misses the mark in consequence of this elementary confusion. The point I want to make is rather different. Admitting that the "imperatives" of a moral code can- not in fact be used as a practical moral criterion, I would ask whether it is still not a direct consequence of the identification of the "morally legislative reason" with a reason I, and every man, have in possession that they ought to provide such a criterion, and whether therefore the manifest fact that they do not is not in itself a refutation of the "hypothesis" which demands the making of the false inference. The further comment I would make on the familiar facts is this, and it is the comment which naturally suggests itself to anyone who remembers Aristotle's admirable discussion of the relation between "practical goodness of intellect" and what Aristotle calls "goodness of character (ἠθικὴ ἀρετή, *virtus moralis*).[1] The facts must not be taken to mean merely that unless we keep the spirit of duti- fulness alive by being daily dutiful in small matters, we are not very likely to have the strength to do our duty in the difficult situations when they arise; that he who is careless in small things is likely to be careless, or worse, in great; though this is true enough. We must add that unless we live in the spirit of duty in the "small matters" of every day, we shall not be likely even to see what the path of duty is when the great responsibilities are laid upon us and we have to react to them. It is only as we become more and more personally moralised by faithful performance of already known duties that the full demand of duty upon us is progressively disclosed. We learn what the law of the moral life is by obeying

[1] *E.N.* 1144 a, 23 ff.

it; clear knowledge does not precede performance, but follows upon it. This, not the mere complexity of the conditions under which actual choices have to be made, is the chief ground of objection to Kant's singular contention that no honest man can ever be in doubt or perplexity about the path of duty.[1] I may be honest enough at the present moment in my desire to walk in the path of duty, but the price of past carelessness is too often inability to see which path is the path of duty.

Thus, again, we are pointed to the conclusion that the "reason" which, in the last resort, prescribes the law of duty is not ours in possession; it is a reason which is only communicated to us in part and gradually, and that in proportion to our faithfulness to the revelations already received. We do not make the law, we discover it and assent to it, and it is for that reason that no attitude to the source of the law is adequate, unless it has passed from mere respect into that unqualified reverence which we know as adoration and worship. And we cannot worship what is no richer in quality than our own self; we can only worship that which is already all, and more than all, we mean when we speak of ourselves as living, intelligent, moral, and personal. For that which we worship must be capable of continuing to sustain our worship, however much farther we may progress along the road which has already led us into such personal moral life as we enjoy. Thus viewed, the "supreme good" takes on the full character of a living, spiritual, and personal God, and the life of fulfilment of duty the character of a daily appropriation of the riches of God. The discharge of duty is seen to be the road to deiformity.

(5) This, again, means that we can make no hard-and-fast distinction of principle between the life of

---

[1] Kant, *Grundlegung zur Metaphysik der Sitten*, i. (*Werke*, iv. 251).

discharge of duty and the life of specifically religious faith. Faith is not a voluntary supplement, or appendage, to dutiful living, but its very breath of life. It would be misrepresenting the facts to think of the simple discharge of duty in the occupations of every day as a walking by sight, to be set in sharp contrast with the walking by faith characteristic of religion. To have a real and living faith means simply to be ready to stake yourself on what you know you cannot demonstrate, to be ready to stand by your conviction when all the appearances are against it. Now, it is not only in what are commonly called "religious" matters that this attitude is demanded of us, though, no doubt, it is there that its presence is most obvious, since it is so plain that a religion which means anything to a man's life means conviction of the truth of a view about the whole order of things which goes far beyond all that any man could propose to demonstrate. If we do not so readily discover the presence of the same element of faith in the unseen in the simple discharge of ordinary duty, the reason is probably that we are commonly contented with too low a standard of the dutiful. We mistake for dutiful action action which is merely "according to duty", adopted for the reason that it is customary and conventional, and so "in the line of least resistance". But a morality reduced to acquiescence in the safe and customary, because it is the easier course, would be a morality from which all the life had evaporated. To perform even the simplest and most familiar act of duty in the dutiful spirit means to recognise it as the thing which is supremely worth while and would remain supremely worth while, were my whole existence at stake; of no act can it be demonstrated that it has this character of the supremely worth while. Of the heavier acceptances and surrenders of the moral life it is obviously true that in every one of them a man is risking the loss of his *anima*, and it is never demonstrable that the losing will end in a finding. The *appearances* are the other way, and that is why the acceptance, or surrender, needs a hero to make it. Even the call, for example, to what men call a "wider sphere of action" may, for all I know, or can prove, when I have to accept or decline it, be an invitation to expend my energy on a task to which I am not adequate, to the loss and deterioration of my personality. I may be taking myself where fatal trials and temptations await me, where the "contagion of the world's slow stain" will have more power upon me. The moral life, followed with a single mind, constantly calls us to put to the hazard not only health or comfort, but the soul itself. If we escape its perils, we escape in the strength of a faith which "appearances" cannot daunt.

It would be a total misconception to contrast the life of ethics as lived in the clear daylight with the life of religion as one of twilight, mystery, and danger. All these are to be found in the ethical life itself. There is the twilight; for, as we have seen, it is only gradually and in part that "conscience" provides light for our path; it enables us, at the best, to see where to plant our feet for the next step, but leaves the more distant scene in darkness. There is the mystery; for, in difficult cases, even the next step has so often to be taken with uncertain misgivings and the mental qualification, "God forgive me, if I am deciding wrong". There is the danger; since it may be the very foundations of our moral life which will be imperilled by a false step. If we allow ourselves to listen to the insidious suggestion that assent is only to be given to "clear and distinct ideas", we shall, of course, have to resign ourselves to going through life without a religion; but we shall equally have to go through life without action. A worthy moral life, no less than the acceptance of a religion, is an adventure by an uncertain light, and the theses of Pragmatism contain at least this much truth, that clearer insight has to be obtained by first acting in the dim light we have, much as, in St. Anselm's formula, belief in the verities of religion precedes the understanding of them. The attitude of practical piety is here only a further continuation and completion of that which has been already adopted in the simple resolution to live dutifully. That resolution itself, formally no more than a determination to act up to the standard of the best, so far as known, works out in the end into the life which draws its continual inspiration from contact with the living God, and is in steady process of transfiguration into the likeness of the source from which its stream is fed. The rule to look "not to what I am, but to what I shall be", of itself expands into the rule of looking not to myself, but to Him from whom what I shall be must come. *Werde der du bist* is but an imperfect transcription of an older maxim, ἕπου θεῷ.

MORAL EVIL AND SIN

Si dixerimus quoniam peccatum non habemus, ipsi nos seducimus.

I am myself indifferent honest, but yet I could accuse me of such things that it were better my mother had not borne me.—SHAKESPEARE.

IT is a commonplace to say that the most outstanding defect of ordinary philosophical treatises on ethics is their usually inadequate treatment of the problem of moral evil. Most writers on the subject seem to think they have done all that is to be expected of them when they have tried to tell us what the good for man is and what virtue, or the moral law, demands of us. What they set before us is either a theory of the good, or, it may be, a *Tugendlehre* or *Pflichtlehre*, and not much more. Even when the writer formally styles his exposition a "theory of good *and* evil", it is *good* of which he has most to say; evil usually comes off with a perfunctory consideration, and sometimes, as in Dr. G. E. Moore's influential *Principia Ethica*, is barely mentioned. So much is this the case that in many generally excellent moral treatises the very word *sin* never occurs, and the notion of sinfulness, or wickedness, is represented as a distinctively theological supplementation to, if not a theological distortion of, the plain facts of the moral life. It might not be going much too far to say that, of the major philosophers who have dealt expressly and at length with the moral life of man (independently of a theological tradition), there

163

are only two, though they are two of the greatest,
Plato and Kant, whose language reveals a keen and
constant sense of human sinfulness. Certainly, one
would look in vain for such a sense in the work of most
of the best-known of these philosophers. It is not in
Aristotle, nor in Descartes, nor in Spinoza, nor in
Leibniz, nor in Hegel; least of all in the breezy and
easy-tempered David Hume.[1] It is not even prominent in such vigorous champions of an "eternal
and immutable" morality as Cudworth, Clarke and
Price. The exceeding sinfulness of man is not one of
their themes, and this is the more noteworthy that they
are divines of a Church which teaches a dogma of
"original sin", and professional preachers of a religion
of redemption. They would, no doubt, if questioned,
have given a formal assent to the proposition that
actual human nature is "fallen through sin", but it is
hard to believe that the assent would have been more
than formal. I do not think I shall be seriously misrepresenting the habitual outlook of most moralists by
saying that they take it very much as an obvious and
regrettable incident of human life that we so often
do what we ought not to do, but as nothing more than
a regrettable incident. If they do not approach the
spectacle of human wrongdoing in the spirit of such
a maxim as "Better luck next time", or even, "There's
no use in crying over spilt milk", at any rate they
tend to the view that our misdeeds are just things to

---

[1] I do not forget Schopenhauer, but I think it would be true to say that his
attention is given almost exclusively to "original" sin, to the exclusion of
"actual", and that, with him, original sin itself receives a metaphysical interpretation which evacuates the meaning. When, for example, he quotes Calderon to
the effect that

"el mayor pecado
Del hombre es haber nacido",

he forgets that Calderon was a Christian priest, to whom the words meant
something very different from a thesis in metaphysics.

be put right and avoided for the future, and that there
is something morbid in troubling ourselves greatly
over them, when once we have done our best to "make
good", by repairing the consequences of the past and
reforming our habits. Amendment, attended perhaps
with confession, virtually becomes, with them, the
whole of penitence; the contrition which makes itself
heard in the "penitential" Psalms seems almost unknown to "philosophical" ethics.

I would not suggest that this attitude to the problem
is wholly without its historical justification. The traditional Christian dogma of original sin, its consequences
and the mode of its transmission, as shaped in the West
by St. Augustine, has always seemed to me, even in
the moderated form in which it persists in the Thomist
theology, manifestly the most vulnerable part of the
whole Christian account of the relations of God and
man, and to call more imperatively than any other part
of the theological system for reconstruction in the light
of philosophy and history. It would be ludicrous, if it
were less sad, to see the Anglican communion at this
moment fiercely engaged in polemics over eucharistic
doctrines, where the differences are almost entirely
about words, but apparently unconcerned by the fact
that the language of its Baptismal office, if it means
anything, seems to assert that millions of infants are
condemned by a just judge to irretrievable exclusion
from true felicity for a fault committed, as Pascal put
it, by someone else thousands of years before their
birth.[1] And yet, if we look more closely at the matter,

---

[1] The difficulty is not so apparent in St. Thomas, since he expressly teaches
that the infant in *limbo* suffers only a *poena damni*, unattended by any
poena sensus. But this does not seem to me to remove the root of the difficulty,
which is, in fact, Augustine's division of evil into the two species of *malum
culpae* and *malum poenae*. St. Thomas himself contrives, in his discussion of
"vengeance", to bring all the "unmerited sufferings" of good men under the head
of *poena* by arguing that they are "medicinal to the soul" (*S.T.* ii.ᵃ ii.ᵃᵉ q. 109,

there is something doubly strange about the current ready acceptance of the fact of human misconduct. From the speculative point of view there is a real problem here, a problem which has been set in the clearest light by the Platonic Socrates. It surely is plain, as Socrates is always contending in the dialogues,[1] that though a man may, and often does, prefer the show or the reputation of power, or riches, or beauty, or learning to the actual possession of them, there is just one case in which no man prefers shadow to substance. No one wants the show of happiness, good, felicity; we all want the substance; we want to enjoy good, not to be believed to enjoy it; to be happy, not to seem happy. We have to reconcile this patent and undeniable fact with the other equally undeniable fact that all of us, in practice, so constantly take the shadow and let the reality go. No one in his senses can suppose that we act thus with our eyes open. There can be no real escape from Socrates' conclusion that the wrongdoer acts from "ignorance", in the sense in which Socrates used the phrase; he mistakes for the highest good something which is not the highest good, is misled by a deceptive appearance of good. I confess that all the attempted defences of the reality of "unreasonable action" impress me as mere sporting with words. If we look not to words but to facts, it is incredible to me that evil should ever be chosen just because it is recognised for what it is. If I asked any man the reason why he preferred A to B, I should think it a complete explanation to be told "because I see that A is so much better than B", even if I thought that "perception" an illusion. If I

---

art. 4 resp.), but unless we accept Augustine's forensic view of the implication of unborn manhood in the sin of the first man, this is merely playing fast and loose with the notion of *poena*. And if we did accept this Augustinian view, could we logically object to his condemnation of infants wholesale to the "fire"?

[1] Cf. *Gorgias*, 466 E 1 ff.

received the answer "because I see A to be worse than B", I should certainly refuse to take my interlocutor seriously; I should suppose that he was "playing" with my question. There is a legend that Henry II. of England on his death-bed deliberately blasphemed God in order to ensure his own damnation. "Since thou", he is made to say, "hast taken from me the thing I most delight in, Le Mans, I will deprive thee of the thing in me thou hast most delight in, my soul." If any man, neither insane nor delirious, ever has behaved in this fashion, I can only say that, in fact, if not in words, he must have pronounced the revengeful frustration of God's purpose a good worth purchasing at the cost of his own ruin. He must have thought it would be truer happiness to look up out of the flames and see the Creator disappointed than to enjoy the delights of Paradise, but forgo wreaking his spite.

Yet the explanation that the choice of evil is due to ignorance or mistake only throws the difficulty back one stage. The problem of wrong choice, with this explanation, becomes a part of the more general problem of false judgement, or error, and this problem is itself a perplexing one. The real difficulty for the epistemologist is created, as Plato suggests in the *Theaetetus* and Descartes indicates more plainly in his *Fourth Meditation*, not by true judgement, but by error. Why do we ever judge falsely about anything? Descartes tries to answer the question, as you may remember, by saying "because we allow ourselves to make assertions when the evidence for them is inconclusive". But we may ask, as Spinoza said,[1] how it comes that we do this. If we perceived the insufficiency of the evidence, we could not give assured assent to the conclusion. We cannot make ourselves believe true what we see

---

[1] Spinoza, *Ep*. lix. (*V.V.L.*), to Tschirnhaus.

to be false, or believe proved what we see not to be proved. Why then does a creature, *ex hypothesi* endowed with "understanding", the power to discern the true from the false, not habitually discern that insufficient evidence *is* insufficient? Why, in particular, does the merely relatively and temporarily good ever impose itself on us as the absolute best? We all, to be sure, know how the evolutionist answers the question. He will tell us that the answer is that our own reason and judgement are themselves in course of development, things still in the making, not things made and completed. Judgement is untrustworthy and mistaken because it is, at every moment, making itself, and the method by which it makes itself is one of trial and learning from the consequences of error. We learn to think truly or to do right by thinking falsely or acting wrongly and having to "take the consequences", thus coming to readjust our ways of thinking, or acting, to the situation our error, or misconduct, has created. In both cases the process of correction is never fully completed, but in both it can be, and is, carried steadily further and further "without limit".

Whether this solution of the speculative problem of error is as satisfactory as it is simple is a question I must not raise here. For the present it is sufficient for my purpose to ask the more restricted question whether, as applied to the special case of *moral* error, it does anything like justice to the whole of the familiar facts of life. Does it really "save the appearances"? I think it is fairly clear that it does nothing of the kind. I cannot, indeed, undertake to offer demonstration on such a point; in matters of practice, as Aristotle should long ago have taught us, strict demonstration has no place. But I think it possible to show that any ethical doctrine which minimises the seriousness of human sinfulness

is incompatible with notorious facts of a moral psychology which any of us may verify in his own personal
experience, and that these facts cannot be disposed of
by treating them as illusion bred of antecedent theological prepossession. Our moral reaction to "wickedness" appears to me to be a genuinely ethical reaction,
and yet to bear witness to the impossibility of prevent-
ing the ethical habit of mind, once thoroughly awakened,
from developing spontaneously into a habit which
must be regarded as specifically religious. It is not, so
far as I can see, theology which has contaminated ethics
with the notion of *sin*; it is morality which has brought
the notion into theology.

The "naturalistic" interpretations of moral misdoing
may take more forms than one, and we may meet some
of them in philosophies based on metaphysical speculations which the consistently naturalistic thinker would
be careful to repudiate. Moral badness may be thought
of as no more than temporary or permanent failure to
keep up to the standard of adjustment of action to
situation already reached in our society, and, in the
main, in our personal conduct; as "atavistic" regression
to the ruder practice of a more "primitive" age. The
bad man may be regarded simply as a "barbarian"
among civilised surroundings, or an "animal" among
men. This is, in fact, the form in which the naturalistic
conception of sin most readily recommends itself to
the thoroughgoing evolutionist. But the same thought
may show itself in connection with a completely non-
evolutionist metaphysic, when sin is treated as nothing
more than a breach of a reasonable law. Thus Dr.
McTaggart, who regards the universe as a vast complex of persons all underived and ultimate, stands in
his metaphysic at the opposite pole from the evolutionist. From his point of view all "evolution" *seems*

to be, but really *is* not, and all judgements that anything
has "evolved", is "evolving" or will "evolve", are,
strictly speaking, false judgements. But McTaggart's
view of moral wrongdoing, pithily condensed by himself into the statement that it is good there should be
rules of conduct, good that we should have the spirit
to break them, and good that the birch should descend
on us when we do so,[1] is frankly naturalistic. It is
against every view of this easy-going type that I would
enter a protest in the name of a sound moral psychology. The point I am anxious to enforce is that, in
more ways than one, our human expression of wrong-
doing and guilt is so singularly unlike anything we can
detect in the pre-human world that we are bound to
treat it as something strictly *sui generis* and *human*,
not generically animal. If we could really succeed in
proving the existence of the same specific experience
in any of our humbler congeners, what we should have
shown would be, not that sin can be adequately described by the categories of "naturalism", but that
some of the creatures we have supposed to be "mere
animals" are more than we have taken them to be, that
the categories of naturalism will not even do all the
work moralists like T. H. Green have been willing to
concede.

There would be nothing necessarily paradoxical in
such a conclusion. We cannot be too careful to remember what "naturalists", good and bad, are too prone
to forget, that our notion of an "animal" is a highly
artificial one, constructed by starting with specifically
human experience, and leaving out of account the
features which strike us as most intimately human.
We have got at our conception of the animal's life by
trying to construct the whole of a comparative series

[1] *Studies in Hegelian Cosmology*, p. 174.

in which we really know only the first terms.[1] It is possible enough, proceeding in this way, to leave out too much. Any limit we construct in this way may be a merely "ideal limit" never to be met in actual fact. But if we commit the mistake of assuming that the ideal limit is actual fact, we clearly must not expect subsequently to be able to show the identity of actual human experiences with imagined experiences which are not even those of a real "animal". What it is like to be a non-human animal we do not know, and at best can only conjecture. The one thing we have no right to do is to mutilate the known facts of the only life with which we are directly and intimately acquainted on the strength of our conjectures about a life we can never experience.

Presuming, then, that "animals" really are very much what a naturalistic account assumes them to be, but being careful to remember that such an account may be inadequate, we may, I think, specify five familiar characteristics which distinguish our human experience of guilt and wrongdoing from anything which — at least on the naturalistic account of the matter—is to be found in the infra-human world.

(1) In the first place, it is characteristic of the human sense of guilt that it always involves condemnation of our own selves and our own doings, and is thus radically different from any discontent with our surroundings. As Butler says,[2] when he is contrasting self-condemnation with mere discontent, the one re-

---

[1] And this procedure may always involve error. To take a trivial example, I give you the first three terms of a series as 1, 3, 9, and ask you to say what the fourth and other terms, which I have not given, are. I am almost certain to be told that the fourth term is 27, the fifth 81, and so forth. But this may be a mere mistake; the fourth term may have been 25. I may have intended the series of which the "general term" is $1 + (n-1) \cdot 2^{n-1}$, not that of which the "general term" is 3^{n-1}.

[2] *Dissertation of the Nature of Virtue* (ed. Gladstone, § 8).

gards our "conduct", the other our "condition". Butler is here thinking of a case such as that of a man who forfeits an expected inheritance through his own folly or ill-behaviour, and of dissatisfaction which expresses itself in an explicit judgement. He means that there is a vast difference between the reflective judgements of the man who finds himself disappointed by a senile freak of the testator and the man who knows he has caused himself to be disinherited for his idleness, profligacy, or ingratitude. The one pronounces himself unfortunate, the other, if he has any vestiges of a conscience, owns himself deservedly punished. I take it Butler would not have denied that the same kind of difference may be found at a less articulate stage of mental development, at which no explicit judgement is formed either on our conduct or on our condition. There may be some analogy between the total mental reaction of a young child who is disappointed of a holiday by the rain and that of one who is deprived of the holiday as a punishment for quarrelling with his brothers and sisters, but we all remember our own childhood well enough to know that the reactions are not identical. If they were, it would be unintelligible how, at a later stage, the familiar explicit distinction between unmerited "hard luck" and deserved unhappiness should ever have been developed. We should not even remark it, as we do, as a common feature of human nature, that men so regularly try to awaken our pity for their misfortunes by dwelling on the theme of their being due "to no fault of their own".

The point is so obvious that I should think it needless to dwell on it but for the fact that so eminent a philosopher as F. H. Bradley has, in one passage of his best-known work, hinted that something at least analogous to and continuous with moral self-condemnation may already be found in germ in the sulky brooding of a beast of prey which has missed its "kill".[1] In Bradley's mouth the words, I suppose, are not meant to have a naturalistic significance. His meaning is probably not that a man oppressed by the sense of personal misdoing is no more than a sulky and disappointed brute, but rather that the brute may conceivably be something more than merely disappointed and sulky. But it must not be forgotten that *if* the tiger which has missed its spring is *only* disappointed and sulky, there is a gulf which cannot be bridged between the tiger's state of mind and that of the youngest child who knows the specific "feel" of naughtiness. The suggestion which Bradley's words at least *ought* to imply is that the tiger is sulky and dissatisfied with *itself*, not merely with the general state of things, however rudimentary its self-disapproval may be. I should suppose that such a suggestion is one which will never be capable either of definite proof or of certain disproof. But if it is sound, it follows at once that a tiger is something very much more like a moral person than has ever been supposed by those who have undertaken to derive human morality from "animal" origins. The attractiveness of the derivation for a certain type of mind lies precisely in its apparent minimalisation of the "nature" it requires us to accept as given fact; its success would require us not to minimalise, but to maximalise, "nature".

(2) A more striking difference between the moral life of man and what appears to be the mental life of animals is found when we consider the human attitude to our own unsatisfactory past. Something has already been said on this by way of anticipation, but we may treat the matter at this stage a little more in detail.

---

[1] *Appearance and Reality*, p. 431 n.

Nothing is more characteristic of the human sense of guilt than its *indelibility*, its power of asserting itself with unabated poignancy in spite of all lapse of time and all changes in the self and its environment. It is only a man with the "mentality" of the animal who can reconcile himself to the comfortable view that what he has done amiss is "washed off" by punishment, or "made good" by subsequent better conduct, and so no longer any present concern of his life. From the point of view of secular society and its criminal law, it is no doubt true that the past is past, if the discipline of life has corrected a man's evil passions and habits, and the actual mischief he has done to individuals, or the community at large, has been compensated. So far we can understand the view that the criminal who has "purged" his offence and made restitution ought to be free from all reproach for his past. It is not for us to cast it in his teeth. But the point which, as it seems to me, all the moralists who treat the conduct of life as no more than a matter between the individual and "society" customarily overlook is that an offender who has been genuinely moralised by experience of the way of transgressors is never satisfied to take this view of *himself*. We may have lost the right to reproach him; he does not cease to reproach himself. He may know quite well that the "hurt" he has done to his victims has been abundantly compensated and that he has himself become a different man, and is no longer in danger of offending in the old way. But even if his past has been forgotten, or condoned by every one else, he does not himself forget or condone it. He is never secure, and does not seek to be secure, against the recurrence of the old self-condemnation in all the intensity of its bitterness. It is not likely that St. Paul's converts or fellow-apostles remembered

against him the part he had played in the death of
Stephen; from their point of view he had "made
good" many times over. But we see from his own
language that he had neither forgotten nor condoned.
Now the kind of experience which led St. Paul to
speak of himself, with the near prospect of crown-
ing his apostolate by martyrdom before him, as the
greatest of sinners, seems to me to be one which we all
can detect in ourselves, sometimes in forms fantastic
enough. There are old misdoings, often they are such
as any kindly outside observer would dismiss as mere
trivialities, not infrequently they date from childhood
itself, which can haunt and torment us all through life.
The sting of them, often enough, does not seem to
lie in any social harm or distress they have occasioned,
nor yet in the apprehension that we are now tainted by
the particular moral defect they reveal. It is sometimes
the juvenile misdeeds which were not taken seriously
to heart by anyone at the time, caused no appreciable
hurt to anyone, and were prompted by cupidities and
tempers which have long since died out with the march
of time, that can wound most in the remembrance.
This goes a long way to explain why the best men
find that penitence and self-humiliation are no mere
occasional or temporary accompaniments of their experience, but a constant and ever-present feature in
the moral life.

I know, of course, that the numerous exponents of a
morality of "healthy-mindedness" would simply dismiss all such experiences as "morbid"—a convenient
way of burking serious thought by parrot-like repetition of a disparaging epithet—or account for them
all as due to an illegitimate influence of theological
"superstition" on our ethical outlook. Against the
charge of morbidity it should be enough to reply that,

if you allow yourself to dismiss any *universal* characteristic of life as "morbid", you lose the very basis for an intelligible distinction between health and disease. If we cannot take *quod semper, quod ubique, quod ab omnibus* as the standard of health and normality, what is to be our criterion of the normal and the morbid? If all men without exception are mad, how are we to draw the distinction between the sane man and insane? Whether the sense of the indelibility of *some* moral misdoing is in fact a universal feature of human experience can, of course, only be decided in one way. Each of us must ask himself whether there are not *some* episodes in his own past about which he himself feels it.

I do not mean to say that the feeling of which we are speaking is not, like other feelings, subject to strange aberrations. The memories which give me the keenest pang when they recur need not be memories of the worst acts I have committed. I may have forgotten, or may take credit to myself for, deeds which I should recognise to be the worst of my life, if my insight into good and evil were more penetrating. But these large possibilities of aberration no more prove the sense of personal guilt a "morbid" delusion than our sense of beauty is proved illusory by the indubitable facts that it is often powerfully affected by objects which, as we discover for ourselves, when our aesthetic perception has been refined and deepened, had little real beauty, and that from the dullness of our perceptions we often let exquisite beauty go unrecognised. The facts "are beyond dispute", but an intelligent man does not infer from them that beauty is an illusion, or that sensitiveness to it is not a real and very specific character of our human experience. In the same way, when a speaker says, as I have heard a distinguished scholar say, perhaps not wholly in earnest, that he has no such sense of sin as books tell of, and can only suppose that it is something of the same kind as his own discomfort on the recollection of a humiliating "social blunder", he is really bearing witness against himself. He is testifying that he has the feeling all the time, though it may, in his case, be attached to the wrong objects, exactly as the man who is thrown into transports of delight by the second-rate in literature or music really has a sense of beauty, though an untrained and ill-regulated sense.

Further, it should be evident that the attempt, while admitting the actuality of the sense of guilt, to explain it away as a consequence of the importation of non-moral "theological" superstition into the ethical domain, is a pure fallacy of *hysteron proteron*. This point has been made so clearly and finally by Professor Gilbert Murray[1] that I make no apology for openly borrowing his example. If we examine the poetry of Homer—and the same thing will be found true of any literature which reveals much of human thought and feeling—we shall note that there are some kinds of conduct, even if they are few, which are regarded as specially unpardonable and certain to provoke the anger of the gods, the unseen guardians of the moral law. To put poison on your arrows seems to be one of these offences. The poisoned arrow appears to horrify the Homeric Achaean much as "poison gas" horrified us when it first made its appearance in the recent War. According to *Odyssey a*, Odysseus was denied by his friend when he requested a "deadly drug" for this purpose: "he gave it not, for he felt an awe of the gods who live for ever".[2] Now whence, as Murray asks,

---

[1] In his *Rise of the Greek Epic*.

[2] *Odyssey a*, 262:

ἀλλ' ὁ μὲν οὔ οἱ
δῶκεν, ἐπεί ῥα θεοὺς νεμεσίζετο αἰὲν ἐόντας.

has this conviction that the gods will not forgive the man who poisons his arrows come? Obviously not from observation of the experienced course of events. It can never have been the case that all users of poisoned arrows were remarked to come to mysterious and horrible ends, only to be accounted for as due to the anger of unseen beings. The order of thought, as Murray says, must have been that the poisoning of arrows is so hateful a practice that I should certainly take vengeance for it, were I a god; presumably, then, the real gods feel and act as I should do in their place. Therefore, I must never take this kind of advantage or have anything to do with others who take it. The crime is not believed unpardonable because it has first been believed that, as a fact, it is not pardoned. It is believed to be in fact never pardoned because it is first felt that it ought not to be pardoned.

The same thing is true about other offences which Homer treats as peculiarly unforgivable. They are all forms of what the Greeks of a later time called ὕβρις, taking full advantage of your superiority against the peculiarly helpless, orphans, beggars, strangers in the land, that is, those who have no visible human backer to do them right. (We see the same thing in the Old Testament in the special stress laid upon the duty of considerateness to orphan, widow, alien in the land.) In all these cases, it is plainly a strictly ethical sense of the enormity and indelibility of the guilt which has led to the belief, by no means directly suggested by observed facts, that it has its unseen avengers. And I would add that we cannot account for this antecedent moral conviction by any appeal to considerations of social utility. The facts in question, on the contrary, fairly *prove* that morality has its source elsewhere than in "usefulness". Poisoned arrows are eminently useful to the group which has tribal enemies to resist and can command a supply of an effective poison. It is not ill-treatment of the widow or the defenceless alien, but ill-treatment of a valuable member of the tribe that should be the great offence, if moral codes were no more than rules of social utility. Many of us, I trust, to-day agree that the last war has revealed new and unsuspected depths of turpitude in mankind, against which we must be strenuously on our guard in all time to come. But the reason for our unqualified detestation of "scientific warfare" and all its devil's paraphernalia of bombs and poisons is not regard for social utility; it is our conviction that the whole thing is a *disgrace* to human nature.

If we may fairly regard this sense of indelible guilt as a genuine feature of distinctively human life, it seems to me, as I have already hinted more briefly, to reveal the presence in man of something we never detect in the animals. Animals, it is often remarked, and sometimes with a suggestion of envy, have no sense of sin. I am not sure that the statement would be admitted without fuller qualification by all observers. There are those who profess that they can detect in their dogs, after some breach of the customary discipline of the household, signs of a shame and uneasiness which might seem analogous with what we men call consciousness of guilt. Thus I have known it maintained that a dog which has transgressed in the matter of cleanliness sometimes seems to be not merely offended by the result, or apprehensive of punishment, but actually ashamed of itself. The question of fact would be hard to settle, and must be left to the determination of experts in animal psychology, of whom I am not one. But I must repeat a remark which has been already made and is, I think, of fundamental importance. We are in grave danger of being misled if we base our conceptions of an animal's psychology on the conduct of just those animals which have been most successfully made companions of man in his daily life, our domesticated and civilised dogs. We have to allow for the real possibility that the naturalistic account of human conduct itself is wholly inadequate. If it is, then man is something more than an animal, and constant and familiar association with the life of man may consequently have, in a lesser degree, made the highly domesticated dog something more than an "animal" too. If he has some *analogon* in his life to what we know in ourselves as morality, the reason may be that by association with man, who is a moral person, he has become what he could never have become of himself. To understand the real limitations of a purely animal life we should surely, as a matter of method, start from consideration of animals which have *not* been subjected to the possibly transfiguring influence of association with man; our standard dog should be "yellow dog Dingo". If we neglect this caution we may obviously be led into a glaring *petitio principii*. You must not argue that the behaviour of the dog domesticated by man is sufficient proof that our human morality is only a development from beginnings all to be found in the infra-human animals, unless you can first establish a merely naturalistic theory of the genesis of human morality itself, and thus your argument from the behaviour of your dog presupposes the very thesis it is meant to establish.

Still, even if we neglect the, as I think, necessary caution which has just been given, we yet seem to detect a real difference between human morality and anything which the extremest believer in the *quasi*-morality of the more highly domesticated animals can

fairly claim for them. Even if it is true that an animal
admitted to human fellowship does on occasion show
signs of feeling ashamed of itself, there seems no
sufficient reason to believe that there is any memory
of the shame which can be effective after the creature
has been duly punished and restored to favour again.
When that has happened, the animal's past seems, as
has been said already in a rather different context,
to be not only dead, but fairly buried. Now we, too,
speak of our "dead" past, but, as I have already said,
it is only the "criminal" who thinks of his past as
buried and done with when he has undergone his
appointed punishment. That he can thus feel at ease
with the past, which has been "paid for", is the very
thing which most certainly proves that he has not really
become a "new man". If he had become a "new man",
he would have to say, in the language of the familiar
hymn,

> Could my zeal no respite know,
> Could my tears for ever flow,
> All for sin could not atone.

The familiar human sense of guilt thus points directly
to that complication of the eternal and the temporal
which is characteristic of moral aspiration. To be
merely temporal would be to live wholly in the present
moment, to be, in the phrase I once heard wittily used
of a certain politician, "incapable of acquiring a past".
If our life were a mere pulse or episode in the "passage
of nature", the past, once past, would be left behind,
dead and done for. That is just what it is not and what
we must not aspire to make it. The man who is truly
aspiring to a better moral life is not aiming at "forgetting the past", painful as the memory of it may be.
If that were all his purpose, drink would probably
serve his end better than moral effort. It may be neces-

sary, at certain stages of his progress, that he should
be warned not to "brood" on the details of the past,
but simple unconsciousness of it is not the condition he
wishes to attain. Forgetting may be seasonable in its
time, but what we really aim at is a state in which we
can remember and yet feel no pang in the remembrance, because we see how all the evil has "worked
for good". Dante[1] has taken the point rightly when
he makes his ex-troubadour in Paradise recall his
disordered youth, not with shame and pain, but with
thanksgiving for the grace which has transmuted a
personality with such beginnings. Because we are
creatures with a passion for eternity, our characteristic moral endeavour is not to forget or cancel the
past, but to make it, with all that is worst in it, an
actual instrument to the achieving of a stable personality that will not pass. Whether our personal moral
effort, unaided by an antecedent free movement from
the side of the eternal to meet us, can achieve this task
is another question. It may be thought that the recurrent stings of guilt, odd as are the disguises they
sometimes assume, are just consequences of our secret
consciousness that the task of complete transmutation
cannot be achieved in our own unaided strength.

(3) A further peculiarity of the genuinely ethical
attitude towards sin seems to me to be that recognition
of our guilt is regularly attended by what we may call
a *demand* for punishment. In days now gone by, it
used to be a commonplace of the average sermon that
"sin *must* be punished", "God *must* execute justice on
the wrongdoer". Utterances of this kind are out of
fashion to-day, and I should certainly not care to re-

---

[1] *Paradiso*, ix. 103:

    "Non però qui si pente, ma si ride,
      Non de la colpa, ch' a mente non torna,
      Ma del valor ch' ordinò e provide."

habilitate some of the ethical and theological tenets with which it was customary to connect them. But I own they appear to me to be prompted by a genuinely ethical feeling and to contain an important truth, though in a form readily liable to unethical perversions. They have the same value, and are open to the same misunderstandings as the old doctrine, also now much out of fashion, of the *retributive* character of punishment; a doctrine really indispensable to sound ethics. We have to remark that the notion of retribution, fundamental in this way of thinking, has nothing to do, except accidentally, with the gratification of revengeful passion; any psychological analysis based on the common confusion between retribution and revenge is a falsification of facts. Revenge is essentially a *personal* gratification to be enjoyed by a party who conceives himself to have been in some way aggrieved or damaged. It follows, therefore, that if punishment is mere vengeance, its proper measure is the material detriment, or the sentimental grievance felt by the party who has been damaged or affronted. If he feels no deep resentment, or is ready to compromise his resentment for some material or sentimental offset, there can be no reason why the revenge should be exacted. The detriment or affront is his own personal affair, with which no one but himself is deeply concerned. We have only to look at the way in which, as society becomes more and more moralised, the development of a satisfactory system of penal law depends on the withdrawal of the initiative in bringing offences to punishment from the parties immediately concerned and the lodging of it with bodies representative of the community at large, as well as on the substitution of a reasonable and "objective" for a personal and arbitrary standard of penalties, to see that throughout the whole process retribution becomes more prominent and more certain in proportion as the feature of satisfaction for the desire of personal vengeance sinks into the background. It would be a mistake to suppose that the process is no more than one of suppressing the excesses to which personal vengeance may provoke an aggrieved party, though this is one side of it.

It is true that when the initiative in the punishment of homicide is taken out of the hands of the family of the deceased it is no longer possible for the avenger of blood to gratify his passion by torturing the culprit; but it is equally true that the main motive for the change of practice has, in fact, been not so much the desire to avoid excessive severities as the desire to make it impossible for the shedder of blood to escape lightly by compounding with the relatives of his victim. If we look at the actual working of the system by which it is left to private persons who feel themselves aggrieved to bring offenders to justice, as we see it in operation in historical societies, what most seriously outrages our civilised sense of justice, I make bold to say, is not that some offenders meet with excessive and inhuman treatment, but that most offenders escape so lightly. The prevalent mischief in the arrangement by which murder, for example, goes unpunished, unless the relatives of the murdered man initiate proceedings, is that most murders are either disregarded or compounded for by what we judge a wholly inadequate "blood-price". It is even possible, with such a system, for the powerful and violent to take the view that their crimes are "well worth" the very moderate cost of patching them up. Men in general are more indolent and covetous, and less vindictive than they are supposed to be when the transition from private to public initiative in the prosecution of crimes is traced to a growing fear of undue cruelty. We may fairly doubt whether, when all is said, the penalties for serious crimes are not, on the whole, severer as well as more certain in highly moralised than in more imperfectly moralised societies.[1]

Again, it would not be true to say that the change on which we are commenting leaves the connection between revenge and punishment unaffected, and merely substitutes the larger group of the community for the private person, or the smaller group of relatives, friends or associates, as the party exacting satisfaction for revengeful feeling. This is, no doubt, a small part of the truth. As we become increasingly humanised, we do learn to see more clearly how the interests of all are bound up together, and how the wrong which immediately falls on one member of the community more indirectly inflicts some injury on the others. But this is far from being the whole of the truth. It has to be added that the punishment of an offence by the agents of a

---

[1] Thus it comes as a shock to us when we first discover that, as recently as 1685 in our own country, perjuries like those of Oates, who deliberately for gain swore away the lives of innocent men, were legally only punishable as misdemeanours. We feel that they ought to have been capital felonies. It is absurd to pretend that suffering inflicted is made just punishment by the circumstances that the suffering is either (1) salutary to the sufferer, or (2) conducive to the general social welfare, or by both. It might be highly salutary to me to learn to bear the loss of eyesight, or to be reduced to extreme poverty, but it would be no "just penalty" if I were sentenced to lose my property, or my eyes, on that ground. And if I am sentenced to penal servitude for a crime, the sentence does not cease to be just because it is foreseen that my character will deteriorate Dartmoor. It is arguable that it would be socially beneficial to deepen the sense of responsibility in ambitious politicians by hanging ministers whose conduct of affairs is proved by the event to have been infatuated; it is quite another question whether the procedure would be just punishment. Justice is no more possible in a society which refuses to recognise retribution than chastity in one where

> "man and woman,
> Their common bondage burst, may freely borrow
> From lawless love a solace for their sorrow".

It is arguable that in such a society there may be something better than either of these virtues, but not that it possesses *them*. To do Shelley justice, he never pretended to regard chastity as a virtue. Would that utilitarians had been as honest, or as clear-headed, about justice.

civilised society is, in principle, not a "revenge". We ourselves should be profoundly disturbed if homicides and forgers were not brought to justice, and we should not be disturbed merely because we thought our own chance of being murdered or cheated increased by the negligence of the authorities. Hume's moral theory is far from being the last word of ethics, but it has at least the merit of putting the "disinterested" character of moral judgements beyond dispute. But when the murderer and the forger are brought to justice, no section of a civilised society enjoys the pleasant feeling of gratified personal revenge. It is in the novels of Dickens, not in real life, that men get a thrill of personal satisfaction when Fagin is driven mad by the near prospect of the gallows, or Uriah Heep sent to solitary confinement. And I believe we should all agree to reject as immoral the view that if society felt so inclined it would be at liberty to compound with a criminal, as a man who has only his personal vindictiveness to gratify, and prefers making a profit to getting the gratification of vindictive feeling, may quite reasonably do. If this were our attitude to crime and criminals, I cannot help thinking there would be a much greater general readiness to "let the offender off" than serious men actually exhibit. We might have to reckon, on behalf of almost every criminal, with the regular defence that his crime can be argued to have been actually beneficial to the community, and that the benefit more than outweighs the indirect detriment caused by the encouragement that acquittal may give to future potential criminals. And in some cases, I believe, such a defence could be made good. It might be no more than the truth, in some cases of deliberate murder, that society had benefited much more by the removal of a bad and dangerous man than it stood to lose by the very

slight encouragement afforded to intending murderers
by an acquittal in this special case and on these special
grounds.

Yet I cannot think a sober moralist would contend
that the badness of a murdered man's character should
be a recognised ground for condoning murder.[1] The
reason given by Macaulay for condemning the illegal
punishment of so complete a scoundrel as Oates, that
illegal penalties inflicted on notorious villains are likely
to be made precedents for similar illegalities in the case
of less hardened offenders, though sound enough, does
not go to the root of the matter. The villain, villain as
he is, has his rights, and they must not be violated,
even though it were certain that the precedent would
not be abused. Morality is, indeed, society's great
weapon for self-protection, but it is something very
much more than a device for social self-protection; its
intrinsic character must not be confounded with this
obvious external effect.

What we all feel at bottom, I believe, is that the sentence of society, or of a court of law, inflicting punishment on an offender, if it is really a just sentence,
is only the repetition of one which the offender, if his
moral being remains sound at the centre, must already
have passed against himself. We recognise the justice
of a social penalty decreed upon us, when and if we
have already sat in judgement on ourselves. Similarly,
when pious men say that God "must" punish wrong-
doing, they are giving expression to a *demand* for punishment which they find in their own hearts. We may
understand the matter better in the light of our personal

---

[1] Thus society probably gains considerably when a professional blackmailer is
murdered by one of his victims. But I cannot believe that any one would seriously
desire to see it made a good legal defence against a charge of murder to prove
that the victim had lived by blackmail, even apart from the danger that such a
defence might often be pleaded in cases where it would be materially false.

feelings about our lapses from the standard of the best in things of which no society can possibly take cognisance. When, for example, we are convicted by our own conscience of disloyalty to a friend, even were it only a disloyalty of secret thought, it is intolerable to us that our friend should go on, in ignorance of the fault, treating us with the same trust as though it had never been committed. We feel that we *must* make confession of it, and that we should be poor creatures if we congratulated ourselves on the absence of evidence of the fault and the certainty that it cannot come to our friend's knowledge, so long as we keep our own counsel. If we confess the fault and our friend treats it with careless condonation, our situation is made still worse. We feel that he is treating us as beings who are not fully human and accountable, creatures from whom nothing better than treachery was to be expected, and this puts an end to all possibility of all genuine human love and friendship. If we are capable of them, they ought to be expected of us, and our lapses into treason *ought* to make a difference to our friend's attitude towards us. We may look forward to forgiveness, when we have earned it, or as freely given for the sake of some third party honoured and loved by both ourselves and the friend we have injured, but genuine forgiveness must, *of course*, involve, on the side of the forgiving party, the awareness that there has been something to forgive. We measure the moral nobility of the forgiveness by the magnitude of the fault to be forgiven. Forgiveness of injuries, prompted by love, is one thing; easy condonation, really based on contempt, a very different thing. He to whom much is forgiven, the Gospel tells us, will love much; we cannot love much because something has been lightly condoned to us. We appreciate a great forgiveness only because we credit the forgiver with a true estimate of the gravity of the act he loves us well enough to forgive.[1]

At the cost of a brief digression, I would remark here that what we have just said needs to be kept carefully in mind in estimating the ethical bearings of the Christian doctrine of the remission of sins. Two different objections are taken to the doctrine on professedly ethical grounds, and both seem to me morally superficial. On the one hand, it is urged that there is something morally offensive in the doctrine that God's justice demands any penalties for human wrongdoing, and that the remission of sins is only effected, as Christian theology teaches, at an immense price, is purchased by the death of the God-man. Justice, we are told, is unworthy of a God; a God should simply "let us all off", and it should cost him nothing to do it. On the other side, it is also said that *any* remission is unworthy of a God. For remission is "letting off", and it is always immoral that anyone should be "let off" any part of the full consequences of his acts. Both criticisms, I believe, arise from a confusion between forgiveness and condonation, and one destroys the other. Mere light condonation, such as that ascribed to God in the Persian scoffer's quatrain about the potter who is a "good fellow", or by the saying of the scientific man who informed us some years ago that God "does not concern himself with our *peccadillos*", is a wholly unethical attitude. A God who "lets us off", because He does not care what such insects do or do not do, would be a God who despised us, and with whom we could have no vivifying relations. We could not draw any real inspiration towards good from

---

[1] May this not explain why, as Macaulay says, so little gratitude was ever called forth by the "cold magnanimity" of William III. to useful but treacherous persons? The pardoned offenders felt that the pardoner despised them, and pardoned them because he despised them too completely to be moved by their treacheries. Naturally, then, they felt little or no gratitude.

whatever relations we may have with a being who thinks
so little of us that he does not care what we may do.
Indeed such a being would be morally on a lower level
than ourselves, who may not care what we do as profoundly as we ought, but at any rate do care to some
extent. A "great first cause" of so unspiritual a kind
would plainly be no fit recipient of respect, to say nothing of adoration, from beings with a moral nature.
Still less would such a being be an unseen friend and
helper of man. For the paradox of Socrates in the
Gorgias[1] is no more than the truth. The offender who is
simply "let off" remains worse in himself, and so further
from true felicity, than the offender who is "brought to
book". It is good for us, and not bad, if the power which
rules the universe takes account of what we are in our
moral being; only on that condition can we expect that
experience of life will be a discipline into moral good.

It is often said—it is not for me to judge with how
much justice—that the Moslem confuses forgiveness
with mere condonation, a "letting-off" from a penalty
which is to be had for the simple ejaculation of an
astaghfiru 'llāh without any change of heart.[2] *If* this is
true, the Moslem must mean by divine forgiveness something quite alien to the spirit of genuine Christianity.
From the moralist's point of view it is a recommenda-
tion, not a defect, of the Christian conception that it
insists on the *justice* of God, which is but another name
for the fact that God is good, and, being good, cares for
the participation of His creatures in the absolute good
which He Himself possesses. It is because Christians
think of their God as "just in all His ways" that they
can also believe that His purpose with them is to make

---

[1] *Gorgias*, 472 e.
[2] Cf. Lane, *Modern Egyptians*, ch. xiii. (pp. 285-7 of edition published by
Gardner, 1895).

them a new creation, not simply to let them loose on a new environment. He makes them happy by first enabling them to "merit" their happiness. Because He is just, His forgiveness is no mere indifference, but a genuine moral forgiveness which means so much to Himself that it can remake the very self of the recipient, as, in a lesser degree, a man's self may be cleansed and remade by receiving a fellow-man's forgiveness for a grievous wrong, though never by being "let off" as a creature from whom nothing can be expected except that he should behave after his worthless kind.

The rival criticism is equally beside the mark. Careless condonation is rightly regarded as proof of moral indifference to justice. But we do not charge a man with injustice when he has been cruelly wronged, and yet, with full knowledge of the wrong that has been done, forgives because he loves. To be "let off" our disloyalties and infidelities because our friends expect no faith or loyalty and, at heart, do not much care whether faith and loyalty are shown, would be morally enervating and ruinous to any of us; to be forgiven by a friend with a finer sense of the loyalty of true friendship than our own may be morally regenerating to all but the "wholly incurable", if indeed there are incurables. Thus the Christian paradox that God is at once the supremely just and also the great forgiver of iniquities, so far from creating an ethical difficulty, is exactly what we should expect to find in a religion which has one of its roots in the ethical conviction of the absoluteness of moral "values". To boggle at it is proof that such religion as one has has not risen far above the level of naturalism.

(4) A further very striking and characteristic feature of our actual experience of the moral life, not always made sufficiently prominent in writing about ethics,

though abundantly witnessed to by the universal language of mankind, is our recognition of the peculiarly *polluting* quality of moral guilt. The vocabulary of all languages is full of expressions which prove how spontaneously men speak of whatever most offends their conscience in the same phraseology which they use about defilement by what is loathsome to sight, touch or smell. In all languages we find grave offences against the really living moral standard spoken of as things "filthy", "dirty", "stinking". The same feeling reveals itself in the numerous ritual practices of all ages which treat various forms of moral guilt, exactly like so many physical pollutions or infections, as things to be actually washed off by ablutions, or banished by fumigation, much as we fumigate, or destroy by fire, objects suspected of reeking with noxious germs. As Dr. Edwyn Bevan says, in his most suggestive essay on *Dirt*,[1] the philosophers in general have taken far too little account of the fact that this specific emotional reaction seems characteristic of humanity in all ages and at all levels of civilisation. They tend to treat the "moral sense" too exclusively as a sense of obligation, and the mental disquiet occasioned by wrongdoing as only an uneasy consciousness of violated or neglected obligation. They seem hardly even to have tried to fathom the significance of the standing association in popular language between "sin" and "uncleanness". "The man who is sorry for having done wrong does not only feel that he has violated an obligation; he feels unclean."

As Dr. Bevan goes on to say, this notion of the "dirty", whether in the physical realm or in the moral, suggests very interesting questions for the psychologist. In the realm of the senses, the "dirty" is often that which, because it is the vehicle of infection, is also

---

[1] E. Bevan, *Hellenism and Christianity*, pp. 152 ff.

dangerous. Yet it is certain that it is by no means always the most noxious things which are regarded as peculiarly filthy or dirty.[1] As Dr. Bevan says, there is nothing particularly noxious about human saliva as such; we do not feel ourselves infected by its permanent presence in our own mouths, and we are well aware that we do not expose ourselves to any kind of infection by contact with healthy saliva expelled from the mouth of another person. Yet we should probably all think it a dirty practice to wash ourselves in water in which another, or we ourselves, had just cleansed the teeth; we do not shrink to anything like the same extent from washing ourselves in water in which we or others have cleansed the hands, though the probability that the water contains noxious matter may be much greater in this case. The point might have been made more apparent by recalling the familiar fact that though a European has no scruple about washing his face in the water in which he has just washed his hands, and usually no serious scruple about plunging his face in that in which he is bathing his whole body, a scrupulous Indian Moslem thinks it polluting to wash himself in water which has been poured into a basin, because this involves allowing the face to come in contact with that which has been "defiled" by previous contact with the *sordes* of less honourable parts. Similarly the least refined among us would be pretty certainly withheld by an almost in-

---

[1] This state of things has its spiritual counterpart also. It is not always the sins which are most destructive of our moral being which are commonly abhorred as particularly "vile". Gross sexual offences, marked pettinesses, are commonly felt as "viler" than the much more ruinous sins of spiritual pride and self-complacency. This has been remarked by von Hügel, and long before him by St. Thomas (*S.T.* ii^a ii^ae q. 117, art. 2 ad 2um "non semper in actibus humanis illud est gravius quod est turpius. Decor enim hominis est ex ratione; et ideo turpiora sunt peccata carnalia, quibus caro dominatur rationi, quamvis peccata spiritualia sint graviora, quia procedunt ex majori contemptu"). The same consideration explains why in Dante's Hell Ulysses and Bertrand de Born are placed lower down than Semiramis or Cleopatra, or Brunetto Latini. See *infra*.

vincible disgust from relieving severe thirst by drinking a liquid into which another, or even he himself, had spit; and in all societies, to spit on the skin or clothes of another is to offer him the most unpardonable, because the "dirtiest", of insults. Any ordinary Briton would rather a ruffian should strike him a severe blow than that he should spit in his face, though the first insult may be also a dangerous assault, while the second is normally harmless. And the same thing is true of moral "dirt". The "dirtiest" sins of civilised men are regularly sexual offences of various kinds, though the users of this language may be quite alive to the truth that aberrations commonly directly connected with unhappy physical constitution or condition—as these offences usually are—are far less ruinous to the moral life of the soul than the great "spiritual" sins—pride, cruelty, fraud, treachery. Cruelty is, as all moralists would admit, a more evil thing than any kind of mere perverted carnal appetite, and if we were angels, would presumably revolt us more. Yet in man, it seems clear, though calculating cruelty may awaken the severer reflective condemnation, it has to be excessive indeed before it arouses anything like the same *disgust*. What commonly revolts one in the character even of a Nero, as depicted in the Roman anti-Caesarean literary tradition, is not so much the stories of deliberate cruelty—which does not, in fact, seem to have been one of Nero's vices—as the anecdotes of a morbid and "unnatural" lust.

It would be interesting, with Dr. Bevan, to carry the attempt to analyse our repugnance to the morally "polluting" further, and to try to indicate its specific *differentia* more exactly, but that inquiry would take us too far away from our principal theme. For my own purpose I must be content to repeat one of Dr. Bevan's conclusions,[1] and to call attention to some inferences which seem to be justified. The physically "dirty" seems to be primarily *excrement* from our own bodies, and secondarily whatever we have come to associate in any way with the thought of such excrement. I would support this illuminating remark by adding that any calling, however honourable and beneficial, which brings its practitioner into regular contact with any of these *excreta* of the human body also seems to awaken in all of us a repugnance based on the feeling that the occupation is "dirty" work. Thus the physician is constantly compelled, for purposes of diagnosis, to examine specimens of the urine of his patients. We know that this work is an indispensable part of the routine of an ennobling and beneficent profession, that it involves no actual infection of the physician's person, and that there are many occupations, none of which revolt us, that bring the craftsman constantly into contact with matter much more noxious and much more directly unpleasant to our senses; but I believe we all have the secret feeling that this particular part of the physician's work is "disgusting" and "dirty". We should shrink from practising it ourselves, and it breeds a recognisable shrinking from the man who does practise it, a repugnance we only overcome by reflection and reasoning, or by a real effort to relegate our knowledge of the fact to the limbo of the unconscious.

Yet—and this is the point Dr. Bevan is specially anxious to make—the excretions which excite this violent disgust are only disgusting to us when they have been *expelled* from the organism. So long as they remain in it, they are not dirty. I do not regard my own body as dirty or disgusting, unless I am morbidly "cynical", by reason of the permanent presence

[1] *Op. cit.* p. 151.

within it of the very materials which, when once they
have been expelled, are regarded as the vilest of
"filth". There may be seen in this a striking illustration of that close association of thought exhibited by
so much of the traditional vocabulary, between the
holy and the unclean. The experience is seen in the
attitude of all human beings who have an articulate
moral tradition to that which has to do with the sexual
side of life. It is at once "holy", as the source of the
renewal and continuance of life itself, and yet is,
in some mysterious way, "polluting". To quote Dr.
Bevan, "It is the same act which in one moral context is the very type of impurity and in another context
is the sacrament of love and life. It would seem as if
some slight change in circumstances could transfer
its character straight away from one end of the moral
scale to the other. . . . Deep at the bottom of all our
sense of uncleanness, of dirt, is the feeling, primitive,
irresolvable, universal, of the sanctity of the body.
Nothing in the material world can properly be dirty,
except the body. We speak of a 'dirty road', but in an
uninhabited world moist clay would be no more dirty
than hard rock; it is the possibility of clay adhering to
a foot which makes it mire."[1]

Now the same thing is true, *mutatis mutandis*, of the
morally "dirty". At the root of our sense of moral
foulness lies a "primitive and universal" feeling about
the sanctity of the rational soul. Nothing can be
morally dirty but an *anima rationalis*. I may illustrate, perhaps, from a distaste which I detect very
readily in myself and suspect to be no personal
idiosyncrasy. There is one part of any zoological
garden which I find it almost intolerable to visit, that
devoted to the monkeys, and what makes observation

[1] *Op. cit.* p. 153.

of monkeys so repugnant to me is, more than anything else, the preoccupation of the creatures with
the functions of sex. Yet I do not know that the preoccupation is really more patent in monkeys than it
is, for example, in our domestic dogs, whose corresponding behaviour gives me no conscious uneasiness.
What makes behaviour in a monkey disgusting to me
when the same behaviour does not disgust me in the
dog? So far as I can see, only the suggestion conveyed
by the monkey's general physique, but not by the
dog's, that the creature is half-human, that it has, as
the dog has not, a human soul to be smirched.

And this reflection leads, naturally, as I think,
to another. From a strictly naturalistic point of view
all repugnance to "dirt" is no more than a "subjective" illusion. Dirt is only what it has been called
by someone, "matter in the wrong place", and there
is no "objective" distinction between one corporeal
"substance" and another in respect of cleanness or
uncleanness. Matter which is in the "wrong" place has
only to be removed to its proper place—and all matter
has its proper place—and it ceases forthwith to be
"dirt", just as the "refuse" of an industry ceases to be
refuse, and is considered a valuable "by-product",
when it becomes the "raw material" of a second
industry. If the purely naturalistic conception of man
were an adequate one, then, we might expect that as
we learn more and more, as our scientific knowledge of
nature advances, to make some employment of every
kind of body, the notion of the "dirty" would be
gradually eliminated from our thinking. In a society
where science had called into existence a plentiful
supply of industries working on "refuse", we might
expect that the right place would be progressively
found for all forms of matter; there would no longer

be any "dirt", and in the end the very word "dirt" would disappear from language. We should learn to talk not of dirt, but of highly valuable "by-products" everywhere. Yet in actual fact the progress of science does not seem to have this result, of banishing the notion of "dirt" and the emotional reaction against it from men's lives. A cultivated Indian Moslem, Dr. Bevan says, thinks it an unspeakable pollution to bring into contact with the human mouth a tooth-brush made of bristles of one unclean creature, the pig, set in a bone of a second unclean creature, the dog. But a European does not feel himself "dirty" because he cleans his teeth with a brush made of these materials.[1] Yet, though the European has learned to think clean some things which the Indian Moslem regards as polluted, he has also learned to shrink from a great deal which does not offend Moslems as dirty. He is revolted, as Sir Richard Burton remarks that Moslems in general are not, by a "dirty" nose. I should suppose that we may take it as reasonably certain that, though our more "enlightened" posterity may come to live down disgust with some things we now regard as dirty, they will equally be astonished to read of our indifference to much they will have learned to think repulsive dirt; for example, the carbon-loaded atmosphere of our industrial cities.

We see the same thing in connection with the morally "dirty". As our code of moral values becomes more conscious and more coherent, and so, as we say, is progressively "rationalised", we do not find that our sense of the "foulness" of sin is steadily giving place to an unemotional view of it as merely "unsuitable response", action in the wrong place. What actually happens is rather that our notion of the "polluting" is transferred

[1] *Op. cit.* p. 147.

to fresh types of action. It costs us some trouble to-day to put ourselves back at the point of view of a hero in Greek tragedy who regards himself as morally unspeakably polluted by a homicide which he has committed, like Heracles, in a fit of madness, or even an "incestuous" marriage, like that of Oedipus, contracted in simple and unavoidable ignorance of the facts. The *situation* of Heracles or Oedipus, of course, distresses us intensely, but we cannot really "go along with" their sense of their moral foulness. But we have also developed a new sense of honour which would feel as an uneffaceable stain deeds which the ancient world left unreprobated, or even admired. To us, with our tradition of the chivalrous, there are comparatively few heroes of Greek epic story or Old Testament narrative who do not seem to have something of the "dirty fellow" about them.[1] *Noblesse oblige* is a maxim with a significance which is steadily being extended and is very far from being exhausted by any interpretation yet put upon it. And it is not merely that the range of acts to which the principle is felt to apply is an ever widening one. As the range of applicability widens, the principle itself acquires a deeper inwardness at every fresh stage in the process. It is not the overt act alone, but the unworthy desire or thought, even the desire which is regularly repressed before it can influence action, the thought which arises only to be dismissed, that our "honour" feels as a stain.

A fine sense of honour, no less than a genuine piety, demands the "cleansing of the thoughts of the heart by the infusion of a holy spirit", a remaking of the natural self and its interests from their centre. Here we have,

---

[1] We all feel this about Achilles' treatment of Hector, and I own to something of the same feeling in myself about David slinging his stones against a Philistine who was expecting to be met honourably with lance and sword.

as it seems to me, plain proof that the identification of the moral good with mere beneficent social activities is a superficial falsification of moral experience. If the whole of our aim as persons with moral aspirations were merely to act for the promotion of "social welfare", I can see no reason why our discontent with our own character should demand the purification of the inner man with all this intensity. So long as our unworthier thoughts and contemplations lead to no consequences in overt action, I cannot see why, on such an interpretation of morality, they should not be regarded as exempt from the judgement of conscience. Why should they not be smilingly dismissed with the reflection, *neque semper arcum Tendit Apollo*? Indeed, it might actually be pleaded that some indulgence in such thoughts and fancies is a *useful* practice for the man who is to do good, as providing a harmless discharge for tendencies which, if too vigorously repressed, are likely to take their revenge in explosive action. I myself have heard grossness in the conversation of our lighter hours defended, and I believe sincerely defended, by this plea of the need for a safety-valve. The gross in action, I have been told, are commonly reticent in speech, and the reticent in speech may be presumed to be secretly gross in act.

It might, of course, be replied to this last remark that even if we mean by morality no more than the promotion of social welfare, still we need to be careful about day-dreaming because our day-dreams are likely to come true in our conduct. I cannot think this of itself an adequate basis for regulation of the internal motions of imagination and desire. I should rather suppose that, if a day-dream is fantastic enough, one may safely disregard its possible influence on action, exactly as we may and do disregard dreams of the night. If I allowed myself to enjoy an "Alnaschar's dream" of unbounded wealth and sensual luxury, or to take pleasure in imagining myself a world-conqueror, my knowledge that I have not the remotest chance of becoming a multi-millionaire or a Napoleon would be quite enough to ensure that my imagination should remain a mere game of the mind with itself and should have no appreciable influence on my conduct towards my fellow-men. And yet, as it also seems to me, any serious morality is bound to treat the enjoyment of the dreams themselves, apart from any possible "consequences", as a fault calling for vigorous correction. And the reason is not far to see. "As a man thinketh in his heart, so *is* he", for the aspiration in which all moral goodness has its source is not a mere endeavour to *do*, but an aspiration to *be*. Or, if objection is taken to that distinction, I would at least say that the aspiration is not directed on any merely outward-issuing doing.

The right discharge of social function itself seems to be most regularly and most successfully attained when it arises from concern with the purification of the inner springs of our personal being. For that reason alone, I would urge, any moral theory which makes the notion of right conduct, the fulfilment of the precepts of a law of action, rather than the notion of good, the attainment of a personality of the highest absolute worth, primary would lead, if seriously acted on, to a lowering of the standard of outward-going action itself. Even if such a morality conceives its supreme law of action with the austerity of Kant, it leaves it at least a possibility that a man might say, truthfully and sincerely, "All this have I done from my youth up; I have been indeed a *profitable* servant"; there is no sufficient place left for the recognition that humility of spirit is the most exquisite flower of the moral life.

Even the Kantian morality, hard as it would be of achievement, would, I conceive, tend to make the habitually dutiful man into something of a high-minded Pharisee. If the criticism be thought too severe, I would only remark that the "stoical" tone of Kant's practical philosophy is matter of commonplace, and that the Stoics of literature are, almost without exception, Pharisees, unless, like Seneca, they have actual grave violations of their own precepts on their conscience. To be at once truly virtuous and truly humble is something beyond them.

At this point I think it may be in place to say a word in reply to a highly fashionable current criticism of the morality of true inwardness. It is common to represent such a morality as a life of preoccupation with mere negations. We hear Christian morality depreciated for its concern with purity of heart and will, on the ground that, as is alleged, it sets up "doing no particular harm" as its ideal. It is usual to make this a point of contact with the "superior" Greek conception of virtue, or goodness, as something positive, as efficiency in doing something definite. I presume that writers who are fond of the antithesis may fairly be taken to imply a preference for the man who has visible and palpable results of his mingling in the world's business to show, no matter with what stains of vice, or even downright crime, he comes out of the bustle, as against the man who has kept his ideal of personal being high, but cannot point to any very definite positive achievements. There is, perhaps, a touch of this temper about Hegel's well-known gibe at the schoolmaster who thinks himself a greater than Alexander, because, though he has taken no cities, he can keep his temper and has never murdered a friend in a tipsy brawl.[1] There is more than

_____
[1] If it is his, I have not succeeded in verifying the reference.

a touch of it in the numerous writers who invite us to
regard a coarse-grained political adventurer of genius
like Caesar as one of the greatest in the kingdom of
ends, on the strength of the real or alleged social benefits
which have resulted from his pursuit of personal ambition, and still more in Nietzsche's fantastic glorification
of Alcibiades, who effected nothing but the ruin of the
society which allowed him to embark it on a grandiose
criminal adventure.

I would not deny that this glorification of "efficiency"
has elements of truth in it, when it appears merely as
a reaction against the confusion of virtue with abstention from definite and recognisable ways of doing social
harm. But I am sure that when it is taken as anything
more than such a protest, it is morally mischievous.
In the first place, it is a mere caricature to represent
the ideal of inward purity as meaning only abstention
from recognised wrong-doing. It is an endeavour to *be*
something very real and positive indeed, and can only
be taken to be a "negative ideal" though a double confusion. It is true that, for reasons which have already
been pretty fully given, we cannot say in detail what
the man who is aiming at becoming "as like as possible
to God" is striving to be. This is not because he is striving to become something without positive character,
but because the character he is seeking to acquire is
too *rich* in positive content to admit of exhaustion by
any formula, and because that content only discloses
itself very gradually as the aspiration succeeds. Again,
though it is true that such a life must have its negative
aspect, since it is an unending "putting off of the old
man", this correcting of the old self is not undertaken
for its own sake, but as the indispensable means to a
remaking: the "old man" is put off, not that we may
be "unclothed", but that we may be "clothed upon",

re-made in the image of the "new". To use a homely simile, you cannot take a bath without stripping yourself; but when a man comes home soiled with work and takes off his dirty working-clothes to step into the bath, his intention is not to remain naked, but to assume the clean raiment of family life and civilised intercourse. Seeing how much of the soil of the world we habitually contract in our daily life, I cannot believe that exhortations to care less than the little most of us do care about ceasing to do evil are likely to be very productive of doing good.

Further, those who have most to say in praise of the ideal of "positive efficiency" too often forget that the "positive" achievement of a life cannot be measured by a standard so crude as that of readily ascertainable specific results. Dr. Inge has truly said more than once that the most effective work in the way of "social amelioration" has usually been due to men who were all the while thinking primarily of something else. An example in point is the beneficent effect on art, literature, and social conditions in general directly traceable to the personality of St. Francis of Assisi, who all through his life troubled himself very little about any of the three. The same thing is equally true of the moral effects of any individual life of quiet goodness. It is not usually the persons who are most definitely preoccupied with this or that project of social reform as the great business of life, still less those who proclaim that their main interest is that of "making their neighbours better" in general, who actually most often send us away from contact with them better men than we were before. More commonly the best influence in our lives is that of quiet and unpretending persons who were quite unconscious of any intention to moralise us directly, and of whom we might find it hard to say just what special "good habit" or reform of our practice we owe to them, though we may feel certain that we "owe our souls" to them. The goodness of the tree, no doubt, is proved by the goodness of its fruit, but the fruit is not usually very precisely discerned by our imperfect vision. And Hegel's smart gibe misses the point. The schoolmaster who prefers himself to Alexander is, indeed, presumably a self-satisfied prig. If he were not a prig, the comparison would not be likely to suggest itself to him, or if it did, his verdict on himself would be less confident, did he remember, before passing it, as he should, that the real question is whether he would have mastered his temper better than Alexander in Alexander's position and with Alexander's temptations. But it still remains true that Alexander might have done much more for the world than he did, if he had known how to keep the strain of the savage in himself under better restraint, and so had not deprived himself of his wisest and most devoted counsellors. And it is not a preposterous view that, though in the eyes of the average man a schoolmaster may seem a little figure and a great conqueror an imposing one, there may be schoolmasters who are greater "in the kingdom of heaven" than Alexander or Napoleon. Plato would certainly have said that there are or may be; and if we desire the authority of a great name to support our considerations, Plato's name may count for as much as Hegel's. In fact, many at least of us would say that however much the world owes to Alexander, it owes much more to Plato, and Plato himself, when all is said, was a kind of pedagogue. Like Johnson, "he keepit a schule and ca'd it an Academy". The element of truth in Hegel's *mot* reduces to little more than this, that a schoolmaster who was really a greater man morally than Alexander would be very unlikely to be conscious of the fact. We must not introduce into moral valuation that pernicious heresy of judgement by grossly palpable results which has worked so much havoc with education wherever it has prevailed.

(5) This rather desultory consideration of the implications of the sense of guilt may be brought to a close with one further consideration. What is the *subiectum* we feel to be defiled and polluted by contact with that which awakens our sense of guilt, or wounds our sense of honour? Assuredly nothing which we could plausibly represent as primitive and elemental human nature; the merely "natural" man, not yet caught up in the advance of the moralising process, if such a creature ever existed, must have known nothing of either sin or honour; the sense of both is itself a product of the moralising process. If a man could be serious with the proposal to "return to nature" by expelling what Nietzsche, with his unfortunate itch for journalistic epigram, has taught a generation to call "moralic acid" from his system, his first task would have to be to divest himself once for all of shame, honour, and chivalry. Modern advocates of *Herrenmoral* take a sentimental pleasure in contemplating themselves as lions or eagles; but the lion and eagle of their fancy have never existed except in the bestiaries and romances. The real lion and the real eagle are not the chivalrous beasts of fable who disdain to harm a virgin or to taste carrion; they are as much mere creatures of their appetites as the wolf and the vulture.[1] Nor is it my own person as it actually exists that is the object of this unqualified and solicitous reverence. That, in many a case, already bears the stain of so many disgraces that I might well

---

[1] So much at least was correctly understood by the "horned Siegfrieds" who provoked Nietzsche's disgust by trying to act out his theories. No doubt, they were young blackguards, but the humour of the situation is precisely that no one could be a "superman" without being something of a blackguard, while the inventor of the "superman" was at heart, after all, a "Christian gentleman".

feel that one more spot could not add much to its un-cleanness. What is defiled by sin and dishonour is the self I aspire yet to possess as my own, *quando che sia*. The poignant shame which goes with consciousness of guilt or dishonour gets its pungency from the contrast with my ideal of what I, as a person, may be and am shaped to be, and this is why we all feel guilt and dishonour to be things much more intimate to ourselves than they would be if they were adequately described as mere infractions of an impersonal law. What is amiss with all of us is not merely that we have *done* this or that which we should not have done, or omitted this or that which "regulations" call on us to do, but that the very fountain of our moral personality is poisoned.

Whether Adam ever "fell" or not, *I* am a "fallen creature", and I know it. Our moral task is no mere business of canalising or embanking the course of a stream; it has to begin higher up with the purification of the bitter waters at their source. Hence, when we feel as we ought to feel about the evil in ourselves, we cannot help recognising that our position is not so much that of someone who has broken a wise and salutary regulation, as of one who has insulted or proved false to a person of supreme excellence, entitled to whole-hearted devotion. Similarly, even in lives in which the thought of sin as a personal offence against the living divine majesty is not operative, we all know that an adequate sense of the dishonour attaching to treason to a principle or a cause can only be awakened when one succeeds in "personifying" the cause or the principle. To make a man feel the shame of treason to the cause of his country as he ought to feel it, you must first make him accept a figure like that of Britannia as something very much more than a convenient abbreviatory symbol for "the system of social institutions and traditions in which I have been brought up"; if he is to care as he ought to care, he must somehow be got, in spite of himself, to feel that Britannia is a living person. Just so, if we are to think adequately of the shame of disloyalty to our best spiritual ideal, we have to learn to think of that ideal as already embodied in the living and personal God, and of falsehood as personal disloyalty and ingratitude to God. It is just because so many of our modern philosophical moralists are afraid to make the idea of God frankly central in their theories of conduct that their treatment of guilt is inadequate to the actual moral experiences of men with any depth of character.

It is easy to say that passionate loyalty can be and is awakened by the imaginative personification of Britannia, though no one really believes in the personification, and that, in the same way, the practical necessity of *imagining* moral guilt as an offence against a personal living God proves nothing as to the truth of such a conception. But the two cases are only imperfectly analogical. There may be no such actual person as Britannia, but we should remember that the loyalties symbolised and summed up for the patriotic Briton in the figure of Britannia are themselves, in the main, loyalties to persons. The symbolic figure represents the body of a man's attachments to a host of those whom he loves and respects, and has respected and loved from his childhood. Britannia means for him all his intensest and most deeply rooted loyalties to persons at once. If you could find a man without any of these personal devotions, a man to whom Britannia was *only* a "figure of speech" for a set of impersonal institutions of which he approved—the House of Commons, the Assizes, the Quarter Sessions, the Coroner's Inquest,

and the like—I wonder how much power the figure
would have to brace him for the great endurances and
the great sacrifices. Not, I should suspect, very much.

Now the moral life, adequately conceived, is a life
of unremitting endurances and sacrifices which go
beyond anything that would be demanded by loyalty
to our personal attachments to fellow-men, and may,
at any moment, require the sacrifice of the most intimate of these attachments to a higher loyalty. Can
this supreme loyalty be felt towards any object but one
with which we stand in a *personal* relation more intimate than any that could come into competition with
it? Can it be demanded, and, if demanded, is it likely
to be displayed? To my own mind the answer is clear.
The supreme endurances and surrenders can be made,
but they can only be made by love, and who can really
love a code or a system of institutions? Who could love
the Categorical Imperative or the *Code Napoléon* or the
perfected social organisation of a distant future? The
more patent it is that it may be a good man's duty not
to let love of friend, or mistress, or wife, or mother, be
the paramount and final influence in all his choices, the
more patent also, it seems to me, that this final motive
must be found in another and a supreme love, and that
such a love, like all loves, must have its real personal
object. Thus once more I find myself forced back on
the conclusion that, to be truly itself, the moral life
must have as its last motive love to God, and so become
transfigured into the life of religious faith and devotion.
For the moralist, belief in the true and living God cannot be relegated to the position of an "extra", which
we may perhaps be allowed on sufferance to add to our
respect for duty or regard for the good of our fellow-
men, if physicist, biologist, and anthropologist will be
kind enough to raise no objection. Belief in the absolute

reality of God, and love for the God in whom we believe, are at the heart of living morality. The good of our fellow-men is unworthily thought of when we do not conceive that good as a life of knowledge of God and transformation by the knowledge into the likeness of God. And the love which arises from our belief is the one motive adequate to secure the full and whole-hearted discharge of the duties laid on us by our ideal.

If moralists are at times ready to compound with the naturalist on easier terms, the reason, I suspect, is that they have not always the courage of their convictions as moralists. They are not quite sure at heart whether the moral life is quite as much "hard fact" as the facts of which the natural sciences treat. If a man is seriously convinced that of all facts those of our own moral struggle are the most immediately sure and certain, that we have more intimate assurance of the reality of love and hate, virtue and vice, than of the reality of atoms or electrons, I do not believe he is in much danger of reducing Theism to the level of a metaphysical speculation or a "permitted" hypothesis.

VI

THE INITIATIVE OF THE ETERNAL

And why not grace? Why not God's grace, Hay? . . . We walk upon it, we breathe it; we live and die by it; it makes the nails and axles of the universe; and a puppy in pyjamas prefers self-conceit!—R. L. STEVENSON.

AMONG the writings accepted by antiquity as Platonic there is a curious fragment of a few pages called *Cleitophon* which raises a perturbing question. (Its authenticity has been generally denied throughout the last hundred years on grounds which, if not absolutely conclusive, are reasonably cogent.) The writer, whoever he may have been, urges that there is a formidable practical defect in the familiar Socratic doctrine of ethics. Socrates can succeed in convincing an auditor beyond all doubt of the supreme importance of having the right moral ideal and being in dead earnest with the business of "making the soul as good as possible". But when we go on to ask what are the steps to be taken in setting about this chief business of life, Socrates has nothing to tell us. He has convinced us, to speak in a metaphor, of the necessity of knowing the true route across the troubled and uncharted waters of life, but he cannot tell us how to set our vessel's course. In this respect, Cleitophon is made to say, even the slap-dash Thrasymachus has the advantage of Socrates. Whatever we may think of the goal Thrasymachus sets before us, at least he can give us definite directions for reaching it. It looks, then, as if Socrates has an unrivalled gift of awakening the "unconverted", but no message of guidance for the once awakened.[1]

As the fragment breaks off at this point, and has the appearance of never having been completed, we do not know how the writer meant to treat the difficulty he has raised. Conceivably his intention was to urge that the seemingly annihilating criticism is, after all, not valid, and it would not be difficult to suggest the line of argument he might have adopted for this purpose.[2] But his difficulty may be restated in a way which indicates the existence of a real standing limitation inherent in all moral theory, so long as it is content to remain *moral* theory and nothing more. It would not, indeed, be a sound criticism if it were taken to mean only that the moralist can give no such precise and specific instructions for living a good life as the boat-builder can furnish for the construction of a sea-worthy craft, or the physician for correcting a definite physical defect by regimen and diet. For it might be properly retorted that the physician, too, *can* give no precise directions for securing a lifetime of physical well-being, and that the moralist is not confined to mere generalities when the problem before him is that of getting the mastery of a specific evil propensity or habit. When his problem is narrowed down to the treatment of a particular fault, such as impatience of temper or undue cupidity for some particular carnal gratification, he, like the physician, can suggest useful special rules of hygiene. The serious difficulty is

---

[1] *Op. cit.* 410 B-C νομίσας σε τὸ μὲν προτρέπειν εἰς ἀρετῆς ἐπιμέλειαν κάλλιστ᾽ ἀνθρώπων δύνασθαι, δυοῖν δὲ θάτερον, ἢ τοσοῦτον μόνον δύνασθαι, μακρότερον δὲ οὐδὲν . . . ταὐτὸν δὴ καί σοί τις ἐπενέγκοι τάχ᾽ ἂν περὶ δικαιοσύνης, ὡς οὐ μᾶλλον ὄντι δικαιοσύνης ἐπιστήμονι, διότι καλῶς αὐτὴν ἐγκωμιάζεις· οὐ μὴν τό γε ἐμὸν οὕτως ἔχει· δυοῖν δὲ θάτερον, ἢ οὐκ εἰδέναι σε ἢ οὐκ ἐθέλειν αὐτῆς ἐμοὶ κοινωνεῖν. διὰ ταῦτα δὴ καὶ πρὸς Θρασύμαχον οἶμαι πορεύσομαι καὶ ἄλλοσε ὅποι δύναμαι.

[2] Cf. my *Plato, the Man and His Work*[3], Appendix, p. 537.

more fundamental. How are our desires for what, in our moments of insight, we can recognise intellectually to be the best to be made effectual enough to compete victoriously in practice with our strong concupiscences for things our understanding can clearly enough see to be not good, or, at any rate, not best? It may be true to say with Socrates that we all at heart desire good, or felicity, and nothing else; the trouble is that the desire is commonly a languid one, and yet has to become a "passion" if real progress in good is to be made. What is to supply the driving force which will fan languid and faint desire for the best into a flame? How are we to be made to care enough for the highest?

Mankind in general, and individual persons in particular, will not be regenerated unless moral aspiration becomes an overpowering passion; and how is such devotion to be secured? There may be a few men, like Socrates himself, in whom the intellectual discernment of a better seems directly able to arouse a passion for its attainment, but these are the exceptions among mankind, not the rule. It is the common experience of most of us that we assent pretty readily to the theses that ends to which the life of another man is consecrated are worthier than those we are pursuing ourselves, that we should be better men if we cared less for things we actually care a great deal about, and more for others in which our interest is actually lukewarm, or, again, if we could only get rid of what we know to be our special infirmities and vices. But our assent to these theses often provokes at best only a passing wish that we were men of different mould; it does not usually stimulate to devoted and unremitting labour at the task of the remaking of the self. For the work of life we need not only a vision of good, but adequate motivation to live by the vision. Mere philosophy tends to regard its business as confined to the delineation of the moral ideal, and to disclaim all pretension to the harder achievement of supplying the motive for devotion. In this sense, at least, ethics has always been what Bradley insisted it ought to be, a speculative, not a practical pursuit.

There can, of course, be no objection to the view that, for the convenience of the student, there should be this division of labour. There is no reason why the man who is trying to become a better man should be compelled also to work at the task of analysing the moral ideal which inspires him, or the man who is trying to analyse the good forced also to play the part of a preacher of righteousness, any more than a convalescent should study medicine, or a medical student convalesce. Each task is likely to be most effectually executed if the two are kept distinct. Thus we have no right to blame the moral philosopher if, on grounds of method, he confines himself to the attempt to tell us what, in principle, the best life for man is. To be sure, unless he is also seriously trying to live that life himself, his statements about its character are bound to be gravely defective. Yet he may have a special superior intellectual penetration, not shared by better but less reflective men, though some of these men may be actually living the best life more effectually than himself, just as we know that, though a man of a prosaic turn of mind will never be a good critic of poetry, the best critic is usually not a great poet, and the great poet often shows himself a mediocre critic. So far there is some real justification for the claim of Schopenhauer that he could depict sanctity without being himself a saint. But the very admission that the moral philosopher is not necessarily saint or hero in the same degree in which he is a good philosopher,

while the men who are heroes and saints may have no
articulate philosophy, involves the further admission
that moral philosophy itself is not rightfully entitled to
the position of supreme mistress and directress of human
action. A φιλοσοφία which is to be what Socrates and
Plato meant φιλοσοφία to be, the sovereign guide and
support of life, must supply adequate motivation to the
pursuit of the apprehended good as well as a sound
conception of that good. The problem is whether this
adequate motivation can be found anywhere in a life
of response to solicitations to action which come solely
from the human and infra-human environment, or
whether it has not rather to be sought in actual contact
with a strictly superhuman source.

This is an issue which seems to be forced upon us
whenever we study the ethical deliverances of the greatest philosophers, not as youthful aspirants to qualify for
the rank of doctors in spiritual medicine, but as patients
seeking spiritual truth with a view to our own moral
health. The doubt expressed by the writer of the fragment *Cleitophon*, whether the exhortations of a Socrates
can really do more than make his hearers, like himself,
eloquent preachers of the necessity of "care for the
soul", whether they can actually contribute anything
to the cure of the diseased moral personality,[1] is not to
be stifled. Plato, for example, may convince us that only
the man who makes "follow God" his rule will ever
achieve true felicity. But suppose that a man—and this
is the case with all of us for much of the time and with
many of us all the time—does not care very much about
"following God", how is he to be got to care? Diotima
in the *Symposium* may be quite right when she teaches

[1] *Op. cit.* 409 B ἰατρική πού τις λέγεται τέχνη·ταύτης δ᾽ ἐστὶν διττὰ τὰ ἀποτελού-
μενα, τὸ μὲν ἰατροὺς ἀεὶ πρὸς τοῖς οὖσιν ἑτέρους ἐξεργάζεσθαι, τὸ δὲ ὑγίειαν . . .
τῆς δὴ δικαιοσύνης ὡσαύτως τὸ μὲν δικαίους ἔστω ποιεῖν . . . τὸ δ᾽ ἕτερον, ὃ δύναται
ποιεῖν ἡμῖν ἔργον ὁ δίκαιος, τί τοῦτό φαμεν ;

that the man who has once entered the right path by becoming awake to all that the beauty of one beautiful person means has only to "follow his nose" persistently enough, to find that his nose will lead him into the presence of the eternal Beauty. But to take even the first step on this road, you must first be already awakened from the deep sleep in which we all begin by being immersed, and what is it that effects the wakening? Aristotle's careful discussion of moral weakness (ἀκρασία) —the condition popularly described as knowing the good but doing the evil you know to be evil—raises the same question in a still acuter form. According to Aristotle, the man who yields to the suggestions of his worse nature is in a state analogous to that of a sleep-walker, or a man in his cups. He *talks* as though he knew the major premiss of the "syllogism of action", but his talk is mere babbling of words, with no more significance behind it than a drunken man's scraps of verse, or the apparently intelligent reply of a sleep-walker to a question.[1] When the man has recovered from his infatuation he will say the same things again, but with the difference that there will now be intelligent purpose behind his articulations, his words will really express his thought. And Aristotle goes on to suggest that there is a rhythm of spiritual waking and slumber in the moral life, exactly as there is a periodic rhythm of waking and sleeping in the bodily life.[2] We cannot help asking with some bitterness whether, when all is said, the exaltation of "practical intellect" really comes to no more than this singularly lame conclusion. Cannot a man be so effectually awakened that he will not often or lightly fall back into periodical sleep? Must we all be morally "in our cups" when the appointed hour comes round? If

[1] *E.N.* 1147 b 9 ff.
[2] *E.N.* 1147 b 6 (with Burnet's note *in loc.*).

we must, the analysis of the "best life for man" is much
of a mockery; it is only a picture of a heaven which we
may be sure none of us will reach. We find the same
thing once more in Kant. Kant has set the life of
"heteronomy", the life in which intelligence is only what
Hume had maintained it ought to be, an ingenious
minister to imperious lusts and cupidities, in the strongest contrast with the life of "autonomy", the life in
which intelligence is pursuing an end which is its own,
and is thus master in its own house. But what he never
explains is how the man who is assumed to be, at the
start, bound hand and foot in the chains of "inclination"
is ever to get loose from them. It is to no purpose to
urge that the chains will fall off of themselves if a man
once cultivates the spirit of unqualified reverence for
the law of duty. The whole problem is how a man who is
absolutely under the domination of "inclination" ever
comes to exhibit pure "reverence for duty", uncontami-
nated by all "inclination", in any the least and most
trivial act of life.

Kant is admirably clear on the point that such reverence will never be produced by any demonstration,
however successful, that the results of wrong-doing are
unhappy, since no man can be made disinterested by
an appeal to self-interest, and, for this reason, he, like
Socrates in the *Republic*, proposes a revolutionary reform in the moral teaching of the nursery.[1] What he does
not explain is how, if human nature in the as yet un-
moralised child is what he takes it to be, the appeal to
reverence for duty on which he would base the earliest
moral instruction is ever to "get home". The famous
Kantian mythus of the "ante-temporal" intelligible
act of choice which fixes our status as sheep or goats
once and for all[2] is no more than a confession that no

---

[1] *Kdpr V*. ii. Th. (*Werke*[2], v. 158 ff.).   [2] *Werke*[2], vi. 125.

explanation is forthcoming. At bottom Kant is merely reverting to the Augustinian nightmare of the *massa perditionis*, though he tries to "save the face" of his Deity by pretending that it is we who "reprobate" ourselves for all eternity.

Perhaps the difficulty is seen at its acutest in the ethics of Spinoza, as has been powerfully urged by a recent expositor, Mr. Guzzo.[1] As Spinoza conceives the moral problem, true virtue and true felicity, which are in the end the same thing, depend wholly on ability to base our conduct on "adequate" thought, a true conception of ourselves and our place in the cosmic system. But we all, without exception, have to begin life with highly inaccurate and inadequate conceptions, and to base our action on them; hence our unavoidable condition is initially that of "bondage" in which every man is a potential enemy and source of peril to every other, because all are rival competitors for the false goods which are competitive in character, and so only to be enjoyed by me on condition that I can exclude the rest of mankind from enjoyment. Now, if this is universally the "state of man by nature", how do we even begin to advance towards that true and adequate conception of human good which, as Spinoza agrees with T. H. Green in teaching, would disclose the truth that real good is not only non-competitive but can only be enjoyed by oneself in proportion as it is enjoyed by all? We might, as Mr. Guzzo says, conceive two possible alternative answers to the question. We might think that human regeneration begins in an intellectual enlightenment. Reflection might be supposed to convince my understanding of the inadequacy of my old notions of good and bad, and lead me to replace them by more rational conceptions. It is, one might suppose, a conse-

---

[1] Guzzo, *Il pensiero di Spinoza*, pp. 290 ff.

quence of this intellectual enlightenment that as the belief that the "competitive goods" are the worthiest objects of pursuit fades, attachment to them and lust after them will likewise fade, and thus there will be an end of the "passions" which made human life a chaos of mutual jealousies and aggressions. The cleansing of the "heart", in that case, would be an effect of an initial illumination of the intellect. But progress from bondage to freedom by *this* route is stopped completely by Spinoza's express declaration that our thought never can be adequate *until* we have emancipated ourselves from "passion",[1] the purification of emotion being thus called for as a pre-condition of the enlightenment.

Shall we say, then, that our deliverance is effected by the opposite route? That an elevated emotional mood, an *attachment* to something better than the "goods" coveted by the average sensual man, comes first and produces clarification of "practical" thinking as its effect? That it is noble emotion which purges the films from the vision of the "eye of the soul"? No doubt, we might point to examples from actual life where this process seems to be taking place under our observation, cases in which "passionate" devotion to a worthy person, or a worthy cause, seems to work a transformation of a man's whole outlook on life and estimate of its goods. But, again, Spinoza is debarred from accepting such an analysis of what happens in these cases by one of his own doctrines. So long as we have false and "inadequate" ideas, he holds, we are and must be at the mercy of "passion", the unworthy emotion and desire which are the inevitable outcome of false intellectual

---

[1] *Ethica*, iv. 14 "vera boni et mali cognitio, *quatenus vera*, nullum affectum coercere potest, *sed tantum quatenus ut affectus* consideratur". In other words, our emotions must be engaged on behalf of "true good" as a pre-condition of our recognition of it as such. See on this point Guzzo, *op. cit.* 146 ff.

presuppositions.[1] There are thus only two conceivable paths from bondage to freedom, and both seem to be barred. False thinking and unworthy action go together. So long as we think falsely we cannot act worthily, and therefore the regeneration cannot begin with the "passional" side of our nature. But equally it cannot begin with a "day of Damascus" in which the eye of the soul beholds a new and transcendent light, for it is our unworthy passions and the habits of action in which they have become embodied that *are* themselves the "scales" on the eyes of understanding.

In the sequel, it is true, Spinoza seems to fall back on one of the very ways to freedom which he has barred against himself. The practical rules laid down in the early proposition of *Ethics* v. are all rules for contemplating what befalls us as the inevitable result of a chain of causation which embraces the whole history of the universe, and where no link could be other than it is. Spinoza trusts to this speculative intellectual vision of all things as necessary to effect a practical moral regeneration for two reasons. When every event in an infinite series is thought of as playing its part in causing our joys and sorrows, it will be only a vanishingly small part of the effect we shall attribute to each particular member of the series, and this, it is held, will eliminate partial jealousies, rivalries, and hatreds, thus leading to settled contentment and general good will. Further, the same line of thinking will lead us, in the end, to regard God as the one real cause of everything which happens, and "no one can hate God", and thus we are led to "intellectual love of God" as our standing emotional habit.[2] But I think it may be replied that the line of reflection Spinoza recommends really leads to the conclusion that any specific

---

[1] *Ethica*, iv. 17 schol., v. 20 schol.　　　　[2] *Ethica*, v. 18, 32.

person, act, or event must be as impotent and unimportant for good as for evil. The strictly "logical"
consequence of preoccupation with the thought that no
one agent or event plays any decisive part in effecting
our felicity or misery should be not a spirit of universal
cheerfulness or good will, but one of sullen, or apathetic,
indifference to all events and agents alike. And similarly, the identification of God with an indifferent and
non-ethical first source of good and evil alike ought
in consistency to lead to unconcern about God, and is
only too likely in practice, in the case of those whose
lot in the world is a hard one, to beget downright
hatred of God. Spinoza's recommendations are as
likely to lead to blasphemy as to piety, and in most
cases likeliest of all to lead to the dull apathy which
wiser men know as *acedia* and reckon among "deadly
sins". If Spinoza was led by them to the *amor intellec-
tualis Dei*, the manifest reason is to be found not in
his philosophy, but in his personality. Like more than
one other great philosopher, he clearly had a personal
religion which finds no adequate expression in his
professed metaphysic. The source of his actual piety
towards God and the happiness it brought him is not
to be found in the doctrine of *Deus-substantia* expounded in the *First Part* of the *Ethics*; we have to
look for it in deep impressions of early life based on
intimate membership of a Jewish family and a Jewish
community, familiar with utterances of psalmists
and prophets who most emphatically did not identify
Deus and *Natura*, but gave whole-hearted adoration
to the *Deus absconditus* who sits above the water-
spouts, "rage they never so horribly". There is something in Spinoza's Deity of the God of Abraham,
Isaac, and Jacob, as well as of the *Dieu des savants
et des philosophes*.

You see the point I am concerned to make. If a man is to be raised in his whole being above his present unsatisfactory level, it is not enough that he should be able to conceive of a self better than that he now possesses. The "ideal" must be able to draw him with an overpowering force; it must be an *efficient* as well as a final cause.[1] And it is only an efficient cause when the recognition of its goodness is accompanied by faith in its existence as the most assured of realities. The old Aristotelian principle that *ens in potentia* can only be "reduced to act" by that which is itself "in act", after all, holds good. The separation of existence and value uncritically acquiesced in by so many of our contemporary thinkers would be fatal to moral progress towards good in any man who should seriously believe in such a separation, where the important purposes of life are concerned. It is from its acknowledged and overpowering reality that the valuable draws its motive power. As Dr. Whitehead has recently said,[2] "There is no such thing as mere value. Value is the word I use for the intrinsic reality of an event."

We get here a hint of the true solution of the apparently desperate problem, how comes a man, being what at this moment he is and having just the worth he has, neither more nor less, at once to conceive the ideal of the better and to be drawn to it. If a man were really "what he now is", if his being were really a *being* and not rather a *becoming*, and a becoming open to the influence and pressure of the eternal Being which envelops all becomings, if in fact a man were a true Leibnizian "monad", self-developing and self-contained, the process would be wholly unintelligible.

---

[1] As Kant says, the "good will" must be a *will*, not a mere *wish*. The problem is how it is to become more than a fleeting wish.

[2] *Science and the Modern World*, p. 136.

It is actually intelligible only because the human "monad", in spite of Leibniz's denials, *has* "windows", and windows which are open to the Infinite. To be quite plain, in all moral advance the *ultimate* "efficient cause" must be the real eternal source of both becoming and value. The initiative in the process of "assimilation to God" must come from the side of the eternal; it must be God who first comes to meet us, and who, all through the moral life itself, "works in us", in a sense which is more than metaphorical. Our moral endeavours must be genuinely ours, but they must be responses to intimate actual contacts in which a real God moves outward to meet His creatures, and by the contact at once sustains and inspires the appropriate response on the creature's part.

But to say as much as this is to say that the everyday moral life of simple discharge of recognised duty transcends the artificial limits we set to it, for our intellectual convenience, when we discriminate between morality and religion. Such a life itself is, after all, from first to last, a life inspired by "faith". The notion that whereas religion makes the demand for faith in the beyond and dimly descried, morality does not, but is a matter of walking in the full daylight, can only arise when we mistakenly think of moral virtue as being nothing more than the routine practice of a set of duties which are perfectly familiar to us all, from our inheritance of social rules and traditions. The life of genuine morality is always something indefinitely more than this. It involves a progress which is not merely improvement in the performance of tasks we have always known to be incumbent on us, or the correction of faults which we have seen, or could have seen, at any moment to be faults. In truth, with every step taken towards a life of more habitual loyalty to known duty, or correction of known faults, we also discern new and unexpected duties with claims on our loyalty, and unsuspected faults calling for correction. Every self-surrender not only receives its reward in the enrichment of the personality we had set on the hazard; it also points the way to undreamed-of greater surrenders. Consequently, the common saying of the old poets, that the uphill road to the dwelling of virtue is steep at first, but becomes easier at each successive step, is a dangerous half-truth; the gradient is really growing steeper all the time. Years of self-discipline may make it easier for a man to practise duties he once shirked or ignored, or to avoid vicious courses which were once alluring, but they also bring their own fresh demands with them, and compliance with the new demands "costs" more than compliance with the old. The way of life does not merely begin as a *via crucis*, it remains a *via crucis* all through. The attempt to walk that road simply in my own strength is as likely to be fatal to my moral being if I make it late as if I make it early. Morality itself, when taken in earnest, thus leads direct to the same problems about "grace" and "nature", "faith" and "works", with which we are familiar in the history of Christianity, the religion which stands supreme above all others in its "inwardness" and takes the thought of regeneration of the self from its centre with unqualified seriousness.

At the risk of a short digression from our immediate topic, it may be worth while to point out that this problem of divine initiative equally arises outside the strictly practical domain of the moral and religious conduct of life. It even meets us, in a more external form, in the course of reflection on nature and natural causality. We may readily illustrate the point from the natural theology of Aristotle, the least "inward" of all philosophers of the first order of greatness. Of all great metaphysicians Aristotle is perhaps the one of whom we can most safely say that his vision in metaphysics is in least danger of being distorted by excessive pre-occupation with the problems of the moral life. No one can reasonably suspect him of being unduly inclined by personal temperament to over-ethicise his metaphysic, since he is curiously devoid of the moral inspiration so manifest in Plato and Kant, and, with a good deal of detriment to logical consistency, in Spinoza. So far as the *Nicomachean Ethics* go, indeed, their doctrine is excellent enough. Aristotle has a high standard of personal behaviour, and is anxious that it should be faithfully lived up to; his practical counsel on the formation of good habits and the avoidance of bad is admirable in its common sense. A society trained as he would have it trained would be eminently law-abiding, orderly, and decent. Yet his treatment of "practice" has always been felt to be wholly devoid of "inwardness". His morality is a highly "this-world" affair of setting up a manifestly sensible rule of be-haviour and observing the rule carefully. Only in one matter does he get perceptibly beyond this very "external" conception of the moral life—in the matter of the analysis of the personal affections on which the worthiest human friendship is based. The sense of sin, so conspicuous in Platonic and Christian ethics, is conspicuously wanting in him, and he seems to have no idea of any moral life which aims at more than the punctual discharge of the social obligations which must be enforced, if a community is to be free from serious disorders. It is not from him that we learn of the moral life as a pilgrimage from bondage to freedom, or an escape from the intolerable burden of an unworthy selfhood. We can hardly say that he feels, as Plato,

Spinoza, or Kant felt, that there is any grievous burden or bondage to escape from. The *Hang zum Bösen* in the human heart is not a reality to him. And the reason is not far to seek. Aristotle's interest in human life itself is at best secondary. What he really cares intensely for is the scientific contemplation of the natural world; he values morality chiefly as a means to something other than itself. A well-ordered πόλις, fair-dealing neighbours, and a good personal character are but pre-requisites indispensable if the "fine flower" of the community are to have the security, quiet, and leisure they require, in order to devote themselves to cosmology and astronomy. You cannot give your heart to the prosecution of such studies if you are all the while set on the enjoyment of sensual pleasures, or the accumulation of wealth, if you are at the mercy of ill-educated neighbours, or if your city is incessantly contending with enemies from without, or distracted by the factions of the malcontents within. But the supreme business of life is to be neither saint nor hero; it is to be something like a President or Fellow of a Royal Society.[1]

Yet the problem we might imagine evaded by this relegation of the life of moral inwardness to a wholly secondary position breaks out even in the theology of Aristotle. The one and only purpose for which his philosophy requires God is a strictly naturalistic one. God is there, not to supply moral initiative by the drawings of "grace", nor even to provide an ideal of perfected personality, to which we might aspire in our own strength. Aristotle, as you know, thinks it actually absurd to ascribe moral personality to his God. God is wanted simply to provide initiative and support for a

---

[1] Cf. *E.N.* 1178 b 3 τῷ δὲ θεωροῦντι οὐδένος τῶν τοιούτων (*sc.* τῶν ἐκτὸς ἀγαθῶν) πρός γε τὴν ἐνέργειαν χρεία . . . ᾗ δ' ἄνθρωπός ἐστιν καὶ πλείοσι συζῇ, αἱρεῖται τὰ κατὰ τὴν ἀρετὴν πράττειν.

physical movement, the supposed eternal and uniform diurnal revolution of the outermost "heaven". One could not well go much further in the reduction of God to a mere "unknown x", necessary to complete a system of sidereal mechanics, and so having the same *status* as the problematical "cause of gravity" mentioned in the *Scholium Generale* at the end of Newton's *Principia*. Yet Aristotle, if we are to take him at his word, goes rather further. His God is to be only the "First Mover", the postulated solution of a real or supposed problem in dynamics. But the movement he initiates and supports apparently involves no outgoing activity on his own part. We are told that he moves the "first heaven" in the same way in which the object of concupiscence or love moves love or concupiscence.[1] The point of the comparison is that, in both cases, the whole process falls wholly within the being who is "moved". To repeat an illustration I have used elsewhere, the Princess of Tripoli, in a sense, "moved" Jauffré Rudel, by supplying the initiative for his famous voyage. Yet it may well have been the case that the Princess was not so much as aware of the existence of her lover. And, since Aristotle insists that the life of God is one unbroken contemplation of a single object, himself, to the exclusion of all others, it would seem to follow that God does not even know of that existence of the "heaven" which he "moves".[2]

As a fact of history, this was the interpretation put on the doctrine by the soundest Aristotelian expositor of antiquity, Alexander of Aphrodisias. Alexander was careful to explain that God, in Aristotle's system, is only the τελικὴ αἰτία, the "final" cause, of the diurnal

---

[1] *Metaphys.*, 1072 a 26 ff.

[2] It would be unjustifiable to interpret Aristotle in the light of the later scholastic doctrine that God, *cognoscendo se, et alia cognoscit. That* presupposes the Trinity.

revolution; the universe finds its satisfaction, exercises its function, in executing this uniform unending revolution, and this is the only way in which there is any connection between the world and God. That one does not need to be biassed by specifically Christian sentiment to find this doctrine of a merely self-absorbed Deity intolerable is shown by the zeal with which it is denounced, for example, by the learned Neo-Platonic scholar Simplicius. Simplicius is no Christian—in fact he was one of the sturdy pagans who migrated to Persia from antipathy to Christianity when the schools of Athens were closed by Justinian—but he is a Platonist, and as such determined to find nothing in Aristotle incompatible with the definitely ethical and theistic philosophy of Plato. Accordingly, he sets himself to argue more ingeniously than successfully for an interpretation by which God shall be less completely cut off from contact with the world.[1] If Simplicius cannot break with Aristotle in his exaltation of the "theoretical life, he is bound, as a Neo-Platonist, to give his supreme principle, as an essential consequence of its inward activity of self-concentration, a further outgoing activity, in virtue of which it παράγει, produces, creates, the world. Thus the attempt to adjust Aristotle with Plato leads directly up to the recognition of what is now called divine "transcendence" and the problem of the relation of this transcendence to the divine "immanence". This problem may occupy us further in the sequel, but for the present I would be content merely to note that no philosophy of pure "immanence" can take the moral life seriously. The special problem of the ultimate source of initiative towards the morally better, which is familiar in theology as the problem of "grace", is

[1] See the polemic on this point in his commentary on the *Physics* (Diels, pp. 1360-1363).

but the particular form assumed by the more general problem of "transcendence" when raised with special reference to human personal activities. The metaphysical denial of divine transcendence carries with it self-righteousness in morality, as well as Pelagianism in theological speculation. (It is only just to add that exclusive insistence on transcendence has its dangers too; it leads to "supralapsarian" theology and an antinomian "going as you please" in morality. Such is the price we have to pay for over-simplification of our problems.)

I must be content, then, at the risk of being thought, as Socrates anticipates in the *Phaedo* that he may be thought in a similar case, *"naïf and rather simple"*,[1] to insist on one point. A man cannot receive the power to rise above his present moral level from his own inherent strength, because the process is one of rising above himself, and, in the moral as in the physical world, you cannot lift yourself by the hair of your own head. Nothing can rise in virtue of its inherent gravity. And, again, you cannot borrow strength from an ideal which is only an ideal, a value without actuality. If the ideal indeed draws you upward, and unless it does so it is not *your* ideal, it does this because it is not divorced from reality, but is more real than anything else you know. It is what we too often call the "actual", that which we are here and now, that is relatively unreal. It is relatively unreal because our life is a becoming, and therefore the so-called actual is always slipping away into the no longer actual. To-day's actuality is to-morrow's "dead past". The "ideal" is above becoming, and escapes this fate. We cannot say of it that the ideal of to-day gives place to the different ideal of to-morrow by becoming to-morrow's mere actuality. As we make

[1] *Phaedo*, 100 D 3 τοῦτο δὲ ἁπλῶς καὶ ἀτέχνως καὶ ἴσως εὐήθως ἔχω παρ' ἐμαυτῷ.

moral progress, we do not reach and pass the ideal of to-day, and say good-bye to it. What happens is that we discover to-morrow that to-day's ideal "had more in it" than we had supposed. Life is not a succession of excursions, each with a destination which is reached and left behind; it is a single journey towards a goal which, in what we see of life, or should see if its duration could be indefinitely prolonged, is never finally reached. The task of putting off temporality can no more be finished at a given date than the evaluation of a "surd" can ever be completed by writing down the last significant digit of the unending "decimal".

A great deal of otherwise admirable ethical literature seems to me to commit a fundamental error by conceiving of the moral life too simply, as a giving *expression*, through outward speech and action, to our inward personality. The real task is not merely that; it is rather the task of the reshaping and transfiguration of the inward personality itself, and the initiative to *such* an undertaking manifestly cannot come simply from within the personality which is to be remade. It must come in the end from contact with an ἀρχὴ κινήσεως which lies outside and around what is, at any given time, internal to the self, and the whole problem is how to live on this source in such a way that it is steadily drawn more and more into the self and yet never brought completely within it. When St. Paul writes to his converts that the life he is now living is "not I, but Christ alive in me", he is using the language of exalted religious adoration, but a not dissimilar statement, pitched in a lower key, would be in principle true of the life of any man who is seriously trying, in however humble a fashion, to be a "better man". Morality itself, taken in earnest, thus involves the "supernatural", in the proper sense of that word, as its environment and daily nutriment. A

morality without an ultimate source of initiative in the
eternal would amount to a prolonged attempt to breathe
in vacuo, or to feed one's body on its own fat. We all
know what would happen to an animal if it always
"hibernated", or if it had to inhale endlessly air which
had already passed through its lungs; yet, except in
the New Testament and in Plato, the indispensability
of τροφή from without for the moral life seems never to
have found adequate recognition.

To say this is not in any way to deny the equal indispensability of personal effort and persistence for all
moral and spiritual progress. Not only may "tasks in
hours of insight willed" be fulfilled in hours of "dry-
ness" and gloom, but we may add that they never will
be fulfilled in any other and easier fashion. The re-
fashioning of personality will no more take place in a
man without sheer hard work and endurance on his own
part than a great work of art will ever be thrown off
without effort in an hour of indolence. *In sudore vultus
tui comedes panem.* But the question is about the hours
of insight themselves, and the inspiration which is received in them. And with regard to them the truth
seems to be that vision, in the moral as in the physical
world, presupposes a real object of vision. The revelation of physical beauty begins not with a discovery of
the beauty of the visual organ, but with perception of
the loveliness of the colours and lines of things seen. In
like manner discernment of "moral" beauty begins
with the contemplation of an object which *gives* itself to
the inward eye. In moral and physical vision alike, we
have first to look *away* from ourselves. If we are to grow
into the likeness of the thing we contemplate, this can
only be because the thing we contemplate is *not*, in the
first instance, the thing we are; it is not *in rerum natura*
at all.

Here, in fact, we have a characteristic of the moral life which removes it definitely from the domain of "nature", even as understood by a thinker like Dr. Whitehead, who is thoroughly in earnest with the conception of nature as an unresting "becoming". It is true that such a conception as this breaks once for all with that uncritical materialism which confuses the "real" with the contents of a "cross-section" of space[1] "at the moment t"; it brings us back to the Leibnizian view of nature as a system in which every constituent is weighted by the whole "past" and pregnant with the whole "future", and so delivers us from confusion of the infinite riches of the real with the poverty-stricken abstraction "nature at a given instant". But even the Leibnizian has to admit that, though every "monad" may be big with the future, we can only read the future of the system by the light of its past; the way in which its members have become what they are is our only clue to what they will yet become. In moral experience it is different. We do not first decipher from the past the route towards the better future, and then take the path so deciphered. It is very often *après coup*, after we have already taken the decisive movement for the better, that we discern by later reflection the continuity of the path we have traversed. In a moral interpretation of history it is actually by the consideration of the future that we discover the true significance of the past. It is not nature but super-nature that can say "what I do thou knowest not now, but thou shalt know hereafter".

I do not, of course, forget that, in the study of the natural sciences themselves, the true significance of the stages by which an organ or structure has been developed can only be comprehended properly when we first know the function the developed organ or structure is

[1] Or, rather, of the spatial-temporal continuum.

to discharge, and that this lies in the future relatively to the process of development. But relatively to us who are fashioning the natural sciences, the function is not in the future. For us the functioning organ must be already there and functioning, if we are to read its pre-history by its own light. But in all moral appreciation the *ex hypothesi* unattained ideal of the best is always actually apprehended, in however vague a fashion. *Der Mensch ist etwas, das überwunden werden muss.* Perhaps; but we have not to wait until the problematical "superman" appears before we can pronounce on the question whether Nietzsche's *Weg zum Übermenschen* is the road to heaven or to hell.

If the considerations so far urged are sound, we may proceed to formulate some important conclusions concerning the type of doctrine about God which ought to characterise any "natural" theology which takes the moral being of man into account as part, and the most important part, of what it regards as the φύσις, *natura*, or given reality which is not to be paltered with or explained away.

(1) Since the moral life, rightly conceived, is no mere readjustment of outward reactions of a self, given once and for all, to its environment, but a reconstruction of the whole personality round a new centre, an ethical religion is inevitably, in the jargon made popular by William James, a religion for the "twice-born". *Thou must be born again* is the central proposition of all genuine morality, and it is therefore indispensable to an ethical theology that it should conceive its God not only as the Maker who has brought man, like the rest of the creatures, into temporal actuality, but as the source and sustainer of the aspirations by which man is made a *new* creature and puts off his first merely self-contained and temporally confined selfhood. God, that

is, to use language technical in the thought of Christianity, must be conceived not only as Creator, but also as Redeemer and Sanctifier. From the ethical point of view, acquirement of our heritage of true personality demands something much more than the correction of bad habits and the formation of good; it demands the transformation of what is best in its own kind into something which is good in a higher kind, and it is here that most of us come so lamentably short in our practice.

To illustrate the point more fully by an example, let us consider any morally valuable institution, such as permanent human marriage. So long as we see nothing in the *consortium totius vitae* but an excellent social arrangement for the rearing of successive generations of the physically and mentally sound, and the maintenance of social quiet and order by the canalisation of a dangerous source of jealousies and rivalries, we are thinking what is true enough, but still we are not thinking worthily of human marriage. It is the fact that, as Milton says, it is the source of our best natural affections, and that by it

> adulterous lust was driv'n from men
> Among the bestial herds to raunge;[1]

but this is less than half of the truth. The Greek formula that the end of matrimony is παιδοποιία γνησίων τέκνων, the perpetuation of the civic life, in fact, even when the words are made to mean the utmost that can be fairly read into them, does not exhaust all the significance of the conception of Roman lawyers that *matrimonium* is *consortium totius vitae*. The end conceived as a partnership in the whole of life, a complete sharing of all interests such that every joy and every

[1] *P.L.* iv. 753.

sorrow is the joy or the sorrow of *two*, is something which immeasurably transcends the mere association of man and woman in the work of bringing a new generation of public-spirited citizens into the world and preparing them for maturity. It already involves a genuine enriching transformation of personality, and one which, if we will be honest with ourselves, most of us must, to our shame, confess ourselves to attain only very imperfectly and with grievous lapses. It is hard, terribly hard, not to have some interests which are not thus completely shared, some joys and sorrows, hopes and fears which remain incommunicable, even in the most successful of family lives. And so long as there is this hard core of unshared experiences, the ideal of the *Institutes* remains something not wholly realised or even in process of steady realisation, however true it may be that the failure to realise it may be traceable to no voluntary fault of the parties concerned. The interest from which a man's wife, or a woman's husband, is shut out, remains as an obstacle to the ethical transfiguration of personality from the form of *I* to that of *We*.

But, further, so long as we think of the life which is to be "shared" only as one of secular and temporal joys and sorrows, we are not yet thinking of it as it is in its full ethical significance; our conception is still only very imperfectly moralised and humanised. The complete transfiguration of the animal into the human is only effected when the shared life is itself a life of common aspiration after the supreme moral good. In such a life it is not enough that there should be nothing which would commonly be recognised as a clash of incompatible interests, or that either party should feel pleasure and pain in the pleasure and pain of the other. Every incident and every act of the rightly shared life would be one in which either party was assistant and co-operant with the endeavour of the other towards the putting on of a personality purified from the last taint of native egotism and secured against mutability, a ministrant to the other of a spiritual sacrament.

We do not, except in a distressingly inadequate fashion, find ourselves attaining such an ideal; if we did, it would not be the fact, as it so often is, that the least animal and most human of our personal affections prove, to the noble mind, the sources of the most dangerous temptations to be false, for the sake of a loved person, to the demands of the ideal for the supreme surrenders. It would not be a duty demanded of the dutifully minded man that he must be prepared, if the call comes, to *forsake* parents and wife and children, since when personality had become what it ought to be and is always striving to be, the parent, or wife, or child would not feel the surrender to be a forsaking. It would be impossible any longer to say

> I could not love thee, dear, so much
> Loved I not honour more,

since the two loves contrasted by the poet would be too completely one to be opposed, even in thought. Only where such an ideal had become matter of fact would it be possible, from the ethical point of view, to pronounce the most intimate and devoted of human attachments an unqualified good. And the ideal simply cannot become matter of fact in our natural life.

The reason is not merely that our moral will is infirm and suffers constantly recurring lapses, true as this is. Even if we could always presuppose a maximum of good will, the conditions under which we have to gain insight into another's personality set limits to the insight so gained. For those who love to be thus entirely at one, it would be needed that each should read the other's personality to its depths with the knowledge of direct and infallible vision, and in the life we are conversant with there is no such *scientia visionis* of one another, nor even of ourselves. There is always something hidden from us in those who have stood longest most near to ourselves; there are things hidden from us in our very selves. Thus it is only the bare truth that realisation of the moral ideal in the simplest relations of human life is a thing impossible, if it has to be achieved purely by our own strength, and in the light of our own insight; as divines have said, every marriage—and we might add every other personal relation of life—is an adventure which is only kept from ending in disaster by the perpetual influence of transforming and sanctifying grace. So long as any human relation rests for its support on a basis of un- transformed "nature", it must inevitably be numbered among the things of which we must expect, sooner or later, to have to say, "I have no more pleasure in them".

(2) Now if this is so, the God of a Theism which is definitely ethical cannot be thought of as related to man, and the system of creatures generally, simply as Creator or a "great First Cause". If natural religion be taken, as it was taken in the eighteenth century, to mean no more than recognition of such a "First Cause", it becomes a mere hypothesis for cosmology and loses all moral significance. In doing so it loses its right to the name "religion", and all that remains to be said of it has been said in five words in the title of one of Blake's tracts, *There is no natural religion*. On this point enough has been said already in connection with our comments on the theology of Aristotle. But it is equally true that the God of a true ethical Theism

cannot be thought of adequately as no more than an embodied, or personalised, moral end, as the "great example" whom we are to follow—a representation common in philosophies of a Platonising type. It is, indeed, already much that God should be thought of in this way; we are already delivered from the depreciation of moral values inevitably prompted by a merely cosmological theology into which God enters, as with Aristotle, as a non-ethical being. We have an inspiring rule and an end set before us which we cannot simply reach and leave behind, when we are commanded to "follow God", to grow, as nearly as may be, into the likeness of that which the "father and maker of all" eternally is. But with all its moral elevation the conception fails us when we ask how this work of becoming like God is to be set about.

The first step towards the "conversion" of the soul from the world to God, as we learn from the Platonic Socrates, is that knowledge of self which is also the knowledge of our own ignorance of true good. How do we pass from the discovery that we are in this miserable and shameful ignorance of the one thing it is incumbent on us to know to apprehension of the scale of true good? How do we get even so far beyond our initial complete ignorance as to be able to say that a good soul is immeasurably better than a good body, and a good body than abundance of possessions? We know how the Augustinian doctrine, which is Christian as well as Platonic, answers the question. It does so by its conception, traceable back to the New Testament, that God Himself is the *lumen intellectus*, a view which has been, in substance, that of all the classical British moral philosophers from Cudworth to Green, and seems, in fact, to be, in principle, the only solution of the difficulty. We know our true good, which is no other than

God Himself, by obscure, but none the less real and impressive, personal contacts with God. Without this real contact with the eternal, the process of winning a true personality could not be begun. Any such view further implies that because God is the *lumen intellectus*, He is also the inspirer of endeavour in all of us, since each of us, as Socrates, Plato, and Aristotle agree in teaching, always endeavours after what appears to him his *good*. An ethical Theism has then to conceive God as the "efficient", as well as the "exemplary" cause of the whole moral life. From its humblest beginnings that life is, at every step, one of transformation into the likeness of that which we contemplate.

(3) This may seem an obvious point, but it carries far-reaching applications. If God is not only the goal, but the author and sustainer of moral effort, the whole moral endeavour of man must be a response to what we can only call a movement from the other side. It is, indeed, our own because it is the response of such moral personality as we already possess, but none the less it is a *response* to a divine initiative. In that language of human social relations on which we have to fall back whenever we try to speak of these matters, we love God because God first loved us. The "good shepherd" does not leave his strayed sheep to find its own way back; he goes out into the darkness and dangers of the wilderness to find it. When we use such language, we know, of course, that we are speaking "anthropomorphically", and that all "anthropomorphic" utterances about the divine are imperfect and attended with danger. But the attempt to expel anthropomorphism from our language about God is attended with worse dangers. Indeed, since we, who have fashioned language, are men, the only language we can use or understand is necessarily anthropomorphic, no matter what its

reference may be. We can see nothing outside ourselves, except through a human medium. Even when we talk of "inanimate nature" we never really succeed in getting quite rid of "anthropomorphism".

This was patent enough in the ordinary old-fashioned textbooks with their free employment of such words as "force", "constraint", "cause"; it is only half-hidden even in the phraseology of the thoroughgoing "positivists" of science who have demanded that physics shall be denuded of the last rags of a terminology which goes beyond the extreme abstractness of pure kinematics. No one has yet succeeded, and no one ever will succeed, in banishing the notions of change and process even from a natural science reduced to pure kinematics. And change is as completely an anthropomorphic conception as "force". If there is any living philosopher of whom we could say that the elimination of the anthropomorphic is a passion with him we must say it of Professor Alexander. Yet when Professor Alexander finds himself called on to assign a reason for the unceasing "emergence" of novel and, according to him, always brighter and better orders of existents, he finds the reason in what he calls the "restlessness" of space-time, thus simply transferring to his ultimates Locke's doctrine of the "greatest present uneasiness" as the standing incentive to action. If this notion of "restlessness" as the source of progressive efforts after betterment is not anthropomorphic, or rather, perhaps, theriomorphic, one would be glad to know what is.[1]

It ought to be obvious that we cannot speak at all of the superhuman or the infrahuman except in terms which derive all their significance, in the first instance, from that with which alone we are immediately familiar

[1] S. Alexander, *Space, Time and Deity*, ii. 345 ff.

from its presence in our own experience of living and striving—the strictly human. We cannot make our science or our theology really non-anthropomorphic, even if we would. Our choice is between speaking of the divine in terms of what is richest and most fully human in our own lives, or in terms of what is poorest and least human. And there should be no difficulty in making the choice, if once we are in earnest, as any genuine recognition of the moral life of man as a manifestation of the real compels us to be, with the notion of the divine as an efficient cause, and, in the end, *the* "first" efficient cause, of human moral advance. We *must* think of the divine on the analogy of all that is richest and most human, not only in our actual character, but in the better we aspire to be. The danger incurred when we represent God, for example, as standing to us in the relation of a noble human lover to the object of his love is not that we are attributing too much to God—it is the "natural" sciences in which *that* kind of risk is real —but that we are attributing too little. For so much of what we call love, when we speak "after the manner of men," is unworthy of the name.

Sometimes we mean by the word little more than a mere *amor concupiscentiae*, a carnal passion in which we care for the object only as an instrument of our own enjoyment and as nothing more.[1] When we mean more, as, thank God, most of us usually do, we still do not always discriminate very clearly between a "love" which is still mainly infrahuman and is concerned chiefly with "taking" and the love which is primarily anxious to "give". There are presumably few human

[1] Cf.

"He will hold thee, when his passion shall have spent its novel force,
  Something better than his dog, a little dearer than his horse."

Even this, however, is something. There are men who "love" a woman, or a fellow-man, much as an epicure "loves" truffles or claret.

relations in which the two are not inextricably bound up together. We talk, for example, of Lear's feeling for his daughters, as Lear himself does, as a "love" of peculiar intensity. But Lear's vehement fury of recoil at the first manifestations of coldness and ingratitude on the other side shows that, if he is to be called a passionate lover at all, his passion is overwhelmingly of the kind which is much more eager to take than to give. He calls himself, indeed, a father whose kind old heart "gave all", but the words are profoundly untrue. He gave, what after all cost him little, kingdoms, because he wanted to take what he cared more about, caresses and *câlineries*. Brought face to face, in the case of Cordelia, with the love which really gives all, he confuses it with want of "natural affection". At heart, Lear is as much one of "nature's takers" as Goneril or Regan, though the thing he lusts to take is less sordid.

Again, even when we are alive to the distinction between the taker's love and the giver's love, we continually confuse the love which aims at giving what is best with that which is content to give the second-rate or third-rate. We do not distinguish, as we ought, between a seeing love and a blind. By a loving father we mean, only too often, more precisely one whose only desire is to give his children what they like rather than what is good for them. In especial, we are apt to be blind to the reality of a love which demands high performance and lays hard tasks on its recipient, for the sake of the strength and beauty of personal character which are not to be had on easier terms. We confuse love with weakness, and this confusion is the source of a great deal of the current literary revolt against the idea of God.

It is held either that all love must be weak indulgence, and that the conception of God as loving us is therefore an unworthy one, or, on the other side, that the undeni-

able hardness of the tasks life sets to the best men is
proof that the author of life is profoundly unloving, and
so morally inferior to ourselves. The source of all this
confusion is the assumption that, if we speak of God's
love for men, we are not to interpret such language in
the light of the strongest and wisest human love, but in
that of weak and unwise love. That error arises not from
too much anthropomorphism, but from too little, from
readiness to think of God in terms of something lower
than our highest human standard of excellence. An
ethical theology is necessarily anthropomorphic, in the
sense that it interprets God and God's ways by the
analogy of all that is most nobly human, and always
with the further caution that as a completely humanised
man would be all we can picture to ourselves of what is
admirable in man and something more, which we cannot yet picture because we ourselves are so far from
being wholly humanised, so God is all that perfect
human excellence would be and abundantly more. Thus
the simple statement that God, whose initiative is the
source of all our advance in good, loves man as a father
loves his children is inaccurate only because it ascribes
too little to God. It falls short because no actual human
father loves his children with a love which is wholly bent
on giving, wholly wise and wholly unspoiled by facile
sentimentality.

(4) The main point on which I would wish to be clear,
however, is that to think ethically of God means to break
finally with the bad "deistic" tradition which finds its
clearest expression in the Aristotelian theology. The
God of a truly moral Theism cannot be a purely self-
centred being, "making eyes at Himself", to borrow a
phrase from Bradley, like some Narcissus. His fundamental activity must involve expansion. And when we
would think of His action upon the world, we can only

think of it as a life in which He gives Himself freely and generously to His creatures that they may be able to give themselves to Him. As Timaeus says in Plato[1] the very reason why there is a world of creatures at all is that the All-good is wholly free from φθόνος, the "dog-in-the-manger" spirit which seeks to engross felicity to itself, and therefore makes the creatures for His goodness to flow out upon. He cannot be wholly blessed, except in blessing.

I may, perhaps, be reminded at this point that, on a *prima facie* view, the tradition of Christian orthodoxy would seem to be at variance with the spirit of what has just been said. It is notorious that Christian theologians have all but unanimously agreed in rejecting the view, characteristic of Neo-Platonism, that the world of creatures emanates, or emerges, from the Creator by some sort of "natural necessity"; creation, they have taught, is a freely willed act of God. He might conceivably have willed to create no world at all, or to create one different in every detail from that which is actual. Not a few eminent Christian philosophers and theologians have gone still further. They have denied that the divine choice to create the actual world is due to its superior goodness when compared with other possible worlds, and some of them apparently have even denied that there is any reason whatever for the choice, thus apparently making both the existence of a world of creatures and its specific character the outcome of something like a divine "whim". Against all such language I would venture, with due modesty, to suggest that both the rival doctrines of a necessitated creation and of a capricious creation rest, in the end, on confusion of thought. It is important to an ethical Theism to insist that there is no necessity external and

[1] *Tim.* 29 E 1, ἀγαθὸς ἦν, ἀγαθῷ δὲ οὐδεὶς περὶ οὐδένος οὐδέποτε ἐγγίγνεται φθόνος.

superior to the Creator; He neither creates because He is constrained to create, nor gives the created world the structure it actually has because that structure is dictated by antecedent conditions. He is the foundation and absolute *prius* of all actuality and all possibility, and He is all, and more than all, we understand by an intelligent and righteous will. To safeguard such a Theism it is needful that we should clearly repudiate the suggestion, which haunts all philosophies of the Neo-Platonic type, that the Creator "has" to create, and to create the world we know, so to say, "willy-nilly", and this cannot be better done than by saying that creation is an act of free and intelligent choice.

But when we go on to add that, therefore, "God might have willed to create no world at all, or might have willed to create an entirely different world", we are, it seems to me, at least on the verge of a dangerous fallacy of ambiguity. We may mean only to give a piquant expression to the thought that the world is and is what it is because God is and is what He is. But we may also mean, and theologians seem sometimes actually to have meant, that God might be the God He is and yet that His creative will might be absent from His being, or might be other than it is. And if we mean this, then, I should say, we are introducing into the divine being itself the element of contingency, or, what comes to the same thing, we are making a distinction, and a *real* distinction, between God and God's will. That is, we are reintroducing the distinction between the possible and the actual into that which we also recognise as the foundation of both possibility and actuality, and so allowing ourselves to forget that God's will *is* God, that *Deus est suum velle*. When once we understand that this distinction can have no place within the being of God, it seems to make no real difference whether we say that God produces the creatures by an act of free will, or, with Spinoza,[1] that He produces them "by the law of *his own* nature", since in God, who is the absolute *prius*, there can be no distinction between *Deus* and *deitas*, such as there is in us, who are always *in fieri*, between the man and the humanity he is ever "putting on", but has never fully put on. In us it is true that there is a distinction between *natura* and *voluntas*, for the simple reason that we have to become true persons with a reasonable will by a gradual and difficult process; in God, who does not become but is, the distinction seems to have no place. My objection to Spinoza's formula would be based not on what it asserts but on what it denies. It asserts, truly as it seems to me, that God acts "by the law of his own nature", but falsely sets such action in God in opposition to "free action", as though the complete identity of *voluntas* and *natura* were not itself the very ideal of perfect freedom.[2]

Whatever may be thought of these remarks, it seems at least plain that anxiety to banish the last vestiges of egoistic self-concentration from the idea of God must have been at work all through the formative period of Christian doctrine in leading up to the final elaboration of the great theological dogma of the Trinity. Why, we may reasonably ask, was the Church so profoundly

---

[1] *Ethica*, i. 16 *ex necessitate divinae naturae infinita infinitis modis* (*hoc est omnia quae sub intellectum infinitum cadere possunt*) *sequi debent;* i. 17 *Deus ex solis suae naturae legibus, et a nemine coactus agit*. But I regard it as mere confusion to say that "all that can be known by an infinite intellect is actual", and, as Spinoza adds at i. 33, that "things could not have been produced by God in any order other than that in which they have been produced".

[2] On the other hand, I find myself in full agreement with the conclusion of St. Thomas (*Quaest. disp. de potentia* q. 3, art. 15), that things have proceeded from God *per arbitrium voluntatis*, and with the reason he gives for the conclusion, but dissatisfied with the rejection of the alternative *per necessitatem naturae*, unless it is understood that "nature" is here taken to be something other than "the nature of God". I desire more emphasis to be laid on what St. Thomas himself asserts, that *voluntas* and *natura, prout in Deo sunt*, are *secundum rem idem*.

dissatisfied with what looks, at first sight, the simple
and intelligible doctrine of an "economic Trinity", a
trinity of "parts" sustained by God as successively the
Creator, the Redeemer, and the Sanctifier? Why were
the thinkers who gave orthodox Christianity its pattern
driven, we might say in spite of themselves, to make
the distinctions of "persons" something more than a
distinction of simple temporal *rôles*, to make it "essential" and eternal? And what did they mean by introducing the supreme difficulty involved in the culminat-
ing assertion that, in spite of this essential and eternal
distinction, there is a perfect *circumincession* of the
three "persons", such that each eternally contains and
is contained in each? Was it from mere caprice that the
apparently simple and intelligible was persistently rejected for the admittedly mysterious and paradoxical?
The typical eighteenth-century answer to the question
is that of Gibbon,[1] that contradiction and nonsense
have an inherent attractiveness of their own for an
ambitious "priesthood" bent on enslaving the human
mind; the consecration of gibberish is the supreme
triumph of a caste set on domination. Such an explanation can only satisfy an age which thinks so unhistoric-
ally as to mistake the makers of a great theological
tradition for designing and clear-sighted hypocrites
not themselves imposed on by their own decisions, and
nothing can be clearer than the historical fact that if
the Christian divines who drew up the standard formula
were indeed canonising gibberish, they at least believed ardently themselves in their own gibberish.

---

[1] *Decline and Fall*, c. xxi. "an eager spirit of curiosity urged them to explore
the secrets of the abyss; and the pride of the professors, and of their disciples, was
satisfied with the science of words . . . the Christians proved a numerous and
disciplined society; and the jurisdiction of their laws and magistrates was strictly
exercised over the minds of the faithful . . . the authority of a theologian was
determined by his ecclesiastical rank", etc., etc.

The real source of their most paradoxical definitions seems to me to have been mainly ethical. It was felt that the doctrine of an "economic" Trinity does not make *giving* as fully and inwardly characteristic of the divine life as it requires to be made. With such a doctrine, the giving and self-emptying may, no doubt, be real, but it remains something external, an incident arising from the relation of the Creator to a creation which has somehow "gone off the lines". Room is left for the thought that if there had been no "fall", if the creature had not "gone wrong", there is no inherent reason why the divine activity should have been one of utter and complete self-bestowal, and thus the possibility is left open of regarding that activity, even in its relation to the creatures we know with all their faults and defects, as not penetrating the inmost depths of the divine life. The god of such a theology may, after all, have a core of self-centredness; he may be, like a magnified Stoic sage who, when all is said, at bottom "keeps himself to himself", in spite of his apparent preoccupation with the "common" good, always at heart frigid and unsympathetic, because the thing of highest worth in the scale of goods is just that in himself which he never shares.

This, I take it, is the reason which would not let Christian divines rest until they had declared that the "personal" distinctions are eternal, internal, and essential to the divine being itself. The thought was not merely that, as was generally assumed, creation had only happened some few thousand years before their own time, and that *some* activity must be found for the divine which has no beginning. There was, further, a consideration which would still remain, even if the world of creatures were held to be without beginning. The divine, infinite, and eternal can only com-

municate to the created and finite so much of itself
as the creature can receive without ceasing to be a
creature. Hence if the world of finite creatures is the
only object on which the divine activity of giving can
be exercised, the riches of the divine nature must
remain as good as uncommunicated; in its foundations
the divine life must be egoistic. To love with the love
that gives must be only a surface characteristic of the
life of God. And since such isolated selfhood is unethical, there is no room for the ethical in the inmost
life of God, when it is conceived thus. To make room
for the ethical we have to think of the divine, even
apart from its relation to the creatures, as having a
life in which there is, within the Godhead itself, an
object adequate to the complete and absolute reception
of an activity of giving which extends to the whole
fullness of the divine nature, so that there is nothing
which is not imparted and nothing which is not received. Because the mutual love in which each party
bestows himself freely and completely and is freely and
completely received is ethically the supreme spiritual
activity, the life of God is thought of as involving an
internal distinction as well as an internal unity, in
order that the whole activity of the divine life may be
one of perfect and unlimited self-bestowal.

> Est totus in Nato Pater,
> in Patre totus Filius;
> Natoque plenus et Patri
> inest utrique Spiritus.[1]

The motives which led to the foundation of the doctrine of *circumincession*, called by Gibbon the "darkest
corner of the whole theological abyss",[2] cease to be so
perplexing if we regard them as arising in the attempt

---

[1] *Paris Breviary*, Office Hymn for *Lauds* of Trinity Sunday.
[2] *Decline and Fall*, c. xxi. n. 59.

to say what God must be if we are to take the moral
relations of persons as the least hopelessly inadequate
clue to the inmost character of the real.

(5) These observations, however, are by the way.
A point of more immediate moment is that, in the
recognition that a moral Theism must take account
of the initiative of the divine, and so reckon seriously
with grace, free movement outward on the divine
side, as the ultimate source of human moral endeavour
itself, we are implicitly abandoning the deep-seated
prejudice that there is any real opposition in principle
between "philosophical" or "natural", and "historical"
or "revealed" theology, or between a philosophical and
an institutional religion. If it is true that our most
inchoate visions of an ideal good are themselves the
issue of actual imperfect contacts with a divine reality,
then the supposed opposition becomes only a distinction, and, I would add, a distinction which it is a
mistake to make too rigid. All our moral vision of
good may be truly said to be due, in the end, to revelation, self-communication on the part of the divine
reality, and it will become impossible to deny that the
value of what is revealed regularly depends on the
capacity of the recipient to whom the disclosure is
made. *Quidquid recipitur recipitur ad modum reci-
pientis.* And clearly, again, no metaphysician has
the right to pretend to determine *a priori* beforehand
what form the contacts with the divine from which
living inspiration to good arises must take. That we
must be content to learn from the event. Since they
are all contacts *in caligine*, we should be prepared to
find that their occasions are often such as might have
been thought unlikely and surprising; it is of the
nature of the case that they should, for example, occur
in the lives of the "babes and sucklings" and should

appear mere foolishness to the worldly-wise. It is no derogation from the genuinely supernatural character of these self-disclosures of God to men to say that the "rationalistic" attempt to judge of them otherwise than by the effects, where they are accepted, on a man's life, is of a piece with the similar less often advanced pretence to say what *must* be the quarter in which "original genius" of any kind should be looked for, or in what strange and unexpected ways it may disclose its presence.

The true distinction will not be between a certain type of religious life or theological belief which is complete in itself and justifiable by "human reason", and another which is wholly non-rational or super-rational and has simply to be accepted on authority of some kind. The true distinction will be rather between that in the divine which is generally disclosed to men with a very commonplace level of moral insight and practice and that which is only directly disclosed to special recipients, why selected we cannot always say, and justifies itself, in the end, by its practical effect in the inward reconstitution of the lives of those who accept the disclosure in good faith. There is no philosophical justification for confining the channels by which the divine may disclose itself, or the persons to whom the disclosure may be made, within limits marked out antecedently by a human theorist.

We may not, for instance, assume that whereas the vision of the divine in Hebrew prophecy must have come simply by "revelation", the insight of the Hellenic moralists must everywhere have a less exalted source; or, again, that though a man cannot afford to lose the religious guidance and support of the lessons of great poets and philosophers, he can afford to dispense, and it will make for his spiritual progress to dispense, with membership of a society of worshippers with a definite tradition of doctrine and worship. We may not assume at this stage of our discussion that the highest attainments in the spiritual life can only be mediated through membership of some specific community and participation in its distinctive rites, but neither have we any right to deny the truth of this assumption on general and *a priori* grounds. It may be that in every religion, as it actually exists in the life of the community which lives by it, there are apprehensions involving real and direct contacts with the divine, and that thus, in the end, every religion contains its basis of "revealed" truth. Yet it does not follow that the quality of all the revelations is the same, nor even that among the revelations of the divine to be found in the history of mankind there may not be some one which corrects and integrates the partial lights of the rest, while not itself calling for correction by any "higher synthesis". In that case there will be, as Christians claim that there is, an historical religion which is, in principle, final and absolute, and not a mere best among many good, or a best as yet accessible. But these are problems which will concern us further in the sequel.

So it may perfectly well be that direct access to the divine has been provided for men in countless ways. Perhaps the "one true light" may at times be caught in the "tavern", though the poet from whom the sentiment comes[1] has generally been regarded as a light-hearted mocker by those who know him at first-hand. And no doubt it is better to catch a distant glimpse of the light in the tavern than to miss it altogether in the temple. Yet it may also be that though many who worship in the

[1] For the original verses see Whinfield's text of Omar Khayyám, quatrain 262. ("To speak in secret with Thee in taverns is better than to offer prayer without Thee in the *mihráb*. 'Tis in Thy will, O Thou, beginning and end at once of Thy creatures, to burn me, and in Thy will to cherish me.")

temple are blind to the light, he who refuses to cross its threshold will never enjoy the fullest illuminations. That the Highest should communicate spiritual life to us through the institutions of a particular society with their physical instruments may be strange, but no stranger than that poetical and musical genius of the first order should make its appearance in the seemingly untoward circumstances among which it often displays itself. Could we have been told at the beginning of the last century that the world was on the eve of receiving the gift of a supreme poet with a direct vision of beauty which would inspire and support the poetic literature of a hundred years and still remain unexhausted, probably the last place where we should have been predisposed to look for the man who was to make us see beauty again would have been the quarter from which John Keats actually emerged. We might not have been clear about the fact even in 1821, when the poet's own short life had come to an end; we know now, because we see the facts in the light of the influence he has exercised, and thus know, for example, how all that is best in Tennyson comes out of Keats.

So it is with the institutions of a living religion. What they are we can only judge by the quality of the life they bring into the world. Antecedently we might be disposed to say, for example, that the ritual breaking and pouring and sharing of bread and wine would be very unlikely to mediate, to those who participate in it with simple and humble hearts, a quality of life they could win in no other fashion. But whether it is so or no cannot be decided by consideration of antecedent probabilities; the appeal has to be made to the effects revealed in the lives of the worshippers. We cannot come to the philosophic study of religion or of theology, the theory of the life of which religion is the practice, with too open minds. It would be very unsafe to infer that what claims to be a special self-disclosure of the divine must be what it claims to be, *because* it is surprising. But it would probably be a good rule to say that God does "move in a mysterious way", and that the most unlikely thing of all would be that a true religion should contain *no* surprises. But this, again, is a thought we shall need to develop further.

VII

THE DESTINY OF THE INDIVIDUAL

Ψυχῆς πείρατα οὐκ ἂν ἐξεύροιο πᾶσαν ἐπιπορευόμενος ὁδόν.—HERACLITUS.

Videmus nunc per speculum in aenigmate.

THE question we are now to consider has only too often been treated as the central and supreme issue in all religion. There is a type of mind—it is exemplified in men like F. W. H. Myers, or, at a much higher intellectual level, Dr. McTaggart—which apparently feels no imperious necessity to worship, but is anxiously beset by the old question, "If a man die, shall he live again?" Such minds have no difficulty in acquiescing in a world without God, but are deeply revolted by the suggestion that their own personality may not be able to survive the shock of bodily dissolution. With them proof of the immortality of the soul, drawn either from general metaphysical postulates or from alleged empirical evidence of the continued activity of the dead, tends to replace the whole of theology. In the many hundred pages of Myers' *Human Personality* there are, so far as I recollect, very few references to the existence of God. Dr. McTaggart has even professed to produce proof that theistic belief is almost certainly false, and quite certainly superfluous.[1]

I suppose I need hardly remind you that this attitude of mind is diametrically opposed to that characteristic of the Christian religion, and almost as completely

[1] *Some Dogmas of Religion*, cc. vi.-viii.; *Nature of Existence*, ii. c. 43.

opposed to the great Platonic tradition in metaphysics. In both Christianity and Platonism, it is the thought of God as at once the source of being and the goal of moral endeavour, the A and Ω, that is central; the high prospects both hold out to the individual man who "perseveres to the end", or, as the *Phaedrus* has it, chooses the "philosopher's" life thrice in succession,[1] are, in the end, based on their conception of the God into whose likeness it is man's vocation to grow; with both it is *deiformity*, not mere endless continuance, which is held out to man as the prize of his calling. If I have delayed discussion of human immortality so long, my reason is that I find myself wholly at one with the Christian and Platonic tradition on this issue. Apart from an adequate doctrine of God, it is, as I believe, impossible to find any secure foundation for a doctrine of human immortality, or any ground for thinking the prospect of such immortality attractive. When we consider human personality as we are actually acquainted with it in ourselves, apart from convictions about the vocation of man based on the identification of the *summum bonum* with the living and eternal God, we are treating personality, after all, in a purely naturalistic fashion, and, as far as I can see, a merely naturalistic perseverance in existence, even if it could be made probable, might well be, like the deathlessness of a Struldbrug, the supreme curse. On that point I may be allowed to refer once for all to the imaginative development of the theme in the *intermezzo* intercalated between the eighth and ninth chapters of Jean Paul Richter's *Siebenkäs*, so admirably rendered by Carlyle.[2]

Thus I do not propose to concern myself here with either of two very familiar types of argument for human

---

[1] *Phaedrus*, 249 A.
[2] At the end of the 1830 *Essay* on Jean Paul Friedrich Richter.

immortality, the metaphysical argument from the alleged character of the soul as a simple substance, or a primitive fountain of internally originated motion, and what we may, without prejudice, call the empirical argument from the real or alleged facts of necromancy. For neither line of argument, be its cogency what it may, has any real connection with the subject of all our reflections, the light thrown on man's nature and status, and consequently on his destiny, by study of his specifically moral being. As to the metaphysical argument, it is enough to say, what would probably be conceded by almost all careful metaphysicians, that, even if we grant, as we could hardly do without a great deal of preliminary discussion, that the soul is a simple substance, or a primitive fount of movement, it does not necessarily follow that it is imperishable. All that necessarily follows is that if the soul vanishes from the sum total of the actual, its disappearance must be strictly instantaneous; it must perish, if it perishes at all, by annihilation or inanition, not by dissolution. This is, in fact, all that Leibniz, for example, ventures to assert of his spiritual simple atoms or monads. When we further seek to complete the argument by proving that annihilation may be excluded from the range of possibilities, either we have to fall back, as Leibniz does, on the appeal to the known goodness of God, or we fall into the materialistic fallacy of arguing that the self is a bit of "mind-stuff" and that the annihilation of "stuff" is inconceivable. Reasoning of this kind may have seemed plausible in days when the conservation of mass could be taken as a first principle too axiomatic to call for discussion; in our own time, when distinguished physicists are declaring that the doctrine of conservation of mass is only a deduction from the conservation of energy—itself no necessity of thought—and is only true under

restrictions,[1] and distinguished astronomers can propose to employ the notion of a progressive annihilation
of mass as a key to the life-history of the stars,[2] we
clearly cannot repose much confidence in the extension
to "mind-stuff" of an apparently antiquated physical
prepossession. Even if we could, it is plain that survival
as a "bare monad", or a bit of "mind-stuff", or a mere
initiator of movements, is not a destiny which can inspire a man with hope or stir him to noble living. The
hope of immortality has been morally inspiring only
when immortality has been understood to mean persistence after physical dissolution of the moral and intellectual character which has been slowly built up in the
course of this present life through struggle and sacrifice,
and the prospect of building further on the same foundations elsewhere. What we want is to "see of the travail of our souls and be satisfied", and this is just what
no *mere* doctrine of the "natural immortality" of the
soul can ensure. Even Leibniz ends by resting his hopes
not on anything he believes himself to have proved
about the nature of a simple monad, but on the unde-
monstrated conviction that a good God will not allow
monads which have attained the status of moral and
intelligent persons to fall back to the level of "mere"
monads.[3]

The same considerations apply equally to those
alleged facts of necromancy on which the "spiritists" of
all ages are accustomed to rely. It must be doubtful
whether, in any case, when we have excluded everything which can be most probably accounted for by
conscious or unconscious fraud, or by obscure, and as

[1] Eddington, *Space, Time and Gravitation*, pp. 141-2; *Nature of Physical World*, 50, 59.
[2] J. H. Jeans in *Evolution in the Light of Modern Knowledge*, p. 14; *Universe Around Us*, 182-90.
[3] See Leibniz, *New System*, 5, 8; *Principles of Nature and Grace*, 14, 15.

yet ill-understood, communication between embodied
minds, very much of the supposed facts is left. If anything is left, I still must agree with critics like Bradley
that there is always a plurality of alternative hypotheses
open to us. To prove, if it can be proved, that I am in
communication with an intelligence other than that of
an incarnate human person, is by no means to prove
that I am communing with the "mighty dead". The
traditional view of the Church that all such communications, if genuine, come from "the devil" may perhaps
be over-hasty, but is certainly incapable of refutation,
if the name "devil" is used widely enough to cover
possible low-grade personalities which are merely silly
or mischievous, as well as those which are actually
morally wicked. And even if we could exclude, as we
cannot, the possibility that all genuine communications from "the other side" come either from freakish
imps or from wicked beings laying cunning plots for
our moral ruin, the prospects held out to us by spiritists
are not of a kind to rejoice a true man. Myers may be
right, though it is hard not to doubt his complete satisfaction on the point,[1] when he says that mediumistic
communications show no trace of actual moral de-
pravity; but one has only to read the journals which
profess to record these messages to be satisfied that,
at all events, they display a distressingly low level of
intelligence. They are mostly a medley of sentimental
gush and twaddling sermonising. If their authors are,
as it is often alleged that they are, the great moral and
intellectual heroes of our past, it would seem that the
brightest prospect the unseen world has to offer is that
of a gradual declension of mankind into an undying

---

[1] F. H. Bradley expressed himself to me, at the time of publication of Myers'
book, as highly indignant at the omission from the long discussion of "possession"
of any reference to its commonest form, "diabolic possession".

society of trivial sentimental bores. Some of us might prefer Dante's Hell, where the damned at least retain something of human dignity. One would rather be Farinata on his couch of fire than Shakespeare complacently dictating drivel. Fortunately my subject relieves me from any necessity of prosecuting this argument further. What we are now concerned with is the light thrown on man's destiny by his moral being, and we may fairly say at the outset that if our moral being indicates anything about our inmost nature and its destiny, we may be confident that that destiny is not to persist either as "bare monads", or as talkers of wordy twaddle of which we should have been ashamed even when "the eternal substance" of our souls was half subdued to its prison in the "sinful flesh".

The limits we have thus prescribed to ourselves, then, demand that we confine our attention strictly to an examination of what is known as the "moral" argument for immortality. And here we find ourselves confronted at the outset by the assertion of a formidable body of contemporary students of philosophy that a "moral" argument must be worthless, from the very nature of the case. It will be instructive to consider the reasons given for this contention by so eminent a philosopher as Dr. McTaggart. Since McTaggart was in fact eager to establish a doctrine of immortality, and made immortality a leading feature in his interpretation of the world, we may be sure that rejection of the "moral" argument does not, in his case, arise from any secret bias against the conclusion it has been used to prove. He would presumably have been glad to reinforce a belief which he ardently cherished by any legitimate argument in its favour. If *he* denies the validity of the "moral proof", the denial must be based on sincere conviction of its worthlessness, and such a conviction on the part of an exceptionally subtle and acute dialectician is reasonably felt to constitute at least a strong antecedent presumption against the line of reasoning so condemned, and must therefore be faced seriously.

Dr. McTaggart has explained fully what he means by a moral argument and why he thinks all moral arguments about human destiny worthless.[1] By a moral argument he says he means an argument by which we infer that some state of things must be real on the ground that it is highly desirable that it should be real. Thus the moral argument for immortality is taken to be to the following effect: "It is so good that we should be immortal that it must be true that we are immortal"; or, "The extinction of human personality at death is so great an evil that we cannot conceive it to occur". McTaggart's comment is, briefly, that so much that would be good is unreal, and so much that is bad is real, that we have no right to say that anything whatever is so bad that it cannot be real, or so good that it must be real.[2] In a world where there is so much evil as there undeniably is in the actual world, nothing is "too bad to be true". Now, undeniably this looks, at first sight, a telling, perhaps an overwhelmingly convincing criticism, though we may note that it is not specially novel, since it is merely the moral of Voltaire's *Candide* compressed into an epigram. But on reflection I believe we shall find that the reasoning of Voltaire and McTaggart is very far from being as convincing as it looks. It is to be observed that McTaggart's

---

[1] *Some Dogmas of Religion*, pp. 53 ff.

[2] It is only fair to say that McTaggart only denies our right to assume as a premiss the proposition that "reality is not hopelessly evil". He holds that it can be demonstrated, or at least proved sufficiently, that the good in the universe is enormously preponderant over the evil. But we must first prove human immortality, among other things, before we can advance to this conclusion. This, however, is enough to invalidate all "moral" arguments for immortality itself.

quarrel is not with the expressed premiss of the reasoning. He at least takes no exception to the statement
that it would be very good that human persons should
be immortal and very bad that they should not. What
he objects to is not the explicit premiss of fact, but the
implied premiss of principle, that what is supremely
good *must* also be fact. For my own part I should have
thought that the proposition thus allowed to pass without examination is itself questionable, unless it is safe-
guarded by a good many restrictions. I do not feel at
all sure that unending existence might not be a very
bad thing. Huxley, we remember, once wrote that he
found the thought of hell less depressing than that of
annihilation. But I believe that if we asked ourselves
the question whether we should prefer for one whom
we loved and respected endless existence in the ice of
Dante's *Giudecca*, or in the sufferings of cancer, or in a
state of idiocy, to cessation of all being, there can be
no doubt what our answer would be. We should welcome, or at least accept, the cessation of our friend's
existence as a "blessed relief" from cruel suffering;
we would rather think that a teacher whose character
and intellect we had reverenced was now nothing at
all than that he was still surviving as a "driveller and
a show".[1] A great thinker, now himself deceased, once
remarked to me that his first words on hearing of the
death of his mother, a lady of brilliant parts whose
mind had been enfeebled in her last years, were "Thank
God!"

It is surely still more certain that most of us would
prefer that a beloved son or sister should be clean cut
off out of the land of the living than that he or she
should continue to live and to enjoy a life of degraded

---

[1] Or undergoing the doom Dante inflicts on the man who had taught him *come
l'uom s'etterna*.

"animalism", or sordid dishonesty. A decent man, with
no real belief in any future life, would probably much
rather see a much-loved daughter "in her grave", as
our proverbial phrase is, than see her flaunting it as
the most famous and flattered harlot of London, or
New York, or Paris. It may be replied that *in a man's
own case*, when it comes to the point, experience shows
that the love of life is so strong that he will usually
consent to live even with deep dishonour, if he cannot
live with honour. And I own that I have no confidence
that sudden "fear of the dark" might not make a
recreant of me in this matter. But for the purposes of
our present argument, what we are concerned with is
not the *strength* of unreasoned cravings and instincts,
but the character of a reflective judgement of good,
and for that very reason, it is our judgement on cases
other than our own, where the mere instinct of self-
preservation does not come into the account, that I
take to be decisive. It is plain, I think, from these cases
that we do not seriously judge immortality to be good at
all, unless we have some guarantee of its quality. And
if Huxley had said that he would rather think of, say,
an infant son or daughter who had died unbaptized
as burning with the *massa perditionis*, than as having
ceased to be, frankly I should refuse to believe him.

Next, as to McTaggart's argument that in a world
where there is so much evil we have no right to say
that anything whatever is "too bad to be true". To
my mind, this argument is vitiated by a transparent
fallacy, introduced by the words "so much". It is
assumed that we know how bad the various evils to
which the argument appeals, are. In other words,
it is assumed that we already know their final upshot.
But this is never the case, unless, indeed, we admit
"faith", as McTaggart does not, as a source of know-

ledge. To take an obvious example. Few things in the actual world would be judged more manifestly and gravely bad than acute, prolonged, and sordid suffering, wholly undeserved and productive, so far as can be seen, of nothing good for the sufferer or for anyone else. But since we do not "see to the end" in any case, we cannot assert *as a fact of experience* that the upshot of the worst the world has to show in this kind may not be, as on the Christian theory it will be, the production of an overwhelming good, for the virtuous sufferer and for others, which perhaps could not have been produced in any other way. It is at least *possible* that the world's worst victims may yet live to smile at the worst that has befallen them, or even to feel that they would not on any account have been without it. Even within the limits of our own vision of life, it often enough happens that a man comes in the end to give thanks for what had seemed his most intolerable afflictions as the best things his life has brought him. And so I should reply to McTaggart that until we know whether what we see of a man's life, between cradle and grave, is all there is to see, we are not in a position to say how bad the things the argument pronounces very bad are. None of them are incompatible with the belief, which was, in fact, McTaggart's own, that reality is overwhelmingly good. But *if* what we see of man's life is all there is to see, that is, if there is nothing beyond the grave, then, and only then, I confess, it becomes undeniable that history is a scene where dubious good is achieved at the cost of intolerable evil. I submit, then, that we are not entitled to argue from the actuality of evils which, for anything we *know*, may flower in overwhelming good to the possibility that the actual is so constituted that evil cannot be overcome by good, and that

McTaggart's attack on the "moral argument" is therefore unsound in principle. It only seems conclusive to him because he has *ab initio* excluded God from his metaphysical scheme.[1]

In fact what lies at the bottom of McTaggart's distrust is simply the unexamined assumption that value and fact are two wholly disconnected realms.[2] If it were so, obviously no proposition about value or goodness, however true, could be a relevant premiss in any argument, demonstrative or probable, which concludes to fact. We have already tried to satisfy ourselves that this divorce of value from actuality is itself a mere product of unreflecting prejudice and that the very point of all genuine religion is that it expressly asserts, as morality tacitly implies, the conjunction of the two. To have a religion, or at least to have an ethical religion, means to believe seriously that though many things may be too bad to be true, nothing is too good to be true. If we sometimes think otherwise, it is because the things we pronounce too good to be true are not really as good as we take them to be. Thus a man offers us some panacea for the body politic and promises that, by adopting it, we shall attain the New Jerusalem within a generation. We may *say* that such promises are "too good to be true", but it does not take much reflection to see that they are really not good enough. It would not be good, in the actual state of our civilisation, that society should be deprived of the incentives to industry,

---

[1] It might be said that McTaggart virtually admits what is here contended for, when, in the passage referred to, he confines his objection to the introduction of a premiss affirming the goodness of "reality" in the initial stage of the argument. I should reply that it is my conviction that unless the proposition is admitted in the initial stage, it will not be possible to establish it at all. I cannot believe that the reasoning of the second volume of the *Nature of Existence* would have appeared probative to its author had he not all along subconsciously made the very "venture of faith" which he wishes to discredit.

[2] And the assumption is one which McTaggart's own philosophy is a continuous attempt to disprove.

patience, self-denial, and brotherly help which are provided by the inevitable imperfections of our social system. A moralist, if he could be offered the opportunity of, *e.g.*, abolishing all bodily disease at a stroke, might reasonably hesitate to avail himself of it. He might feel the gravest doubt whether radiant physical health for the whole community, not accompanied by a miraculous moral rebirth, would not tend to lower its moral status, by depriving it of graces of character far more exalted in the scale of goods than physical well-being.

And, after all, to say that nothing is too good to be true is only to show as much faith in the divine nature as good men habitually show in human nature. It may be doubted whether there are not some things too bad to be credible of any man, even of the worst, but no one who has within him the faith in human nature without which life would not be worth living would admit that there are deeds which are, in the strict sense of the words, too good to be achieved, calls of duty too arduous ever to be obeyed. At the most, a man who has the faith in the possibilities of his kind necessary to save him from an immoral cynicism would only say of the great moral responsibilities that compliance with duty is hard and is only achieved by the few heroic souls, and by them only when they do not confide solely in their own strength. Also it is a recurrent and a joyful surprise to find that when the occasions for the supreme heroisms arise, so many whom most observers would have judged as mere "average" men, or something worse, rise to the occasion. We as a nation are not likely soon to forget the revelations of unsuspected capacity for heroism in the ordinary person which came to us during the War of 1914–1918, and I cannot doubt that every nation engaged in that struggle on either side has much the same story to tell. Naturally the disclosure was a double-edged one. We also learned with shame and distress that very horrible and bestial things could be done by men who normally conduct themselves in more ordinary situations without gross criminality.[1] We learned, too, that the temptation to shirk burdens and dangers, or even to make one's private market out of the public necessity, could prove too powerful for the integrity of some whom we should have thought above suspicion. Probably we all learned to be at least a little more uncomfortable about our own moral standing. Yet, on the whole, the revelation of good was more impressive than the disclosure of evil. The worst misdeeds established against offenders were all of a type with which we had been made acquainted by the lives of our "criminal classes". More men fell low than perhaps we had expected, but I doubt if any fell lower than we already knew men could fall; multitudes rose higher than we had dared to hope they had it in them to rise. To doubt whether something may not be too good to be true is really to doubt whether the things which are possible with men may not be impossible with God.

We may, then, dismiss this initial objection to the principle implied in the "moral" argument for human immortality. The real question we have to consider is whether the moral being of man in fact *is* such that it affords indications, or at any rate a presumption, that he is destined to survive the shock men call death, and, if so, what further light ethics can throw on the quality

---

[1] I am not thinking so much of bad conduct on the part of our opponents— though I am perfectly convinced by the evidence for *some* of this—as of bad conduct on our own side, such as the now admitted circulation, for purposes of propaganda, of discreditable stories against the enemy which were apparently not believed by the persons responsible for their circulation.

of human life beyond the grave. We must be prepared to find that any light we can discover reveals very little and leaves natural curiosity far from satisfied. It may illumine no more than the next few steps of the road to be trodden through life. Yet this would be indirectly a considerable gain for theory as well as for practice. If there should be a real further "revelation", or self-disclosure of the divine, among the religious faiths of mankind, agreement or discrepancy with what we can learn from ethics may well be the touchstone by which we can safely distinguish the genuine light of revelation from specious but misleading counterfeits.

To what, then, speaking generally and roughly, does the moral evidence for human survival of death amount? There are two preliminary considerations on which it seems desirable to make some remarks. If we take the expression "moral argument" in the widest sense, it may fairly be held to cover two familiar lines of thought on which the defenders of the hope of immortality have laid weight, the argument from the *consensus gentium* and also the direct appeal to the real or alleged universality of the wish for continuance as evidence of its own fulfilment. Neither line of argument can be regarded as manifestly conclusive, yet we may fairly doubt whether either deserves the unqualified rejection both often receive from philosophers in our own day.

(1) First, then, as to the argument from the presumed *wish* for immortality to its reality. It is interesting to note how powerfully this reasoning often appeals to minds we might have supposed to be impervious to the rather different type of argument from *consensus*. The case of Shelley affords an apt illustration. No one could well be less inclined to accept a widespread belief on the ground that it is widespread and therefore, presumably, natural than Shelley. Those who knew him

intimately have recorded that it was a favourite saying with him that "everyone's saying a thing is true
does not make it true", and, apart from this testimony,
his works bear abundant witness to a deeply rooted
suspiciousness of all widely received traditions which
amounted to something like a positive disease. From
the moralist's special point of view—and it was a point
of view from which the poet himself always professed to
desire to be appreciated—it is Shelley's most obvious
intellectual defect that he never seems to have been able
to understand the value of a moral tradition, supported
by the practice of generations of civilised men and the
approval of the most eminent reflective thinkers, as witness to its own fundamental soundness. The very fact
that a practice or a belief had been a permanent factor
in shaping the civilised society of Western Europe actually seems to have operated with him as a reason for
suspecting its validity. Theoretically, indeed, he maintained only that a belief may be false, or a custom baneful, in spite of its apparently universal acceptance; but
in practice, when he came to deal with specific beliefs
or customs, he habitually tended to assume that what
all men accept must be false or pernicious just *because*
everyone accepts it.

A typical example of this eccentricity is his notorious
and singular craze, revealed no less by his private correspondence than by his poems, for the glorification of
incest. The reasons which have led civilised societies to
condemn the practice so vehemently and unequivocally,
or at least some of these reasons, are so obvious and so
weighty that one can hardly suppose them to have been
ignored by Shelley or any other man not an imbecile.
In this matter there seems to be no ground whatever for
the poet's challenge to the universal tradition of civilised Europe, beyond a prejudice against it based on its

very universality. From a mind so constituted we might have expected a similar acrimonious rejection of the hope of immortality, just on the plea that so widely diffused a hope must be one of the illusions of the "tribe". Yet we find Shelley, in fact, in the notes to *Hellas*, manifestly cherishing the hope in the very act of declaring it to have no foundation beyond a wish. "Let it be not supposed", he says, "that I mean to dogmatise upon a subject concerning which all men are equally ignorant. That there is a true solution of the riddle, and that in our present state that solution is not attainable by us, are propositions which may be regarded as equally certain : meanwhile as it is the province of the poet to attach himself to those ideas which exalt and ennoble humanity, let him be permitted to have conjectured the condition of that futurity to which we are all impelled by an inextinguishable thirst for immortality. Until better arguments can be produced than sophisms which disgrace the cause, this desire itself must remain the strongest and the only presumption that eternity is the inheritance of every thinking being." Even apart from the light thrown on such a passage by recorded utterances of the poet in conversation, which cannot all be ascribed to the invention of his associates, it is manifest that the words are written in good faith by one who himself shares in the desire of which he speaks as a universal and inextinguishable thirst, and that when the desire is said to be the "strongest" presumption of its own fulfilment—a remark logically superfluous when it is also declared to be the only such presumption—there is no ironical *arrière-pensée*. The poet seriously means to say that this "only presumption" really is a strong one.

Now it might plausibly be urged on the other side that the poet's statement of the alleged facts is an exaggeration. Appeal might be made to the apparent acquiescence of millions of the human race in religions which are said to contemplate the extinction of human personality as the crown of felicity, to the notorious absence of all reference to the hope of the world to come from all but the very latest parts of the Old Testament scriptures, and other similar facts, in support of the view that what Shelley represents as a deep-seated aspiration of universal humanity only exists, to any marked degree, within the limits of a special civilisation —our own—which owes its moral tradition to the specific influences of Greek philosophy and Christian theology. And it might further be contended, even more forcibly to-day than a century ago, that the "desire" is not universal even within this particular civilisation itself. We must all know among our own personal acquaintance, intelligent and virtuous persons who appear to be quite indifferent to the prospect of a life to come, and possibly some who even seem to regard any such prospect with actual repugnance.[1]

I own that personally I am not as deeply impressed as some moralists seem to be, by this alleged counter-evidence. The evidence supposed to be afforded by the wide prevalence of a religion like Buddhism, for example, may well strike the layman in these studies as at least ambiguous. The experts seem at any rate to be far from certain as to the real meaning of the Founder's teaching, and it is significant that, in its development into a widespread religion, Buddhism has no more been able than Judaism to retain an attitude of negation or mere agnosticism towards human destiny after death. Similarly, we may set against arguments drawn from the theoretical attitude of the agnostics of our own civilisation a fair counter-argument founded on the

[1] Cf. McTaggart, *Some Dogmas of Religion*, p. 57.

curious inability of these very agnostics to be fully consistent with themselves. No one, I take it, has ever denied that Spinoza's metaphysic expressly excludes the admission of any sort of persistence of the individual person after the physical dissolution of his body. Yet it is quite impossible to read the famous series of propositions in the *Vth Part* of the *Ethics* which deal with the "eternity of the mind", without perceiving that the writer of these propositions has a personal faith which is his supreme inspiration in life and is quite unjustified by his professed philosophy.[1] Spinoza's "way of life" is based on the conviction that the wise and virtuous "mind" has a prerogative of "eternity", not shared by any other "finite mode"; if Spinoza's metaphysic is sound, no "mode" can be eternal except in a sense in which all are eternal alike. No one, again, will credit Renan with anything but a strict agnosticism in theory; yet it is impossible, I should conceive, to mistake the tone of the dedication of the *Vie de Jésus* to the author's dead sister for that of empty decorative rhetoric.

Thus, when all legitimate deductions have been made, I confess that the "inextinguishable thirst" for immortality of which Shelley speaks does, to my mind, remain a very impressive fact. It is impressive specially for two reasons: (*a*) it seems to be felt as acutely by men who have drunk deep of a long inheritance of science and philosophy as by men who have never learned to think or question, and is therefore emphatically not one of those aspirations which are automatically destroyed by mere progress in intellectual development; (*b*) and, again, even those who profess themselves, no doubt with sincerity, to be most emancipated from reverence for the traditions of a human past never seem able, in

[1] Cf. C. D. Broad, *Five Types of Ethical Theory*, pp. 15-16, and T. Whittaker, *Transcendence in Spinoza* in MIND, N.S. 151.

their moments of high emotion, when they have forgotten the demands of an official *credo*, and are most near to saying what they really in their hearts believe, to escape the use of language which either means nothing or means that this aspiration is alive in the speaker. On the whole, then, I think we must accept it as fact that the aspiration towards the "unseen" future is *allgemein-menschlich*, and "natural", in the sense in which abhorrence of cannibalism or incest is natural. Individual exceptions, or even exceptions extending to the whole of special minor social groups, prove no more in the first case than they prove in the other two—viz., that there are abnormal individuals, and that special conditions may lead to the prevalence of an abnormality over a whole restricted social group.

Still, even when so much is granted, we must expect to be met by the objection that a wish may be universal in the fullest sense in which we can call any characteristic of human life universal, and yet may be doomed to mere disappointment. That everyone wishes for a certain thing is no proof that anyone will ever get it. A man might, as Aristotle remarks, wish never to die at all, and, as I suppose every priest knows, all of us in certain moods fiercely resent the necessity of dying as an "infamy of our nature". Yet most of us, like Aristotle, are agreed to regard this craving as a wish for the merely impossible.

There is, indeed, a counter-assertion of which too much, perhaps, has been made. It has been urged that a *universal* wish must be regarded as the expression of a "natural instinct", and that it is not "nature's" way to provide creatures with instincts which are destined to have no fulfilment. Stated thus baldly, the reasoning does not appear very impressive. Without going into the very difficult questions of the proper definition of "instinct" and the worth of "instinct" as explanatory hypotheses in biology and psychology—topics on which much that is impressive was said in this place by my eminent precursor, Dr. Lloyd Morgan[1]—we may certainly retort, with truth, that the "instincts" of which the argument speaks are very often not fulfilled in the most obvious sense of the word fulfilment. Thus the attraction of male and female animal to one another is "instinctive" in the sense of the argument now under consideration, and the fulfilment of the "instinctive" craving would be said to be found in the propagation of a new generation of the species. But the "instinct" itself, as felt by the pairing male and female, is not an instinct to procreate, but an instinct to *mate*, and when it gives rise to a conscious wish, the wish is not primarily a wish for the offspring but a wish for the partner. We see this clearly enough in our own human life. There are those who unite because they are lovers, and those who unite because they want sons or daughters; in most cases, perhaps, the two motives are conjoined, but commonly with a predominance of the one or the other. But the most ardent lovers are not usually those who are most desirous of progeny, nor the persons in whom the passion for paternity or maternity is consciously strongest the typical lovers of "romance". (It has been said of Burns, and, I conceive, with truth, that he had an exceptionally strong and sincere passion for paternity. But though the orators of our Burns clubs might resent the remark, it is equally true that Burns had no passion for "love", and that we cannot understand either his life or his poetry unless we recognise that fact.) In literature, we note, the great lovers are mostly sterile; the typical fathers and mothers are of quite a different spiritual

---

[1] See *Life, Mind and Spirit*, lect. v.

pattern from the Lancelots and Tristrams and Helens and Didos. And in life itself, it is a source of tragedy when the man or woman with the temperament of the lifelong lover discovers that maternity or paternity is the supreme passion of the "other party". The now too notorious "Oedipus-complex" may probably be no more than a singularly ugly piece of pseudo-scientific mythology, but its inverse is a familiar fact of life. We need no myth to explain why fathers are often secretly jealous of their sons, or mothers of their daughters.

Thus it is readily intelligible why a sceptic should seek to disable the argument from the supposed "instinct" for immortality by the retort that the "inextinguishable thirst" is really no more than an expression of the primitive "instinct of self-preservation", and that it gets all the fulfilment it ever need get in the part this "instinct" plays in securing and prolonging our life here in the body. The real question, as I think, is untouched by these superficial logomachies. We have to ask whether it is clear that the widespread belief in the world to come could so much as be causally accounted for on these lines as the product of a wish or "instinct" of any kind whatsoever. And this brings me to a more general consideration of the *consensus gentium* and its presumable foundation. If the "naturalistic" "explanation" of the *consensus* breaks down even as an account of its origin, *a fortiori* it can do nothing to discredit its value.

(2) Now there are certain features about this widespread belief, testified to by the general prevalence among mankind of theories about the land of the dead and practices intended to facilitate the reception of the dying in that region, or to secure their position there, which it seems hard to reconcile with any form of the "naturalistic" theory of the sources of these

beliefs and practices. I speak, of course, as a layman in these matters, and mean to be referring only to certain outstanding features of what appears to be historically the belief and practice of the human race in the earliest stage of its existence as yet known to us with any certainty. But I believe it may fairly be said, without much danger of contradiction from those who know, that, in the view of the world which we loosely call "primitive", because we find it already widely diffused among peoples whose civilisation is the least developed known to us, and because we cannot say at present what views, if any, may have preceded it, the survival of the mysterious thing called the soul is universally taken as a matter of course, and it is also taken as a matter of course that this continued existence is a continuance of the same kind of life we know on our side of death. The chief remains a chief, the hunter a hunter, the common man a common man, the slave, where slavery has found a footing, a slave "yonder", as he was "here". Future existence is not, as we who have inherited the traditions of philosophy and Christianity are prone to assume that it must be, *better* existence, or existence "at a higher level"; still less is the world to come a scene in which the "wrongs" of this world are "put right". At most existence in that world is the old familiar kind of existence with some obstacles and disappointments removed; the hunter roams through "happy hunting-grounds", where the game is more plentiful and the hunter's aim more regularly successful.

Often enough the whole colouring of the picture is a gloomy one, as in Homer and the most ancient parts of the Old Testament, where the condition which awaits the dead is a mere joyless shadowy prolongation of their occupations here, and to "go

down to the pit" is the inevitable worst which comes
to us all in our time. It may be urged, with a great
deal of force, that these Homeric and Hebraic conceptions reproduce the ideas of an age in which belief
is fading, and that the Greek ghost, as we can still
see from Attic tragedy, and presumably the Israelite
ghost too, had once been thought of as a much more
real being. But so far as our evidence goes, it is much
clearer that these ghosts were thought of as formidable to the survivors than that they were ever supposed to have themselves an enjoyable or enviable
lot. And when we further consider what kind of life
men must have led, in the distant prehistoric times,
when they were mainly engrossed in a grim struggle
for bare existence against a hostile, or at least a
"stepmotherly", nature, I find it very hard to believe
that the *wish* for the prolongation can have been an
adequate cause of the general belief in the fact.

It might, no doubt, be replied that the word "wish"
is out of place; we are not dealing with a conscious
wish, but with a primary impulse more fundamental and
persistent than any wish, the native fierce resistance of
the living body to its own dissolution, in virtue of which
a drowning or choking man will still make a furious
physical fight for life, even though it may have been
deliberate preference of death to life which brought
him into the water or the gas-poisoned atmosphere.
Yet I own to a still unremoved difficulty in understanding how a supposedly unconscious organic impulse
could of itself—as the explanation implies—give occasion to a widely diffused conscious aspiration which, in
its turn, coloured, and still colours, men's whole attitude
to their world, in view of the conditions which must have
made life anything but enjoyable to the great majority
of men in the earliest age of the conflict with a niggardly

"Nature". Indeed, it might be *à propos* to reflect that, according at least to one version of the curious "psychology of the unconscious" now fashionable, the supreme "unconscious impulse" of every organism is precisely to get rid of its own existence as *this* organism; all are "unconsciously" trying to die in every act of their lives. It seems to me, then, that "naturalistic" theories are manifestly inadequate as causal explanations of the apparent universality with which men who have not acquired an artificial scepticism accept the "spirit-world" as fact, and that the inadequacy cannot be removed by attempts to get behind conscious wish to an unconscious original *libido* which each theorist is free to interpret just as he pleases.

Though I am perhaps diverging from our special topic in adding the remark, I seem to myself to detect the same inadequacy in the more old-fashioned naturalistic theories which lay no special stress on wish or *libido*. It looks at first plausible, for example, to find the origin of our belief that the dead are not wholly lost to us simply in our dreams about them; the man I saw and spoke with "in dream" last night, clearly still is something and somewhere. What such a theory leaves unexplained is why mankind should feel the concern they do feel in their waking life for the denizens of the dream-world and for their own destiny when they come to inhabit that world themselves. In general, it cannot have taken long to discover that the stone, or arrow, with which I was wounded in last night's dream leaves me uninjured to-day, that the possessions into which I came then vanished at my waking, that my living friend has not made the promise uttered by his "double" in my dream, and the like. Why, then, should my dreams about the *dead* long retain an importance and significance which has already been lost by my dreams about the living? Why do I go on practising rites based on the conviction that I really see and hear my dead father in my dreams, so long after I have lost the belief that I really see my living contemporaries when I dream about them?

Again, I dream that my dead father complains to me of being cold and hungry. But do I not equally dream that I feed him and warm him at my fire? Why does not the dream-feeding discharge my obligations in relation to the dream-hunger? Why must I make a visit with an offering of food to my father's tomb when I awake from my dream? I confess there seems to me to be a problem here for which the "naturalist" neither provides, nor attempts to provide, any solution. Thus it seems to me that the way in which personal continuance is apparently taken for granted as something obvious in what is called the "primitive" view of life and the world is a singularly impressive fact, not by any means adequately accounted for by any of the "naturalistic" explanations. So far the appeal to the *consensus gentium* does seem to have more significance than it is at present fashionable to admit.

But the main point on which I am concerned to lay stress is that, be their origin what it may, these beliefs in a continued existence much of the same kind as that we now lead on earth, perhaps without some of our present "disagreeables", are wholly different in quality from definitely *ethical* convictions. Their sources are not specifically ethical, and the kind of immortality they hold out to us is non-moral. It is neither a source of moral inspiration nor an implication of the objectivity of right and wrong. If we were asked to believe in a life to come simply on the alleged ground that we should all very much like to have a perfect and unending "good time", it would be pertinent to make two points in reply.   (1) We can easily wish for what we know, or think we know, to be entirely impossible. The elderly can easily wish, and literature is full of eloquent expressions of the wish, like the famous chorus of Euripides' *Heracles*,[1] that they could have their flaming youth over again, or perhaps even that they could combine all the freshness of its ardours with the insight which has come to age through experience. Yet all of us, except the few who base wild aspirations on experiments done with extracts of monkey-glands, are probably convinced that rejuvenescence in late life is fully as impossible as Nicodemus thought it, and we are, I suppose, convinced, without any exceptions whatever, that at any rate the combination of the ardour of youth with the wisdom of age is impossible, since the ardour depends for its specific quality on the fact that the young adventurer is breaking new paths, sailing an uncharted sea, where experience is not at hand to prescribe his course. It is just this sense of dangerous adventure into the unknown and unexperienced which gives our youth its peculiar charm; the youth *plus* age of some of our dreams would be only the not very delectable "youth" of Meredith's Adrian Harley.

(2) Again, it might be said, though we may all have these wishes at times, it is very doubtful whether a wise man or a good man would really choose to have them gratified. In the wise and good such yearnings are likely at most to be arrested in their incipient stage as mere "velleities"; they will not rise to the level of serious and steady *voluntas*. When we reach a certain level of moral ripeness, we can see that the gratification would not really be a good thing for us; hence such moods cease to represent our genuine self, just as the

---

[1] Euripides, *H.F.* 655 εἰ δὲ θεοῖς ἦν ξύνεσις | καὶ σοφία κατ' ἄνδρας, | δίδυμον ἂν ἥβαν ἔφερον | φανερὸν χαρακτῆρ' ἀρετᾶς | ὅσοισιν μέτα, κτλ.

dreams in which we occasionally find ourselves back
in childhood, with the hope and fears of childhood,
cease to represent it. Wishes which are specifically unethical cannot figure as the basis of a "moral" argument for anything, since they cease to be even real
wishes in proportion as we put on morality. If there
is an ethical justification for anticipations of a future
beyond death, it cannot be founded on the mere consideration that all or many of us more or less passionately wish for such a future. A *moral* argument for
immortality should take the form of an argument that
the destruction of our human personalities must stultify
the whole moral life by making its supreme end unattainable. If this conviction can be justified, it clearly
affords anyone who believes that the moral life is
identical with the truly human life the best of reasons
for holding that there is a destiny of the moral person
beyond what we can now see. But the argument has,
of course, no weight for anyone who denies that the
life of morality is the fullest expression of our distinctive character as human, and therefore cannot profess to be a *demonstration* valid for everyone who will
accept the general laws of logic and the merely "non-
moral" facts of existence, though it may rightly be
treated as decisive by all believers in the absoluteness
of the demands of the moral law. From their point of
view, the argument will be, succinctly formulated, that
since the moral law can rightfully command us to live
as aspirants to eternity, eternity must really be our
destination. This, if it can indeed be made out, is, I
must hold, an absolutely valid ground for those who
believe in unconditional moral obligation to believe
also in a coresponding attainable moral goal.

It is, you will observe, in substance the contention on
which Kant relies when he introduces into the *Critique of*

Practical Reason as a postulate presupposed in morality that very belief in the immortal "soul" which he had done his best to prove indemonstrable in the *Critique of Pure Reason*. It is, in fact, a legitimate inference from the reality of a function to the reality of the environment where the function will find its use.

The real problem to be faced is not whether reasoning of this kind from the reality of function to the reality of the environment in which it can function is valid. To raise doubts on that point would be fatal to the admission of enough rationality into the cause of things to make science itself possible. The real question is rather whether in fact examination of the moral life reveals the reality of any such functions. The issue is raised with the utmost clarity by the proposition of St. Thomas[1] that "the final felicity of man is not to be obtained in this present life". *If* this is true, then, always on the fundamental presupposition of the moralist that there is no absolute disjunction of "fact" from "value", the conclusion is obvious; the true destiny of man is not to be found "in this present life" either.

But it may be asserted, in direct opposition to St. Thomas, that human felicity *can* be obtained in this life—in fact that it can be obtained nowhere else, since it proves on analysis to consist altogether in the exercise of activities correlated with the experienced temporal environment of the human organism, and in nothing else. Here it is, I should say, that we find ourselves face to face with the supreme practical issue. Is "highest human good" conceivable simply in terms of the activities we exercise, and the environment with which we are familiar in this our temporal and embodied life, or is the moral end one which defies complete resolution into the successful prosecution of any or all of these "secular"

[1] *S.C.G.* iii. 48.

activities, much as a "surd" defies complete expression
in the form of a terminated or recurrent decimal fraction? Is the world about us what Wordsworth called it
in the verse which moved Shelley's disgust, the "home
of all of us", where "we find our happiness, or not at
all", or is it what it has been called by so many, a place
of exile, an Egypt where there may be "flesh-pots",
but where we have no free citizenship? Is it our great
business to "make ourselves at home" in it, or to escape
from it, even though the road should lead out through
a barren and dry land where no water is? Both views
cannot be equally true, and neither is, on the face of it,
visibly so false that a man must be a fool to acquiesce
in it. And since we have to live somehow, we cannot in
action adopt a "non-committal" course of simple agnosticism. We must act on the one assumption or on the
other; *il faut parier*. Our attitude on the question of
man's destiny not only may, but must, in the end be
determined by the choice we make between the view
of the world familiar to us from the literature of Platonism and that represented on the whole and with qualifications by Aristotle, and without any qualification at
all by the persuasive voices of the *mondains* and secu-
larists of all ages.

Manifestly our whole practical rule of life will be
different according to the choice we make. If the
Platonic and Christian view is true, it must follow "as
the night the day" that we dare not lose our hearts to
any temporal good. The rule of detachment will be
the obvious supreme rule of successful living; the moral
task of man will be to learn so to use and prize temporal
good as to make it a ladder of ascent to a good which
is more than "for a season", *ita per temporalia transire
ut non amittamus aeterna*. If the numerous moralists who
take the other side are right, the moral business of man

will be wholly to secure the temporal goods, the only goods there are, in the life of "practice". There will be plenty of room for care and delicate discrimination in preferring the higher of these goods to the lower, but there will be no justification for any sacrifice of temporal good to "some better thing" which, on the theory, must be an illusion. In *this* morality, at its best, there will be no room for the injunction, "love not the world, nor the things of the world".

I cannot think, as Dr. McTaggart appears to have done, that this difference is merely one of ethical speculative theory; it must, as it seems to me, directly affect the most momentous practical choices we are called on to make in the conduct of our lives. From a strictly "this-world" point of view, for example, the whole purpose which dominated a life like that of St. Francis must be pronounced to be fantastic. It might be admitted that incidentally, very much against the intention of St. Francis himself, the Franciscan movement, with its varied repercussions on economics, art, letters, and politics, was in fact productive of a vast amount of what a discerning secularistic moralist would recognise to be true good, but in principle this will merely illustrate the familiar proposition that good, and even an overplus of good, may arise from what is itself not good, or even actually evil. In principle, Francis will be in exactly the same position as Caesar or Alexander, on the supposition that Caesar and Alexander were men whose actual aims were perverse and largely evil, though they were so situated that in serving their perverse personal aims they inevitably benefited humanity. From the anti-secularistic point of view it is at least conceivable that this verdict should be exactly reversed and that we ought rather to say that while incidentally, owing to personal limitations, Francis may have drawn the distinction between the temporal and the eternal too crudely, and thus rejected as illusion much which is true eternal good, in principle he was right. It may be the evil, not the good, in the Franciscan movement which will prove to be the merely incidental and unintended.

To put the point more generally, though on any interpretation of life which is not merely flippant, morality will demand a good deal of genuine sacrifice, the sacrifice of real and definite temporal good will, to the secularist, never be justified except where there is at least a reasonable hope of securing a definite secular better.[1] If there is good which is better than anything secular, this restriction will lose its justification, and it may be a plain duty, for some men at least, and possibly for all men, to sacrifice definite secular good for something different in kind and only dimly apprehended, with the certainty that the sacrifice will never be compensated by any gain in the same kind. It is this apparently *unreasonable* choice that St. Paul calls the "foolishness" of this world; the question is whether St. Paul was right in saying that this foolishness of the world is wisdom with God.

Let us try to state the problem in the form most favourable for the secularist; we do not, I hope, want to gain an easy victory over a "man of straw" of our own manufacture. Under the head of secular good, then, I mean now to include everything which can be really attained and enjoyed in human life on the assumption that human life means no more than existence as a member of the human species, under the conditions imposed on us by place and time, as part

---

[1] And this is just the view taken, *e.g.*, by Mill in his *Utilitarianism*: "The only self-renunciation which it [the utilitarian morality] applauds is devotion to the happiness, or to some of the means of happiness, of others" (12th ed. p. 24).

of the "complex event we call nature". Thus I mean the phrase, in the present context, to cover not only physical health, longevity, comfort, and fertility, but the minimising of all the ills which attend disharmony with our physical environment and friction with other members of our social world, as well as the satisfaction of our interests in natural knowledge and sensible beauty. The ideal proposed for valuation shall be that of the progressive establishment of a human society on earth in which want, disease, physical pain and mental deficiency are, if not abolished, at least reduced to a minimum, offences against the social order obviated by a sound tradition of human good will and solidarity, and art and natural science made the delight and business of everyone. It may fairly be said that such a conception of a secularist ideal, if it sins at all, sins rather by generosity than by niggardliness. The question I wish to propound is this—allowing our secularist's ideal thus to include everything which has been recognised as good by a high-minded Utilitarianism like that of Mill, or an aesthetic Utopianism like that of William Morris, is the perpetuation of such a social life of humanity through the largest vista of successive generations a wholly satisfactory final aim for moral aspiration? Or do we all feel that, if the Utopia became fact, we should not, after all, have attained the best, that there would be missing something elusive and impossible to define precisely, and that something *the* thing without which everything else loses its value? May it not be that all along, if we make humanitarianism, however generous, our supreme rule of life, we are living only for a second-best?

I state the problem in this way in order to make it quite clear that there is one cheap and common line of adverse criticism which merely misses the point. The demand for a "felicity beyond this life" has too often been represented as having its roots in a vulgar personal selfishness. Hegel, according to Heine's story, talked with contempt of the man who expects a *Trinkgeld* beyond the grave for not having beaten his mother, and I observe that in the most recent study of Ethics which has come into my hands, Professor Laird's excellent *Study in Moral Theory*, the same conception is made prominent as one of the alleged bases of the moral argument for immortality, which the author is anxious to deprecate.[1] I confess that this demand that "virtue" shall receive a "reward" does not seem to come legitimately into the argument, and I should gravely doubt whether it has ever been the real inspiration of the hope of immortality in any mind of the first order. There may be some persons who seriously reason in the way derided by Bradley, "if I am not to be paid hereafter for living virtuously, virtue will involve genuine self-denial, and morality will turn out not to be the same thing as prudent self-seeking".[2] But I do not believe that such reasoning is common. Even those who speak most often of "reward" probably do their own thought an injustice by the language in which they express it. And I might remark in passing that, when this language is employed, it is most often not used by a man about himself. It is much more common to say of another that he has "passed to his reward" than it is to speak of myself as expecting my reward, and the fact should not be insignificant to a really acute psychologist.

But be those who clamour for their personal *Trink-*

---

[1] *Op. cit.* p. 312, with its pleasantries about "medals" bestowed for doing our duty.

[2] *Appearance and Reality*, p. 508.

geld many or few, it is not thus that Plato and Kant and other great moralists who have championed the cause of hope have spoken. Their thought has not been that morality and decency are a disagreeable task only to be made tolerable by high pay, but that the good which the virtuous man seeks is of a kind not expressible in the currency of secularism. It is not that he demands the "Union rate of wages" for his good performances and abstentions from mischief, but that the social utility of his life has been all along a by-product achieved in the process of aiming at something different, something which is merely illusory, if the secularist estimate of human nature and its destiny is the correct one. No one denies that there are real sacrifices to be made; the question is whether they are all, in the end, sacrifices to idols.

Nowhere does this come out more plainly than in the familiar New Testament language about sacrifice. Bradley once caricatured the current hopes of heaven by representing the believer as saying to the sinners of this age, "You sin now, we are going to sin hereafter". But this is, of course, caricature, and conscious caricature. The hope of "sinning hereafter",[1] if it is a hope entertained by anyone, is at least not the hope of what a Christian or a Platonist means by heaven. We are told in the New Testament that we must be prepared to cut off the right hand or put out the right eye, if they "offend" us, since it is good for us to enter into life with one hand or one eye rather than to perish with two. It is not suggested that the hand we have cut off, or the eye we have put out, grows again miraculously as we enter the gates of life. For the man whose conception of good is exhausted by the

---

[1] I regret that I have failed to verify this reference, but I believe I have attributed the phrase to its true author.

kind of good that may have to be sacrificed, there is
no promise of any kind of "compensation" such as he
could appreciate. The whole point of the language is
that the sacrifice *is* sacrifice of a good and that it is
irrevocable. The cutting off of the right hand may,
for example, in a given instance symbolise the sort
of choice which haunted the imagination of T. H.
Green, the deliberate abandonment of a promising
literary or artistic career for one of useful but dull
drudgery as a sanitary engineer, or a civil servant.
A man who makes the hard choice *may* enter into a life
from which he would have been debarred if he had
evaded the choice, but it is not suggested that he will
hereafter be, "in eternity", all the more an artist or a
scholar. Or, again, the call of duty may come between
a man and the supreme personal love of his life.
He may "make his soul" by following this call of duty,
but it is the modern sentimental novelist, not Christ,
who tells him that he will some day be repaid by being
once more the Romeo to his old Juliet "in eternity".

Indeed, it is constantly urged further, with some inconsistency, against the Platonist or Christian who takes
his convictions seriously that he pushes the demand for
sacrifices to a fantastic extreme. The humanitarian of
the type of Mill admits that, as the world goes, in its
present very imperfect condition, the best men must be
willing to make considerable sacrifice of genuine good;
they may often, as Mill phrases it, have to do without
happiness. But there is a restriction which Mill is careful
to mention. The sacrifice is only justifiable at the bar of
reason when there is the prospect that a surplus of good
of *the kind thus sacrificed* will be secured for someone
else, and if we assume, as humanitarians like Mill
regularly do, that all the great outstanding evils of
life are due to bad physical and social conditions, and

therefore removable, as science indicates improved methods of grappling with hindrances of both kinds, and the gradual perfection of our social system diminishes the competition of "classes", it fairly follows that the demand for the making of such sacrifices will be diminished beyond all assignable limits. As we approach the ideal humanitarian state, the sacrifice of "my own happiness" to anything else will steadily tend to disappear from human experience; the way of virtue will come, in the end, to be for everyone the flowery path.

Now this view of the place of self-denial and sacrifice in life is wholly different from that of the Platonist, to say nothing of the Christian. Both conceive the supreme good, or felicity, of man in a way which makes it incommensurable with the enjoyments the humanitarian calls collectively "happiness", since both look upon the task of right living as a remaking of character round a new centre. It is not a man's circumstances, according to this view, but his personality which must be unmade and remade if felicity is to be obtained. He must grow into a personality which has its centre not in the competitive finite selfhood with which we all begin, but in the infinite and eternal. Every stage in the process is a dying out of the natural man into the spiritual man, and in all of us the natural man "dies hard". Hence the "war in the members" is no temporary incident in the moral history of man, but its fundamental and persistent character. The demand for "costing" sacrifice can never be eliminated by the application of physical science to the abolition of disease and want, or by the introduction of an improved set of social institutions. Amelioration of this kind, at the most, will provide men and women with better opportunities of making the most of their humanity—if they choose to do so, and do not grow

weary of their choice. The "naughting" of one merely
natural concupiscent self is not, in the end, undertaken
for the purpose of providing gratifications for the
concupiscence of some other such selves, but because
it is the only way into true life for all selves. In principle, even if Utopia could be realised to-morrow, the
"naughting" of the natural man would still remain
imperative. However delightful our temporal environment might be in Utopia, it would still be the "work
of a man" not to lose his heart to it, to use it and pass
through it without setting up his rest. And here, again,
there would be no convenient compromising and calculating and striking of a balance.

After all, on the premisses of secularistic humanitarianism, the desires of the natural man are to be
accepted without qualification as right and to be
gratified, when they do not seriously clash with the
similar desires of other specimens of the natural man;
hence for many or most of us life is, on the whole, a
business which only calls for real sacrifice and self-
denial at intervals and as the exception. The opposite
view, be it right or wrong, is that we have the "old
man", who must be "put off", with us all the time, and
our business with him is not merely to see that he makes
no one else unduly uncomfortable by his methods
of enjoying himself, but to see that the sentence of
death is duly executed upon him. The end, in fact, is
to "follow God"; the things which humanitarianism
regards as supreme ends-in-themselves are, at best,
subordinate incidents in the attainment of an end
which humanitarianism leaves out of account. *This*
end is not pleasing yourself without prejudice to the
equal claim of your neighbour to please himself; it
is wholly different from any kind of self-pleasing.
Hence, entirely apart from any question of interfer-

ence with one's neighbour, the moral life, so conceived, is a life in which denial of self is demanded at
all times and in all situations, if we are to become what
we aspire to be. And hence, again, the Christian
demand for a purity of the secret places of the heart,
which means much more than abstinence from the
gratification of desires it would be socially harmful to
satisfy, and the violent metaphor by which such a life
can be called one of "concrucifixion" with Christ.

We do not conceive of such a life rightly if we think
of it as inspired by the purpose of pleasing the natural
self of any man; it is the life of one who means what
Nietzsche merely said, *der Mensch ist etwas, das
überwunden werden muss*. The thought which in fact
inspires it is the conviction that each of us only becomes
human in the full moral sense of the word, in so far as
he forgets about pleasing himself or pleasing other
men, in his determination to serve God. This is all
through life a hard task, and one in which we all fail
shamefully, for two reasons, that we all begin with an
imperious passion for gratifying ourselves, getting "what
we want" as the supreme end of ends, and also that
we may miss the mark of "pleasing God" and putting
on a true moral personality in either of two contrasted
ways, the way of Epicurus or the way of Stylites.
The task is to use our inheritance of environment and
natural endowment in such a way as to attain true
spiritual manhood; we fail in this task alike whether
we make lower good a principal end or refuse to make
it an instrument towards something better. We do not
need the psycho-analyst to tell us that it is the same
libido of the natural self that displays itself alike in the
abandonment of the victim of unrestrained passion
and in the self-torture of the "pillar-saint". The kinship of lust and cruelty is an old and familiar fact with

obvious implications. If I certainly cannot make sure of pleasing God by doing what I like, it is also hopeless to propose to please Him by making it a rule to do what I loathe. I am more likely to gratify only an evil pride which is as incompatible as any "carnality" with the single eye and the pure heart.

All this, however, is by the way. The main question for us at the moment is whether we really are unavoidably driven, when we consult the witness of conscience, to admit that the ideal of good which has inspired our historical moral achievements proves on examination to be something not included in good as good can be legitimately conceived by the humanitarian. Is devotion to the temporal welfare of human society the sufficient justification of the imperatives of morality? If it is not, then, unless we admit—and the admission would be fatal to all moral philosophy—that moral imperatives cannot and need not be justified at all, and so have no genuine obligatoriness about them, we must be prepared to admit that there is good rational ground for anticipating a destination of human persons which is ignored when such persons are thought of as merely transient; morality will thus bear a real witness of its own to the presence of the seeds of immortality in us.

You see, no doubt, what is the objection a Platonist or Christian philosopher has to face. We may expect to be told that sufficient justification is provided for all the imperatives of an earnest and elevated morality if we take as our supreme good the retention and further development of all the inheritance the human race has won in its slow and painful struggle out of the savagery with which certified history begins. We can set ourselves to play the part of men in the transmission of science, and art, and sound social morality to our successors, and the slow improvement at once of the traditions we have received in all these matters, and of man's physical estate. None of us will accomplish much, and no single age will accomplish much, for the execution of this task, but we have a reasonable prospect that the work may be continued through an enormous number of generations, and imagination has no right to set any limits to the cumulative result.

It may, indeed, be said that we have no certainty that our efforts may not be neutralised by some stupendous unforeseen cosmic convulsion of nature, or, still more probably, by a wanton self-destruction of humanity in national or class conflicts. But the reply to this suggestion is obvious; if the past history of mankind affords no grounds for induction to the future, we are wholly in the dark about the probability of this dismal end to history, and need not distress ourselves unduly with mere bad dreams: if the past does justify induction, it is at least a probable contention that mankind will prove equal, in the future as in the past, to recovery from their worst set-backs. And if it is argued that, at any rate, our planet must sooner or later become unfitted to support life, and that human moral civilisation and all its products must therefore be some day as though they had never been at all, we may even be told that this prophecy itself is based on physical theories which have never been *proved* to be true, and so may turn out to be mistaken, and that, in any case, the good achieved has been great and real good while it lasted. As Professor Laird[1] ingeniously pleads, the argument of those who say "since to-morrow we shall die, there is no worth in anything beneath the glimpses of the moon; so let us eat and drink and be merry" refutes itself. For even they

[1] *Study in Moral Theory*, p. 311.

assume that our perishability leaves untouched one judgement about "value", the judgement that while we *are* here it is better to eat, drink, and be merry than to fast, go thirsty, and be miserable. But why should any judgement of worth be affected if this one retains its validity? On these lines it is argued by many, most recently and persuasively by Professor Laird, that the absoluteness and rationality of moral obligation affords no ground whatever for the "great hope" of the Platonist and the Christian.

But now, is the case quite as simple as Professor Laird, for one, takes it to be? The ingenious flanking argument just cited from him strikes me, at least, as more ingenious than solid. What if the unnamed opponents to whom it is addressed had the full courage of their convictions? If indeed they draw from their premisses the conclusion Professor Laird expects them to draw, the usual conclusion of the unthinking man, I own they stand convicted of glaring inconsistency. But suppose they say—and it is what I have myself only too often been tempted to say when depressed by the apparently formidable presumptions of our impermanence—"since to-morrow we die, and there will, sooner or later, be a morrow when all the persons, nay, all the sentient beings we can conceivably affect in any way by anything we do, will be dead, it really does not matter a jot whether to-day we or anyone else eat and drink, or go hungry and thirsty: there *are* no values at all, and good is a mere illusion". I shall, no doubt, eat to-day when I feel the pinch of hunger, even though I know I am appointed to be hanged to-morrow and believe that this will be the last of me. But in so eating, in so much as breathing, I am only providing one more object-lesson in the fundamental unreasonableness of all human behaviour.

As I say, I admit that in moments when the thought

of the apparently inevitable final frustration of all human endeavour has weighed heavily on me, it has never occurred to me personally to draw the conclusion "let us eat and drink and be merry", but rather to say "nothing has any value, and the one rational state of mind is sheer indifference", and this conclusion would paralyse not only all morally good action, but all consciously purposive action whatsoever. Nor do I think I am exceptional in feeling thus. I suspect Huxley meant the same thing when he said that he would prefer life in hell to annihilation. Dr. Bevan[1] expresses the same thought by his saying that he can endure to see life tragic, but cannot endure to see it trivial.

How would Professor Laird meet this more logical employment of the argument he wishes to dispose of? I presume by a mere assertion that he himself perceives that, even if we were all certain of extinction to-morrow, it would still be better to eat our meals to-day. He would be of the mind of the condemned murderers, who, if the newspapers can be trusted—though it is surely questionable whether they can—usually "make a hearty breakfast" immediately before being hanged. But would he go the length of the felon of the anecdote, who asked to have an umbrella held over him on the way to the gallows, because "it was a drizzly morning, and he was apt to take cold"? If it really "all comes to the same thing in the end" whatever we do, as we must anticipate if there is in reality no sort of connection between fact and value, then, I confess, to set assertion against assertion, I do not see why it is more reasonable to be hanged on a full stomach than on an empty. Once more I want

---

[1] *Hellenism and Christianity*, p. 173. Cf. the complaint of Arnold that

> "Each day brings its petty dust
> Our soon-choked souls to fill,
> And we forget because we must
> And not because we will."

to protest against the dogmatic assumption that there is a divorce between the two.

I am not in the least perturbed when Professor Laird goes on, as he does, to insist that the world of the actual is visibly full of things which are valueless or downright bad. To pronounce anything valueless, I should need to know the whole of its contribution to the scheme of things. This is true even of specifically moral evil. I may say of Judas, or of Nero, that they were bad men and did bad acts, but before I could go on to say that a world which contains Judas and Nero is less valuable than an alternative world which would not include them, I should have to know, as I assuredly do not know, that the total effect, including the moral effect, of the presence of Nero and Judas in the scheme of things has not been a good which would have been missing without them. The world might contain as much evil as you please, provided that all this evil serves as opportunity for a sufficient overplus of good, and yet be not only the "best of possible worlds"—that need not be saying much for it—but unspeakably glorious and good. Until you are in a position to *prove* that there is actual evil which is not turned to "glorious gain"—and no one can prove this—you cannot appeal to the admitted presence in things of evil which, to us while we are immersed in it, seems intolerable, as any proof that "the good" is not the ultimate *raison d'être* of all things.

Indeed I think Professor Laird may fairly be cited as evidence against himself. Unlike some of the moralists who would make human good a merely terrene and temporary affair, Professor Laird is very much in earnest indeed with the problem of the right conduct of human life, and as uncompromising as Kant himself on the absolute and unconditional character of moral obligation. He nobly refuses even to hear of the possible clash of a man's "moral" duty as a man and citizen with alleged extra-moral obligations of art or science. As he says,[1] an artistic or scientific imperative, if it is really imperative at all, is itself a moral imperative. The man who is a conscientious and industrious historian, or physicist, or painter, but a bad husband or bad friend, is simply doing what we all do, discharging one part of his moral duty and neglecting another. In fact, though Professor Laird does not put the point in this way, Kant was simply right when he assigned the primacy to the "practical reason" on the ground that *all* interest is practical. And, again, Professor Laird fully agrees with the common verdict that nothing can be a duty unless the performance of it is possible. All imperatives are moral, and no imperative commands the impossible. And, finally, all moral imperatives are included under the supreme formula that it is a man's absolute and unconditional duty to make the best of himself.[2] I cannot well suspect Professor Laird of writing the sentence with the suppressed ironical qualification that, though we do well not to say so, the man will always be "making the best of a bad job". On these premises it seems to me clear that *if* the "best" at which the moral struggle aims all through really is a best which cannot be achieved in a temporal environment, the supreme moral imperative is not justified, as Professor Laird himself rightly insists that all imperatives ought to be, unless the temporal environment of man is not his only or his ultimate environment. It is a true, if a homely saying, that you cannot make a silk purse of a sow's ear, and ought not to waste energy and ingenuity on the attempt.

---

[1] *A Study in Moral Theory*, p. 58.
[2] *Op. cit.* p. 56, "The ultimate moral question for any of us is the best use of the whole of our resources, capacities, and opportunities"; p. 201, "It is self-evident that anyone ought to do the best he is able to do, and that, if any given action is not the best he can do, then it cannot be his duty to do it".

Thus, after considering the attempts which have been made, with more or less subtlety, to stop discussion *in limine*, I find myself at last brought face to face with the central issue : assuming ourselves to be satisfied of the genuine authoritativeness of the imperative which commands us to make the best of ourselves, are we obeying it by devotion to the attainment and extension of distinctively secular good, even if we rate the possibilities of such attainment and extension as high as they have ever been rated by the most optimistic humanitarians? For more than one reason, it seems to me, we must say *NO*, and must therefore conclude that secular good is not the adequate object of the moral quest, which yet must have its adequate object, if it is to be justified as rational.

(1) An obvious feature of all moral aspiration is that, however it conceives the good on which it is directed, it at least always conceives it as something which is a secure and abiding possession, inseparable from our very personality, something, as Aristotle said, which is οἰκεῖον καὶ δυσαφαίρετον, "our very own, not lightly to be taken away". A man who is at the mercy of his circumstances is morally, so far, a slave, not a free man, and one thing at least which a sound morality ought to achieve for us is to make us free. And to be free we must be masters not only of our fortunes, but of our moods and passions, in other words, of all that is mutable and temporal within us as well as without us. Short of this we have no security that our character and personality may not be wrecked at any time by the unforeseeable calamities the course of events may bring with it, or the unforeseeable changes our own individual being may suffer. To attain the good at all a man must be master of his fate and himself. And if man is a merely temporal being, and nothing more, he can be master of neither.

The old Epicureans were often ridiculed by their rivals for their assertion that their ideal "sage" would be thoroughly happy, even if he were being roasted alive. Even in the "bull of Phalaris", he must be able to say "how delightsome this is", "how I am enjoying myself".[1] But, as Dr. Bevan reminds us,[2] the bull of Phalaris is, after all, not an impossible contingency, and we might add that there are lingering and torturing afflictions, fully comparable with the "bull", which are only too often actual, and a morality is defective if it cannot teach serenity and cheerfulness even in these extreme cases. The true paradox is not so much that the "sage" should be undismayed by the prospect of the "bull", but that he should be so, if his "good" is no more than what Epicurus declared it to be, "a healthy condition of the flesh and a confident expectation of its continuance".[3] Contingencies much less unusual than consignment to the bull of Phalaris are enough to make both constituents of *that* good impossible.

To put the point quite generally, we should do no injustice to a purely secular interpretation of the good if we said that the secular moral ideal is to "have a good *time*", taking care, of course, not to identify a "good time" with the satisfaction of our grosser cupidities. The sting of the phrase lies in the introduction of the "time" into the matter. No man is really free so long as he is dependent on having a good time, since he can

---

[1] Cicero, *Tusculans*, ii. 7. 17 sed Epicuro homini aspero et duro non est hoc satis, in Phalaridis tauro si erit, dicet: quam suave est, quam hoc non curo. Seneca, *Epist. Moral.* 66. 18 Epicurus quoque ait sapientem, si in Phalaridis tauro peruratur, exclamaturum: dulce est et ad me nihil pertinet. (For further references of the same kind in Cicero, Seneca, Lactantius, see Usener, *Epicurea*, pp. 338-339.)

[2] *Hellenism and Christianity*, pp. 170-1.

[3] Metrodorus, Fr. 5 (Koerte) ἀγαθὸν ψυχῆς τί ἄλλο ἢ τὸ σαρκὸς εὐσταθὲς κατάστημα καὶ τὸ περὶ ταύτης πιστὸν ἔλπισμα ; Epicurus Fr. 68 (Usener) τὸ γὰρ εὐσταθὲς σαρκὸς κατάστημα καὶ τὸ περὶ ταύτης ἔλπισμα τὴν ἀκροτάτην χαρὰν καὶ βεβαιότητα ἔχει τοῖς ἐπιλογίϚεσθαι δυναμένοις.

guarantee neither the continuance of the environment on which he relies for such a good, nor that of the inner moods of soul in which he will find contentment in it. The elementary requirement that our morality shall make us independent of change and circumstance should be enough to prevent confusion of the good at which a "virtuous" man, as such, is aiming, whether he knows it or not, with any combination of goods which are, from their very nature, *temporanea*, πρόσκαιρα.

There are two ways in which we might try to turn the edge of this reflection, neither, as it seems to me, satisfactory. One might conceivably urge that permanency through an interval of time, though something quite different from eternity, is all we need demand of the good, and that where moralists and philosophers have demanded more, it has been from mental confusion. And permanency, it may be said, unlike eternity, can be secured under favourable conditions. It is, after all, possible to anticipate with a considerable probability a lifelong fruition of the good things you personally care for, just as you can, by prudent investment, make it "as good as certain" that you will have a lifelong income sufficient for your wants. And if you take care to form the right kind of habits, you can also anticipate, again with high probability, that the kind of life which satisfies you now will continue to satisfy you. What is more, a whole generation may have the same sort of confidence that the general structure of their "civilisation" will not only "last their time", but be perpetuated to, and improved by, succeeding generations. A general collapse of the foundations of Western European civilisation, for example, is a contingency so remote that its bare logical possibility need not give us any uneasiness.

No doubt there is something in these consolations,

so long as we do not examine them too narrowly. But I cannot believe they will stand really close scrutiny. Even the assurance that "Western civilisation" will last our time and our children's time is hardly likely to rank as even an approximate certainty with us, who have seen the great war of 1914–18 and the years of danger and insecurity which have followed and are following. And if there had been no "great war", still the humanitarian cannot really "make quick-coming death a little thing". It is not merely that we know that each of us will soon have to die himself; the sting of our mortality is that the same fate equally awaits the children on whom the humanitarian tells us we should set all our hopes, and their children after them. If all things human are utterly perishable, the moral would seem to be the uncheering one:

> Reck little, then, I counsel you
> What any son of man can do;
> Because a log of wood will last
> While many a life of man goes past,
> And all is over in short space.

Or, in graver language, "as soon as thou scatterest them, they are even as a sleep, and fade away suddenly like the grass. . . . We bring our years to an end as a tale that is told."

The thought is hardly one which can reasonably evoke a high estimate of any good which the passing generations can achieve in their brief passage across the stage, or any very thorough endeavour after it. If our life is no more than the strutting of a player through his part in a short scene, sheer quietism would seem to be the attitude towards it indicated by reason and reflection. One might add that, from the point of view of secularistic humanitarianism itself, the best of temporal good seems to be most certainly attained by those who have set their hearts on something different. When I am told that, if you must set your heart on the future at all, you should set it on your children,[1] I cannot but repeat that all human experience seems to show that devotion to children or wife, party or country, is only regularly fruitful of the good it desires when the devotion is kept on the hither side of idolatry. It sounds a hard saying when we are told in the Gospel that the man who would enter life must be prepared to forsake parents and wife and children and lands, but we all recognise the truth of a similar thought, pitched in a lower key,

> I could not love thee, dear, so much,
> Loved I not honour more.

The rule of all wise and profitable love of everything that passes is to love without losing one's heart. He who wishes for the true good of wife or child or country must love them dearly, but there will be something he loves more; if there is not, his love will carry in it the seeds of a curse for the very beings he loves most. To make a god of one's child is to spoil the child of your idolatry; to make "my country, right or wrong," the principle of your action is to do what lies in you to turn your country into one which is not worth loving. And to be devoted exclusively to the good of the "next age", like those who set their hearts on "Socialism in our lifetime", or the "evangelisation of the world in the next generation", is pretty certainly not the best way to provide the "next age" with either the worthiest of social systems or the soundest of gospels. The true secret of life is to love these things well, but to love something else better. And we have only to think of the various names we give to that something else the love of which keeps all our loves for particular things sane and sweet, to see that, whether we call it "God", or "beauty", or "the right",

---

[1] Bosanquet, *Science and Philosophy*, p. 334.

or "honour", by all these different names we mean something which is "not of this world", but stands above and untouched by the temporality and mutability it transfigures.

Once more, the same moral may be pointed in a rather different way. When a man sets his heart, to the best of his power, on the good of the successive generations of mankind, what is the "good" he desires for them? It, no doubt, includes such good things as greater average longevity, a higher standard of physical health, better economic conditions, a more general diffusion of the love of knowledge and beauty, and the like. But, besides these identifiable particular "goods", does not the "good" always include something more, something we could not define or describe, but still felt to be of greater importance than all the particular "goods"? We desire, rationally enough, that the coming generations should be healthier than our own, should know more truth, should find the world fuller of things of beauty, and should not have to wrestle, as we have, with the presence of disease, dirt, penury, and ignorance. But we desire even more that the men and women of the future should be *better* men and women than ourselves, or, at least, if we do not actually desire this ardently, we censure ourselves for our moral lukewarmness. And this means, among other things, that they should be *more* devoted than we are ourselves to the promotion of good for generations which will still be for them future and unborn. We desire that our descendants should have the same difficulties to grapple with as ourselves, or even worse difficulties, but should face them with a higher self-devotion, rather than that they should enjoy all the other goods which have just been enumerated a hundredfold, but fall behind ourselves in the spirit of sacrifice. We do not, unless in consciously unmoral moods, desire for them, any more than for ourselves, increase of good things in possession at the cost of an inferior moral personality; it is not our ideal for them that they should "fleet the time carelessly", like the heroes of socialistic Utopias.

This simple consideration that we do not want our children, or our children's children, "to fleet the time carelessly" leads at once to a dilemma, if we think of man as capable only of temporal and secular goods which can be particularised. If what we really prize as the thing to be won by our own unselfishness is some kind of temporal Utopia, it seems rational to agree with one of the speakers in Mr. Lowes Dickinson's dialogue,[1] that we should set ourselves to fashion the Utopia for our contemporaries and our children, who do exist and in whom we can take a personal interest, not to sacrifice their best chances of good for the benefit of a remote posterity which may conceivably never exist at all, and in which we can take no sort of personal concern. It seems preposterous, if all human good is temporal, to demand that every one of a countless succession of generations should sacrifice the enjoyment of it in order that it may be possible for beings belonging to a problematic and indefinitely distant future. But if we act on this advice, plainly, we must at least go on to draw the hazardous inference that moral goodness itself is no part of the "good for man", but a mere means to nonmoral good.[2] For the generation for which the Utopia is created will be simply entering on an inheritance which it is merely to enjoy in possession; it has no *work* to do, and moral goodness is wholly concerned with the doing of the work by the pre-millenarian generations. The happiness of the favoured generation is, in fact,

---

[1] G. Lowes Dickinson, *Meaning of Good*, pp. 111 ff.
[2] Cf. *op. cit.* p. 136.

bought at the price of the destruction of moral personality, and, from the moralist's point of view, the world,
or a thousand worlds, is not well won at the cost of
human souls.

On the other hand, if the moral goodness *we* value,
genuine moral personality, is what we specially desire
to see produced abundantly in those who are to succeed
us on the stage of history, we cannot find our aspirations
realised in the life of a society where there is no call
for risk, adventure, and sacrifice. If personality of the
quality we prize is to subsist under temporal conditions
at all, there must be the stimulus to its development in the
form of sufferings to be relieved, dangers to be faced,
wrongs to be redressed, ignorance and ugliness to be
overcome. It is certain enough that, in any imaginable
generation,

> Pity would be no more,
> If we did not make somebody poor,
> And mercy no more would be,
> If all were as happy as we.

And thus the humanitarian, unless he is willing to
sacrifice personality to possessions, would seem to be
compelled to introduce into his Utopia with his left
hand the very conditions he is trying to exclude with
his right. His rule would seem to be, in a very singular
sense, not to let his right hand know what his left hand
does. At least, like Penelope, he would spend the
night busily undoing the results of the day's work.
The moral life would become a hopeless task of creating
wrongs that they might be put right.

I state what may be called the fundamental paradox of humanitarianism thus crudely and baldly of set
purpose, because the very baldness of the statement
sets the paradoxicality of the position in bold relief.
Its point is that you cannot overvalue the highest tem-

poral good, nor promote it for humanity too ardently, so long as you care more yourself, and labour as far as is in you that mankind shall care more, for something else. You may have it all in possession without detriment to your moral being, so long as you hold it with a loose hand, and do not close the fingers on it. Every iota of it will go, in its due time, from you and from every son of man down to the last-born, and any part of it may go at any moment, and one must be ready to let it go without reluctancy. For the business of man as a moral being is, after all, a simple one; it is the "making of his soul", a making impossible except at the cost of the steady unmaking of the "private self", whose real defect is precisely that its centre lies in some possession which must not be surrendered. What makes our "finite selfhood" the contradiction so many moralists have called it is not that no self or subject is identical *numero* with another, that there are *many* selves, but that each clings to some possession which it dares not let go for fear of losing the very core of personality.[1] Yet, as we may all learn from experience of such surrenders as we actually make, it is just in letting go the cherished possession, when the call comes, that we learn the real strength and richness of the personality which can let so much go and yet survive, because it is not tethered. What we should really learn from these experiences is that there is that in our personality which is not fettered to any temporal good and can emerge enriched, not impoverished, from the surrender of them all. The good on which personality feeds, and severed from which it would die of inanition, is something which is not any nor all of the describable and imaginable goods circumscribed by place and time.

---

[1] This is what Goethe personifies as Frau Sorge in the closing scenes of *Faust*.

One side of this thought, the conviction that the world is what Keats called it, a valley of soul-making, and that the soul is made by surrenders, has been expounded, with a power I can only contemplate with admiring envy, in Professor Bosanquet's well-known lectures on the *Value and Destiny of the Individual*. But Bosanquet seems to me to have ignored the other half of the same thought. When all is said, he holds out as the ultimate goal to be reached by the supreme surrender what seems to be merely the resolution of moral personality into nothing. True personality, it would appear, is made only to be lost in the very act. This, I am convinced, is a misreading of the facts to be interpreted. The natural interpretation would rather be that as the self which is enriched by partial surrenders remains *my* self, though its centre is increasingly displaced from my exclusive possessions, so the self to be won by the supreme surrender of all that is temporal is still *my* self, though its centre has become the one and abiding eternal. Heaven, to put it pictorially, is not a realm of selves, each clinging pertinaciously to some secret possession which it will share with no other, but Heaven is a realm of selves for all that, selves whose whole life is one of the supreme adventure, losing themselves in God, but with the result that in the very plunge out of self they find, not nothing, but themselves, and themselves with a richer content.

Need I say much about that other way of dealing with the problem created by the transience of all temporal good illustrated, for example, by Mr. Bertrand Russell's only too famous essay on *The Free Man's Worship*?[1] It is, in a sense, a desperate way of trying to escape from temporality. We are to

---

[1] B. Russell, *Philosophical Essays*, pp. 59 ff.

recognise to the full the unsatisfactoriness of the temporal, and at the same time to lift ourselves above it by a quietistic scorn for a reality which is as much inferior to ourselves in worth as it is superior in brute force. The "free man" is to be Prometheus on his rock—a Prometheus after the fashion of Shelley rather than of Aeschylus—despising the "omnipotent matter" which Mr. Russell sets in the place of Zeus. To some of Mr. Russell's readers, I know, this attitude of contempt for the stupid "omnipotence" which produces intelligence, beauty, and goodness only to crush them, has seemed sublime; at the risk of being dismissed in such quarters as a *Durchschnittsmensch*, I must own that the pose strikes me as rather one of solemn conscious futility. If the case of man were really thus, "silence after grievous things" would be more becoming than any rhetoric, even Mr. Russell's, or, if words there must be, one phrase of Johnson's would be sufficient, "a man knows it must be; it will do no good to whine".

But I should like to make the further comment that the state of soul described in Mr. Russell's essay seems to leave no real place for either freedom or worship. Freedom is excluded by the fact that the standing attitude of our latest Prometheus to his Zeus, "omnipotent matter", is one of scorn and conscious superiority, "proud defiance". Now scorn and inner freedom simply will not keep house together, as Shelley was aware when he made *his* Prometheus expressly disclaim any feeling of contempt for his tormentor.[1] He who scorns, in fact, suffers from a double unfreedom. He must be conscious of the obtrusive and unwelcome presence of the object of his contempt, and thus he cannot get away from what

[1] *Prometheus Unbound*, i. I. 53.

Spinoza, with more insight, reckons as one of the "passive affects" which inhibit and make unfree.[1] And this is not all: to feel scorn, a man must also be concomitantly conscious of himself and of his own superiority, and this is to be more or less of a bitter "prig". To be free you must get rid of *all* preoccupation with yourself, and for that very reason a "superior person" never is really free.

Again, the scorner, with his consciousness of his own superiority, cannot really know what it is to "worship". Worship is for the *sancti et humiles corde*, and one only knows it when one's mind is filled by an object which leaves no room for consciousness of one's self by the side of it. This, by the way, is also why Kant's attitude to the moral law and its source never really rises into worship. To be conscious of the moral law as an unconditional imperative is, as Kant himself knew, to be conscious of yourself as inhibited by it. To use the fashionable jargon of to-day, an "inferiority-complex" is attended by a painful awareness of the self as depressed and thwarted. Worship is possible only when one can forget one's self and one's own inferiority; it is this which gives it its character of free and joyous *abandon*. All worship is at heart an incipient *iubilus*.

But the main comment I would make on the whole attitude is that morally it is condemned by the simple consideration that it is bound to hinder the production of good works. As Spinoza reminds us,[2] *Laetari* and *bene agere* go together; a view of the world which makes simple-minded joyousness impossible cannot be the view required for men whose lives are to be fruitful in good works, and therefore, *if* our moral life discloses anything whatever about the framework of

[1] *Ethica*, iv. 46 Corr. I, Schol.   [2] *Ethica*, iv. 73 Schol.

reality in which it is set, such a view cannot be the truth. If the real world indeed meets the moralist's demand on it, it must be a world to be met neither with scorn nor with resignation, but accepted and welcomed with single-hearted joyfulness.

If the inmost secret of the moral life is that it is a life of "making the best" of ourselves, of achieving, out of the crude and conflicting stresses and tensions with which we start, a genuine personality which is free and its own master, and if the price which has to be paid for every advance towards such freedom is surrender, then, as it seems to me, we can think of such a life as not condemned in principle to futility only on one condition. The condition is that we anticipate the completion of the process as found in the winning of a personality absolutely above circumstance and mutability by a supreme surrender of the whole realm of merely temporal values, as dying out of time into a real eternity. What such an eternal life would be like is, of course, more than we can imagine, since all our imaginations are borrowed from the temporal. What we imagine we imagine as a tissue of "events", though some of the events may be "slow-moving". Still, imaginable or not, and the human imagination is no criterion of the real—that dying out of the temporal into the eternal which writers like Suso spoke of as "passing away into the high god-head" must be real, and must be no mere negation, but the final affirmation of the moral self, if morality itself is to be, in the end, more than a futility. What is put off in such an achievement of the moral end must be not personality or individuality, but that inner division of the soul against itself which makes the tragedy of life and leaves us here mere imperfect fragments of persons.

In the traditional language of Christianity, it is the life of the "flesh" which must be surrendered if eternal life, the life of the "spirit", is to be won. And this opposition the "flesh", as we see from St. Paul's description of its characteristic "works", includes a great deal more than we commonly mean by "carnality". To live to the flesh is to make our supreme good of anything which is no more than the gratification of incidental passions and desires, followed merely because I happen, for my own particular, to feel them strongly, though they are incapable of justification by the standard of absolute good. It is to take "I want it" as a last and sufficient legitimation of any pursuit. In this sense of the word, a life directed to the prosecution of science or art, or to the enjoyment of the social relations of the family, or the friendly circle, may itself be one of living to the flesh, if I follow science as no more than a means of satisfying curiosity, or art as a mere profession, or a mere hobby, or am interested in the members of my family or circle of friends merely because they happen to be there, and to be mine. To die to the life of the flesh need not mean that I am not to find my vocation in life in the pursuit of science, or in the filling of my place in a family and social group. To "spiritualise" such a life is so to live it as to achieve for myself, and to help others in achieving, a moral personality, proof against all shocks and all disappointments. Any life so lived ceases to have as its inspiring motive a lesser and circumscribed loyalty which may be a hindrance to the supreme loyalty to the best, and becomes itself an expression of the supreme loyalty. Yet, at the same time, all loyalties but the supreme loyalty *may* become clogs upon us, and all are therefore conditioned. Even if no actual conflict arises, they are all loyalties to objects which endure only for a time, and the good man whom morality contemplates must not be left without anything to live for, if one and all of these objects should be taken from him. Like Mary, he must choose as his object of supreme loyalty a good part which cannot be taken away. In that sense we might accept the poetic phrase

> Ich hab' mein Sach auf Nichts gestellt;
> Drum ist's so wohl mir in der Welt

as our motto.

I know well enough, of course, that few or none of us actually live up to this moral ideal. It is pitiful to think what a little thing will make shipwreck of the life of any of us by taking away some minor good to which we cling over-passionately. Yet if we are morally reflective creatures, we have at least the grace to be heartily ashamed of ourselves when the failure of one of these temporal attachments tears up our life by the roots. And my argument is concerned not with our sorry practice, but with what we know our practice ought to be. Hence I feel bound to hold that the plain fact that there is no loyalty to the best of temporal goods which it may not become a duty to subordinate to the supreme loyalty to Good itself is ground for the conviction that we have a good, and consequently a destiny which is not expressible at all in terms of duration, and yet must be attainable, if it be true that the moral life itself is no dream or illusion, but the most insistent of realities.

If this is so, there are important consequences to be drawn, and I would indicate some of them very briefly. It will follow that our possession of a moral being gives us a right to a reasonable hope that the attainment of a truly free personality, in which we rise above contingency and uncertainty, because we have learned the lesson of surrender, really lies before us. This will, of course, involve the hope and conviction that the crown of moral attainment remains secure, even against the shock of that general dissolution of our bodily organism which we call death. Free personality is manifestly not to be completely won while we are in the body, "servile to all the skiey influences"; while the "displacement of a grain of sand in the urethra" can stultify a man's highest intelligence and purpose, he is obviously very much in chains, and if the moral order is a reality, we cannot believe that he wins his freedom only in the moment of ceasing to be anything at all. But this rational moral hope is strictly limited by its character and foundation. It is a hope that we shall win our way into a true free moral personality as our final and inalienable good, and we can say no more than this. What it is to enter on the fruition of eternal life we cannot so much as imagine: *trasumanar significar per verba Non si poria*. At the most we can only say that such a life would have always and in perfection the quality we experience now, rarely and imperfectly, when we have made one of those surrenders which we find it so hard to make, and have made it heartily and with a will.

Perhaps an illustration may be taken from an experience which must have come to many during the war of 1914–1918. There are probably among my audience some who, as young men rejoicing in their youth and all its promise of a full and varied life, then made, from sheer loyalty to a higher good, the surrender of hazarding all they prized most to play a man's part in their country's struggle, and made it with the full sense of the preciousness of all they were setting on the hazard, and yet gladly and ungrudgingly. I take it that if any man can recall, as perhaps it is hardly possible he should, what the quality of his life was when he was making the choice, he knows by analogy what is the abiding character of eternal life, as a life in which, to use the traditional language of noble livers, the soul is "oned" with the Most High, or, to fall back on words which perhaps come home more directly to modern men at large, in which one has ceased to be one of the world's takers and become finally a giver, and so, in fact, has found the good part which nothing can take away, because one has no longer anything which is a mere private possession to be shared with no one, but lives wholly by bestowing.

I cannot myself see anything self-contradictory in the conception of a community of many members each of whom has his own special individuality as a recipient of the infinitely varied and manifold graces of the Bestower of all good, and yet keeps back nothing, but is a channel through which all he has received flows out freely on all his fellows. Such, I take it, would be the "life of gods and godlike men", in which the "flesh", the world's grabber, is once and for all dead, and there is no life but that of spirit.

If this is what an eternal life satisfying the aspirations in which morality has its source would be, it follows that ethical considerations can do nothing to confirm anticipations not covered by such a conception, and may actually negative imaginations which prove to be inconsistent with it. In any conception of our destiny which appeals to morality as its sanction, or one of its sanctions, there will inevitably be the touch of austerity which is as characteristic of sound morality as of serious art. I confess that not a few of our current imaginative forecasts of "immortality" seem to me to be tainted with moral superficiality. They do no sufficient justice to what experience reveals to us all in varying measures, the indispensability of detachment and surrender as the one pathway into ascending life. We are all too prone to forget that the road to life is, from first to last, a "purgative" way. I know that so rare and delicate a thinker as the late Mr. Clutton-Brock[1] has declared that what most of us need is not so much purgation as enrichment. But I cannot help thinking that this sharp contrast between the two is a misleading antithesis which its author would have found it hard to defend as it stands. Certainly, enrichment is the obvious need of us all; our moral life is dreadfully poverty-stricken; it is our curse that our loves are so few and so feeble. But, so far as I can see, it is regularly by purgation and simplification that enrichment has to be won. Our loves are deepened and enlarged in the same proportion in which our hungry cupidities are suppressed. We love too little and too feebly because we lust—I use the word in its wide old acceptation—so passionately and for so much. Our problem is to learn to live by our loves and not by our cupidities; the second must be surrendered that the first may flourish. We shall never be truly rich until we have learned the lesson that *unum est necessarium.*

And I see no reason in the nature of things to suppose that the surrender of the bodily life with all its accidents, which each of us has to make at death, need be the end of the process. It would be more natural, to my mind, to think that even the vanishing of the so-called "bodily" lusts with the body itself leaves a hard purgation still in front of most of us. There are such things as unwise personal attachments, involving no element of physical "appetite", to unworthy objects, undue and disordinate

[1] See a passage in the composite volume *Immortality: an Essay in Discovery* (London, 1917), pp. 234-6.

devotions to supra-personal objects short of the highest, rooted prejudices and false judgements, and I cannot see why removal from the body should, of itself, purge us of these defects. A Nelson, in the life beyond the grave, would, I take it, have to unlearn an exclusive idolatry of England and an irrational animosity against "the French", an Aristotle to overcome a one-sided superiority to simple and unlettered loving souls, before either could enter fully into life, and in both cases the lesson involves a great purification and simplification.

Hence there seems to me to be a profound truth, unaffected by the secondary errors grafted upon it by the demand for detailed imagining of the unimaginable, in the central thought of the doctrine of Purgatory, a doctrine which I believe to be really held, in one form or another, by the thoughtful even in communities which nominally repudiate it.[1] I cannot conceive that most of us, with our narrow range of understanding and sympathies, our senseless antipathies and indifferences, and our conventional moral outlook, could ever be fitted by the mere fact of escape from the physical limitations of the body to enter at once into the eternal life of the simply loving souls. I should think it more probable—always with deference to wiser judgements —that death leaves us, as it finds us, still far too much takers and too little givers, and that the process of purgation, begun in this life in all who have made any progress in good, needs, for all but the very few, to be continued and intensified, and that, for most of us, this means severe discipline. It may be well to have got rid of the crude imagination of "Purgatory-fire" as a "torment", and still better to have lost the belief that

---

[1] Thus the Articles of the Anglican Church repudiate "the Romish doctrine of Purgatory", whatever that may be; but Anglicans who think at all, regularly, as I should say, believe in a Purgatory, whether they call it by that name or not.

one can purchase remission of the torment by cash payment into an ecclesiastical treasury, but the main thought that the hardest part of the work of putting off temporality may, for most of us, lie on the further side of the physical change called death seems to me eminently sound. It is a true philosophical instinct which has regularly led great Christian theologians to look for our final consummation not only beyond the dissolution of the body, but beyond the great closing of history at the "Day of Doom". The popular theology of our own country, which finds expression in hymns, according to which the "faithful dead" enter "into immediate rest", has done only too much to deprive the doctrine of immortality of moral seriousness, but it is not the theology of the great divines of any section of the Church.

Still more frivolous, to my own mind, are the attempts made, independently of theology, to construct a doctrine of human immortality apart from a profoundly ethical conception of God, and from the conviction that the true basis of a wise and good man's hopes for himself must be found in aspiration after unification of the human will with the divine. I have spoken sufficiently already of the moral triviality and tediousness of most of the alleged revelations of "spiritualism" about the eternity of boredom which awaits us all. The same criticism seems to me applicable to all attempts to base our highest hopes on the so-called "oriental" lore of transmigration and reincarnation. There is no particular reason for entertaining these speculations as more than doubtful fancies, unless they can be shown to be involved by our conviction that the moral end must be capable of achievement, and from the moralist's point of view they would seem to make the very possibility of achievement questionable. If we

think of the supposed series of births as actually unending, it is clear that the moral end, if we have divined
its character rightly, is never attained. The doctrine,
so taken, converts eternity into the mere repetition of
temporality and thus holds out as a boon what the
morally aspiring man most wants to escape, bondage
to the round of circumstance. In this respect, indeed,
the old Orphicism has the advantage of some of its
modern substitutes; it did, apparently, contemplate, as
the prize of those who have trodden the way of purgation to the end, escape from the "weary wheel". Origen
is alleged, truly or falsely, to have flirted with the fancy
that, in a coming age, Christ and Caiaphas may change
places; in our own days F. W. H. Myers could gravely
give the preference to Buddhism over Christianity in
one respect, on the ground that the former teaches, or
is said to teach, that the Buddha had "often been in
hell for his sins".[1] But clearly the ethical implication
of such fancies is highly dubious. They mean that free
spiritual personality is only achieved to be lost again;
our completest moral victories are only passing incidents in a campaign which ends in nothing. A sane
moralist may or may not be a believer in the dogmatic
theology of Christianity; in either case he can hardly
be blind to the ethical superiority of the religion which
teaches that, "Christ being risen from the dead, dieth
no more; death"—the supreme external manifestation
of temporality—"hath no more dominion over him".

On the other side, if the "wheel" is ever to be escaped,
there seems to be no reason why the episode in our
moral ascent which is terminated at death should
necessarily be repeated. There may be many stages,
and hard stages, still before us in our journey, but
why should we assume that one march has to be accom-

---

[1] *Human Personality*, ii. 289.

plished twice? One would more naturally suppose, though all supposals are uncertain, that no day's march repeats itself, just as within the life we know there is no recurrence of childhood, or adolescence, or the prime of manhood. I own that it is surprising to me to find a philosopher of the distinction of Dr. McTaggart favouring speculations of this type, on the ground that they provide opportunity for the making of a diversity of experiments in living. They give us, he says, the prospect of being Galahad in one life and Tristram in another.[1] Now I do not know in what order Dr. McTaggart would propose to take these two lives, but, for my own part, I cannot conceive that it would be anything but an apostacy and a return to the flesh-pots of Egypt for one who had been Galahad to lead the life of Tristram, and though Tristram might come, after long and bitter purgation in the fires of adversity, to be something like Galahad, it could only be when he had thoroughly learned the lesson that it is not good to be Tristram. The kind of immortality contemplated is radically unethical; it is not an advance towards the achieving of a free personality, and therefore leaves no room for that giving and hazarding all that a man has by which free personality is won. Dr. McTaggart's immortals, in fact, may put on in succession the masks of Galahad and Tristram, and, for all I know, of Mordred too, but all through these are only "impersonations"; there is no growing personality behind them. And hence Dr. McTaggart is strictly consistent in refusing to allow any weight to "moral" arguments for such an immortality, for the future he anticipates is, after all, a non-moral one. It may be a future of unending duration, but, against Dr. McTaggart's own intention, it does not seem to have the quality of eternity

---

[1] *Some Dogmas of Religion*, p. 138.

about it. I should expect such a cycle of adventures to leave men, as it finds them, "quick-change artists".

It is true, as I know, that Dr. McTaggart proposes to be certain on metaphysical grounds, most fully explained in the second volume of *The Nature of Existence*, that the succession of impersonations must culminate in a "timeless" perfection for each of us. But I am far from understanding clearly what "perfection" can mean in such a context. Whatever it means, it seems to be deprived of genuine moral significance by the consideration that, according to the system, it is something fated to happen to us, not something to be won by personal effort. Apparently we have it thrust upon us, whether we will or no, as Malvolio's greatness was thrust on him.[1]

It seems to me important, again, to realise that if the only sort of continuation of life into the unseen for which we can hope to find justification in the analysis of the moral good is the completion of the process of putting off the temporal to put on the eternal, it follows that we do not know how much which, at our present stage in the pilgrimage, appears as though the very roots of our personality were twined about it may not have to be let go before the eternal is really put on, in the full measure possible to men. To speak imaginatively, we may reasonably anticipate that the law of dying into life holds good for Heaven itself, as well as for Earth and Purgatory. Like T. H. Green,[2] I see no difficulty in conceiving of a society where there is no longer wrong to be put right in the relations of the members to one another, nor evil to be burnt away out of the individual desire and will. But even in such a community there need not cease to be differences of

---

[1] Cf. the utterances on this point in *Studies in Hegelian Cosmology*, c. iv.
[2] *Prolegomena to Ethics*, pp. 195, 328.

insight between the members, and, arguing by analogy from what we see of the life of personality, the deepest insight would be the reward of the completest self-abandonment, the most adventurous loss of self in the "divine dark" of the Godhead. There, no doubt, the dark would have its own special quality; it would not arise, as so often with us now, from the resistance of obstinately self-centred will to the rays of the spiritual sun, from coldness of heart, but from the very unapproachableness of the light itself. That dark would be a "deep, but *dazzling* darkness". And one would return from every adventure of the spirit simply enriched with a fuller insight, and a more vivid life, not, as we too often do from our present imperfectly pure adventures, maimed and numbed. And, again, the return would make us more and more complete givers and bestowers of all we had won by the adventure on every member of the society. But the rule would still be, there as here, that it is only he who will lose himself beyond rescue who finds himself to eternal life. The difference between the eternal life of face-to-face vision and the life of time, where we see only *per speculum in aenigmate*, would lie in the completeness of the abandonment of self and the consequent enrichment without compensatory loss with which the soul returns from the adventures.

While the self is still bound up in temporality, the self-abandonment is never quite complete, and by consequence the adventure always entails some element of loss amidst all its profit; there is always love which, because it has not been wholly converted from mere lusting into love, has to be starved. In eternity, all loves would be wholly subordinated to the supreme and irresistible love of God; all would be ventured and, for that very reason, all would be found to be completed and satisfied. But *how* they would find this completion is just what cannot be known by anticipation; that is the "transhumanisation" of humanity of which Dante[1] says that it cannot be expressed *per verba*, and it is because any imagined Paradise, like Dante's own, is an attempted description of the undescribable, a would-be "evaluation" of the everlasting "surd", that all such imaginings leave us with some sense of hollowness. Even Dante's must, at moments, have suggested to most of us the disquieting reflection that it has an unfortunate resemblance with a glorified firework night at the Crystal Palace, or a gaudy celebration of the Vespers of Our Lady. In principle, the note of austerity characteristic of all true morality is not silenced by the hope of Heaven. We cannot say of any of the relations to which we cling most fondly how much they might need to be transfigured to find their completion in eternity.

This is the answer to the kind of sceptical puzzles with which play is made in *Appearance and Reality*.[2] Bradley asks, for example, whether two men who had buried their quarrel in a woman's grave would be friends in the resurrection, or whether all of us would be content to sit down among the angels without recovering our dogs. The question only has serious point for those who sympathise with what Bradley calls modern Christendom's "repeal of the austere sentence" of the Gospel.[3] I venture to think that if modern Christians really abolish the "sentence" in question, that "in the resurrection they neither marry nor are given in marriage", they are so far false both to their professed Christianity and to the fundamentals of a sound ethics. How all the loves which go to the making of moral personality are to be completed in a society where the

---

[1] *Paradiso*, i. 70.   [2] *Op. cit.* p. 509.   [3] *Loc. cit.*

love of God is supreme, we have no means of saying; Bradley's difficulty arises from the assumption that, if completed at all, they must be completed in some way of which we, who are still distracted by conflicting loves, can form a clear picture. And this is false in principle and is the very error of the Sadducees, who erred "not knowing the scriptures nor the *power* of God". Though this particular difficulty, I should have supposed, does sometimes find its solution even on earth. Even here, at our best, we do find doors of escape from "all the little emptiness" of merely competitive loves, so far as we learn to set our hearts more on giving than on taking. Eternal life in fruition would be a life which is all giving without taking, and therefore also all receiving; we think falsely of it if we import into it any relation not consonant with this principle.

It would not be honest to leave this subject without some reference to a further matter upon which clear thinking is much needed—the old problem of the fate of the "finally impenitent". If we are to think ethically of human destiny, we must be prepared to face the possibility that there may be those who obstinately shut the windows of the soul against all influences from the divine, until they have made themselves impervious to them. A man may conceivably so harden himself against good that he ends by becoming incapable of it, or by sheer protracted sloth he may lose the power to make the surrender by which we die into true personality. At least we have, as moralists, no right to say that such a thing is intrinsically inconceivable. If it is conceivable, then it is conceivable that a man may finally and irretrievably miss the very end to which his being is ordained. There may be a definitive "second death" which is a death not into eternity, but into complete and hopeless temporality. We may, indeed, hope

that none of us will ever actually incur this fate, that
the long-suffering and bountifulness of the Giver of all
good will, in the end, break down the wilfulness and
sluggishness of the least responsive among us. But I
do not see how we can be confident that it is so, and I
am sure that if anything can frustrate attainment of
our final good, it is the besotted fancy that this good
is bound to come to us, unstriven for, in the course of
things, whether we choose or not, and that we may
therefore neglect the arduous business of the "making
of the soul". No dictum can be morally shallower than
the often-repeated current assertion that "Hell" is only
a nightmare begotten of superstitious fear of bad and
vindictive gods.

Historically this is *obviously* untrue; it is clear, from
considerations already dwelt on in an earlier lecture,
that the belief that sinners are punished in Hell, like
the belief that they are exposed to special "judgements"
in this present life, is no induction from a misunderstood experience, but the expression, in crude forms,
of a real *a priori* ethical conviction. Men argue that
there *is* a Hell because they are convinced, on moral
grounds, that there *ought* to be one, if eternal justice is
not to be mocked. It is the faith that there is a moral
order in the world, and that it is founded on justice, that
is the parent of belief in retribution beyond the grave.
What is felt to be morally intolerable is that by the mere
fact of dying betimes the impenitent wrong-doer should
triumphantly escape the operation of a law of universal
justice. As Plato puts it, in his admonition to the young
man who is led to the denial of God's moral government of the world by the spectacle of apparently successful lifelong transgression, "You shall assuredly never
be passed over by God's judgement, not though you
make yourself never so small, and hide in the bowels

of the earth, or exalt yourself to heaven: you must pay the penalty due, either while you are still with us, or after your departure hence, in the house of Hades, or, it may be, by removal to some still more desolate region".[1] Belief in a penal and retributory Hell, as contrasted with the older and non-ethical conception of a shadowy continuation of this present existence in a ghost-world, arises directly from the moralisation of men's outlook on the future, though it may take ages of deepening moral reflection before the misdeeds which are held to receive their deserts hereafter come to be identified wholly with what men with a lofty ethical rule of life recognise as moral guilt, in distinction from ceremonial and ritual shortcomings. And in principle, as we can readily see, the rose-coloured anticipations of an easy-going unethical Universalism are as illogical as unethical.

If there is a supreme good for man which yet is not to be attained without personal effort, it must follow that the man who refuses, or persistently neglects, to make the effort towards that good imperils his felicity. He is trying to live in an environment for which *he* is not designed, and to which he cannot adapt himself without ceasing to be truly man. "Heaven" is, of all others, the society in which such a man would be most utterly "in the wrong place"; he would there be the proverbial "fish out of the water", and consequently miserable. It is idle to fancy that God, if He liked, could make the criminal, or the sensualist, or the trifler, happy by translating him to Heaven. To quote Plato once more, the supreme law needed to ensure moral order in the world is a very simple one; it is that men, like liquids, "find their level"; they are drawn, as by a sort of moral gravitation, into the company of the like-

[1] *Laws*, 905 A.

minded, and so they "do and have done to them what
it befits them to do and to endure".[1] There we have
the reality of which the various pictures of the fires
of Hell are so many imaginative symbols, and in a
morally ordered world it could be no otherwise. It is in
mercy, not in wrath, that the way of the transgressor
is made hard. There is a *bottom* of truth in a modern
poet's paradox that God's mercy

> I do think it well,
> Is flashed back from the brazen gates of Hell,[2]

and in the better-known words of a greater poet, that
the maker of the dreadful realm was

> La divina potestate,
> La somma sapienza e il primo amore.[3]

Once more we must remember that we are not to
take our symbols for facts. We do not *know* that any
man actually has sinned, or will sin, himself into complete death to the supreme good, and it is not surprising that Christian theologians, with no desire to be un-
orthodox, have sometimes reminded us that the united
Christian Church has never formally condemned the
doctrine of universal restoration, achieved through grim
experience of the way of the transgressor, taught by
some of the most eminent among the early Fathers.
And, again, we do not know what the ultimate consequences of complete absorption in mere temporality
would be. It is tempting to suppose that the culmina-
tion of such a process would be such a forfeiting of
personality that the consciousness of the man who has
wholly lost *lo ben dell' intelletto* would resemble that of
Leibniz's "mere monad", or, as I think Baron von
Hügel has said somewhere, would be like mere aware-

---

[1] *Laws*, 904 B-E.   [2] Francis Thompson, *The Child-woman*.
[3] Dante, *Inferno*, iii. 5-6.

ness of what Bergson calls "clock-time". Thus, by refusing to deepen his personality, a man would end by losing even what personality he has; "from him that hath not" there would literally be taken away "even that he hath". And we could not imagine that such a process would be anything but grievous in the extreme to the man who, by his own fault, brought it upon himself, just as any one of us would be profoundly unhappy if he found himself steadily declining into physical and mental imbecility, with the knowledge that he had brought his fate on himself by his own vices.

All this is speculation about the unknown, and, as one of our divines sensibly says, it is not very profitable to speculate about a future which must receive us and may prove to be singularly unlike anything we had conjectured. But it should be plain that a genuinely ethical faith can have nothing to do with theories devised simply to get rid of the principle that the way of transgressors, in a reasonably ordered universe, is necessarily hard, and that if eternal life is a thing that has to be won, there is always the grim possibility that it may be lost. A creed constructed to reassure the careless can hardly be a morally sound creed. We need to contemplate the possibility of Hell not, as superficial caricaturists represent, in order to have the pleasure of consigning our enemies, or our neighbours, to it, but to warn ourselves against the risks we run by disloyalty to the best. I venture to think that this may be a sound ethical reason for dissatisfaction with the rather fashionable conception of a "conditional" immortality, which does not pertain to man as man, but may be achieved by a select few. To say nothing of the danger of spiritual pride involved, as the history of Gnosticism in its manifold forms shows, in any such distinction, all such theories seem to me to ignore that deep division of the soul, as we find it, against itself which testifies to man's double environment—temporal and eternal. They conceive man as primarily a being with a strictly natural environment and destiny. This seems to me in conflict with our moral experience; the division of the soul against itself, its inability ever to be wholly content with natural good, are not, so far as I can see, peculiarities of a few, but are written large on the inner life of us all. And in principle Aristotle[1] appears to me to be right when he denies that some members of a γένος can be perishable and others imperishable. A bad-living man, after all, or a carelessly living man, is not a "mere animal", and it is not reasonable to anticipate for him a mere animal's destiny.

The difficulty becomes acute when we remember that we have to take into account not two classes of men only, but three. There are those who seem never to have been awakened out of mere worldliness, those who have been wakened by the call of the eternal and have followed it, and there are also those who have heard the call and refused to follow, or have followed for a time and turned back. To me, as to von Hügel,[2] it seems clear that the troublous problem is that of the destiny of this third class, the "apostates", who make the "great refusal".

I have indeed owned already to a doubt about the very existence of men who not only *seem*, but *are*, wholly unawakened. It is not clear to me that there are any merely "animal" men, who have *never* felt, however obscurely, the solicitation of a more than temporal good. But *if* there are such men, it would be conceivable that their destiny should be as limited as the good to which they respond. Their destination

[1] *Met.* 1058 b 26.   [2] *Essays and Addresses* (First Series), pp. 195 ff.

might conceivably be that suggested by von Hügel, unending enjoyment of a purely temporal good in a *Limbo* which is technically, indeed, "Hell", but is, in fact, a more satisfactory habitat than Europe, even in the pre-war days.

But there is no doubt whatever about the existence of men who are "spiritually awake" and yet false to the good to which they are awake. James Boswell may serve as a tragic historical example of the class, and it is well with any of us whose conscience does not misgive him that he may be in the same group. What I find clearly incompatible with an ethical faith is the easy belief that the destiny of the "awakened" man who obstinately persists in disobedience to the heavenly vision can possibly be the same as that of the man, if there is one, whose "vegetable" slumber has never been disturbed at all. Good nature is surely at variance with ethics when it suggests that the man who chooses known evil, and persists in his choice, remains on the moral level of the "human animal" who makes no genuine choices. What the "second death" may be, I trust none of us may ever find out, but in a morally ordered world it must surely be a terrible possibility.

The world does not become unethical because it contains potentialities of tragedy; there is the possibility of the tragic in all ethical situations. It would become an unethical world if it were so constituted as to make human choice merely frivolous; μέγας ὁ ἀγών, οὐχ ὅσος δοκεῖ, τὸ χρηστὸν ἢ κακὸν γενέσθαι.

Hence there seems to me to be something seriously unethical in the view that we stand to win eternal life if we make our choice rightly, but to lose only temporal good if we persist in choosing wrongly. There is something, to my mind, unsuited to the moral dignity of man in the thought that the end of the man hardened in wrong is the "end of a dog"; it is worthier of humanity that there should be no escape from the law that, for good or bad, we gravitate to our likes and "do and have done to us what is befitting". We are here in our life somewhere on a ladder, where there are as many rungs below us as above. Happily, we know that he who has descended very far and very often may begin to climb again, and may even outstrip some who had long been above him, but that every descent will be followed by a reascent seems to me to be what we may possibly hope, but have no sure ground for affirming.

As Glaucon said long ago to Socrates,[1] there are always the disquieting examples which seem to show that even exceeding wickedness does not tend of itself to impair intense intellectual vitality. Stupidity and animality are not the special characteristics of the "incurables", the greatly bad men who are the curse of humanity. It is perhaps not clear that even the sturdiest theistic optimism absolutely requires us to expect the complete elimination from the world of the spirit

der stets das Böse will, und stets das Gute schafft.

Even if this should be an implication of the ethical view of the world, at least it does not carry with it the further implication that we can escape the full consequences of our persistent evil-doing by simply "paying the debt of nature". A living divine was recently reported, correctly or not, to have declared that "if there are really diabolical men, no doubt, their destiny is perdition, but I should hope that such men are very few". I should like myself to hope that there are none such, but there is just one man, of the many whom I have known, about whom I feel it is salutary not to be over-sanguine, myself.

---

[1] *Republic*, 610 D 5.

VIII

OTHER-WORLDLINESS

As Birds robb'd of their native wood,
  Although their Diet may be fine,
Yet neither sing, nor like their food,
  But with the thought of home do pine;

So do I mourn and hang my head,
  And though thou dost me fullness give,
Yet look I for far better bread,
  Because by this man cannot live.
                                    VAUGHAN.

Exeamus igitur ad eum extra castra.

THROUGHOUT our past argument we have repeatedly
spoken of the contrast between the eternal and the
secular, or temporal, as something familiar and fundamental in the common experiences of the moral life.
We have thus assumed that there is an element of the
"other-worldly" present throughout in the common
everyday life of the simple good neighbour and honest
citizen, that it is a duty for all of us to practice other-
worldliness, and not to live as though "this" world
were the only world there is. It may be well to pause
here and ask ourselves to what practical rule of conduct
such an assumption commits us, and whether that rule
indeed has the sanction of the morality by which we all
live. What is the true relation of the "other" world to
the whole system in which we find ourselves bound up
by the fact that we are members of a great animal
"kingdom", existing in a definite space-time region of

the universe, and members, moreover, of a historical society of humanity, living and deceased. We cannot but remember that while this thought of the dual citizenship of man, as at once a "child of nature" and a being who is something more than "natural", has inspired the practical teaching of the greatest of philosophical moralists from Plato to Kant, it is also fashionable among reputable philosophers to decry this so-called "dualism" as a fatal error, and to find in it the central flaw of Platonism, the "excrescence" on Kant's doctrine which had to be cut away by the surgery of Fichte and Hegel before the critical philosophy could bear its true fruits.[1] There are not two worlds, it is often said, but only one; that "other world is just this world rightly understood": it is the death of all morality to direct our aims or set our hopes on a *saeculum venturum*, just as Bosanquet has said that it is the death of idealism to project its ideals into the *future*.

The same radical conflict of standpoints meets us in the estimation of poetry, and the arts generally. We are told, to be sure, of the "consecration and the poet's dream", and of the "light that never was on sea or land" as the aspiration of all high artistic endeavour; to say that a poet, or a painter, however admirable his work may be in other respects, is "of the earth earthy", is felt as denying his claim to rank among the greatest, even by critics wholly free from prepossessions in favour of any specifically theological interpretation of the world, just as the most unqualified opponents of

---

[1] "If Aristotle is limited and thwarted in his idealism by the want of formulae more elastic than those proper to number and magnitude, he less frequently lapses into the false dualism of soul and body, mind and matter, ideas and things, which made Plato, against his principles, a mystic, and which has clung like a body of death to Platonising philosophy ever since" (T. H. Green, *Works*, iii. 47). "The conception of a Ruler of the world, apparently external to the spirit of man, and of a future life, continued in Kant's philosophy as survivals, though they are, in my judgement, quite unessential to it" (Bosanquet, *Science and Philosophy*, p. 349).

any intrusion of theology into the field of ethics commonly regard it as an imputation on a man's moral theory or practice to call either "worldly". Yet, on the other side, a modern poet whom most of us would be inclined to call the reverse of a "worldling" or "worldly-wise" person, could make it his boast that

> Earth of the earth is hidden by my clay.

And it is the commonest of disparagements to say of poets and artists that they lose themselves in a world of dreams, or that their work has no contact with the coarse, brutal, fetid, but living world of common flesh and blood.

The curious fact, disclosed by this universal linguistic usage, is that, in the conduct of the life of business and social relations, we plainly agree that it is a duty to be, in some intelligible sense, a "man of the world", and yet a grave defect to be "worldly". The good man ought, if the phrase may be allowed, to be an unworldly man of the world. And, as if to warn us that we are not dealing with some mere confusion of thought, due to the imperfect emancipation of morality from the foreign control of a "moribund" theology, we find just the same seemingly paradoxical combination of qualities demanded, in the name of art, from poets, painters or musicians. They also, if they are to rank with the immortals, are to be men of this world without being worldly-minded. It is just where men believe themselves to find both qualities in perfect balance, for example in Shakespeare, or it may be in Goethe, that they confess the presence of supreme genius. It is made a claim for Shakespeare that his thought moves in the world of the actual, not in a beautiful but fanciful kingdom of dreams; *he* at least is no "ineffectual angel". But it would be felt at once to be an absurd charac-

terisation of him to call him, what we all agree to call
his brilliant contemporary Bacon, "worldly-minded".
We are commanded by our own religion, in language
familiar to us all, to be *in* the world and yet out of it.

Shakespeare was no divine, nor, so far as it is possible
to discern his personality behind his work, does he
seem likely to have felt the specifically religious aspiration to a supernatural "holiness"; yet it would be hard
to find a better phrase by which to describe the character of his ripest work. *Macbeth*, or even *The Tempest*,
deals with a life which is "of this world", the life of men
and women of flesh and blood, not that of angels or
devils, nor yet of elves or fairies. Macbeth may have
his traffic with demons; yet he is no "devil incarnate",
but a man, with a man's temptations and crimes, and
also with a man's qualities of heroism and resolution.
Ferdinand and Miranda meet and love in an enchanted
island, but they are "sublunary lovers", after all. Their
life is to be lived out in the world of common realities, and it is to be the "practical life" of marriage, the
family and mundane affairs at large. "Pictures in
their eyes to get" will most certainly not be all *their* propagation,[1] and their maturity, as the poet is careful to
let us know, has before it the very business-like task of
adjusting the affairs of two communities on a sound
basis. Milan has been thrust from Milan that his heirs
may become rulers of Naples. Even Prospero, who had

---

[1] Donne, *The Extasie*:

> "So to' entergraft our hands, as yet
>   Was all the meanes to make us one,
> And pictures in our eyes to get
>   Was all our propagation."

Contrast the tone of Prospero's warning (*Tempest* iv. 1, 51):

> "Look, thou be true; do not give dalliance
> Too much the rein: the strongest oaths are straw
> To the fire i' the blood: be more abstemious,
> Or else, good night your vow!"

once neglected his duties as duke to bury himself in his library of books of magic, has learned a more practical wisdom by the event. His island is a temporary place of refuge, not a home, and the great object to which his wizardry has been made instrumental is to effect his return to the world which "is the home of all of us".

Yet, for all this, worldliness is the last charge we should be likely to make against *Macbeth* or *The Tempest*. Shakespeare can, of course, be worldly enough when he pleases. Falstaff and Prince Hal, for example, think and speak, from first to last, "like men of this world", and it is just their fundamental earthiness which makes the second repellent and the first, at his brightest, a creature to whom no one could lose his heart. But it is not in such characters that we see Shakespeare's measure of humanity, nor, I would add, to them that we must believe their creator's heart to be given. Macbeth sinks into a hell of murderous frustrated ambition against which a man like Falstaff is secured by his very carnality; yet, even in his ruin, it is Macbeth, not Falstaff, who ennobles our conception of humanity by the revelation of what a man can be, for good or evil. The Beatrices and Rosalinds of Shakespeare's earlier days are, at bottom, "good girls" enough; the Cleopatra of his maturity is an incarnate corruption; yet, with all the corruption, Cleopatra has the touch of a quality which the earlier sympathetic heroines do not reveal. She has, as no Rosalind nor Portia of them all had, "immortal longings", windows of the soul open on Heaven and on Hell, and the difference makes her not less, but more, a revelation of the universal woman in all women. The presence of something which is not "of this world" in her makes her the more overpoweringly real. If there are good and evil characters in Shakespeare's gallery of whom we could say with some measure of justice that they are dreams rather than solid realities, we must say this of just the more ordinary good and bad figures of his less fully mature work.

By the side of Othello, Henry Vth is unreal, Brutus is unreal; all the earlier women are dreams and fantasies by the side of Lady Macbeth or Cleopatra. It is just where the figures, for good or evil, impress us with the sense of being something more than earthly that we feel the poet's grip on the realities of our "moral being" firmest. Othello and Macbeth are not, like so many characters in Shakespeare's earlier work, merely playing their parts in a pleasant interlude, nor, like even Henry Vth, walking in a pageant in honour of England. They are fighting for their lives in a battle where the stakes are Heaven and Hell, and it is because the battle is so grim and the stakes so fearful that we feel that the fight is being waged, not in fairyland, but in the real waking world of our common life. And if anyone should fancy that *The Tempest*, at any rate, is only a dream of an enchanted island, he must be curiously blind to the truth that, there too, the same battle is being waged, however fantastic the weapons, for the souls of a criminal king and his more criminal counsellors.

> You are three men of sin, whom Destiny—
> That hath to instrument this lower world
> And what is in't—the never-surfeited sea
> Hath caused to belch you up; and on this island
> Where man doth not inhabit, you 'mongst men
> Being most unfit to live . . .
>   . . . whose wraths to guard you from—
> Which here, in this most desolate isle, else falls
> Upon your heads—is nothing but heart-sorrow
> And a clear life ensuing.

The words are spoken by Ariel in the disguise of a

Harpy, but they fix us at the heart of real life. The element of the fantastical is in their setting, not in their sense. Similarly we misread the famous words of Prospero, that

> We are such stuff
> As dreams are made on, and our little life
> Is rounded with a sleep,

if we hear nothing more than an echo of the Horatian *pulvis et umbra sumus*. They would be both trivial and misplaced if we did not understand that there is an infinite seriousness behind the seeming futility of the parts man plays in the brief puppet-show. It is the tension between the sense of this underlying earnest and the apparent vanity of life that explains the speaker's reference to the "beating mind" from which his words come.

We are not to be surprised, then, if the same problem of a life which has to be lived out in "this world", with all its apparent tangle of accident and restricted incidental issue, and yet is directed on an end which redeems life from tedium and frivolity, precisely because this world cannot exhaust it, reappears, in principle, in the most measured and sober rule of practice a moralist can devise. We shall expect to find that life may be marred in practice in either of two ways. It is marred if we lose ourselves in concentration on a mere manageable success which we, or our children, can see with our own eyes; if we mistake the proverb of the bird in the hand for the last word of moral wisdom. It is marred in another way, if we lose our sense of the imperatively necessary "here and now", the duty of the moment, in preoccupation with what lies beyond every now and every here. We need to learn the double lesson that there is no more certain way of being unfaithful in much than to be careless of being faithful in little—for there are, indeed, no mere "littles" in the moral world—and no more certain way of being unfaithful in little than to be satisfied with aiming at little. In fact, we need to reconsider and state more correctly a familiar formula which has already been used in a context where it was accurate enough for the immediate purpose. The true rule of life, we said, was to combine detachment with attachment, to use and love all goods but the highest without losing our hearts to them, that when the call to let them go comes to us we may be able to obey without breaking our hearts. But, if we would speak with a nicer accuracy, we must rather say that the rule is not simply to make the best use of the lower and temporal goods, while they last, and then to let them go with a will; it is to use them in such fashion that the very using is itself an act of devotion to the higher and more abiding. It is not enough that whole-hearted possession should be *followed*, in due time, by equally whole-hearted surrender; there is a more excellent way which unites possession and surrender in the same act.

This is the most difficult of achievements for us, who, even in what is called the autumn of our lives, are mostly mere beginners in the pilgrimage from the seen to the eternal, but it is a task which we must essay, unless our lives are to end in moral failure. Unless we have at least a beginning with the lesson, the division of the self against itself is not even on the way to be healed. We are still at the mercy of the before and after, still "in our sins". We have found, it may be, an answer to the two first of R. Hillel's pithy questions, "If I am not for myself who is for me, and if I am only for myself, where is the good of me?" The third still confronts us, unsolved and insistent—"And if not now, when?"

Let me illustrate what I mean by a concrete example which I have used elsewhere.[1] "A man discharges the duty of a husband and a parent in a secular spirit, if he has no aim beyond giving his wife a 'happy time of it' and bringing up his children to enjoy a lucrative, honourable or comfortable existence from youth to old age". I interrupt the self-quotation to add that a man would still be discharging *these* offices in a secular spirit if, Indian fashion, he had it in mind, later on, when the work has been done, to retire to the forests, and there give his old age to retired meditation. The more excellent way—one says it with shame, as one reflects on the failure in one's own practice—is that indicated in the sequel of the quotation, to which I return: "Marriage and parenthood become charged with a sacramental spirit, and the discharge of their obligations a *Christian* duty, when the 'principal intention' of parents is to set forward a family in the way to know and love God, and to be spiritual temples for His indwelling". Where such an end is attained, and so far as it is attained, the "flesh" is not merely "suppressed" in the interest of the "spirit", it is made the minister of the spirit, as "necessity", in Plato's *Timaeus*, is made the Creator's "workman",[2] perfectly subdued to His purpose in the ordering of the world. Where it is not achieved there is a double failure. A man, for instance, cannot set his son forward on the way to know and love God, except by bringing him up to some definite honourable and useful life of service to a specific community; but, again, he cannot bring him up to render the service adequately if

---

[1] *Essays Catholic and Critical*, p. 81.

[2] ὑπηρέτης. Cf. Plato, *Tim.* 46 C 7 ταῦτ' οὖν πάντα ἐστιν τῶν συναιτίων οἷς θεὸς ὑπηρετοῦσιν χρῆται τὴν τοῦ ἀρίστου κατὰ τὸ δυνατὸν ἰδέαν ἀποτελῶν, 68 E 4 χρώμενος μὲν ταῖς περὶ ταῦτα αἰτίαις ὑπηρετούσαις, τὸ δὲ εὖ τεκταινόμενος ἐν πᾶσιν τοῖς γιγνομένοις αὐτός.

he himself looks, and teaches his son to look, to no end
beyond that definite service to that specific community.

If, for example, a man wants his son to give of his
best to Scotland as a public servant, it is not enough
that he should educate the son to be a public servant;
he must be even more concerned that the lad should be
a good Scotsman than that he should be a good civil
servant. And if he would have the boy a good Scotsman, he must make it a still more vital concern that he
shall become a true man. And a true man's ultimate
loyalty cannot even be to "humanity". There are
services which I must not render, even to "the well-
being of humanity". If I may indulge once more in
self-quotation,[1] "it may be argued that for the good of
the human race I ought to be prepared to sacrifice
the very independence of my native land, but for no
advantage to the whole body of mankind may I insult
justice by knowingly giving sentence or verdict against
the innocent".

In a word, just as the only way to be a thoroughly
good professional man is to aim at being something
more than a professional man—for example, at being
a good citizen—and the only way to be a thoroughly
good citizen is to aim at being, at any rate, a "good
European", or something of the kind, so the only way
to be a good man or a good "citizen of the world" is
again to aim at being something more. I believe no
moral theory can ignore this without identifying
morality with mere conventional respectability, and so
stultifying itself. For we may take it as certain that a
moral code which enjoins respectability as the supreme
obligation will not long ensure that its followers shall
remain even respectable. As T. H. Green[2] says of

[1] *Essays Catholic and Critical*, p. 61.
[2] *Works*, i. 371 (*Introduction to Hume*, II.).

Hume, it is because he derationalises respectability that "he can find . . . no room for the higher morality. . . . An 'ideal' theory of ethics tampers with its only sure foundation when it depreciates respectability." Green goes on to say, in impressive words, that "there is no other 'enthusiasm of humanity' than one which has travelled the common highway of reason, the life of the good neighbour and honest citizen, and can never forget that it is still only on a further stage of the same journey".

But it is obviously implied in such a statement that the goal of the "journey", though it may not disclose itself to the traveller's conscious vision until many stages of the way have been achieved, from the first lay beyond anything which can be adequately described as "citizenship" or "neighbourliness", and therefore beyond the horizon of the "temporal" world. Thus, in spite of a certain tendency to minimise the "supernatural" factor in the moral life, a tendency which leads him from time to time to depreciate the significance of moral crises and "conversions", and, on occasion, to caricature Platonism, Green bears witness, one might almost say *malgré lui*,[1] to the impossibility of getting the note of "other-worldliness" out of a genuine practical morality.

At the same time, it is equally clear that there is no way of effectively "having our citizenship in heaven" except the way of discharging the specific duties of this place and this time *as* duties which have an ultimate source of obligatoriness lying beyond the now and here, thus making God, in the scholastic phrase, our "principal intention"[2] in the discharge of those homely duties.

---

[1] Or, more truly one might say, *malgré la tradition hegélienne*, to which Green, happily, was not completely subdued.

[2] Not necessarily our conscious intention. "The supernatural should not be directly identified and measured by the amount of its conscious, explicit refer-

You cannot do justice to the demands of morality itself
if you follow the lead of Aristotle by bisecting human
life into a "service of the divine" to be achieved by
"speculation", and a lower "practical life" of service to
the human community. This is, in effect, to have one
aim for the working-days of the week and another for
Sundays, to be the honest citizen and good neighbour
on common days, the "thinker" or man of science on
high-days and festivals. In practice such a sundering of
the life of the "divine something in man" from the "life
of man" is bound to degrade both. If our duties as
men and citizens are regarded as something secondary
and inferior, it will not be long before they come to be
discharged in a perfunctory fashion, as tasks to be got
over and out of the way that we may escape with all
speed to the higher work of the study and the laboratory; we shall be too anxious to be good physicists,
or chemists, or metaphysicians to be more than very
second-rate men. Again, by being thus cut off from
the "work of *man*" the speculative life itself becomes
impoverished and loses its seriousness. The resulting
degradation may show itself in a great variety of ways.
In some lives it appears as engrossment in so-called
"religious" duties to the neglect of the simple humani-
ties of life. Then we get the man, for example, who
identifies the "spiritual life" with absorption in ceremonial "devotions", or solitary meditation, at the cost
of forgetting to be a good husband, or father, or neighbour. Or we may consider the type whose prosecution
of the "speculative life" takes the form of preoccupation with a science which has become dehumanised,
the man who pursues knowledge as a mere gratification

· ences to Christ or even simply to God, but by certain qualities . . . of which
heroism, with a keen sense of 'givenness' and of 'I could not do otherwise',
appear to be the chief" (Von Hügel, *Essays and Addresses* [1921], p. 280).

for his curiosity, or even devotes himself to the discovery of new curses for humanity — "poison-gases"
and the like—for discovery's sake.

In principle, the source of the degradation is the
same in all these cases: the devotee of a life of the "divine
element in man", supposed to be severed from the
"work of man", naturally becomes a specialist in something at the cost of failing to "make a *man* of himself".
It is a little strange that Green, of all men, should have
reproached Plato with a "false dualism which has clung
like a body of death to Platonising philosophy ever
since",[1] without reflecting that *this* "dualism" is specifically Aristotelian. Its source is, in fact, the fatal error
of dividing life into a higher sphere of "speculation"
and a lower realm of "practice", which, as it is supposed,
can be kept distinct, and it is against just this fatal
severance of "active good living" from the "higher
spiritual life" that Plato is setting his face when he
insists that neither the "philosopher" nor the "king"
can be what he should be until the two parts are united
in the same person.[2]

There is, then, a sense in which "other-worldliness"
would really be the death of all morality. Morality
withers at once if we are serious with that bisection of
life into one part devoted to the "secular", and another
given to the "eternal", which is made verbally by anyone who draws a sharp distinction between "secular"
and "eternal" interests, or "secular" and "religious"
duties. But there is also a sense in which "other-worldliness" is the very breath of the moral life. If we understood by a "religious" duty a duty which can be discharged otherwise than by making the right response

[1] *Works*, iii. p. 47.

[2] Cf. *Rep.* 497 A 3 οὐδέ γε, εἶπον, τὰ μέγιστα (*sc.* διαπράξεται ὁ φιλόσοφος), μὴ
τυχὼν πολιτείας προσηκούσης· ἐν γὰρ προσεχούσῃ αὐτός τε μᾶλλον αὐξήσεται καὶ μετὰ
τῶν ἰδίων τὰ κοινὰ σώσει.

here and now in a temporal situation, we should have to say that morality recognises no such duties; all duties are acts which it is incumbent to perform in some *now*. But, in another sense, morality recognises no "secular" duties; all its tasks are "religious", in the sense that, to be adequately discharged, they have to be undertaken in a religious spirit, a spirit of loyalty to something which may demand the renunciation, and always does demand the subordination, of every loyalty to concrete temporal individuals and communities. How deeply rooted genuine morality is in such a loyalty to the "other" world we see most clearly, if we consider the glaring and fatal objection to "humanitarianism", that is, to the theory which finds the justification of moral imperatives simply in the representation of them as the claims of a human society, of the present or the future, on the loyalty of its individual members. Perhaps, in view of the unfortunate popularity of a false humanitarianism in current moral speculation, and the grave danger that speculative error of this kind may infect practice, a brief digression may be permissible at this point.

(1) All duties, so we are told by a host of fashionable writers, are *social* duties. And the theory has been sometimes preached, even by those who should know better, to the length of denying that prayer, meditation, participation in the public worship of God, sacramental or other, are duties at all, on the ground that we cannot specify the human persons with reference to whom, or the precise ways in which, these activities are socially beneficial. This is obviously hardly a fair deduction from the premisses of humanitarianism itself. For it might well be that a man's whole discharge of his functions as citizen and neighbour is made much more thorough and single-minded by his hours of private

or public devotion, though we cannot specify any particular person, or group of persons, particularly benefited, or any particular performance which is the direct outcome of this devotion. Indeed—and this is a consideration to be remembered in estimating the social value of the technically "religious" life of the "monk" —the practice of the whole community may be affected in the same way for the better by the presence within it of individuals or groups whose whole activity is given to such devotion.[1]

But there is a criticism which it is not so easy for the humanitarian to dispose of, and this criticism may take several forms. We may ask, for instance, whether it is really true, as some writers are fond of asserting, that a Robinson Crusoe—at any rate an "atheistic" Crusoe— convinced that his restoration to human society is out of the question, ceases to be under any moral obligations; or whether it is true that, if the human race knew itself to be menaced by inevitable destruction in some cosmic cataclysm to-morrow, there would be no moral objection to general abandonment to-day to a frenzy of license. The behaviour of whole populations in times of pestilence or civil war, when a general dissolution of society is apprehended to be at hand, as well as the conduct of castaways, or the disturbing facts which not uncommonly come out at inquests on persons who have joined in a "death pact", seems to show that there is some ground for believing that many men do *de facto* draw the conclusion, "since we must die to-morrow, we cannot be blamed for giving the rein to our lusts to-

---

[1] Cf. Bradley, *Ethical Studies*[2], p. 337: "However secluded the religious life, it may be practical indirectly *if* through the unity of the spiritual body it can be taken as vicarious" (a correction of his own earlier attack on the *religieux*). For a rather reckless development of the view to which objection is taken in the text cp. the essay of Bosanquet, *The Kingdom of God on Earth*, already referred to (*Science and Philosophy*, pp. 333-51).

day". But the question still remains whether to act in this way is not to degrade our personality? If it is, *why* may I not spend my last moments in degrading my personality? We must not say, "because the effects on humanity will be so evil", since *ex hypothesi*, there are not going to be any effects. If our Robinson Crusoe may not "make a beast of himself" on his island— assuming him to be reasonably certain, as he might be, that he will never live to escape from it—this must be because to "make a beast of himself" is something more than an offence against a community from which he has been finally sundered.

Or we may take a different illustration which does not require the introduction of so exceptional a case as that of the solitary. Wanton cruelty is admittedly one of the vilest things we know; any man would be turned out of the most tolerant society of decent men if he were known to be in the habit of getting entertainment from the tormenting of a cat, or even of ants and flies. But *why* is such conduct reasonably held to be unpardonable? Surely not merely on the ground that because, though otherwise innocent, it may easily lead to the habit of practising cruelty towards human beings, or may be taken as an indication that the offender would certainly practice such cruelty if he had the chance. The fact is, at least, doubtful. Persons in southern Europe who show themselves callous to the sufferings of the animals, on the plea that they are not "Christians", and that we may therefore treat them as we please, do not seem to be more indifferent than Northerners to the sufferings of their fellow-men, and we all know the odious type of person whose sensibility to the sufferings of animals is only surpassed by his indifference to those of his own kind. We are familiar with the kind of man who writes indignant letters to the newspapers about the brutality of stamping out hydrophobia at the expense of a temporary muzzling order, or the selfishness of those who object to the intrusion of his dog into a railway compartment. Nor yet can we say that the exceeding vileness of the cruelty is measured by the suffering inflicted on the victim. It must be highly doubtful, for example, whether a fly or an ant is really capable of feeling much in the way of suffering. So far as we can tell, the "corporal sufferance" of the beetle on which we tread is *not* comparable with an ordinary human toothache. Yet the strongest conviction that this is so does not affect our abhorrence of the human being who amuses himself by treading on the beetle or pulling the wings off the fly.[1]

So far as I can see, the real ground of our judgement is not that the creature suffers so much; indeed, I own that personally I should feel some touch of the same repugnance for a man who wantonly defaced the lilies of the field, which presumably do not suffer at all, and I believe I could show this feeling to be justified. But, be that as it may, I feel sure that it is the cruel *man*, rather than the suffering he causes, who is the direct object of our loathing. If there is any foundation for this judgement, it follows that our condemnation of cruelty itself, the very vice specially abhorrent to the humanitarian, has its roots in a supreme loyalty which

[1] Cf. J. Laird, *A Study in Moral Theory*, p. 302. As will be seen, I agree entirely with Prof. Laird in his thesis that "it is not simply the evil effects of cruelty upon humanity that makes the torturer what he is". It will also be seen why I am not satisfied with his own explanation that the "sufferings of the victims who are not men" are the "chief condemnation" of the torturer. In many cases our tendency is to exaggerate these sufferings by imagining what we suppose we should feel if, retaining our own acute sensibility, we were subjected to analogous treatment. We think of the fly deprived of its wing suffering what *we* should suffer if our arm were torn from us, exactly as, in Adam Smith's familiar illustration, we judge of the cheerfulness of the condition of a lunatic who is completely self-satisfied, by imagining what we suppose we should feel, could we *per impossibile* be at once the lunatic and the sane spectator.

is not loyalty to the fellowship of human persons, nor even to the fellowship of sentient creatures.

(2) It is the same with all the virtues which ennoble human life. They are all to be found at their best only where human society is not made the *principal* end and the *supreme* object of loyalty. As has been already said, the noblest national life is impossible where nationality is taken as the ultimate principle of allegiance and *salus rei publicae suprema lex* as the great commandment. So a world-wide federation of mankind would prove morally disappointing and, in fact, would hardly be likely to subsist long, unless it were recognised that there are some prices too heavy to be paid even for the continued existence of federated humanity. Mankind itself is best served by those who feel the duty of serving it to be one they owe to something more august and worthy to be loved than humanity, just as, to use the words of one of our most penetrating critics, "the advance of civilisation is, in truth, a sort of by-product of Christianity—not its chief aim; but we can appeal to history to support us that this progress is most stable and genuine when it is a by-product of a lofty and unworldly idealism".[1] (A considered study of the social, economic, literary, and artistic debt of Europe to St. Francis, or of England to men like Wesley, or the Tractarian leaders, would furnish an interesting commentary.)

The point we are concerned to make, then, is that "other-worldliness" does not mean the neglect of obvious duties of the temporal world in which we are living, for the sake of some wholly different set of obligations. It means the discharge of the duties of the situation as the man who is unworldly sees them, in a spirit of loyalty to a kingdom which is not of this world.

---

[1] Inge, *Personal Life and the Life of Devotion*, p. 84.

We may say, if we please, that, at bottom, "religious" and "secular" duties are the same, but that they may be discharged in a secular or in a religious spirit. Even what are properly called more specifically the "duties of religion" have their secular side, their value in holding the actual community of the living together in a bond of good fellowship. For example, a man who, from intellectual conscientiousness, cuts himself off from the public worship of his society may, in a particular case, have no alternative, if he is to be an honest man, yet his efficiency as good neighbour and citizen will, none the less, often be really impaired.[1] The Oxford latitudinarian tutor of a (probably apocryphal) story, who urged an agnostic undergraduate to communicate with others at the altar, on the ground that "it keeps the College together, like dinner in Hall", was uttering a sentiment which I take to be no less repugnant to Agnostics than to Anglicans. Yet the remark, so far as it goes, is undeniably true. What really shocks a finer nature is not that the statement is untrue, but that it bases an obligation which, if real, ought to have a more august source, on merely secular principles. It treats an act which, to be adequately justified, must be justified by a relation between man and God as though its *raison d'etre* could be furnished by a mere social relation between members of the same college.

We put the same thought from a different point of view when we say, in the fashion of George Herbert, that any so-called secular duty becomes "work for God" when it is done in the spirit of service to Him, and thus acquires a new "sanctification":

---

[1] I remember years ago hearing F. H. Bradley make the point in a conversation on the "ethics of conformity" by asking the question whether an "agnostic" lord of the Manor would not have a duty to attend Church regularly, if the parson were an admirable man whose moral influence for good in the parish would be seriously impaired by the "squire's" non-attendance on his ministrations.

Who sweeps a room as for Thy laws
Makes that and the action fine.

And the principal matter is that "secular" duties
themselves are only then most efficiently performed
when they receive this sanctification. If a room is to
be well swept, an empire well governed, or any other
piece of service to be discharged as well as it can
be, the work must be done by someone who does not
regard the sweeping, or the governing, as its one be-
all and end-all, just as to make any human relation
yield its worthiest fruit, it must not be treated as an all-
sufficient end in itself.[1]

Speaking generally, we may say that we shall not
detect the indispensability of "other-worldliness" in a
sound morality if we look exclusively for evidence
to the moments of tension and crisis, when there is
a direct clash between the embodied loyalties of the
family, the nation, the brotherhood of nations, and an
unembodied loyalty to something which lies beyond
them all. These crises are, after all, exceptional occasions; in the average life of the simple good man they
never present themselves recognisably. He may never
be faced with the clear and sharp alternative of disobeying God to obey man, or disobeying man to obey
God; at any rate, such sharply defined alternatives are
not habitually characteristic of the ordinary dutiful
life. But the other characteristic of the moral life of
which we have been speaking—viz. that the duties
arising from our embodied loyalties are only discharged
to the height when they receive a final consecration
from a loyalty which has no embodiment—is omni-
present and all-pervasive. To serve men with one's

[1] Cf. St. Thomas, *S.T.* ii^a ii^{ae} q. 123, art. 7 resp. dicendum quod duplex est
finis, scilicet proximus et ultimus . . . sic ergo dicendum quod fortis sicut proxi-
mum finem intendit ut similitudinem sui habitus exprimat in actu . . . finis
autem remotus est beatitudo vel Deus.

might, one must do the service "not as to men, but as to the Lord". A morality in which there is not this pervasive and ever-present note of the "other-worldly", I would urge, has already lost that which makes all the difference between a living morality and an ossified conventionalism. It has lost that possibility of adventure which is the soul of morality and science.

Thus, ethically considered, the relation between, "this" world and the "other" is not that the "other" is something wholly foreign which is to follow upon "this" world. The "other" is with us already, seizing on "this" and transforming it, and, by that very fact, providing the element of adventure without which "this" life would sink into a monotonous routine. Eternity is not a time to come after time is over; it is rather, to use the imagery of Heraclitus, the ever-present fire to which time is the fuel. Or we may put the situation in Peripatetic phraseology, if we say that "this" world is to the "other" as matter to form. The moral problem is the problem of educing from, or superinducing on, the familiar stuff of our daily secular life a form or pattern which endows it with the quality of completeness and finality.

Possibly I may make my precise point more clearly by considering the significance of two well-known deliverances which have won a considerable amount of acceptance, the sayings that "it is the death of idealism to project its ideals into the future", and that "the other world is simply this world rightly understood". The first of these sayings, perhaps, bears more directly on the practical business of the right direction of conduct, the second on the speculative question of the philosophical implications of loyal acceptance of the ethical standard. But the spirit of both is the same, and it will clarify our thoughts to ask how far we can accept either.

(1) "It is the death of idealism to transfer its ideals to the future." The words are Professor Bosanquet's, but my object is not to discuss the particular question of the sense in which their author meant them to be understood. There is obviously a sense—though I do not suppose it to be what Bosanquet intended—in which the statement is wholly true. It would be the death of all practical idealism to lose itself in a day-dream of a good and beautiful world, thought of as not here now, but bound, in the nature of things, to arrive in a "good time coming". The business of morality is not to find an escape from the triviality, sordidness, or cruelty of the actual present by dreaming idly of a Utopia; it is to make the present better by reshaping it in the image of the ideal. Or perhaps even that statement is misleading, since we do not and cannot enjoy a clear and well-defined picture of our ideal as embodied in concrete institutions. At best we see two or three steps ahead of us; we know certainly of this or that which is amiss and demands to be righted now and here, and we know the spirit in which the adventure of righting it ought to be undertaken. Contemplation of imaginary Utopias, unless it is undertaken half in play, and more with a view to illustrating the spirit of social goodness than as a programme of actual reform, is probably, in the main, mischievous. It means, according to personal temperament, either cessation from actual strenuous effort to "set the crooked straight", or the frustration of effort by the attempt, characteristic of the *doctrinaire* in all ages, to "canalise" life once and for all. An "ideal" of practical value cannot be a vision of the future, pure and simple, because it must be an inspiration and a call to daily and hourly action now.

And, again, there is a different sense in which the statement would be merely and very dangerously false. The meaning may be—on the lips of some of those who use this language, I suspect that it is—that time, and, along with time, imperfection and evil and the moral struggle are mere illusions. It is a pure mistake to suppose that there is really anything which calls to be put right here and now, for *here* and *now* are themselves illusions. If we could only see things from the "point of view of the Absolute", we should see that what is is already a finished and flawless whole; everything is not only "the best possible under the conditions", but wholly and perfectly good.

Plainly this kind of metaphysical optimism, if we could seriously make it the spirit of our lives, would be the ruin of all practical effort; it would leave us with no rational justification for doing anything in particular, rather than anything else. And, no less plainly, the theory involves a hopeless logical contradiction which makes it as false speculatively as it is pernicious in practice. It asserts the existence of both evil and succession in its very attempt to deny them. For it declares that everyone, except its own adherents at moments when they are under its own sway, is suffering from an "illusion" due to a partial, and therefore falsified, outlook on the world. And it exhorts us to replace this partial view by one taken from "the standpoint of the whole". Thus it says at once that there is no evil and that there is at least the one and all-inclusive evil that we—or most of us—mistakenly believe in the existence of evils; it says that there is in truth no futurity, and also that we should, *for the future*, believe that futurity is an illusion. Reduced to its simplest terms, it in fact maintains that *time* is a word with no significance, an "unmeaning noise". And with this metaphysical view morality too, must become an illusion; for morality is *making* the best of ourselves, our endowments and opportunities, bringing what *ought* to be into actual existence—that or nothing.

If, then, it is false to think of an "ideal" simply as something which is not as yet, but some day will be, it is equally false to think of it as having no reference to futurity. The better is not simply what is yet to be, but it *is* something which is not yet actual, and for that very reason it impresses on us the obligation to act with the intention that it shall be brought about. When all is said, the moral life really is a γένεσις εἰς οὐσίαν, a growth into moral maturity, and its claims on us are bound up with the recognition that "becoming" has its place in reality, no less than "being". Growth is not mere succession or transience, nor even mere transience according to some regular pattern of transition; it is rather the achievement of an identity of pattern which steadily makes itself, within a succession where there was at first random variation.

So far, at least, the nineteenth century evolutionary formulae are clearly sound; as anything grows, it acquires an increasing power of maintaining its own *esse* by increasing skill in self-adaptation to changes in its surroundings. It may begin by being changed almost out of recognition in response to modification without. It only becomes *mature* in the degree to which it learns to meet such modifications by responses which leave it more and more recognisably the same. A thing which had "perfectly adapted" itself would neither remain obstructive and irresponsive against suggestions from without, like a lump of granite, nor take a new impress from every change of circumstance, with the ductibility of an ideally plastic sheet of wax. It would be infinitely rich in artifices of response

to the variations in its surroundings, and yet, under all
the variety of its responses, it would keep the pattern
which was definitely its own, as a profoundly civilised
human society proves its high civilisation by ability
to reproduce its typical institutions without impair-
ment under transplantation to unfamiliar climates.
An Englishman or a Scot, it is said, will remain an
Englishman or a Scot, if you translate him to the
North Pole or the Equator. He carries his pattern
with him wherever he goes. This is sometimes regarded as a mark of "insularity"; to me it seems rather
a presumption of high civilisation. *Plus ça change*,
plus c'est la même chose should be exactly true of the
"perfectly evolved" type; the types which "go under"
are those which either do not know how to change,
or do not know how to be *la même chose* under the
variations.

(2) And this, in principle, decides our verdict on the
second saying, that the "other" world is "the world
rightly understood". The saying may be true or false,
according to the sense put on the word "understood".
We have probably all heard the *mot* which defines a
violin solo as the "dragging of the tail of a dead horse
across the intestines of a dead cat", and perhaps other
sayings which dispose of intimate human relation-
ships in the same fashion. Nor do I doubt that there
really is a type of man to whom a definition like this
would appeal as a correct account of what music
"really is"; what is more than this in the significance
of music to the music-lover, such a man would say, is
simply unreal, a pleasing illusion, perhaps, but still an
illusion which is dissipated by being "understood".
Philosophers of the now, as I hope, diminishing school
who maintain that all nature's apparent wealth of
colour, sound, and scent is somehow merely super-

added by "the mind" to a "reality" which is only a complicated kinematical dance of particles seem committed by their metaphysics to a view of the kind. But we should hardly claim for the serious champion of such a view that he had much "understanding" of the music. In fact, our homely vernacular comment on his utterance would probably be couched in the words, "the man who can say that simply does not understand what music is". To him the "world" in which the man who does "understand" music habitually lives would be simply an "other" world, to which he possesses no key; it is because that world is so wholly "other", that he calls it illusion. From the musical man's point of view, it is his own "world" of beautiful melodic or contra-puntal pattern which is "this" world and the reality; the dead horse and the dead cat belong to what is, to him, an "other" world of the merely irrelevant and "unreal".

The philosopher, with both views before him, has the task of integrating them. From his point of view, neither the melody with its qualitative wealth, nor the dead horse and dead cat, can be dismissed as simply unreal, or belonging to a "world" of illusion. In the one world of the real, as he sees it, there are both the melody and the dead brutes. But they are not connected by a mere "togetherness", and do not stand on the same level. The hairs of the dead horse and the guts of the dead cat, as constituents of the violinist's bow and violin, have a real character which they have not outside that setting, simply as so much dead hair or gut. Further, bow and violin in use are themselves simply *instruments* for the creation of the heard music. What the "Philistine" calls the reality is only the *matter*, the melody itself is the *form* of the whole reality, and the dominant feature in it. The man who discovered how to make the remains of the dead horse and dead cat minister to the musician was not superimposing an illusion on reality; he was revealing to his fellows rich characters of the real world to which they had formerly been deaf, by teaching them *how* dead gut and dead hair enter into the pattern of the real, *how* these "objects" are "ingredient into events".

The long line of discoverers who have gradually fashioned our instruments of music, and the long line of composers and executants who have made them increasingly instrumental to the expression of beautiful patterns, have disclosed to us a world which is startlingly "other" by contrast with all the reality accessible to those who came before them, but the disclosure has been all along a disclosure of the riches contained in the complex pattern of the real world, not a "psychic addition" of steadily accumulating unreality. Only in that sense can the "other" world of music be fairly said to be "this" world of horse-hair and catgut "rightly understood"; and that is not the sense in which those who accuse Platonism, or Christianity, of a false other-worldliness commonly wish the saying to be interpreted. Like all discoverers and inventors, by teaching us what can be done with certain things the musicians have taught us to know what the things "really" are. In a recent bad novel, a materialistic professor was credited with the statement that he himself *was* "four buckets of water and a bagful of salts". But, of course, a living body, even when it is not the body of a distinguished scientific professor, is *not* pailfuls of water and a few salts; it is a living human body. And a violin is *not* so many feet of catgut stretched on a board; what it *is* you learn by hearing a great violinist play great music on it.

We might say, then, that what happens to us as

we learn to appreciate the beautiful, in music or any other art, is that just those features of the rich and complex pattern of reality which were, to begin with, to us an "other" world, dimly descried and dream-like, become increasingly relevant and dominantly real; what was our given "reality" becomes increasingly subordinate and unreal. It is not too much to say that, as we advance in appreciation, substance and shadow exchange parts. And this is also exactly what happens in the process of moral development, as immediate and appetitive goods and circumscribed loyalties give place to the more remote and intellectual goods and the larger loyalties. As in the one case, so in the other, there must always have been the capacity for appreciation, or the transition could never have been effected. But whereas we begin, in both cases, with the dominance of the immediate and obvious, and the appeal of the more remote and ultimate, when it is consciously felt, comes to us as an irruption or invasion from the strange and dim, breaking in on the familiar and firmly grasped, so also, in both cases, the suggesting "environment" to which we are growing more sensitively responsive steadily takes on more and more the character of a "world" in which we habitually live, and are "at home", while the once familiar becomes an "other" from which we are increasingly estranged. Thus it is with the cultivation of a true "public spirit". At first it is with difficulty and on special occasions that we are conscious of a loyalty to something beyond our own narrow circle of relatives and friends; the learning of citizenship is a process by which we come habitually to take the whole body of our fellow-citizens as the community which is to be the standard object of reference in our conduct.

This may seem only a very small advance in moral-

isation, but it is not so small as it looks. How many
of ourselves, for example, in recent years of warfare,
showed that we had not yet learned even to think of
our country as our moral "world", by the contrast
between our readiness to fight to the last man "in the
good cause", so long as the person to be conscripted
was our neighbour, or our neighbour's only son, but
changed our note at once, as the thing "came home
to us", when it looked certain that, unless the struggle
was abandoned, we ourselves, or our own sons, would
have to be called up? It is easy to repeat the language
of devotion to an object which has rightful precedence
over our domestic ties, but far from easy to breathe
an habitual moral atmosphere in which this devotion
is always present and dominant. Yet, as we learn to
breathe that atmosphere, we are steadily coming to
"be at home" with that which once was to us the
"uncanny" and "wholly other", and to find "uncanny"
just what was once the everyday and familiar. But
patriotism is not an illusion or dream superimposed
on a "real" moral world of narrow family attachments;
family affection and patriotism belong, after all, to the
same "world". In learning to let our private family interests be subject to national public spirit, once more
we are discovering, not inventing, a pattern which is
"really" there, embedded in our "real" human nature.

Thus far, then, it seems to me that the saying "the
other world is this world rightly understood" is true.
The whole complex pattern of the one world in which
we live and have our being is made up of the most
varied strands. And it is not simply a pattern with
many and various strands; it is a pattern whose constitutive elements are themselves patterns, reproduc-
ing, in varying degrees of fullness and distinctness, the
characteristic pattern of the whole; and this is why we

can speak of the pattern of the whole as *all*-pervasive, though more clearly discernible in some of the sub-patterns than in others. This is the underlying conception characteristic of all those philosophies, such, for example as that of Plotinus in the ancient, or Leibniz in the modern world, which have made it a capital point that the real world is a hierarchised, or many-levelled, whole. How great a future such a type of philosophy has before itself is suggested by the vigour and originality with which it has been restated, almost at the present moment, by Dr. Whitehead[1] as absolutely necessary for the deliverance of Physics from the confusions of nineteenth-century material-ism, and, again, by the emphasis laid on the concept of "emergence" in the predominantly biological thought of Professor Alexander and Dr. Lloyd Morgan.

It is not my business now, even if it were within my capacity, to criticise these thinkers or to develop their suggestions further. What is to my immediate purpose is just this. The pattern of the one world embraces the whole of our own life and all that sustains it. It is not therefore to be learned only from the physical and the physiological sciences, nor even from the whole body of the sciences, since all of them, at the best, deal only with artificially constructed abstracts from the complex wealth of life, and that real world in which life is set. What is before us to be deciphered is nothing less than the whole of life; to make out its underlying pattern we must take into the account morality, art, religion, as living things. Manifestly, we cannot expect that the pattern of patterns which embraces them all should be discerned by ourselves except in dim and tentative fashion, and even this must remain impossible if we persist in taking so much of the pattern as

---

[1] Whitehead, *Science and the Modern World*, cc. ix.-xi.

is disclosed by the analysis of its more elementary features—those, for example, which are disclosed by a study of sub-patterns common to all merely physical, or even to all merely biological, structures—for the whole.

The "dominant" characters of the pattern should only be recognisable for what they really are when we set ourselves to study it in the light of the richest sub-patterns of all, those of the highest structures known to us, living and *intelligent* creatures; even then our insight must be expected to be very imperfect. The "synthetic philosophy" of Spencer, now fallen "on evil days, and evil tongues", should at least have the credit of having rightly discovered what the true problem of the philosopher is—the detection of a pattern of the whole which repeats itself in, and dominates, the patterns of its parts. The mistake of this philosophy was that it attempted to find this dominant pattern expressed fully and unambiguously in the simplest and poorest of all sub-patterns, those which are disclosed by consideration of merely physical structures. Hence its initial blunder of *defining* "evolution", taken as the key to the whole pattern, in terms of the "integration" and "disintegration" of "matter" and "motion".

Against all such attempts to find the dominant pattern of the real world in the most rudimentary abstractions, I would urge that, as our example of the violin suggests, we only succeed in "understanding" the more rudimentary pattern by recognising it as a subordinate element in the richer and more "concrete". When we say of the man who takes the scraping of the tail of the dead horse across the guts of the dead cat to be the "reality" that he only thinks this because he has no "understanding" of the music, what we mean is that, as we also habitually say, he does not "appreciate "the music, does not know how to "value" it. Our very use of the words *understanding* and *appreciation* as equivalents in such sentences is itself tantamount to denial of the alleged separation between a realm of facts, or actualities, or realities and another realm of values. To understand any partial pattern is the same thing as to appreciate it, to recognise it for what it is, a subordinate arrangement *instrumental* to a richer pattern.

Mere analysis of the violin and the bow into *their* simpler physical components would contribute nothing to this understanding. The "Philistine" in musical matters might successfully analyse the movements of the laws of the bow and the answering vibrations of the strings into a marvellously complicated dance of atoms or electrons. But however far he carried his analysis he would be no nearer "understanding" what happens when great music is greatly rendered at the end of his task than he had been at the beginning. Understanding only comes in when that which the "Philistine" takes to be the whole "pattern of the event" is seen to be only a subordinate and instrumental factor in a richer pattern whose dominant characters are just those which the "Philistine" has *ab initio* excluded from consideration; or, in other words, when the event is considered, to use Platonic language, as one in which ἀνάγκη is the ὑπηρέτης of νοῦς; or yet again, to speak with Aristotle, when the event is contemplated in the light of the *end* which gives it its characteristic *form*.[1]

A hierarchised world like the world of reality, is

---

[1] This is, in fact, the point of the famous chapter of the *Phaedo* (98 B-99 D) so much admired by Leibniz, in which Socrates explains the ground of his dissatisfaction with the doctrine of Anaxagoras. The use of the distinction between νοῦς and ἀνάγκη to make the same point comes, of course, from the *Timaeus* (47 E ff.).

necessarily a teleological world, and for that reason "materialism", in the proper philosophical sense of the term, the substitution of *analysis* into subcomponents for *integration* by reference to a dominating principle as the ideal of explanation, is strictly incompatible with real belief in any genuine "emergence".[1] This is the rock of offence on which, as it seems to me, even so subtly worked out a materialism as that of Professor Alexander, must, in the end, be shipwrecked. Since every event we can observe, from the displacement of a grain of sand to the taking of an heroic resolution like that of the three hundred at Thermopylae, or the planning of a symphony or a cathedral, or the moral transformation of Saul the persecutor into an apostle of the Gentiles, is something which has its own here and now, Professor Alexander exhibits space-time to us as the one reality of which everything is "made". The apostle of the Gentiles, for example, actually *is*, in reality, a complicated space-time pattern and, on the

---

[1] This incompatibility, as I venture to think, *saute aux yeux* all through Dr. Lloyd Morgan's volume on *Emergent Evolution*. Dr. Lloyd Morgan constructs his metaphysical scheme on the basis of two initial postulates: (*a*) Spinoza's doctrine of the independent but exactly correspondent divine "attributes"; (*b*) the reality of the "evolution" of the genuinely novel. But the reason, and the only reason, why Spinoza has to insist on (*a*) is that *he* disbelieves (*b*). If (*b*) is true, there is no reason at all why the "antecedents" of an event which is a "mode" of *cogitatio* must be looked for exclusively among other modes of the one "attribute"; on the other hand, if (*a*) is true, there has never been, and could never have been, any genuine "emergence". It is the second alternative which Spinoza adopts. Nothing can be clearer than that his view is that, *e.g.*, every movement of a living organism is completely explicable without remainder by the laws of kinematics; "adequate knowledge" of such a movement would mean the deduction of it from the attribute of *extensio*, in other words, its complete reduction to a kinematical problem.

This is logical and heroic, though wholly incredible. Dr. Morgan wants to equivocate at pleasure, to "save his face" with the high-and-dry metaphysician by calling in the authority of Spinoza, and with the biologists by zeal for evolution. This is human and pardonable, but neither heroic nor logical. Either kinematics is the one and only key to everything, or it is not; you cannot possibly have it both ways. If Spinoza's philosophy is true, the world is not "hierarchised", and there is no real "evolution"; if there is real "evolution", the world is "hierarchised", and Spinoza's philosophy is false, and cannot be saved as a compliment to his personal moral excellence. *Utrum vultis, Quirites?*

premisses of this philosophy, is nothing else, however much Professor Alexander may protest that he is also a new pattern "emerging" from his "day of Damascus".

In truth, the most poverty-stricken of events is infinitely more than a combination of *heres* and *nows*. To be a space-time pattern is the most rudimentary and general character of the most diverse events, not the full truth about any one of them. It is precisely because another contemporary philosopher, Dr. Whitehead, sees this so clearly that he finds himself driven first to introduce into his own analysis of the simplest facts something over and above the events, viz. the "objects" which are "ingredient" in them, and then, in his description of those objects, to construct a whole hierarchy of "abstractions".

Now this very different rendering of the facts, which involves recognition of the "eternal", and ultimately of God, as an implication of all that happens seems clearly much sounder than Professor Alexander's. By constructing his world out of mere events without "objects" ingredient in them, Professor Alexander involves himself in the difficulty that he has to identify actual processes with the mere fact that *something* is happening, without being in a position to say *what* it is that happens. The cruder and more old-fashioned corporealistic materialism, which did try to deal with this question, by saying that *what* happens is displacement of permanently self-identical little bits of stuff, may have given a very unsatisfactory solution of the problem, but it had at least the merit of seeing that there is a question to be answered where Professor Alexander is content to be wilfully blind. It rightly recoiled from the monstrosity of identifying *all* quality with the material structure of the *ex hypothesi* quality-less, even though, by a blunder, it reduced the list of qualities ascribed to its real world to an inadequate *minimum*.

Dr. Whitehead's theory enables him to do better; he is in a position to find a place in his real world for the infinite variety of characteristic quality with which actual life confronts us. Both he and Professor Alexander are in justifiable revolt against the bisection of this world of qualities into a real and an illusory part. But where the one saves the whole of the experienced physical fact for the real world, the other, whether he knows it or not, empties the real world of all possible content. This is the price which a philosophy has to pay when it begins by assuming that the complete explanation of a fact can be given by assigning its ἀρχαὶ ὡς ὕλη, or, in other words, that we know all about a thing when we can say "what it is made of".

What I am trying to urge, then, is this. The statement that the "other" world is "this" world rightly understood is false and mischievous, if you take it to mean that "this" world can be rightly understood by taking as its dominant pattern some pattern which you have detected by abstractive consideration of a certain restricted selection of characters. But this seems to be meant in fact by most of the philosophers who lay stress on the *dictum*. They have commonly a polemical purpose at the back of their minds; some type of event is to be excluded *a priori* from actuality and relegated to the level of "illusion", on the plea that it will not fit the known pattern of "this" world. The characters to be eliminated in this "high *priori*" way are not the same in all cases. The saying may be used as a plea for dismissing to limbo miracle, or revelation, or divine providence, or prayer, or the anticipation of a future beyond death, or almost anything you please. And,

in some at least of these cases, the effect of the exclusion must be, in the long run, to make a considerable
difference to the regulation of conduct. If, for example,
it is baseless superstition to expect the help of God's
grace in the task of living rightly, or to believe that
human beings have a future beyond the grave, we
should surely do right in regulating our lives on the
assumption that these beliefs and expectations are
illusory, and wrong in acting as though they may be
something more. If they are something more, they
ought to be effective in the regulation of our conduct.

Prudence is, perhaps, too often rated lower than it
deserves to be by modern moralists, from the singular
prejudice that it must be purely selfish in its operation,
though we all know that there is such a thing as
prudent regard for the interests of our children, and
that a man may come short in his conduct as a father
from imprudence, no less than from want of affection.
But even those moralists who most degrade the meaning of prudence have not usually gone so far as to deny
that it would be a moral fault in a man to neglect
insuring his life when he has the opportunity, or to
build his house in a region subject to dangerous earth-
quakes, without taking the probabilities of an earth-
quake into consideration. In the same way, even as
a matter of prudence in the less worthy sense of the
word, a man's practical decisions may be reasonably
affected by his estimate of their probable effect on his
own destiny—unless one is prepared, as I am not, any
more than Butler[1] was, to hold that it is no culpable

---

[1] *Dissertation of the Nature of Virtue*: "It deserves to be considered, whether
men are more at liberty, in point of morals, to make themselves miserable without
reason, than to make other persons so. . . . It should seem that a close concern
about our own interest or happiness, and a reasonable endeavour to secure and
promote it, which is, I think, very much the meaning of the word prudence, in
our language; it should seem that this is virtue, and the contrary behaviour faulty
and blameable." Butler thus agrees with St. Thomas (*S.T.*ii.ªii.ᵃᵉq.4, art 4 resp.),

thing to make one's self miserable without a cause. Still more obviously may it rightly make a serious difference to the way in which a conscientious man will train his children what he expects *their* ultimate destiny to be, and to his view of the good to be promoted for mankind what he anticipates as the outcome of all human action.

When it is said, then, that the "other" world is "this" world rightly understood, I would urge that the statement should only be accepted as true with the important proviso that we can only come to a *right* understanding of "this" world as we advance in incorporating into our conception of it character after character which was originally felt as unfamiliar and belonging to a "beyond". In particular, we shall certainly be led astray if we assume that we already understand the true pattern of "this" world, when we have considered simply the patterns which present themselves in an isolated study of characteristics common to all kinematical systems, or even to all biological organisms. That which we leave out in all such specialisation — for instance, the "imponderables" which make all the difference to the moral and religious life of mankind—is no less constituent of "this" world than what we retain. To understand "this" world rightly, in any full sense, we should need to be omniscient, not merely in the sense of being acquainted with all the "facts", but in the further sense of seeing them all in their right proportions, and thus apprehending correctly the relations of dominance and subordination between them. We properly isolate different features of the whole reality for specialist study, but we should

that prudentia non solum habet rationem virtutis quam habent aliae virtutes intellectuales, sed etiam habet rationem virtutis quam habent virtutes morales, quibus etiam connumeratur.

never allow ourselves to forget that this is a process of artificial isolation, and that, in the full actual situation from which our selection has been made, the dominant factors in the pattern may conceivably be precisely those which the selection, made relative to special purposes of our own, has quite properly left out of the account.

When Laplace, if the famous anecdote be true, told Napoleon that he had omitted all mention of God from the *Mécanique céleste*, on the ground that he "had no need" of the theistic hypothesis, he may have intended a sarcasm, but he said no more than the truth. For the *analysis* of the movements of the planets, it is plainly superfluous and irrelevant to make any reference to a *Creator*, just as it would be irrelevant to introduce a theistic reference into a proof of the Pythagorean theorem. But the silence of Laplace in the one case, like the silence of Euclid in the other, affords not the faintest presumption against the theist's belief that the domination of the whole world-pattern by God is the most significant and pervasive fact in "this" world of actual life.

More generally, when we speak of understanding the world rightly, it is imperatively necessary that we should not be led astray by the Cartesian identification of "understanding rightly" with the reduction of complexity to a few simple types of relation between elements which seem, but only seem, to be self-luminous. The history of science during the last three centuries is itself the sufficient proof that this demand for "clear and distinct ideas" as the sole test of understanding has only one possible issue, the reduction of reality to a kinematical pattern, and the purely kinematical world of mere changes of configuration is the most unreal of unrealities, because it has been deliberately invented on the principle of emptying the world in which we live, and to which we have to respond, of everything which proves its reality by confronting us with an unsolved problem. It is true that, as the philosophical physicists are themselves hastening to inform us, this ideal can never be actually attained in practice. Closer examination reveals that the fundamental assumptions of a kinematical construction never are in fact the absolutely simple and obvious things they were meant to be; the apparent transparency of the deductions is only procured by the device of putting the opaque and "arbitrary" into the initial postulates.

Descartes, for example, proposed to reduce all physical and biological science to kinematics, because to his mind the postulates of an Euclidean geometry of configurations appeared matter of course, "evident by the natural light", and Leibniz cherished the same ideal. Both were condemned to failure in physics as a consequence of the impossibility of admitting into their schemes anything so "arbitrary" and devoid of "evidence by the natural light" as the concept of mass, and the gravitation-formula. Physics could not so much as get on its legs without that initial stiff dose of "arbitrary" brute fact, for which no reason could be assigned. In a sense, the more advanced of the advocates of "relativity" may be said to have realised the Cartesian programme, of the geometricising of physics, which had seemed to be ruined once for all by Newton, since they replace the whole apparatus of "forces" familiar to us in the classical Newtonian mechanics by varying "curvatures" in space-time, and thus do away with the time-honoured distinction between bodies moving "under the action of no forces" and bodies whose movements are deflected or constrained by external "forces".[1] But, as Mr. Meyerson has observed,[2] the programme is only realised by substituting for Descartes' simple and uniform "extension" a space-time continuum as complex and apparently arbitrary as the whole Newtonian scheme of "forces".

If we ever could succeed in eliminating the element of mystery and apparent arbitrariness from our accounts of the real world, we should feel that, in doing so, we had emptied it of its reality and were left with a mere product of our own imagination.[3] The real world is precisely the world in which there are no absolutely closed sub-systems or spheres; every region in it is open to influences from every other. It is the

---

[1] Hence, from the point of view in question, gravitation is the great "irrationality" of the scheme. The Newtonian *Laws of Motion*, it is assumed, are evident by the "natural light"; it is not thinkable that they should not be universally valid. This comes out with exceptional lucidity in Clerk Maxwell's treatment of these laws (*Matter and Motion*, c. iii.). The "first law" is pronounced (art. 41) to be a proposition the denial of which "is in contradiction to the only system of consistent doctrine about space and time which the human mind has been able to form", and it is clear from the reasoning by which this conclusion is reached that Maxwell really means by this that the law is "evident on inspection", that a denial of it must be not merely false, but meaningless. Even of the "third law" it is expressly said (art. 58) that denial of it is not "contrary to experience", and that "Newton's proof" of it is no "appeal to experience and observation, but a deduction of the third law of motion from the first" (in spite of the fact that Newton himself does appeal to facts of common experience—the horse pulling on the rope, etc.—to establish the proposition). The gravitation formula, on the other hand, from the time of Newton onwards, has always been admitted to have no semblance of self-evidence or rational necessity. It has to be accepted as a "brute fact" which might, for all we can see, equally well have been otherwise, and this is why Newton himself, in the well-known *Scholium Generale* at the end of the *Principia*, assumes that there must be a *cause* of gravity, though he is unable to say anything about the character of that cause. He clearly means that the truth of the laws of motion is "evident by the natural light", and so no reason need be given for their validity; this is not the case with the gravitation-formula, and therefore we must demand a reason for its truth.

[2] É. Meyerson, *La Déduction relativiste*, c. 10 (*l'explication globale*), 11 (*la matière*), 23 (*l'évolution de la raison*) especially pp. 314-16.

[3] Cf. Meyerson, *op. cit.* p. 204: "si le géométrique est moins rationnel et plus réel que l'algébrique pur, il est plus rationnel et moins réel que le physique. . . . Et l'ensemble de ces considérations tend certainement à nous confirmer dans cette opinion que c'est bien, en fin de compte, le non-déductible . . . qui apparaît comme constituant l'essence du réel"; p. 205, "la science est réaliste; mais nous savons cependant que d'explication en explication, *elle ne peut aboutir qu'à l'acosmique, à la destruction* de la réalité". (Italics mine.)

pattern of the whole which repeats itself, more or less distinctly, in the pattern of every part, and by consequence, no analysis of any selected part will sufficiently reveal this pattern of the whole. Leibniz may have been wrong in making this an objection to atomism as a physical hypothesis, but he was clearly right in urging against metaphysical atomism the difficulty that it implies the false consequence that the whole pattern of reality could be discovered by sufficiently minute analysis of a single given constituent of the real, *e.g.* the "world-line" of a single atom.[1]

If the views just indicated are sound, every partial system will have a reality beyond it which, because "non-deducible" from any analysis of the system in question, will be, relatively to that system, "another" world. There will be features in the pattern of the whole which could not be discovered by concentration on the analysis of any of the partial patterns, or all of them, and this means—since every part is conditioned by the character of the whole—that such an analysis will always be imperfect, even as an account of the pattern of the part itself.   In our scientific theory, as in our moral life, advance will regularly depend on the absorption into our "world" of what had been initially marked off as belonging to the "other", and consequent transformation of what was originally taken as *our* "world".

Thus, not to recur to the already mentioned example of the device by which exponents of "relativity" have

---

[1] *Primae Veritates* (*Opuscules et Fragments*, ed. Couturat; p. 522), "*Non datur atomus*, imo nullum est corpus tam exiguum, quin sit actu subdivisum. Eo ipso dum patitur ab aliis omnibus totius universi, et effectum aliquem ab omnibus recipit, qui in corpore variationem efficere debet, imo etiam omnes impressiones praeteritas servavit, et futuras praecontinet. Et si quis dicet effectum illum contineri in motibus atomo impressis, . . . huic responderi potest, non tantum debere effectus resultare in atomo ex omnibus universi impressionibus, sed etiam vicissim ex atomo colligi totius universi statum, et ex effectu causam."

transformed the notion of a "geometrical world" by incorporating in that world elements of heterogeneity regarded as foreign to it in the classical rational mechanics, we can see at the present moment that one of the outstanding scientific tasks of the coming generation will pretty certainly be to break down the old isolation of physics and chemistry from biology and physiology, and that the synthesis will not be effected by the reduction of living organisms to the level of kinematical, or even kinetic, configurations, but by the introduction into physics and chemistry of concepts already disclosed in the study of the life-patterns of organisms.[1] It is only in this way that the more "abstract" sciences can hope to lose their present character as analyses of complexes which are products of an artificial isolation, and become, what they aim at being, adequate analyses of the rich actual complex in the midst of which our life is set, accounts of the real world, not of an imaginary "ideal" substitute for that world, which has no being except in the imagination of the laboratory student.[2]

But even when physical and biological science have been successfully integrated, there must remain a final, and still more difficult, integration. Artistic making, moral action, religious adoration, do not belong to a world, or worlds, of their own; they too, no less than movement, chemical combination, growth, reproduction, and death, belong to the one actual world in which all life is lived, and their specific patterns disclose features of its pattern. It will hold

---

[1] I am thinking here more particularly of the demand of Dr. Whitehead that the concept of "organism" shall be introduced into physics (*Science and the Modern World*, 150, 190 al.), and of Professor Eddington's very frank recognition of "indetermination" in nature.

[2] We shall have more to say on this "historicising" of the natural sciences in the penultimate lecture of our second series.

good here also that every real physical, or physiological, process is a moment in the full life of a real
world not made up of *merely* physical, or physiological,
processes; its full actual character will thus only be
understood when we see it as one subordinate strand
in this ampler tissue. And, again, we may expect it
to be true that the resulting account of any actual
process of the kind will be schematic and misleading
in proportion as, for specialist purposes, we have
denuded the actual "happening" of its contents.[1] It
is to the richest and fullest patterns of all that we must
look for the least inadequate glimpses permitted to us
of the pattern of the whole. We should not be safe in
taking either ethics or physiology alone as the key to
a "clear and distinct" comprehension of ὄντα ᾗ ὄντα,
but we shall be less widely astray if we use physiology
as our key to the real than if we relied on kinematics,
and nearer the truth in interpreting the world by the
light of the moral life of responsible and intelligent
creatures than we should be if, with some of our contemporaries, we took our highest "categories" from
physiology. The whole pattern must, no doubt, always
remain incomprehensible to us, but the richer partial
patterns at least indicate to us what are relatively the
dominant features. This is the final justification of the
refusal we long ago made to admit any ultimate dualism of a realm of actuality and a distinct and separate
realm of value. "Values", we meant, are simply the
dominant features in the pattern of reality.

On such a view there can, of course, be no ultimate
distinction between "two worlds". If the accusation

---

[1] Dr. Whitehead's remark (*Science and the Modern World*, p. 116) that "the
electron blindly runs either within or without the body; but it runs within the
body in accordance with its character within the body; that is to say, in accordance
with the general plan of the body, and this plan includes the mental state", is an
apt illustration of the principle we are concerned to maintain.

of "other-worldliness" is meant as a protest against "metaphysical dualism", it hits no man so hard as it does the "naturalist" of that half-hearted type which lacks the courage—or "face"—to deny the legitimacy of judgements of value *in toto*, but attempts to make its peace with morality, art, and religion by relegating "value" to some kingdom of the ideal, supposed to be situated outside the boundaries of the actual. In our view, the so-called "values" must be the most potent of all the "forces" or influences which shape the course of actuality. We indeed only discover their shaping influence when we study the richest of all the partial patterns which are open to our inspection, the life-patterns of the artist, the hero, or the saint. We may be convinced that they also dominate the course of historical development at the sub-human level, the history of the "inorganic" and the merely "organic". But that, if a fact, is a fact not disclosed by inspection of these realms themselves, and this, presumably, is what Hegel really meant when he spoke of the "lapse into immediacy" characteristic of "nature",—the historical but sub-human.

While we are as we are, conviction on this point must remain a matter of "faith", not of "sight", even though the faith may be a firm assurance of the reality of the things which are not seen. If we could *see* by our own direct inspection that the "values" which are fundamental for the spiritual life of man are also the dominant characters in the whole pattern of reality, we should be in present fruition of that "beatific vision" of God, *per essentiam suam* which Christian theologians agree in regarding as reserved for the pilgrim who has reached his home in eternity. What is popularly called the "other" world would once and for all have absorbed for us what we are accustomed to call "this" world.

But, as it is, we are not yet *in patria*; in art, science, morality, religion alike, we are, at best, only on the way thither. The "other" world is being taken gradually up, and is transforming our vision of "this" world, but the transformation is not complete. There are always fresh horizons beyond us, and unsolved enigmas, spots of deepest shade and obscurity, within our temporary horizon.

The tension between *this* world of the familiar and *that* world of the baffling and "unseen" is not peculiar to the experiences of the strenuous noble liver, or the aspirant after the vision of the "Holy"; it is no less characteristic of the experience of the votary of science. Dr. Whitehead is putting his finger on it when he remarks that it is distinctive of the science of to-day by contrast with that of ages which had carried investigation less deep, that no one can say what apparently hopeless nonsense may turn out to be the great scientific truth of to-morrow.[1] It may be, and has been, held that this tension is not only real, but inherent in the very nature of things; that there would no longer be knowledge in a world where nothing was unknown, nor a moral life where evil had ceased to be, and that thus knowledge and goodness would both disappear in the very act of winning a final victory over their opposites. In that case, we should have to pronounce the inspirations to which we owe both what of knowledge and what of genuine virtue we have won in our historical advance to be illusions. There could be no "celestial city", and there would equally be no "Solomon's house". On the suggested conception of human life as an unending battle in which victory is never won, I propose to say something in our next lecture. For the

---

[1] *Science and the Modern World*, p. 166, "Heaven knows what seeming nonsense may not to-morrow be demonstrated truth".

present, I must be content to have offered some defence of the thesis that the concepts of the "other world", and of the transformation of *this* "given" world into the likeness of the "other" as the grand concern of the moral life, are at the root of all sane thinking about the regulation of conduct.

It is important to observe that the thought expressed by this contrast between the "this-worldly", natural, or secular, and the "other-worldly", into which it is our task to transform the given and familiar, is even more fundamental to a metaphysic of morals than the concept of *sin*. As we have seen, the sense of sin committed bears forcible and unmistakable testimony to the real being of the God against whom sin is done. But I think we may say that conclusive testimony to God would be yielded by our moral experience, even if it included no consciousness of committed sin. Sin does more than anything else to estrange man from God, but it cannot be said to be the only, or the primary, source of the consciousness of separateness. Our moral struggle and progress are not merely an attempt to put right what has gone wrong, any more than the struggle of the intellect towards truth is a mere attempt to correct past errors.[1] Ignorance is a more ultimate fact in our lives than error. Even if all our judgements had been true without exception, so far as they went, we should still, in virtue of the very fact that our life is a becoming and a growth, have work enough, and hard work enough, for the intellect to accomplish in the way of extending our mental horizons, integrating truth already discovered with truth in process of disclosure. If it were feasible, as

---

[1] As it would be on the theory that all science is a partial recovery of knowledge possessed in perfection by the first man, prior to his "Fall", or that, as Roger Bacon held (*Opus Maius*, ii. 9) "eisdem personis data est philosophiae plenitudo quibus et lex Dei, scilicet sanctis patriarchis et prophetis a principio mundi."

Descartes fancied it feasible, to acquire a kind of artificial infallibility,[1] it would still be true that the work of extending the system of true judgements to cover the whole range of the knowable would be a slow one, sufficient to task the intelligence of an indefinite number of generations.

And similarly with the practical task of the regulation of conduct, the very fact that our minds grow would entail the consequence that, even in a world where every act was conscientiously regulated, men would have to advance from the execution of regulation by reference to a tiny "circle" to regulation by reference to ever-extending "circles". If as children we were never wilful or naughty, we should still need to learn, as we passed from the nursery to the school, and from the school to the world at large, how to practise towards more comprehensive systems the same loyalty which had moulded our conduct when its effective environment was the little family group, and the lesson would need time for its mastery. Here also there would be ignorance to be overcome, even if sin were eliminated. Apart from the estrangement brought about by actual misdoing, there would still be in our experience a contrast between our familiar special "world", or setting, and an, as yet, mysterious and disturbing "other". In virtue of the fact that we have always, ultimately, the whole of what is for the setting of all our acts, our ethics would still require a note of "other-worldliness"; it would still be our task in life to learn to transfer loyalties from a "here" to a "yonder" and to make that "other" our home. And this task is one which would never be completed in any life of which time or succession remained the dominant formal char-

---

[1] *Meditatio* iv. "possum tamen attenta et saepius iterata meditatione efficere ut . . . habitum quemdam non errandi acquiram."

acter. For it is just in so far as we are creatures of
time and space that the problem arises. It would cease
to exist only if every when and every here could become
our now and here; then, and only then, would the
antithesis of "this" and that "other" have lost all its
significance. It is in this fact that each of us, when all
is said, occupies some regions of the space-time continuum, but not others, that we seem to discern most
obviously the difference between ourselves as creaturely
and our Creator.

It is true, no doubt, that we may widen the range of
what I may call our "effective occupation" of space-
time. It is not bounded by the surface of our bodies, or
the dates of our birth and death. There is a real sense
in which I may be said to occupy all regions of space
and time which my understanding can contemplate,
or my will affect, but there are, for each of us, some
regions of space-time which our knowledge and our
will never pierce; which are, for us, only the unknown
outer darkness. It is true that effects, even from that
outer darkness, register themselves in my body, and
that my body in turn "mirrors" itself in effects even
upon the unknown. Yet this does not make me, in
the full sense, truly all-pervasive. It may be that the
effects of my moving a finger here at this present
moment are felt through all space and all time. But
we must also remember that from any point in the
space-time continuum to any other there are always
alternative routes. The route from the region which
contains the movement of my finger to some other
might be quite different, and yet the region reached
the same. In other words, it is not rigidly true, as the
vulgar determinism assumes it to be, that the "physical
state of the universe" a hundred years, or a hundred
seconds, hence *cannot* be the same if I do not now move

my finger as if I do. This would be true if I were in the strict sense all-pervasive, in no sense confined within some limited region, however vast. But if I were so unconfined I should not be *a* being, I should be *the* Being, not a creature, but the Creator who upholds all things by his power.

To put the point in still another way, the very sense of an "other" lying beyond my horizon is testimony to my utter *dependency*; the consideration that from any region of the continuum to any other there are alternative routes means that, in every act and process which enters into the being of the finite, there is an ineradicable element of real *contingency*, or indetermination. It explains why, for example, in any possible physical theory, the complete system of the laws of motion must contain something which is not the formulation of a logical principle and therefore appears *arbitrary*. Now this constitutes an important point of contact between science, morality, and religion. For religion also, as von Hügel has said,[1] the sense of our own contingency and dependence is even more fundamental than the sense of sin. We can at least conceive that there might be a man who was sinless but still simply man, as we can conceive that there might be a man who had never asserted a false judgement. But even a sinless man would not be God. There would be no chasm between him and God brought about by wrong-doing, but there would still be the unbridgeable gulf between the dependent and the wholly independent. Only a being who had no *locus* in the continuum, and to whom, for that reason, the whole continuum would be equally present, could be independent and free from all contingency, and such a being would not be a "creature".

[1] *Essays and Addresses* (First Series), p. 43.

The thought has been rightly seized by traditional Christian orthodoxy. According to the traditional story, Adam before his transgression was a sinless man, not in the sense in which a brute without intelligence and responsibility is sinless, but in the sense that his intelligence was clouded by no error, his will perverted by no evil appetition; his judgement was sound and his volition right. He was what Dante, through the mouth of Virgil, professes himself to have become once more, after his ascent through the terraces of Purgatory.[1] But for all that, Adam, before the "fall", was not divine, he was man *simpliciter*, a creature of contingency, and so liable to fall from good, not permanently established in it. Those who win through the world to eternal life, indeed, are said by the same theology to be finally and permanently established in good. Yet even they still remain "creatures", though beatified creatures. For their final establishment, as they are well aware, is not a conquest of their own right hand. It is given them, and they receive it gratefully as a free gift. This is why humility persists and is the very vital air of their Paradise. The most exalted simply creaturely figure of Dante's Heaven is also the lowliest, *umile ed alta più che creatura*.[2]

It is manifest that the actual growth of any human individual into genuine moral personality will itself provide numerous illustrations of that integration of partial patterns, and domination of the pattern of the part by that of the whole, of which we have been speaking. In our childhood the proverb that "to-morrow is

---

[1] *Purgatorio*, xxvii. 140,

> "libero, dritto e sano è tuo arbitrio,
> e fallo fora non fare a suo senno."

[2] *Paradiso*, xxxii. 2.

a new day" has a degree of truth which it should not retain beyond childhood. The single day, the lesser divisions of the day, have their own interests and their several patterns, and if we go far back enough, these patterns will be found to have little inner connection with one another beyond one which is unconscious and supplied by the mere fact that they are all dominated by the periodicity of the general rhythm of the organism. As we grow older, we learn by degrees to have a conscious pattern or plan which connects the action-patterns for the whole day, the whole week, and so forth, into a whole larger pattern, and connects them by establishing a subordination among them. As our personality develops, the periodic rhythm of waking and sleep, work and rest, does not cease, but it does become increasingly dominated and regulated by far-reaching purposes which fill our whole life.

We need not be perpetually reflecting on such a life-purpose; indeed, it depends for vigorous and successful prosecution on the thoroughness with which it is so stamped upon our behaviour that we cease to have to attend specially to the work of regulation. Regulation by a pattern of purpose repeating itself with the necessary adjustments in its various partial sub-patterns becomes a matter of habit. But, of course, the domination is all the more really present the less we need to attend consciously to the dominant pattern. To develop a genuine moral personality is to pass from a condition in which there is little more to connect the partial patterns than the periodicity of organic rhythm to one in which this periodicity itself becomes instrumentally subservient to "dominant" pattern. Thus, in an intensely rich personal life, we have not simply, for example, the rhythm of alternate movement and repose, or work and play; the specific character of the

repose or the play is that it is the *kind* of resting or
playing which is congruent with the ever more and
more clearly "emergent" pattern of the unique personal
life.

Even our dreams, I should say, come in this way
to take on the impress of our waking life in various
subtle ways; they become less of a riot and begin to
exhibit traces of organisation. Our imagination is still
at play in our hours of sleep, but the play becomes more
and more definitely the play appropriate to a being
with a distinctive personal character. We are organising a personality strong enough to persist in the face
of the marked organic difference between the waking
and the sleeping condition.[1] There seems no sufficient
ground for denying that this process of organisation
may be carried beyond assignable limits. When we
have liberated our scientific thought, as we should
do, from the "determinist" superstition which treats
actual concrete "becoming" as a secondary consequence of mere displacements of stuff, and have come
to understand that the real and primary fact is this
concrete "becoming", which is lived through, but never
analysed in reflection, except in respect of a few of its
more obvious characters, we shall, I think, see that
here too we have an example of the parallelism of
greater and lesser rhythms.

Sleeping may be the "image of death" in this sense
too, that the life-pattern which can persist undestroyed
through the alternation of waking and sleeping may also
be able to persist, modified but unshattered, through
the vaster change we call the death of the organism.
The Greeks may have been guided by a sounder

---

[1] Perhaps *Socrates* asleep really *is* "the same person" as Socrates awake, in a
sense in which the statement could not be made, without qualification, of me. That
is because he has "lived in φιλοσοφία" (*Phaedo*, 69 C-D), as I, to my shame, have
not.

analogy than we commonly suppose, when they found a symbol of the soul in the butterfly emerging from the cocoon. An entomologist friend has declared to me his own conviction that inspection of the cocoon at a sufficiently early stage reveals no manifest persistence of anatomical structure; the caterpillar appears, for the time being, reduced to a mere featureless pulp. Yet in the end the moth or butterfly emerges with a definite structure somehow reconstituted out of this apparently structureless "mess", and the *imago* of each species emerges with its own specific structure. This may, perhaps, be what befalls the human person after its apparent loss of all traces of individual structure at the dissolution of the visible corporeal frame. What has been taken for a pleasing poetical fancy may be the actual fact, as nearly as fact is expressible in language.

And, similarly, it may be that another thought, familiar to readers of Spinoza, is truer than many of them have supposed. It may well be that, in proportion to our success in organising our character into a personality capable of resisting transformation by revolutions in "circumstance", the "carry-over", so to speak, at death may be more or less complete. The supreme physical shock, which may all but completely unmake the loosely knit or wrongly knit character, may leave the well-developed and finely knit "personality" comparatively unaffected. So that it would be no more than the truth that the man who has made the fullest use of the opportunities for the development of a genuine human personality has the mind in which "the greatest part is eternal". To some of us, the shifty and chameleon-like, and again the merely blockish, who hardly grow at all intellectually or morally, the death of the body may well mean entrance into a realm which is overpoweringly unfamiliar, and where we cannot "be ourselves"; to others it may be escape to a sphere where we find ourselves truly "at home" at last. Then it would be the simple fact to say of such a one,

> Not with lost toil thou labourest through the night!
> Thou mak'st the heaven thou hop'st indeed thy home.[1]

The same dark may well be to the idle servant an "outer darkness where there is weeping and gnashing of teeth", but to the good and faithful servant the *noche amable más que el alborada* which "unites lover and beloved".[2]

---

[1] M. Arnold, *East London*.

[2] S. Juan de la Cruz. The words are from the fifth stanza of the Canción prefixed to the famous work on the *Dark Night of the Soul*:

> "¡Oh noche que guiaste,
> Oh noche amable más que el alborada,
> Oh noche que juntaste
> Amado con amada,
> Amada en el Amado trasformada!"

IX

THE GOAL OF THE MORAL LIFE

All casuall joy doth loud and plainly say,
Only by comming, that it can away.
Only in Heaven joyes strength is never spent;
And accidentall things are permanent:

.   .   .   .   .

This kinde of joy doth every day admit
Degrees of growth, but none of losing it.

DONNE.

I HAVE kept to the end the discussion of a difficulty
which has been stated by no one with more force and
directness than by Bradley in one of the chapters of
Appearance and Reality, where the moral and religious
life itself comes under the sentence of being, after all,
only the appearance, though an exalted appearance,
and not the reality. So far, we have been urging, as I
fear with monotonous persistence, that the familiar
conception of this life as a pilgrimage from the temporal to the eternal is wholly true, and that the reality
of the pilgrimage is itself evidence of the reality of a
goal which is plainly not to be reached, if life under
terrestrial conditions and limitations is the only life we
have. But it may be retorted that the argument is of the
kind called by the Greek logicians λόγοι ἀντιστρέφοντες;
it "cuts both ways", and makes as much against our
conclusion as for it. For if the pilgrimage were ever
to reach its goal, moral goodness, it may be said,
would itself disappear. We are moral beings only because, and so long as, there is a goal beyond us which

386

we have not reached. If we had reached it, there
would be nothing left to inspire effort and prompt
to progress, and characteristically moral life would
come to an end. Morality *is* progress, says Kant, and
many another champion of "life in a world to come",
and without survival of death that progress can never
be completed. Morality *is* progress, replies Bradley,
or, at least, so you tell me. Then *with* endless survival
it must become endless progress, and therefore must
remain everlastingly uncompleted.[1] As an *argumentum
ad hominem*—or perhaps more precisely *ad clerum*—
we are further reminded that in the Christian Heaven
there is no progress, but only fruition; you are at
home, and your journeys are over and done with.
Hence if, like Kant, you base a hope of immortality
on the alleged need of endless life, if there is to be endless progress, you have broken with the teachings of
Christianity.[2]

The conclusion meant to be drawn is that, in any
case, the task we set before ourselves in our moral
life is one which, from its nature, cannot be achieved,
and that the whole of that life is thus based on a salutary illusion. (Religion is dealt with less drastically
than morality, but only, I think, because Bradley
tended habitually to underestimate the closeness of the
connection between morality and religion, to the point

---

[1] *Appearance and Reality*, p. 508: " 'But without endless progress, how reach
perfection?' And *with* endless progress (if that means anything) I answer, how
reach it? Surely perfection and finitude are in principle not compatible. If you are
to be perfect, then you, as such, must be resolved and cease; and endless progress
sounds merely like an attempt indefinitely to put off perfection." I presume that
the criticism is directed particularly against Kant's position in *KdpV*. i, Th. ii.
bk. ii. *Hpst*. iv. (*Werke*, Hartenstein[2], v. 128 ff.).

[2] *Appearance and Reality*, p. 500. "If progress is to be more than relative, and
is something beyond a mere partial phenomenon, then the religion professed most
commonly among us has been abandoned. You cannot be a Christian if you maintain that progress is final and ultimate and the last truth about things. And I urge
this consideration, of course not as an argument from my mouth, but as a way of
bringing home perhaps to some persons their inconsistency."

of almost making the second simply a ἕξις θεωρητική. If it is true, as it seems to be, that theology has a double foundation, in Ontology and in Ethics, Bradley's theology seems to suffer no less gravely from disregard of the ethical foundation than Kant's from neglect of the ontological.) One may add that, as Bradley is clearly aware, the Christian doctrine, which he has invoked to stop the mouth of the Kantian believer in endless progress, must be an illusion too, for it tells us that we *are* to be perfect, as its own supreme practical injunction, and such perfection is certainly not capable of being attained in this moral life, where we are all, more or less, always at the mercy of the unknown and incalculable, and must in the end be defeated by the inevitable falling of the night.

Is there any way for us out of this unwelcome dilemma? It seems to me that there is a way which has long ago been indicated for us by the great philosophers. But the difficulty ought to be fairly faced, if we are not to admit in the end that in taking our life as *moral* beings as a clue to reality we have been simply losing ourselves in a maze from which there is no exit. If, indeed, we could be content to adopt any of the views which make an absolutely sharp distinction between religion and morality—for example, the view that morality is wholly a matter of attaining a "terrestrial felicity" with which religion, as concerned with a strictly "supernatural good", has no concern—there would be no problem for our discussion. We could then, if we pleased, simply concede all that Bradley asserts; we could say that the pursuit of ethical "perfection" is, as he maintains, the pursuit of an impossibility, but that this does not affect conceptions of our future in a land of supernatural blessedness. Heaven, we might say, is not to be won by morality, and it is strictly in keeping with this to hold that moral action is no feature of the life of the denizens of a heavenly Paradise. They have left morality behind them on entering into their reward; to be moral is to be still engaged in "work", but in Heaven there is no more work to be done; one rests from one's labours. But to adopt that position, or any similar position, would be to acquiesce in the very severance of "nature" and "grace" against which the whole of what has gone before has been a protest. For us, at least, that way out is stopped.

The difficulty we must face, then, when reduced to its simplest terms, is this. To live morally is to live to make the good real. But this very statement implies that there is good which is not real and has to be made so. If once we succeeded in making good wholly real and reality wholly good, there would be nothing left for us to live for, as moral beings. The supreme command of all morality is thus a command to make morality itself superfluous. But to aim at the super-session of morality is to be radically immoral, since to be truly moral means to be moral for morality's own sake, to lead the moral life because of its own worth. Or, still more bluntly, morality is unremitting war against evil, but where there is no evil there can be no war against evil. The good man, therefore, must will at once that evil shall exist, that it may be over-come, and also that it shall be overcome, that is that it shall not exist. Thus his whole life is a hopeless attempt to will two incompatibles at once.

Now an irrationalist, like Professor Aliotta,[1] may

---

[1] For the views of Aliotta see his vigorously written manifesto, *La guerra eterna e il dramma dell' esistenza* (Naples, N.D., but apparently published about 1918. I regret that I have not seen the later and revised form of this interesting little book). Professor Aliotta in effect accepts Bradley's thesis and turns it against every form of monistic belief in metaphysics. *Because* there cannot be good where

hold such a view without being much disturbed by it, since he appears to take the view that the whole worth of life depends on the fact that it is an "eternal war", where the issue of the campaign is never decided. It is the fight, not the victory, which gives life its value in his eyes. (Mr. Chesterton has somewhere said virtually the same thing—how he reconciles it with his professed theological views I do not know—when he declared that in life there is no such thing as taking care to be "on the winning side", because "you fight to *find out* which is the winning side".[1]) But such a view should hardly commend itself to any but a very boyishly minded philosopher. When you come to think it out, it means that a thing only becomes good, and so worth fighting about, because someone makes it a bone of contention. The good would not really be good unless there were a party who think otherwise and are ready to fight in the quarrel. This is certainly not in accord with the principles on which reflective men commonly base their conduct. To get men to fight at all, if you are dealing with men who are more than overgrown schoolboys, you have to begin by persuading them that they have a good cause. Men and nations have often waged arduous wars for causes which the

---

there is not also evil, as there cannot be sunlight without shadow, it is inferred, the real world must be the battle-ground for an unending internecine conflict between rival "reals"; the *mundus intelligibilis* is, in fact, a sort of magnified and never-ending *Caporetto*. Theism is rejected explicitly on the ground that, if God is, the issue of the conflict between good and evil is *not* doubtful; the moral struggle, therefore, we are told becomes only a *sham* fight: "Che io mi affatichi o mi abbandoni, è del tutto indifferente: così il mio lavoro, come la mia ignavia rientran egualmente nell' ordine providenziale; e Dio troverà sempre modo (o meglio l' ha già trovato) di accommodare le cose. Il risultato finale del dramma sarà sempre lo stesso: l' eterna divina commedia che si chiude col trionfo definitivo del bene" (*op. cit.* 135). This emphatic insistence on a "moral" argument for atheism is the more impressive that it represents a complete *volteface* on the part of the brilliant Italian author, who had, in 1914, concluded the English edition of his work, *The Idealistic Reaction against Science*, with an "epistemological proof" of the existence of God (*op. cit.* 463 ff.).

[1] *What's Wrong with the World?* p. 12.

"disinterested spectator" has to pronounce thoroughly bad, but surely no people ever put forth its energies steadily and vigorously, at the cost of heavy sacrifices, in a war for a cause recognised by itself to be a bad one. Thus, in the last world-war, our opponents were anxious to justify their attack on Belgium by the plea —quite a good one, if it could have been made out— that the Belgians had in some way violated their own neutrality, and we may feel sure that the argument was not invented simply to make an impression on "neutrals"; those who devised it were, at bottom, trying to convince themselves. To quarrel about nothing is universally recognised as no behaviour for rational and civilised men. They may "find matter in a straw", but only when they can get themselves to believe that it is the straw which "shows how the wind blows". It is not the straw itself, but "honour" that is at stake, and honour is not nothing.

No one seriously behaves as though he believed that a good thing is made good by becoming the argument of a quarrel; men quarrel because they think that they are being wrongfully kept out of the good thing, or that their enjoyment of it is menaced. The only way to dispute this would be to adopt the extreme irrationalist view that life is never really regulated by conscious purpose, but wholly by unconscious *libido*. But a moralist who accepts this position, even if his theory of conduct is a thorough-going "immoralism", stultifies himself. All moral rules, even the rule of ruthless cultivation of the "will to power" and contempt for the "conventions of the herd", are imperatives, addressed to conscious intelligences. It would be waste of breath to formulate them, if we seriously believed that purposes and intentions are not, in the end, the real directive agencies which mould a man's life. Nietzsche's commands are as "categorical" as Kant's.[1]

If we stop short of this excess of irrationalism, which, in fact, would render us unfit to give or receive argument, it must clearly be a really serious question, affecting our whole estimate of the worth of ethics as a source of suggestion for metaphysics, whether the aspirations fundamental to moral action are self-destructive. If they are, we have merely been misguided in supposing that our experience of moral obligation throws any light on human nature or human destiny.

---

[1] It may perhaps be said that these considerations hardly meet the main point of an argument like Aliotta's. Granted that there must be a real good to fight for before men can be expected to fight, does it not take the reality out of the *struggle* to believe that God is on the side of right, and right certain to win? Is not this belief tantamount to a doctrine of absolute predestination, and does not belief in predestination paralyse effort?

We may say (1) All experience shows that in fact even belief in absolute predestination, the so-called *fatum Muhammedanum* of which Kant speaks, does *not* paralyse human effort. The belief that the "Lord of hosts is with us", and that our cause *must* therefore win, has always been found in fact to give men heart for a stubborn contest, as no other belief does.

(2) The popular conception that the predestinationist does not believe in the reality of human "free will"—and it is this conception which underlies Aliotta's argument—seems to be a mere mistake. We can see clearly enough that this was not the case, *e.g.*, with St. Augustine, who was at once the originator of Christian doctrines of predestination, and the most vigorous of assertors of the reality and importance of human will. It is said also to be the case with Mohammedans, though here I can only speak at second-hand. Cf. Otto, *The Idea of the Holy* (E. tr.), pp. 92-3: "In many typical Mohammedan narratives . . . men are *able* to devise and decide and reject; but, however they choose or act, Allah's eternal will is accomplished to the very day and hour that was ordained. The purport of this is precisely, *not* that God and God alone is an active cause, but rather that the activity of the creature, be it never so vigorous and free, is overborne and determined absolutely by the eternal operative purpose." "This is a predestination which presupposes free will just as its foil."

(3) The interest of a fight does not cease for me because I feel sure of the issue. I still have a real concern in being among "those that triumph", or, it may be, among those who perish with their honour unstained. In the final assault on Thermopylae, Leonidas must have "known" who would "win" the pass, and he may conceivably have been equally convinced that the Hellenes would, in the end, come out of the war as victors. Neither assurance removed his interest in fighting a good fight.

It will, I hope, be understood that I am not here expressing any views of my own about predestination. I am only concerned to maintain that even the most absolute predestination is not incompatible with human "free will", and that belief in it neither has, nor logically need have, the consequences supposed by Prof. Aliotta.

In spite of a well-known mot of Bentham, it is plainly
absurd to speak of an obligation to supersede obligation. To say that there "ought to be no *ought*" is only
another way of saying that there really *is* no *ought*;
if there is not, any conclusions based on the conviction
that moral obligation is the most illuminating fact of
human nature will be merely worthless.

We need, therefore, to discuss carefully the question
whether the goal presupposed in moral endeavour
really is such that the reaching of it would destroy
moral personality itself. For my own part, I cannot but
think that the contention rests on a fallacy of ambiguity.
I grant at once that Bradley's criticism is justifiable, if
it is taken as aimed at certain specific ethical theories.
It is, I apprehend, wholly just as a criticism of a
doctrine like that of Herbert Spencer, and there are
indications in the relevant chapters of *Appearance and
Reality* that the writer has Spencer very much in
his mind. (I am thinking of the repeated allusions to
a certain "New Jerusalem".) According to Spencer,
we must remember, obligation is always an indication of some unremoved misadaptation of our agent
to his "environment", and will consequently disappear
in the Spencerian "New Jerusalem", where the agent
is perfectly adapted to an environment apparently
assumed to be absolutely stable, and is therefore no
longer, "evolving", but completely "evolved".[1] This
particular conception had already been submitted by
Bradley to an annihilating criticism in *Ethical Studies*,[2]
where it had been urged that (1) the assumption of the
absolute stability of the "environment" to which the
"evolving" moral community is taken to be "adapting"
itself is glaringly at variance with all we know, or have
reason to believe, about our historical situation as deni-

[1] *Principles of Ethics*, i. 127 ff.   [2] *Ethical Studies*[2], p. 91 n.

zens of this planet; and (2) that, if complete adaptation could ever be reached, there is no reason to believe that it would be permanent; indeed, on Spencer's own arbitrary postulate of the "instability of the homogeneous", one would have to infer that a really complete adaptation must be momentary.

If the concluding divisions of Spencer's *Principles of Ethics* had been published when *Ethical Studies* was written, it may be said that polemic on *this* point would have been superfluous. For we find there that it was Spencer's own belief that complete adaptation by evolution is only attained to be immediately lost again; evolution does not, after all, lead to the establishment of a permanent "moving equilibrium", but begins to undo its own work as soon as the "moving equilibrium" has been reached. It is more to my purpose to remark that Spencer's account of the character of the process during the half of the cycle in which it is advancing in the direction of a momentary "moving equilibrium" seems to be based on a curious misreading of the facts. It is *obviously* not true that as a community advances in moral civilisation its members lose the sense of their reciprocal moral obligations to one another. It would be much nearer the truth to say that what we call "social conscience", the acuteness with which the ordinary good man—good that is, according to the conventional standard of his society—realises these obligations, becomes intensified. And it is not hard to see why this should be so. The less highly developed a society in moral civilisation, the more elementary the rights and claims of which its members are conscious, the narrower also are the limits of the body to which loyalty is habitually paid, and the less clearly does the average member understand the ways in which his own action affects other members of the community. To learn this lesson, we do not need to go back to prehistoric ages, or to compare the working morality of European civilisation with that of contemporary barbarism. We have only to compare our own conceptions of our "social obligations" with those of very excellent men of a hundred years earlier to see that there has been a marked intensification of the sense of obligation between 1825 and 1925.

We may remind ourselves, for example, of the change in the general opinion about the obligation of providing all citizens with the opportunites of education, or of making dwellings sanitary and comely, or of paying a "living wage", to see how great the difference is. Or more simply still, we might contrast the purposes for which we think it imperative that an income-tax should be levied with the views which must have prevailed at the much more recent date at which Gladstone could promise the total abolition of the tax in the event of the return of his party to power. I think that it would, further, be fair to say that, during the last hundred years, we have not merely come to have a more exacting standard of social obligation; we have also come to feel more acutely about our own personal defections from that standard. The "whole law", as we now conceive it, embraces a great deal more than our great-grandfathers supposed, and we are at least as sensitive as they, and probably more so, to the moral urgency of fulfilling the law. As the generations succeed one another, men who wish to have a conscience void of offence find that task more, not less, difficult.

I can only account for Spencer's apparent blindness to such plain facts by supposing him to have reasoned somewhat as follows. Society is engaged in steadily "adapting itself", that is, in putting right what is wrong. Hence in each successive generation of a morally progressive society there is less left to be still put right than there was in the generation before it, and therefore less need for painful and strenuous effort. Further, the *habit* of putting right the wrong grows stronger with practice through the generations.[1] Therefore the conscious sense of effort to be made and duty to be done must be steadily growing fainter. Thus we may look for a climax when there will be no wrongs left to be righted, and the now superfluous sense of obligation will die out.[2]

If this fairly represents Spencer's line of thought, one may make the remark that several dubious assumptions seem to be presupposed. It is taken for granted that a "perfectly evolved condition", in which there is no evil left to be got rid of, can be reached in a finite, though perhaps a very long, time, or, in other words, that the amount of wrong to be righted before a society is "fully evolved" is a fixed finite *quantum*. The "absolute difference" between the amount of evil now present in a society evolving towards "moving equili-

---

[1] I do not suggest that this reasoning is wholly sound, but it would be in keeping with Spencer's own unqualified belief in the "heritability of acquired characteristics".

[2] It is instructive to observe that the writer of the article "State of the Dead" (Christian) in the *Encyclopaedia of Religion and Ethics* describes the final state of the lost in Hell precisely as Spencer describes that of the "perfectly evolved society". "The faculty which, in the case of the finally impenitent, has been wholly and irremediably abused is that of free will, and therefore, whatever else eternal loss may involve, it must involve the loss of this. . . . The lost, deprived of all power of volition and choice, will sink to the rank of necessary agents. . . . Thus they can sin no more, and will perform the will of God unerringly, which will surely be for their good. Moreover, their enjoyment of natural goods, though impaired, will not be destroyed. In fact it even seems possible to regard their condition as one of relative happiness of a purely natural kind." I am not sure how far this anticipation is coherent, since it seems to assert in one breath that the "lost" both are, and are not, genuinely human beings, but there is exactly the same difficulty about Spencer's description of the life of his "millennial" age. There, also, the "fully evolved" men and women have no real choice; their will is always determined *ad unum* by a natural necessity, and Spencer regards this condition as one not only of "relative" but of supreme happiness. The only difference is that the (Anglo-Catholic) writer of the article makes the condition he regards as "damnation", but Spencer as the highest felicity, perpetual. So much for Spencer's courteous standing insinuation that the "orthodox" clergy are "devil-worshippers". But, like most "agnostic" critics, Spencer had probably never troubled to study the religion he satirised.

brium" and zero steadily diminishes as the evolution goes on, and presumably the rate of diminution is also steadily accelerated. No sufficient account is taken of the possibility that the very same progress which introduces superior adaptation in some special respects may bring with it new, and possibly more serious, departure from adaptation in others, though one would have thought this consideration could hardly be missed by a writer who lived through the "industrialisation of England", even without the rival theories of Spencer's antagonist Henry George to call attention to it.

It *seems* to be assumed, again, that moral action consists merely in putting wrongs right, and that if there should ever come a time when there are no more wrongs to be corrected, "practice" will have "done its do". This is a point to which I shall have to recur; for the moment, I would only observe that the assumption seems about as reasonable as it would be to say that the sole task of science is to refute "vulgar errours", and that, if they were all once thoroughly refuted, nothing would be left for science to do, so that in a "fully evolved" society the sense of truth would share the fate of the sense of obligation. Avenarius, if I understand him rightly, actually professed to believe something of this kind. As far as I can fathom the main argument of his chief work, his thesis is that the intellectual evolution of a society will be complete when every "stimulus" evokes a response composed exclusively of expressions of "pure" experience. But response to stimulus only has *significance*, or *meaning*, so long as it contains an element which is not "pure" experience, but *interpretation* of the "experienced". In the final stage, the stimuli contained in the "environment" will evoke "responses" from the members of the "perfectly evolved" society, and some, no doubt, of these re-

sponses will be vocal, reactions of the organs of articu-
lation. But they will have no *meaning*, will *signify*
nothing beyond themselves. They will be knocked out
of us by events, exactly as a roar or a squeak may be
produced from a toy lion or toy bird by pinching it in
the right place.

This seems to me an inevitable consequence of Spencer's premises, though it never occurred to Spencer to
draw the conclusion. Avenarius, if I understand him,
did draw it, and it is just the reckless clear-sightedness
with which he drew it which gives the *Kritik der reinen
Erfahrung* its great value. The book is a final *reductio
ad absurdum* of the attempt to treat intelligence as the
product of the adaptation of a relatively plastic organism to a fixed environment.[1]

Finally, there is in what I take to have been Spencer's thought a gross double confusion of the *fact* of
obligation with the *sense* of being obliged, and of this
sense with the consciousness of a disagreeable *effort*,
as though awareness that "I ought to do this" were
always attended by the thought "but I would much
rather not". The first of the confusions should be
impossible to anyone who refuses to subscribe to the
wholly immoral doctrine that a man escapes his obligations by systematically ignoring them; that a husband,
for example, has no obligation of fidelity to a wife
whom he has married without any thought of being
faithful, and has habitually neglected for other women.
The second only seems plausible through an error of
mal-observation. We are, no doubt, most powerfully
impressed by the "sense of duty" when there are great
sacrifices to be made, when the act to be done is almost

---

[1] Of course, it is very possible that I have misapprehended the main thesis of a
work so difficult and diffuse as the *Kritik der reinen Erfahrung*. But this is what
seems to me to be the conclusion to which the argument inevitably leads.

too hard for human flesh and blood; but in the case of the more usual daily obligations of good citizenship and neighbourliness we are at once aware that the good offices are *incumbent* on us, not works of supererogation, and also that it is pleasant to discharge them. A man may feel the imperativeness of duty with uncommon intensity when the duty is painful or difficult, as he may feel the strength of a personal affection most keenly when he is suffering bereavement. But though, in this sense, "we never know how we loved our friend until we have lost him", this is no proof that we do not love our living friend, or that we are not aware that we love him.[1] In the same way, even if it were true that every step in moral progress leaves us with so many fewer and less formidable temptations to encounter, it would not follow that, as we "go on to be perfect", either our obligations or our sense of them must decrease. If a "fully evolved" society is to mean a society which is fully moralised, such a community would not be one where no one had a sense of obligation; it would be a society in which every member was more thoroughly alive than in any other to the full range of his obligations, and more careful to fulfil them.

But, of course, moral progress no more means the mere putting right of wrongs than intellectual or artistic progress means the simple correction of old errors. The correction of errors is only a subsidiary task for the intellect. Its primary business, which would still remain in illimitable fertility, if there were no more

---

[1] And, similarly, it has been observed that a virtuous man never *feels* the sacredness of an accepted moral maxim so acutely as on those exceptional occasions when he, rightly or wrongly believes that it is a *duty* to depart from it. In ordinary life we tell the truth as a matter of course, without reflecting on the sacredness of truth or the immorality of lying. A good man, convinced that, in his present situation, he ought to keep back the truth, or to equivocate, is likely to be very exceptionally conscious of the sacredness of the general obligation to veracity and candour.

"false opinions" to be corrected, is the exploration of ever new regions of truth. If an artist could overcome all the difficulties created for him by the intractability of the materials through which he has to express himself and by his own limitations and bad mannerisms, if he became a "perfect master" of his instruments and his own moods, there would still be the endless work before him of giving actual embodiment to his vision of beauty. And, in the same way, the moral life would not disappear even from a world in which there were no wrongs left to be righted. Even a society in which no member had anything more to correct in himself, and where "thou shalt love thy neighbour as thyself" were the universally accepted rule of social duty, would still have something to do; it would have the whole work of embodying the love of each for all in the detail of life. It is this, not the mere abolition of abuses, or the elimination of unfavourable circumstances from the environment, which is the paramount business of the moral life.

The description of that life as a phase in "evolution", which is destined to disappear, when and if evolution becomes complete, is thus based on confusion of thought. But it has also to be added that the attempt to represent the "completely adapted" society as a possible product of natural "evolution" is itself inherently absurd. "Evolution" itself is, in its very nature, a becoming, not a being, and it is a double becoming. The "environment" is something which becomes, no less than the "organism", though its rate of becoming may be slower. Evolutionary adaptations are adaptations to a changing, not to a fixed, environment— unless, indeed, you mean by the "environment", as Spencer did not, the intimate presence of the living and abiding God to and in all His creatures. And though the planetary environment, which is all that Spencer takes into account, may usually change very slowly, this need not always be the case. It may be that there are no sudden catastrophic changes on the large scale in the developing organism, but we have to reckon with their possibility as features of the planetary environment. We are not, after all, *assured* against cataclysms which permit of no adaptation, and, even apart from such cataclysms, we have every reason to expect that the society which Spencer calls "fully evolved", because it has adapted itself to a relatively stable environment, must inevitably degenerate again, as changing terrestrial conditions make the maintenance of a high level of civilisation increasingly difficult. A high morality "evolved" after millenniums of struggle would only be won to be lost again in succeeding millenniums. If we may trust the physicists with their "principle of Carnot", the "cave man", or something of the same kind as the "cave man", lies ahead of us, as well as behind us—unless, indeed, the perfectly evolved society should escape an old age of decay by perishing in its prime, either by a "bolt from the blue" or by *felo de se*. Mankind, as their moral life unfolds, are seeking a house eternal and abiding, and it is evident that such a house, if it is to be found at all, must be found in some other world than one where succession and temporality are dominant.[1]

Probably, however, it is Kant rather than Spencer whom Bradley's argument has most particularly in mind. As against Kant, the argument takes the form that the Kantian philosophy enjoins moral faith in

---

[1] Evolution, as conceived by Spencer, is, after all, no genuine *historical* process. The fact is shown by his complete disregard of the "principle of Carnot", which forbids us to regard "becoming" as reversible. On this extraordinary oversight see the pertinent criticisms of James Ward, *Naturalism and Agnosticism*[1], i. 192-195.

immortality on the ground that the particular good morality consists in seeking is one which we can never obtain in a limited time. Morality is the progressive acquisition of self-mastery, complete domination of irrational impulse and inclination by the rational will. But what makes the essential difference between God and man is that irrational inclination and impulse are ineliminable from humanity. We cannot become beings with purely rational wills; all we can do is to make will more and more preponderant over inclination, without ever getting rid of inclination altogether. If we are to achieve anything of moment in this conflict, we must have an endless time for the work, so that we may "approximate without limit" to an ideal we never actually reach. Against such an argument it is pertinent to object that a goal to which you can only make un-ending approximation is, *ex hypothesi*, never attained. On Kant's own showing, the man who makes the exer-cise of the morally good will his aim in life—and no other man is morally "good" —is, at best, the Achilles of Zeno, attempting the impossible task of coming up with the tortoise. Assuming that Zeno's analysis of the problem is correct, we can only say that Achilles shows himself no mathematician by consenting to the race. He should have known that he was trying to do what, from the nature of the case, is not to be done. The sooner he gives up his impossible pursuit, the more rational we shall think him, as we should have thought Hobbes less irrational in his determination to "square the circle" if he had not spent so many decades over the problem. Indeed, we do Achilles an injustice by this suggested comparison, for the tortoise has at least only a finite handicap, and this Achilles steadily re-duces, though he never wipes it out. But God, with no "lower nature" at all, is presumably as infinitely ahead of the Kantian good man after untold millions of years of respect for duty as at their beginning. One is reminded of Pindar's μὴ ματεύσῃ θεὸς γενέσθαι.[1]

Here, again, I confess I find Bradley's comment just. Kant has the merit of seeing far deeper into the real nature of the moral problem than Spencer and the evolutionary moralists in general. The evolutionists as a body seem to me to take a hopelessly "external" view of morality. They appear to regard it as a mere matter of devising an ideally frictionless social machine, which may be counted on to minimise the risks society runs from collision with its physical environment, and perhaps actually to abolish the evils arising from competition between its members. If they can be cheerily optimistic about the coming of a "perfectly evolved" morality, it is only because they set morality no more difficult task. Kant is resolute to demand more from his good man; he will not be satisfied with anything less than the cleansing of the thoughts of the heart, the inner purification of all the sources of will, and he sees clearly that this is not feasible for mankind in general without a discipline extending far beyond the limits of our earthly existence. If we are to be schooled into perfect obedience by the things we suffer, it seems plain that, for most of us, the schooling we get in our three-score years and ten is only a small part of the training we need. We leave this life before we have well learned even our alphabet. But the central difficulty still remains. According to Kant himself, the lesson is always learning, never learned. Hence it is in point to raise the objection that if morality means learning a lesson a man never masters, it should seem that if he once did master it he would cease to be a moral being, since to be moral means to be engaged in learning the lesson.

[1] *Ol.* v. 24.

Thus the duty of a member of the "kingdom of ends" would appear to be to do his utmost to abolish the kingdom of ends itself, and this hardly seems reasonable.

Yet, on reflection, it appears that Kant is really making the same assumption as Spencer, in a subtler way. He, too, is assuming that there would be no moral life to be lived where there was no longer wrong to be put right. His one advantage over Spencer is that he conceives of the process of putting the wrong right in a more inward fashion. The wrong to be righted is no mere misfit of the organism to its environment, but a wrong relation between reason, the higher, and inclination, the lower, element within the moral personality. The unruly motions of the flesh must be brought into subjection to the motions of the spirit. But if the flesh should ever be so completely subdued that it no longer lusted against the spirit, man, as a moral being, would, on Kant's theory of the moral life, have ceased to be. The person in whom the good will was now finally established would no longer be a man, but a god, and this complete transformation of humanity into deity Kant rightly pronounces impossible, thereby, may we not say, revealing that at heart he has retained much more of the old metaphysic, with its distinction between being absolute and in its plenitude, and being contingent and restricted by limitation, than the professions of the *Critique of Pure Reason* would justify. But the point for us is that, however right he may be in holding that the conversion of the creature into the Creator would be an absurdity, in his determination to avoid that absurdity he makes the moral life a battle which never ends in victory, and that all thinkers who do this lay themselves open to Bradley's criticism that such an identification reduces morality itself to the position of an illusion which, for moral reasons, we must be tender of exposing. It is only a secondary further consequence that any testimony the moral life may appear to yield in favour of our immortality must be pronounced worthless. If Achilles can never catch the tortoise, his chances are not improved by giving him a race-course of indefinite length.

Is it, then, really true that it is of the *essentia* of the moral life that it should be a struggle with evil, whether in the form of an environment which is a misfit, or in the more insidious form of "inclinations" which persist in remaining imperfectly subdued?[1] Would the interests which sustain the life of "practice" simply disappear if moral and physical *evil* were really overcome? The question is an important one, since, if we answer it in the spirit of Kant, we shall have to say that a *moral* "rational theology" must definitely reject any doctrine like that taught by Christianity about the final state of the saved; there can be no "Heaven" where those who have come through the struggle "reign with Christ": there may, conceivably, still be an adventure which never finishes, but it is an adventure like the quest of El Dorado, or the philosopher's stone, and such a prospect, I fear, grows less attractive the more steadily it is regarded.

I venture to think that Kant, at any rate, would have come to a different conclusion, if he had not falsified the problem by an over-simplification arising from his distrust of ontology. In his anxiety to build his philosophical theology on ethics and nothing but ethics, he

---

[1] Kant's assumption that there must be such an element of "inclination" in every "creature"—its presence being just what distinguishes the "creature" from the Creator—is a relic of the "Augustinian" doctrine that all "creatures" exhibit the composition of "form" with "matter". He does not consider the rival Thomistic view, which founds "creatureliness" on the distinction between *essentia* and *esse*, the "what" and the "that", and consequently recognises the actual, or possible, existence of creatures (the angels) in whom "form" is uncompounded with "matter". If the Thomistic view is tenable—I do not say that it is, or that it is not —the moral life, as conceived by Kant, would not be possible to an angel.

has misread the lessons of ethics itself. If we look more closely at the problem, I believe we shall see that the elimination of evil and its source in unruly inclination would still leave the ultimate distinction between God and man untouched, and consequently could not affect the essential characteristic of the moral life, that it is a life of *aspiration*. There is a possibility which combines attainment and aspiration, and would thus leave room, within a society of just men made perfect, for a very real and intense moral life. In fact, in our familiar experience of the moral life, as we now have to live it as a life of warfare, we do not see it in its truest character; we see it, as Socrates says in the *Republic*[1] we now see the soul, incrusted with all sorts of accretions which disguise its true lineaments; to discern them, these accretions must be purged away. With the passage from struggle to triumph, morality would no doubt undergo a transfiguration, but it would be a transfiguration and not a transformation.

This, I may remind you, was definitely the conviction of Green, who expressly says, in opposition to the view that the moral life can be simply equated with a life devoted to "reforms", that "the character of the moral reformer is not merely a means to the perfect life, but a phase of the same spiritual principle as must govern that life. But whereas we cannot but suppose that, if the perfect life of mankind were attained, the spiritual principle must have passed out of the phase in which it can appear as a reforming zeal . . . we cannot suppose that, while human life remains human life, it can, even in its most perfect form, be superior to the call for self-abandonment before an ideal of holiness. There is no contradiction in the supposition of a human life purged of vices and with no wrongs left to be set

[1] Plato, *Republic*, 611 C-D.

right. . . . In such a life the question of the reformer, What ought to be done in the way of overt action that is not being done? would no longer be significant. But so long as it is the life of *men*, *i.e.* of beings who are born and grow and die . . . in whom virtue is not born ready-made but has to be formed (however unfailing the process may come to be) through habit and education in conflict with opposing tendencies; so long the contrast must remain for the human soul between itself and the infinite spirit."[1]

Green, as his language shows, is thinking here of life within the limits in which we are acquainted with it, and is apparently willing to concede, for purposes of argument, that "complete adaptation to environment" might be permanently attained in such a life. His point is that though the attainment would do away with the special vocation of the "reformer", or "social worker", it would not, as Spencer supposed, abolish morality and obligation. There would still be something to be lived for, the completer assimilation of the activities of the human spirit to those of the divine, the practice of adoration, humility and the reception of the grace of God. If you choose, by arbitrary definition, to restrict the name *morality* to the life of struggling to "put the crooked straight", you would have to say, indeed, that morality had been transcended, but it would only have been transcended by transfiguration into a life continuous with itself and inspired by the same ideal of "imitating God" which has been operative from the first in producing the most elementary of social and moral "reforms".

Now this, provided only that we substitute, as I think we fairly may, for Green's more specific mention of birth and death a more general reference to becom-

---

[1] *Prolegomena to Ethics*, sect. 302 (p. 328).

ing or succession as that which distinguishes the life of the creature from the life of the Creator, seems to me to be the truth of the matter. The interest which sustains the good man in what he knows now as the conflict with evil of every kind need not be exhausted by the mere removal of evil; the termination of the battle in a decisive victory need not put an end to the activity to which the victory has been due, though it would make a significant difference to the form that activity would assume. To use the language of the devout imagination, the winning of heaven would not leave the pilgrim arrived at the end of his journey with nothing further to do. In heaven itself, though there would be no longer progress *towards* fruition, there might well be progress *in* fruition. Life "there" would be, as life "here" is not, living by vision, as contrasted with living by faith and hope; but might not the vision itself be capable of ever-increasing enrichment?

To put the same thought from rather a different point of view, I do not see why "social service" might not be as characteristic of heaven as of earth, though it would have a rather different quality "there". On earth we have in the main to serve our neighbour by removing the sources of temptation and the other obstacles to the good life put in his way by untoward circumstances, or by the undisciplined cupidities and resentments within his own soul. Each of us has to set others forward, and to be set forward by them, in the way of purification from inordinate devotion to lower good and intensification of devotion to the highest. In the heavenly city, as conceived, for example, by Christianity, there would be no further call for this particular service, since it is a community of persons who are all in love with the highest good. But even in such a heaven, we have heard, one star differs from another in glory. Even in a society where every member was in actual enjoyment of the "beatific vision", it would still remain the fact that some see more of the infinite wealth of the vision than others, but each receives according to the measure of his capacity. We could thus understand that those whose vision is most penetrating might well have a heavenly "social service" to discharge in helping their fellows to see, and might find a deep significance in the speculations of "Dionysius" and his mediaeval followers about the part played by the higher orders of angelic intelligences in "illuminating" those beneath them. When all "see God" face to face, some may yet see more than others, and may be supposed to help those others to see more than they would if left to themselves. A friend whose vision is keener than my own may not only render me valuable help in scaling a mountain-top; when the summit has been reached, his aid may actually enable me to discern the prospect more perfectly than I should have done if I had stood on the peak alone.

There is also another side to the same thought. To many imaginations, I believe, there is something repellent, or at least profoundly depressing, in the current representations of Heaven. It is made to appear as a region where there is no room for the *adventure* which is the very salt of life, the abode of a monotonous self-sameness of boredom. It is not every temperament that expresses itself in the words

> There remaineth a rest for the people of God,
> And I have had troubles enough, for one! [1]

But the conception of Heaven as adventureless is really unjustified. There is no sufficient reason why the disappearance of wrong, within or without ourselves,

---

[1] R. Browning, *Old Pictures in Florence.*

to be put right should put an end to adventure and
novelty. Even in a life where there was direct vision of
God, we can readily understand that no vision could
ever be complete, just because the object of vision is
infinitely rich; there would always be the aspiration to
see further, prompted by the splendour of the vision
already granted, and we may readily conceive, with
von Hügel,[1] of this aspiration as only to be satisfied
by bold adventure in self-forgetfulness. It would be
the spirits who plunge most venturesomely into the
"divine dark", not knowing what it may have to disclose, who would most completely make themselves,
returning from the plunge into the Godhead with
clearer and deeper perceptions, for the nourishment
of their own being and that of their less venturesome
companions.

Thus a life in which the struggle with evil to be put
right was a thing of the far-away past might also
exhibit its continuity with the "militant" life of earth,
by retaining the characteristic notes of social service,
of self-forgetfulness, and of the winning of self by the
adventurous staking of self. Even in Heaven life
would have its astonishing and joyful surprises for
everyone. The "finite God" of some modern speculations might, no doubt, come to bore us badly, because,
since he is finite, we must expect, sooner or later, to
have nothing more to find in him or receive from him,
but this creation of dualistic metaphysics is not the God
of the saints, nor of any considerable religion. One
might recall, in this context, words of John Bunyan,
no less appropriate that they were primarily written
to a rather different purpose: "Christ Jesus has bags
of mercy that were never yet broken up or unsealed.
Hence it is said he has goodness laid up; things reserved

[1] *Essays and Addresses* (First Series), p. 218 ff.

in heaven for him. And if he breaks up one of these bags, who can tell what he can do? Hence his love is said to be such as passes knowledge and that his riches are unsearchable. He has nobody knows what for nobody knows who."[1]

I take it, then, that we need no more suppose there would be any loss of continuity with present conditions in a moral life carried on into a realm from which evil had disappeared than there would be in the pursuit of fresh knowledge by a society whose "vulgar errours" had all been corrected, or the pursuit of art by artists who had attained full mastery over their medium of expression. We have no actual experience of such a state of things, but we can, at least, see that the follower of science who had no longer misconceptions and mistakes to be got rid of, or the artist who had no longer to wrestle with the refractoriness of his materials, the defects of his implements, and the unskilfulness of his own right hand, would still have a boundless field of the unexplored and the unexplained in which to find ample employment for his energies. We do not, in fact, find that the musician or painter who appears to have nothing more to learn about the management of his violin bow or his brush is driven to abandon his art because he has acquired mastery of this kind. He goes on to *use* his mastery, and there is no reason in the nature of the thing why he should not go on to use it indefinitely, for the production of beauty which is perennially new and increasingly *more* beautiful. To think otherwise is to make the mistake of confusing mastery of technique with the whole of art. The same thing is equally true of the business of the moral life.

---

[1] Bunyan, *The Jerusalem Sinner Saved*. Bunyan's immediate purpose is to reassure a sinner who is tempted to despair by the blackness of his record of past transgressions, but the thought lends itself equally well to our present argument.

The moral life does not consist merely, or chiefly, in *getting* into right relations with our fellows or our Maker. In our earthly house we have constantly to be doing that, but it is only the preliminary to the real business, the προοίμιον αὐτοῦ τοῦ νόμου ὃν δεῖ μαθεῖν; the real business is not to establish these relations, but to live in them.

To illustrate the point in the simplest possible way, we may say that we have, for example, to learn to love our parents, our friends, our fellow-men generally. At first our loves are too often languid, and even when they are not languid they are "inordinate", not under the direction of clear-sighted wisdom. But even on earth we have something to do beyond merely un-learning unloving, or unwisely loving, ways. As we learn to love rightly, we have to exercise the love we have learned by giving it actual embodiment in the detail of our lives. And so, if we found ourselves in a world where every one of us had unlearned unloving-ness and foolish loving, one part of the moral business of our life on earth would, no doubt, be done with. We should no longer have the old aversions, or indiffer-ences, or wrongly directed affections to unlearn. But the *main* business of the social life, the putting of wise and right love into act, should remain; we should find occupation enough in *showing* our love, and this would be an occupation continuous with what is morally of highest importance and value in our present life.

This may seem a painfully obvious remark, but I make it for the purpose of entering a protest against what appears to me a gross caricature of the moral life, which is only too fashionable in certain philosophical quarters, and can unfortunately shelter itself behind the authority of at least one recent *clarum et venerabile nomen*. You will doubtless remember how Bosanquet

was given to characterising "morality" as a realm of
" claims and conflicting counter-claims", and using the
description as the basis of a subtle depreciation of the
specifically moral attitude towards life. In fact, religion,
as conceived by Bosanquet, consists precisely in "transcending" this ethical system of claims and counter-
claims, in soaring above morality into something different and better, and, obviously enough, such a view
of the practical life plays straight into the hands of
Bosanquet's favourite metaphysical doctrine that individual human personality is a mere illusion.[1] No one
would desire to speak of Bosanquet except with the
deepest respect, and yet I must protest—*ich kann
nicht anders*—that his habitual description of the moral
life in such language seems to me a misrepresentation
as grotesque as dangerous. (Dangerous because, with
men of less fine moral fibre than Bosanquet himself, it
is apt to engender the delusion that it is "spiritual" to
be a-moral, if not actually immoral, in fact, that one can
be at once "in grace" and leading a careless, or even
an actually bad, moral life. And it is a short and easy
step from this theoretical delusion to practical ill-living.)

I must ask, then, whether, for example, the life of
family affections, or of intimate reciprocal friendship, is
something "super-moral" or not. Has a man who does
not know what it is to be a good father, or son, or husband or friend, really lived the "moral" life? Has any
man done so if he has merely respected the precisely
definable "rights" of his fellow-citizens, without having

---

[1] For Bosanquet's use of such language see, for example, *Value and Destiny
of the Individual*, lecture v. *passim*. I am, of course, aware that it may be said
that the same type of view is equally to be found in Bradley, though not, I think,
quite so consistently adhered to, or so clearly formulated. But I feel bound to
protest against it, wherever found, as leading, if taken seriously, to a confusion
of spiritual religion with an easy "Nature-pantheism" which is at variance with
the real intentions of both philosophers at their best. Green is nobly free from *this*
defect.

lived the "shared life" with any of them; or does not the very suggestion arise from a dangerous confusion of the ethical with the merely juristic point of view? I should myself say that it is just the relations such a man has been unfortunate enough to miss—in many cases, of course, it may really be his misfortune rather than his fault—which are the finest flower and the most perfect expression human history has to show of the ethical spirit. It is not without very good reason that Aristotle's account of the life of "practice" culminates in the description of the φιλία of the good man. In this relation, when obligations cease to be capable of formulation as definite "claims" and "counter-claims", a man is not rising *out of* the realm of morality into something higher; he is finding himself, for the first time, *in* a region where the ethical spirit gets unhampered expression.

Or can it be—as I can scarcely believe—that those who use language like Bosanquet's really believe that the best family life, and the noblest types of friendship, really fall within the system of "claims and counter-claims"? This I should call a mere distortion of the facts. It is just because there is no room in these relations for insistence on claims and counter-claims that they have been the great instruments by which man has been historically moralised. In a business partnership it may be possible to delimit the respective claims and obligations of the parties, and, in view of our human frailty, it is important to do so, though no man would be the best of partners, even in business, if he did not recognise, as conscientious men of business habitually do, that, even here, the spirit of partnership calls for mutual confidences and services which cannot be strictly delimited, nor set out in the letter of any bond. But in the realm of marriage, or in a friendship "based on good-

ness", the relation itself would be merely destroyed by
any attempt to reduce it to the rendering of specific
reciprocal services. A marriage which has the quality
of an ethical marriage is always at the least what the
Roman lawyers called it, a *consortium totius vitae*,[1] and
a friendship which is a matter of the *quid pro quo* is
what Aristotle calls it, only an imitation of the genuine
thing.

So far from morality being the sphere of "claims
and counter-claims", it is only when you begin to rise
out of that region that *any* social relation, even that
of mere "neighbours", begins to acquire a genuinely
ethical character, and in the most truly moralised intimate relations, which do most to make personal character, one has left the region of "claims and counter-
claims" altogether. What you give, or should give, to
your wife, or children, or to your chosen friend, is nothing less than yourself, whole and without reserve,
and you receive, or should receive, the like. If in practice we all come badly short of this ideal, that is not
because the ideal is "super-moral", but because, in
actual fact, we are all only very imperfectly moralised.
It is intolerable that metaphysicians with a spite
against personality, "the noblest gain of Christian
thought",[2] should foist on us a caricature of true moral
personality as a device for reconciling us to their substitution of an impersonal Absolute for God.

What we are now saying is not inconsistent with our
former insistence on the relativity of all loyalties except

---

[1] This is the real and insuperable *ethical* objection—independent, by the way,
of any theology—to the substitution of any kind of *union libre* for marriage. The
terminability of the "free union" is only a consequence of its inner moral vice, that
it is an attempt to give something less than the whole self, to keep back "part of
the price". A relation which *must* be a moral failure, unless it is based on full and
free self-surrender, is undertaken "with a mental reservation". Marriage only
succeeds in being what it can be at its best because both parties enter into it
knowing that there can be no "backing out".

[2] Martineau, *Types of Ethical Theory*, ed. 2, p. xxviii.

the highest. There is a loyalty which each of us must put even before loyalty to the wife of his bosom or the children of his loins, but it is not a loyalty to some supposed inaccessible and impenetrable kernel of his own individuality, and it is a supreme loyalty which is equally recognised by the other party, if the relation between the two human persons is what it ought to be. The fullest recognition that there is such a highest loyalty to someone or something other than this or that human person, or group of persons, does not involve that conception of human personalities as, in the last resort, merely mutually exclusive and repellent which apparently accounts for Bosanquet's depreciation of the moral and his hostility to finite individuality. It is emphatically not true that we must either hold that personality is mere "appearance" or regard the real world as composed of mutually repellent atoms. In truth, the richer your individuality is the more personality you have, the more you have to share with others, and the more urgently you feel the necessity of giving and receiving. It is the shallow, not the deeply and richly human, personalities which are gardens shut up and fountains sealed. No doubt a bountiful nature *may* be driven back on itself by the world's refusal of its gifts, or indifference to them, but it is not the richest in gifts to bestow who are the most easily repulsed. And the due recognition of the higher loyalty is not the same thing as a niggardliness in bestowing. The hero of the song who "loves honour more" is not really offering a gift of less value to his beloved than the idolater who forgets "honour". He is not loving the less because he loves in a fashion more worthy of a man.

Thus I think we may dismiss the conception of the sphere of morality as one of collision between "claims and counter-claims" as a misunderstanding. We may, no doubt, say that where the fulfilment of all loyalties has been ordered by the principle of degree and subordination, so that there remains no conflict of lower with higher, we have got beyond anything that can be significantly called *mere* morality, but we have only done so by learning to be wholly true to the spirit present in all morality. Our moral life, to repeat a distinction already made, may have been transfigured, but it has not been transformed; the victory and the struggle are connected by a continuity of interest, and there is no real ground for the fancy that victory would somehow eliminate finite moral personality. There is nothing unintelligible in the conception of a society of "perfected" persons, where all would be faithful mirrors, each from his own perspective, and, so to say, with his own curvature, of the infinite light and love of their common source, each having his own special contribution to make to the love and joy of all, each bestowing as well as receiving. Thus, in such a life to come as would be life in which man, as a moral being, had found his permanent home, *morality*, as we know it, could not rightly be said to be transcended; what would be transcended is the limit now set to the expression in act of the moral spirit, partly by our dependence on circumstance and physical environment, partly by the fact that all of us are only so imperfectly moralised in the intimate recesses of our souls. There would be no more progress *towards* goodness of environment or character, but there might be abundant progress *in* good, onward movement in the manifestation of the principle of the good life in ever more varied and richer forms.

I take it we might illustrate this distinction between progress *to* and progress *in* from the history of the arts.

Do there not seem to be periods in the life of a man or a people when there is no more to learn about methods of expression, though the periods are not empty or barren, but employed in the actual embodiment of what has been learned in a succession of "masterpieces"? Shakespeare's highest mastery in the tragic art, for example, is shown not in one such masterpiece, but in several—*Macbeth, Othello, King Lear*. We can say of his earlier work that it reveals him advancing, or progressing, towards finding himself as a supreme tragic artist. *Hamlet* has been specially remarked as showing great progress, in this sense, by comparison with *Julius Caesar*, and I believe it will generally be admitted that *Macbeth, Othello, Lear*, all of them show progress by comparison with *Hamlet*. But it does not follow that any one of the supreme three can be said to show progress from any other. It is at least an intelligible statement to say that all are *equally*, though each in its own special way, revelations of achieved mastery.

In fact, the very distinction we seem to be feeling after has long ago been expressly drawn for us by Aristotle. It is just his distinction between a γένεσις, a process of becoming, or development, by which some capacity comes to its full growth, and the ἐνέργεια, or activity by which the capacity, once developed to maturity, exhibits itself as a feature in the world-pattern. In life as we know it morality exhibits both γένεσις and ἐνέργεια inextricably. We are all along—it is to be hoped—growing into morality, *becoming* better men and women, and, at the same time, so far as our character acquires fixity of pattern and organisation, that fixity reveals itself in activities issuing from it. But there is nothing in itself irrational in hoping for a stage in our existence in which finality may have been actually reached, so far as development of personal character is concerned, and yet endless room left for the embodiment of the character so won in varied action. With the disappearance of growth, or becoming, of character we should not have lost our unique personality; we should have at last come into complete possession of it.

If we study the way in which character visibly makes itself under our eyes, we do indeed find that the process is marked by the disappearance of eccentricities and fluctuations; the more completely the individuals who share a common great tradition appropriate all that tradition has to yield, and make it into the stuff of their own personality, the more clearly do a common set of principles stand out as regulative of their life-pattern. Yet the persons do not lose their peculiar individuality. The "prentice work" of two great poets of the same age and language may be much the same kind of thing, and it may be hard, or impossible, to discriminate the manner of the one from that of the other. It is precisely in the work of their maturity that they may show themselves inspired alike by the same traditions and ideals, figures of the same age and the same "movement", while each is yet unmistakably himself and not the other. There might easily have been several men of the same time and the same sort of endowments, any of whom might have been the author of *Love's Labour's Lost*, or the *Two Gentlemen of Verona*; it is conceivable, though less likely, that there might even have been two men at the time of Shakespeare, either of whom might have written *Romeo and Juliet*; it would be much harder to believe that there could have been two contemporaries, either of whom might have given us *Othello* or *Antony and Cleopatra*.

It is the same with goodness. Two great figures of the moral or religious life, belonging to the same era, and subjected to the same general "influence of the age", let us say, by way of example, a Dominic and a Francis, or, if you prefer it, a Mill and a Ruskin, may both be eminently good, but each with his own special way of being good. Francis and Dominic are both definitely thirteenth-century figures, Mill and Ruskin both "Victorian", but the type expresses itself differently in Francis and in Dominic, in Mill and in Ruskin. This much by way of comment on the view that, in a Paradise where all men were sinless, there could be none of the variety, multiformity, and individuality which give zest to life. It seems to me nearer the truth to say that it is just the limitations on "genius" of every kind, deriving from the general character of men's "ages", "centuries", "surroundings", which are the obstacles to complete individuality. In Paradise I should expect individuality to reach its *maximal* expression, if Justinian there is no longer *semper Augustus*,[1] nor Bonaventura a cardinal, nor Cacciaguida a soldier, but one and all are *Menschen mit Menschen*.

There are certain implications of this view which I could wish to set out explicitly before I bring this first half of my programme to its close, always, I trust, with due submission to better judgements.

(1) It is clear that if we have conceived rightly of the kind of final destination of man which would be a real attaining of the moral ideal, the completest transfiguration of "this" world into the "other" of which we can reasonably conceive would not wholly abolish the successiveness of human experience. Even a heavenly life, such as we have tried to imagine, would still be a forward-looking life. The "glorified" would, indeed, no longer be looking forward to a future in which they had

---

[1] Dante, *Paradiso*, vi. 10:

"*Cesare fui e son* Giustiniano.*"

still further to put off the old man with the passions and
the lusts, or in which they would still be waiting for
the "beatific vision", and so far, it is true, that faith and
hope might be said, if not to have ceased, at any rate
to be no longer the dominant notes in life. But there
would still remain an undertone of something analogous
to those virtues, since the blessed would always have
new discoveries awaiting them, more to learn than they
had already found out of the unspeakable riches of the
wisdom of God, and these inexhaustible surprises would
be won, as deeper insight is won here, by humility,
trust and self-surrender, by letting self go, following
an apparently paradoxical inspiration. Heaven—if a
heaven indeed there is—we may safely say, must be a
land of delightful surprises, not a country of Lotus-
eaters where it is always afternoon. And in the same
way, if we are to think morally of Heaven, we should,
I suggest, think of it as a land where charity *grows*,
where each citizen learns to glow more and more with
an understanding love, not only of the common King,
but of his fellow-citizens. In this respect, again, there
would be one lesson mastered before the portals of
Heaven would open to admit us. We should have
learned to love every neighbour who crosses our path,
to hate nothing that God has made, to be indifferent to
none of the mirrors of His light. But even where there
is no ill-will or indifference to interfere with love, it is
still possible for love to grow as understanding grows.

We can see both growths illustrated often enough in
the conditions of our earthly life. As to understanding,
in a sense anyone who is aware of the meaning of the
equation $x^2 + y^2 = k$, or $xy = k$, and knows how to plot
out a graph of the functions, may be said to "understand perfectly" what a circle, or an equilateral hyper-
bola, is; there is no error infecting his thought, and no

further discovery he may make about properties of these curves will lead to any revision of the equations. But the greatest mathematician does not know all the fascinating properties which may be discovered from the equations. It is conceivable that, after so many centuries of geometrical study, the most elegant and attractive of the discoveries still await some geometer of the distant future. And as to love, a brother and sister may love one another with all their hearts in the nursery, and they may also love with all their hearts after the joys and sorrows of a long life; but if one has grown in the right way, one has more "heart" to love with at sixty than one had at ten, because one has so much more insight. There may have been full and complete sympathy at the earlier age, yet there has been progress *in* loving, though not progress, in the supposed case, *from* half-hearted or intermittent love to steady and whole-hearted love. The progress *in* loving has been from a blind to a seeing love.

(2) If our general principles are defensible, we clearly may have to reconsider the worth of a once familiar conception which is now very much out of general favour, the conception of our earthly life as one of *probation*. I know that this thought, the theme of countless sermons in the days of my own youth, is unpalatable to two quite different sets of thinkers, the spiritualists and theosophists, who seem to have no place in their scheme of things for the eternal, and those "absolute Idealists" who rightly perceive that, on their metaphysical theory, time itself must be an illusion. The first party will hear nothing of final beatitude at all, but only of an unending series of promotions in a *cursus honorum*, or even of endless alternations of promotion and disgrace; thus they lay themselves open to all those hostile criticisms of "endless progress" with

which we have just been dealing. The second would have us believe that, if we only knew it, we are already at the end of our road and "in Heaven", though, for some mysterious reason, we are unaware of the fact. But so long as there are such moods within us as indifference and mutual ill-will, this is *manifestly* not the case. If our life is really a journey, it should be clear both that there is a home to be reached, and that we have not yet reached it—indeed, that most of us presumably have a great deal of the worst of the journey still before us.

But if this is so, it is true, again, that the great business of our life here must be to find the right road and to walk in it. As I have said, we do not yet love all the creatures of God, nor even all our human neighbours, and those we do love we too often love "inordinately", not in the right way or the right measure. There is a lesson which has to be learned not only by those who value wealth, or reputation, or power, but by those, for example, who love their own puppy-dog better than their fellow-man. Now, it is at least conceivable that the crisis we call death, in which the mind partner in the mind-body relation is dissociated indefinitely from its fellow, may put the gravest of obstacles in the way of our mastering this lesson. If we have not begun to learn it here, it may be that our subsequent experiences will not be such as to enable us to repair the neglect. (I do not assert that this is so, but I say that we have no assurance that it is not so.) The true nature and extent of the crisis is more than we, who have yet to pass through it, know; but when we reflect on the far-reaching effects of lesser organic crises on our moral being, analogy suggests that the moral consequences of physical death may be still more serious. Hence I cannot think the present-day fashion of minimising the

spiritual significance of death altogether wholesome or
becoming a

> Being breathing thoughtful breath,
> A traveller between life and death.

To be sure, when we remember how often Christianity has been degraded in practice from being the life
of the love of God and His creatures to being a purely
prudential attempt to secure the individual against *post
mortem* suffering, we inevitably feel some sympathy
with some of the motives which account for the fashion;[1]
but it is mere folly to treat our mortality and uncertain
tenure of bodily life as of no moral significance, forgetting that there may well be lessons which must be
learned, if we are ever to attain true felicity, and must
be begun here in the body, or not at all. On this point a
sober moralist must surely feel dissatisfaction with the
attitude expressed when death is compared with "going
from one room to another", and find much more wisdom in the old-fashioned evangelical insistence on the
text that *"now* is the accepted time, and *now* the day
of salvation". None of us *know* that if we wait for to-
morrow, to-morrow may not be too late. There is at any
rate one very real "hell" to which a man may consign
himself, the hell of ever-renewed and ever-baffled endeavour, and a man can never know that he may not
send himself thither by present negligence. Even if he
escapes that doom, in a morally ordered world, we must
believe, neglect to tread the steps of the moral ascent
at the suitable time can only be made good by an ascent
gravely more tedious and more painful. The present
would be a better age than it is if we all lived more in

---

[1] It is painful to note the frequency with which the suggestion that the main
concern of life is to insure myself against future torture recurs in the hymnology
of the Wesleys, or how the same preoccupation seems to haunt Newman in his
Apologia, though, no doubt, the *main* motives in both cases were of a nobler
kind.

the habitual temper of men who remember that they have an account to give.

(3) In trying to develop the thought of a beatitude which includes progress *in* attainment, though not progress *to* attainment, we have not finally succeeded in overcoming the antithesis between time, the successive and fleeting, and eternity, the complete and non-successive. It has been implied that succession would still be a feature in the life of a creature, though a feature steadily decreasing in importance, even in a Paradise of light and love. This was a prominent doctrine of the late Baron von Hügel;[1] how far it would be admitted by the official exponents of the theology of his church, or any other, I do not know, but I feel convinced that in substance, at any rate, it is sound. I may remind you that a distinction which seems to be much the same in principle is made by two great philosophies, each in its own way. The Neo-Platonists, who ascribe *eternity* both to the being and to the operations of Intelligence (νοῦς), and to the being, though not to the operations of souls (ψυχαί), make it a capital point that even "eternity" may not properly be predicated of the supreme source of all being. The One, or God, is actually προαιώνιον, *prae-eternal*.[2] St. Thomas naturally follows the language of Scripture in asserting "eternity" of God, but he is careful to insist that this eternity, in the strict and proper sense of the term, is intrinsic to God. Angels and the beatified in Heaven possess only a "participated eternity", and possess it as a gift from God, which lifts them above their own level. The intrinsic "measure" of the life of spirits, considered apart from

[1] I would refer here to the full exposition of the Baron's views in his study, *Eternal Life* (1912), also to the second essay in *Essays and Addresses*, second series.

[2] See, for a formal exposition of the Neo-Platonist doctrine, Proclus, *Institutio Theologica*, props. 48-55.

this supernatural gift, is neither eternity nor time, but *aevum*, which is spoken of as something intermediate between the two. The difference is explained thus. Eternity is, in the famous phrase of Boethius, "occupation whole and altogether of a life without bounds," *interminabilis vitae tota simul et perfecta possessio*,[1] and thus can have no element of successiveness, no before or after, connected with it. Time is purely successive; what is simply temporal has becoming, not being; its *esse in transmutatione consistit*. *Aevum* is itself "all at once", and so far is like eternity, but it permits of having a before and after "conjoined" with it.[2] Hence St. Thomas says of the angels that they have an *esse substantiale* which is intransmutable, but is conjoined with transmutability *secundum electionem* (since, according to the well-known traditional account, they were subjected to a test, with the result that some of them chose to rebel, others to adhere to good), and conjoined similarly with transmutability of *attention* and, in some sense, of *location* (since angels can descend and reascend).

I do not know whether experts in Thomist philosophy would accept an interpretation that suggests itself, and would make this account of *aevum* exactly what our own argument needs for its purpose. The distinction between former and later which Thomas excludes altogether from eternity should, in strictness, I take it, be interpreted not as the distinction between antecedent and sequent, but as that of past and future. How the world is apprehended by God none of us would venture to say, but we cannot conceive that it is not apprehended as an ordered scheme exhibiting what is fundamental to the moral life, the one-sided and

---

[1] Boethius, *De Consolat.* v. pros. 6.
[2] *S.Th.* I[a] q. x. art. 5. See further I[a] q. x. art. 4, 6.

inversible relation of real causal dependence. In that sense, I take it, there must be a *prius* and *posterius* in the world as apprehended by God. But there is no *prius* or *posterius* in God, or in God's *apprehension* of the world. The whole process, *prius* and *posterius* alike, would fall for God, who never becomes, but is, within a single present, just as in our own experience apprehension of the present is never awareness of an object in which there are no relations of before and after, but always apprehension of a *present* object which embraces a before that has not yet faded into the "past", and an after that has not to emerge from the "future". We all know that it is to some extent a matter of native endowment how extensive a slice of "what is there" we can apprehend as being all at once with all its interrelations, including those of before and after; we know also, I think, that with care and practice one can learn to take in bigger "slices" in this way. We can and do cultivate the power of thus taking in at a single glance more and more of the detail of a situation to which we have to make practical response, or to appreciate the bearing of a proposition in the sciences, without that conscious advance of attention from each step in the argument to the next which we found necessary when we were beginners.

The same thing is seen in the case of appreciation of aesthetic form. There is, I understand, some doubt about the genuineness of the letter in which Mozart is supposed to speak of his ability to hear his own compositions "all at once" by an interior audition, and of the incommunicable rapture of the experience. Yet I imagine it is not really doubtful that the great artist in every kind must really possess some such power of envisaging as a *totum simul*, however imperfectly, what he can only convey to us by means of a detail which he has to elaborate, and we to "follow", in the form of long-drawn-out successiveness. Not to speak of the vision of the artist himself, which is, after all, the artist's secret, if we consider only our own imperfect appreciation and enjoyment of the artist's work when it is already there for us, it seems to me that as we learn to appreciate better, the work we appreciate and enjoy steadily sheds its successiveness. There was first a stage in which single stanzas of the poem, single scenes, or even speeches, of the drama, single phrases of the melody, were all that could fill our minds at one time; appreciation of the whole as a unity with structure had to be won with difficulty and the aid of conscious recollection and reflection. This is afterwards succeeded by a stage at which the impression is made by an inter-related whole, and our judgement of appreciation passed primarily on the whole as such, with a conscious immediacy.

To take an illustration which I purposely make childishly simple. I suppose we all know the sort of person who reads a great work of fiction in the mood appropriate to a railway detective story, for the sake of its surprises, and would have his enjoyment spoiled by any chance remark disclosing the turn the story will take. I had once myself a friend of this type; it was impossible to discuss or describe in his company any work of fiction he had not read, because, as he used to say, "I might some day want to read the book myself, and I shall get no pleasure from it if I know beforehand what is coming". In men of this kind, whose enjoyment depends almost wholly on being perpetually taken by surprise, I suppose we might say the appreciation of narrative and dramatic art is at its lowest. To one who wants to appreciate the art of the story, or the play, the element of mere surprise is a hindrance; it is

an advantage to him to know beforehand what the
incidents to be treated are, that he may be free to concentrate his attention on the structure of the whole.
And, similarly, the great artists are those who depend
least for their effects on the administering of *pure* surprises. What shocks are there in the *Iliad*, or, again,
in *Tom Jones*? Could either of these works be rightly
appreciated by anyone hearing the narrative for the
first time? Fielding, I know, does contrive to keep up a
mystery, though a fairly transparent one, through the
story. But how much does it contribute to the real
merits of his tale, or which of us would find his appreciation of the book affected if the author had taken the
reader into his confidence from the start? It cannot
even be said that Fielding has at least availed himself,
for artistic effect, of the uncertainty whether his hero
will eventually be rewarded with the hand of his mistress. Anyone aware of the literary tradition to which
the book belongs knows from the outset that the pair
are meant to make a match of it. For the matter of that,
most of us, I believe, would not in the least mind if they
did not. What we really care for is that the end of the
story, be it what it may, shall be of a piece with what
has gone before.

These remarks may seem below the dignity of our
theme, but I think they are really in point. They indicate the possibility of a knowledge of the successive
which would involve no uncertainty, and no element
of pure surprise, and yet would apprehend the successive in its order as successive. That is, the successiveness would be *wholly* in the things known; it would
not be a successiveness in the knower, or his knowing.
If we conceive such an apprehension to embrace the
whole of that which happens, it would be knowledge
of the whole course of temporality by a knower to

whom Boethius' definition of eternity would be strictly applicable, a knower possessed of "unbounded life" wholly and all at once. Such apprehension would realise Spinoza's ideal of "knowledge under a form of eternity", but it would not get this quality of eternity, as Spinoza imagined it must, by denuding the known of its temporal form. It would be the knower, not the history he knows, who would have eternity as his proper "form".

Now such knowing as this, so far as I can see, would be quite impossible, in its perfection, for man, or any creature. It would be, as I have said, knowledge from which the last vestige of uncertainty, and capacity for being surprised, had vanished. This does not mean, as Spinoza took it to mean, that such "divine" knowledge would apprehend all events as *necessary*. Since the world of creatures actually is a world of becoming, contingency and partial indetermination, if God apprehended it otherwise, God would be Himself the victim of illusion; this so-called knowledge would not be knowledge. A being in possession of all knowledge must, of course, know the incomplete as incomplete, open alternatives as open alternatives. But the point is that, though there might be contingency enough in what such a knower knows, there would be no contingency in the knower himself. He would, for example, know that at this moment of my life there are alternatives between which I can choose; but, since he sees all at once, he would also know that I am in the act of choosing one of the alternatives by my choice, and which I am choosing. He would not be taken by surprise when I choose.

So, in a sufficiently familiar situation, I myself know, when I make a choice, that I really am choosing, not finding out that choice has been precluded by my circumstances or my "past", and yet I am not taken by surprise by my own choice. Such complete freedom from uncertainty would seem, from the nature of the thing, impossible to a creature. For every creature is not merely set in a background of the uncertain; he also has the uncertain within himself. He is a dependent being who is not his own *raison d'être*, and he cannot sound the whole mystery of the being upon whom he is, in the last resort, dependent. There is more in God than any creature will ever find out. At most a creature can only be assured that nothing still remaining to be found out will belie what has been disclosed.

This, I suggest, is what is really meant by the "participated eternity" enjoyed by creatures in Paradise, in virtue of their direct vision of God. With them "vision" has replaced "faith"; they "behold God *per essentiam suam*"; what they behold is truth, pure and unalloyed, and obscured by no metaphor or irrelevant symbolism, exactly as mathematical truth may be to the mathematician truth without confusion, metaphor or alloy, but they never see all there is to be seen of the *essentia* of God. There is always more to be seen, as there is always more mathematical truth to be discovered. Thus, for any creature, however exalted in goodness and wisdom, there are always possible surprises in store, though in a world from which evil had disappeared the surprises would always be "joyful". But for a being who can be surprised, even if the surprise takes the form of delight "beyond expectation", futurity must remain as an uneliminated feature of experience.

Hence I think von Hügel on the right lines in regarding the life of creatures as one in which successiveness and futurity never wholly vanish, though they may become of decreasing importance "beyond all assignable limit". The tension of anticipation of the unknown would be less pronounced in the higher ranks of a Dantesque empyrean than in the lower, but it would still be there, as the witness to the unbridgeable gulf between the independent and the wholly dependent, Creator and creature. And I find it hard to believe that St. Thomas can have thought otherwise, especially when I note that the eternity in which the beatified participate is made to depend on their vision of God. This "participated" eternity would thus seem to be actually *God's* eternity, as contemplated by the beatified. In virtue of the principle that we become like what we behold, a soul in actual vision of God is assured that it cannot forfeit that vision, for he who *sees* the good can desire nothing else. But there is always also the awareness that there is more to be seen than the soul has yet taken in, and thus the mind's attitude does not cease to be forward-reaching. Complete ἐνέργεια ἀκινησίας, activity, which is rest and nothing but rest, is reserved for the Creator alone. But to say this is not to say that the struggle with the bad is ineradicable from creaturely life.

(4) We must, however, be very careful how we identify the best life, in Aristotelian fashion, with *vita contemplativa*. There are qualifications which must not be forgotten. In such a heaven as we are trying to imagine, the conflict of right with wrong, truth with error, has no place, and thus the "practical life", as understood by Kant and others who simply identify it with this struggle, would be no more. But if we may conceive of a "blessed" life as providing opportunities for progress in vision, to be achieved by intellectual adventure, and to bear fruit in the illumination of others besides the adventurer, then clearly the spirit of the "practical life" continues at this higher level.

Contemplation of the vision is the inspiration of the adventures, and their fruit is neither the righting of wrongs nor the amendment of errors, but enriched contemplation. Yet the adventures themselves are "practice", and the ultimate goal of action is not to pass out of being, but to be made wholly fruitful in contemplative rest. Such a goal is in keeping with the spirit of morality, as the mere disappearance of "action" is not. We make war, as Aristotle said, that we may have peace, and we discharge business that we may have leisure. But peace and well-spent leisure are not the same as sloth and inaction. It would be a false psychology that should treat "contemplation" as passive, in the sense of being inert. To contemplate aright we must, indeed, be wholly *receptive* towards suggestions from without; we must lay the whole self open to the object contemplated, lose the self in it. But to be thus receptive takes all the energy with which a man is endowed. Contemplation and laziness will not keep house together; and we should merely misunderstand the great masters of the mystic way if we supposed their traditional language about "passive contemplation" to mean that our highest felicity is a state comparable with the lazy enjoyment of a hot bath. Rightly understood, the life of fruition of the vision is not the supersession, but the fulfilment, of the life of dutiful practice of the modest virtues of the family, the city and the nation. What is superseded is only the conflict with adverse elements in the self and its environment, and that is only superseded because it has been brought, by God's grace, to a victorious issue.

The very mention of God's grace reminds me that I am touching on matters more properly reserved for the second part of our programme, in which we are to consider the relations between such a natural theology as is directly suggested by reflections on the implications of ethics and the theologies of the historical religions. So long as we are within the bounds of the purely ethical, it may be said, the moral conflict must be thought of as one in which man fights for himself and must win any success he does win by his own unaided efforts. But according to any religion which is not a mere "Pharisaism", no one achieves "eternal life" by his own effort; it is the "gift of God". How, then, can we speak of it, as we have just spoken, as the supersession of the moral struggle by a *moral* victory? I must not now anticipate the course of the reflections with which we shall be occupied later. So I will only add that the paradox, if it is a paradox, is inherent in the *Christian* religion itself. The fruits of the tree of life, and the hidden manna, are expressly spoken of as *gifts*, but they are gifts said to be reserved for victors. "I *have* overcome the world", said One; but it is said in order that each of us also may overcome. We are still the *ecclesia militans*, and *our* victory is still to be won.

INDEX OF PROPER NAMES

END OF VOL. I

Printed in Great Britain by R. & R. CLARK, LIMITED, *Edinburgh.*

By Prof. A. E. TAYLOR

THE PROBLEM OF CONDUCT. A Study in the Phenomenology of Ethics. 8vo. 12s. 6d. net.

WORKS ON PHILOSOPHY

STUDIES IN PHILOSOPHY AND PSYCHOLOGY. By G. F. STOUT, M.A., LL.D., Professor of Logic and Metaphysics, St. Andrews University. 8vo. 15s. net.

KANT'S CRITIQUE OF PURE REASON. Translated by NORMAN KEMP SMITH, D.Phil., LL.D., F.B.A., Professor of Logic and Metaphysics in the University of Edinburgh, author of *A Commentary to Kant's Critique of Pure Reason.* 8vo. 25s. net.

THE GROWTH OF PLATO'S IDEAL THEORY. An Essay. By Sir JAMES GEORGE FRAZER, O.M. 8vo. 7s. 6d. net.

ESSAYS ON THE NATURAL ORIGIN OF THE MIND. By C. A. STRONG, author of "The Origin of Consciousness: An Attempt to Conceive the Mind as a Product of Evolution." 8vo. 12s. net.

ADVENTURES IN PHILOSOPHY AND RELIGION. By JAMES B. PRATT, Ph.D., author of "The Religious Consciousness." Crown 8vo. 8s. 6d. net.

SYSTEMATIC PSYCHOLOGY: PROLEGOMENA. By EDWARD BRADFORD TITCHENER. Crown 8vo. 10s. 6d. net.

MACMILLAN AND CO., LTD., LONDON

WORKS ON RELIGION

THOUGHTS ON SOME QUESTIONS OF THE DAY. A
Charge delivered at his Primary Visitation by WILLIAM
TEMPLE, Archbishop of York. Crown 8vo. 4s. 6d. net.

THE FULLNESS OF SACRIFICE. An Essay in Reconcilia-
tion. By the Right Rev. F. C. N. HICKS, D.D., Bishop of
Gibraltar. 8vo. 15s. net.

THE GOSPEL ACCORDING TO ST. LUKE. The Greek
Text, with Introduction, Notes and Indices by Canon J. M.
CREED, M.A., B.D., Ely Professor of Divinity in the University
of Cambridge. 8vo. 15s. net.

THE GOSPEL AND THE MODERN MIND. By WALTER
R. MATTHEWS, M.A., D.D., Dean of King's College, London.
Re-issue. Crown 8vo. 7s. 6d. net.

MAN AND THE IMAGE OF GOD. By HUBERT M.
FOSTON, D.Lit. (Lond.). Crown 8vo. 7s. 6d. net.

HISTORY OF THE PAPACY IN THE 19TH CENTURY
(1864–1878). By the late J. B. BURY, D.Litt., LL.D.,
Regius Professor of Modern History in the University of
Cambridge. Edited, with a Memoir, by the Rev. R. H.
MURRAY, Litt.D. 8vo. 10s. net.

RABBINIC LITERATURE AND GOSPEL TEACHINGS.
By C. G. MONTEFIORE, Hon. D.Litt. (Oxford), Hon. D.D.
(Manchester). 8vo. 15s. net.

MACMILLAN AND CO., LTD., LONDON